Reconstructing Appalachia

New Directions in Southern History

Series Editors
Peter S. Carmichael, West Virginia University
Michele Gillespie, Wake Forest University
William A. Link, University of Florida

RECONSTRUCTING APPALACHIA

THE CIVIL WAR'S AFTERMATH

EDITED BY ANDREW L. SLAP

Introduction by Gordon B. McKinney

THE UNIVERSITY PRESS OF KENTUCKY

Scholarly publisher for the Commonwealth,
serving Bellarmine University, Berea College, Centre College of Kentucky,
Eastern Kentucky University, The Filson Historical Society, Georgetown College,
Kentucky Historical Society, Kentucky State University, Morehead State University,
Murray State University, Northern Kentucky University, Transylvania University,
University of Kentucky, University of Louisville, and Western Kentucky University.
All rights reserved.

Editorial and Sales Offices: The University Press of Kentucky
663 South Limestone Street, Lexington, Kentucky 40508-4008
www.kentuckypress.com

Maps by Dick Gilbreath, University of Kentucky Cartography Lab.

14 13 12 11 10   5 4 3 2 1

Library of Congress Cataloging-in-Publication Data

Reconstructing Appalachia : the Civil War's aftermath / edited by Andrew L.
Slap ; introduction by Gordon B. McKinney.
    p. cm. — (New directions in southern history)
  Includes bibliographical references and index.
  ISBN 978-0-8131-2581-7 (hardcover : alk. paper)
  1. Appalachian Region, Southern—History—19th century. 2. Appalachian
Region, Southern—Social conditions—19th century. 3. Appalachian Region,
Southern—Economic conditions—19th century. 4. Reconstruction (U.S.
history, 1865–1877) 5. United States—History—Civil War, 1861–1865—
Influence. 6. United States—History—Civil War, 1861–1865—Social aspects.
I. Slap, Andrew L.
  F217.A65R43 2010
  973.8—dc22   2009053154

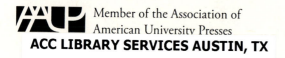

Member of the Association of
American University Presses

Contents

Acknowledgments

The idea for this project first emerged at a Friday afternoon social gathering of colleagues in the history department at East Tennessee State University (ETSU). During the gathering, I casually commented that I could put together an anthology on Appalachia during the Civil War era. Stephen Fritz, a senior member of the department who is usually jovial in social settings, suddenly became serious and told me that was the kind of idea junior faculty should follow through on and not just discuss. I dutifully thought about the idea for the rest of the afternoon, and that evening I called Bob Sandow to get his thoughts. Bob and I talked for more than an hour that Friday evening, after which I e-mailed Pete Carmichael to see if he would be interested in such a project for his series at the University Press of Kentucky. Pete was enthusiastic from the start, and by Monday morning Joyce Harrison, an acquisitions editor at the press, had contacted me. Bob, Pete, and Joyce all helped me conceptualize this project as a sequel to Kenneth W. Noe and Shannon Wilson's seminal *Civil War in Appalachia: Collected Essays,* focusing on the Civil War's aftermath in Appalachia.

My original inspiration for a collection on Civil War–era Appalachia came from the historians who had given talks at the ETSU Civil War Speakers Series, which I started upon arriving at ETSU. Many of the Civil War–era historians in the area naturally focused on Appalachia; Bob Sandow, Anne Marshall, Mary Ella Engel, and Steve Nash were among the numerous historians to give a lecture in the series over the years. The ETSU history department and the Center for Appalachian Studies and Services jointly sponsored these lectures, and center director Roberta Herrin has always been enthusiastic about the series. Dr. Robert and Norma Clark's generous support of the history department has helped make the lecture series possible and thus has directly contributed to this volume. Bob Clark has also audited nine of my courses, including every graduate seminar I have taught, and has improved them all with his keen reading and sharp questions.

It has been a pleasure to work with the University Press of Kentucky in the production of this book. Stephen Wrinn and Anne Dean Watkins quickly dispelled any worries I had when Joyce left the press. Steve and Anne Dean took over the project and did a great job of encouraging me and keeping the project on time. The press also picked good readers for both the proposal and the manuscript. Martin Crawford, Ken Noe, and the anonymous reader all saw promise in this project and offered constructive criticisms that made it better.

I am neither an Appalachianist nor an Appalachian. Thus, at every stage of this project I have been struck by how welcoming and generous Appalachian historians have been to a newcomer to their field. I appreciate the contributors' interest in this project, and getting to know and work with them has been a pleasure. They were extremely patient with a novice editor. I particularly want to thank John Inscoe for his advice on editing a collection of essays and his meticulous reading of my chapter in this volume.

In my six years at ETSU, I have started learning about Appalachia. Some of this education has come from my students, but I have also benefited from being academic director of the local Teaching American History Grant, awarded by the U.S. Department of Education. The grant has enabled me to meet hundreds of area schoolteachers and to travel throughout the region. While beginning work on this volume, I decided that one of the grant's summer institutes for teachers should focus on Altina Waller's wonderful *Feud: Hatfields, McCoys, and Social Change in Appalachia, 1860–1900*. Besides just reading and discussing the book, I wanted the teachers and myself to experience the places and the environment viscerally. Grant director Deborah Montanti encouraged me to follow the vision, and Kevin Barksdale made it possible, taking us on an amazing two-day trip to Matewan, Beckley, Bramwell, and Pocahontas. Kevin, with the help of Paul Lutz and Bill Richardson, enabled us to experience Appalachia in a way few outsiders can. One of the highlights was sitting in rocking chairs on the porch of our hotel in Beckley and listening to upper East Tennessee school teachers discuss the nature of Appalachia. It has become a cliché that research informs teaching, but the combination of my experiences with the Teaching American History Grant and working on this project have certainly improved my understanding of the students at ETSU and thus my teaching.

The collaborative environment of the ETSU history department has made this project more enjoyable and improved this volume. Colleagues such as Steve Fritz and Mel Page regularly offered encouragement and advice. When Dale Schmitt was director of graduate studies, he allowed me to change my general Civil War–era graduate seminar into a post–Civil War Appalachia course at the last minute. I benefited from reading and discussing some of the seminal works in Appalachian history with the graduate students in the course. Kyle Osborn and Meredith Bocian deserve special recognition, as I had the privilege of directing both of their MA theses on Civil War–era East Tennessee. I have learned a great deal about the region's history and how to advise graduate students from Kyle and Meredith. The only reasons Meredith does not have an essay in this collection are that her thesis focused on the antebellum period and she was still working on it when the essays were due. Both have gone on to work with top scholars in Appalachian history, Kyle with John Inscoe and Meredith with Ken Noe. I look forward to watching both Kyle and Meredith's careers develop over the coming years.

Tom Lee is exactly what one hopes for in a colleague. Other than a few wry comments about me trying to make him redundant, Tom encouraged me to pursue this project, agreed to contribute an essay, and did not object when I asked to teach a graduate seminar in his specialty. Tom generously spent time discussing books and Appalachian historiography with me. He read my chapter during finals week so I could meet a deadline, and he greatly improved it with his close reading and insightful analysis.

When I received copies of my first monograph in early 2007, I told Nicole that the next couple of years would be less hectic than the preceding ones had been. A few weeks later I started this project, and Nicole said she would never again believe promises about work being less hectic, though she added that she had never really expected anything else. As always, Nicole's patience and help have made my work possible. Our daughter, Abby, two years old when I began working on this book, did not display much patience; but she did help by occasionally running into my office to play for a few minutes, reminding me of what is important. Maybe it even helped that, unlike her parents, Abby was born in upper East Tennessee and is a native Appalachian.

Introduction

Appalachia, 1865–1910

Gordon B. McKinney

The decades following the Civil War in Appalachia were a time of decline and growth, confusion and organization, poverty and riches. As the work in this volume will demonstrate, our understanding of this complex period is deepening. At the same time, however, scholars and general readers alike have come to recognize that many of our traditional understandings are no longer available to us. This is not a problem unique to observers from our own time; the people who lived in Appalachia from the end of the Civil War until the beginning of the twentieth century felt a similar level of uncertainty. Still, there were a number of broad developments that encouraged people at the time to view the mountain South as a unique region.

The Civil War in the mountains, as described by Andrew L. Slap in chapter 1 of this volume, was a catastrophic experience for the region.[1] The aftermath was also a challenge to all members of mountain society. South of the Ohio River, the region's limited infrastructure was partially eliminated. Both armies destroyed railroad bridges and roadbeds; they also dismantled the rails, engines, and cars for good measure. The farms in western Virginia, West Virginia, East Tennessee, and northern Georgia were stripped of their produce for both men and horses. North Carolina governor Zebulon B. Vance, himself a western North Carolinian, captured the anger of mountain small farmers when he complained to Confederate authorities: "If God Almighty had yet in store another plague worse than all others which he intended to let loose on the Egyptians in case Pharaoh still hardened his heart I am sure it must have been a regiment or so of half-armed, half-disciplined Confederate cavalry."[2] In addition to the material destruction, social entities no longer functioned as they had before the war. Churches, schools, local governments, and militias virtually disappeared during the fighting and could not easily be replaced. While southeastern

Ohio and western Pennsylvania witnessed little of the physical destruction suffered by their southern neighbors, political animosities were present here as well. Opposition to the war and conscription divided neighborhoods and communities, making concerted action difficult.

Equally important was the economic collapse suffered by the region's former slave states. Any agricultural surplus had been consumed, and livestock herds had been decimated. The transportation infrastructure had been weakened. All investments in enslaved persons were lost with emancipation. Confederate money and bonds were now worthless, and many parts of Appalachia had no cash circulating to allow everyday activities to resume. As a result of all of these developments, many residents of the highland South were forced to borrow money at ruinous rates of interest.[3] Consequently, few mountain entrepreneurs had the financial resources to help rebuild the region. While the mountain counties of Pennsylvania and Ohio had fared better during the conflict, even there economic success appeared to accrue to a small number of landowners and industrialists.

Another legacy of the war was the unfortunate fact that the entire region also lacked sufficient human resources to rebuild itself. Tens of thousands of European and African Americans were killed in the military carnage that was part of the war. Sadly, this loss of life was not evenly distributed throughout the mountain counties. As an inducement to enroll in the military, both federal and Confederate governments encouraged men from the same town or county to join companies and regiments together. While this strategy probably improved wartime morale, it could also result in disaster. Martin Crawford cites one example from Ashe County, North Carolina: One company of the Confederate Twenty-sixth Regiment had sixty-six soldiers from Ashe County at the battle of Gettysburg. During the horrific battle in Pennsylvania, eleven of these soldiers were killed or died shortly thereafter, and eight were badly wounded.[4] No community could sustain this kind of loss without suffering economic disruption after the conflict.

As challenging as battlefield casualties were to mountain communities, the internal guerrilla war that took place at home was even more devastating. Phillip Shaw Paludan has documented one of the most searing of these confrontations, in his study of the Shelton Laurel massacre in Madison County, North Carolina.[5] Ken Noe discovered much the same type of activity in southern West Virginia, as did Noel Fisher in his study of East Tennessee.[6] Jonathan Dean Sarris documents numerous outrages directed at civilians by guerrilla bands in Lumpkin and Fannin counties in north

Georgia.[7] One observer was moved to conclude: "The warfare between scattering bodies of irregular troops is conducted on both sides without any regard whatever to the rules of civilized war or the dictates of humanity. . . . The murder of prisoners and noncombatants in cold blood has, I learn, become quite common."[8] This brutality often involved neighbors, kin, and nearby communities, but the animosities developed during the war would not simply disappear when peace arrived. Thus, the disruption of the social and political life of mountain communities was added to the hardships caused by economic dislocation.

When the Confederacy surrendered in April 1865, the people of Appalachia sought to put their world back together. It immediately became apparent that this task would be most difficult. In some parts of the mountains, veterans from opposing armies and guerrilla fighters from both sides now had to coexist and try to put their world back together. T. R. C. Hutton's chapter demonstrates that some soldiers were never able to adjust completely to a nonviolent existence. Veterans like Unionist William Strong and former Confederates in the Ku Klux Klan resorted to physical coercion whenever more peaceful means of accomplishing their ends seemed too slow or uncertain. Local businessmen sought to obtain sufficient capital to open stores and manufacturing operations. The region's farmers planted crops without the assistance of formerly enslaved laborers who were now freed or family members who were now dead or disabled. Confederate constitutions were declared void, and federal laws passed during the conflict were now in force in former Confederate states. Women who had operated as independent farmers and entrepreneurs had to adjust to a resumption of their legal subservience. African Americans who had been emancipated from slavery eagerly sought to explore the meaning of their newfound freedom.

Not unexpectedly, many early attempts at reconciliation and community cooperation failed. Religious societies split by antebellum and wartime controversies remained separate. In addition, African Americans began to form their own distinct denominations.[9] In East Tennessee, Unionists who claimed to have suffered financial damages during the Confederate occupation of the region used the courts to recover their losses and exact revenge on their tormentors. In this volume, Steven E. Nash explains in detail how those who protested Confederate policies in western North Carolina felt adrift as leadership of the anti-Confederate movement allied itself with the increasingly radical national Republican Party. These conservatives increasingly aligned themselves with President Andrew Johnson and the national Democrats.

The region's elite sought to retain its dominance by seizing control of state and local political systems. In many formerly Confederate areas, this meant that many of the people who had created and supported the Confederacy retained positions of power and influence. The outstanding result of this kind of political maneuvering was Georgia's election of former Confederate vice-president Alexander Stephens to the U.S. Senate.[10] Only in Unionist areas like East Tennessee and West Virginia did new southern mountain leadership emerge. The political elite north of the Ohio River were much more secure. Local Republicans were part of the ruling organizations in their states and the nation. Their opposition was also part of a venerable political tradition that often drew upon local leadership and customary behaviors that would sustain them through difficult times.[11]

Northern Republicans reacted very negatively to the reemergence of the old Southern elite. As a result, congressional Republicans, including some from western Pennsylvania and southeastern Ohio, seized control of the political Reconstruction process. Their coalition was unstable, however; in his chapter in this volume, Robert M. Sandow reports that there was a great deal of unrest among voters in western Pennsylvania at the time. Resistance to the draft during the war and efforts to form labor organizations in the 1870s created volatile political allegiances in that region. Through the passage of the Fourteenth and Fifteenth amendments to the U.S. Constitution and the Civil Rights and Reconstruction acts, the Republicans tried to restructure southern politics. Through these measures they disenfranchised the region's elite. All of the people in the mountains who had held civilian or military positions in the Confederacy and those who owned twenty or more slaves were barred from the political process.[12] In addition, all those who had been previously excluded from voting or holding office because of poverty or race were allowed to vote and hold office. This change was often deeply resented. When African Americans sought to vote for the first time in Asheville, North Carolina, in 1866, white residents assaulted them and drove them away from the polls.[13]

Incidents of this type were symptoms of a political structure that encouraged confrontation rather than conciliation. Democrats in parts of Appalachia decried the granting of citizenship rights to African Americans. Many Republicans were not enthusiastic about the enfranchisement of blacks either, but they tolerated the new arrangement because they benefited from it. Some mountain Republican leaders, such as William G. Brownlow, were forced to make abrupt changes in their public positions. Brownlow, a Republican Reconstruction governor, had vehemently opposed making the abolition of slavery a war aim, but during Reconstruction he embraced black voters.[14] In addition, southern Republicans often espoused policies that favored the lower classes in their regions and states. A prime example of this type of initiative was the "stay laws" that were passed by the new legislatures or added to the new constitutions. These enactments allowed the poor to remain on their land even when they could not continue to pay their mortgages.[15] These new issues inflamed voters in both parties and created a hostile atmosphere for most political campaigns during the period.

In addition to the political warfare that threatened community peace, Appalachian regions also experienced the shock of rapid industrialization and urbanization. This trend was particularly noticeable in western Pennsylvania. The conjunction of three rivers and several rail lines made Pittsburgh one of the country's great industrial cities. This ascendancy began during the antebellum period, but the production demands of the Civil War accelerated the city's growth. Because of the ready access to coal in western Pennsylvania, Pittsburgh's rise fueled expansion throughout the entire region. At the same time, the concentration of industrial firms encouraged fierce competition that led to numerous innovations in management and production. These improvements were often introduced by entrepreneurs such as Andrew Carnegie. The result of these innovations was that many of the smaller firms, unable to raise sufficient capital or introduce new systems or products, were taken over by their larger competitors.[16] As these companies grew, they began to require more raw materials that were found in other parts of Appalachia.

At the same time, iron and steel makers elsewhere in Appalachia began to develop their own centers of production. Union soldiers who had noticed the presence of large coal deposits around Chattanooga, Tennessee, during the extended fighting in that region later moved to the area after the war. Some of these transplants, led by H. Clay Evans, started a company that would become Tennessee Coal and Iron.[17] Within a relatively short period of time, Chattanooga became a leading center of iron production. Farther south, the former plantation elite looked for opportunities to restore their economic fortunes through investment. When two railroads crossed tracks in a farmer's field, these investors sought to take advantage of the abundant iron ore and coal found in northern Alabama. They named the new community Birmingham and soon were producing a large quantity of iron as well.[18]

All of these enterprises needed improved transportation and better access to more natural resources. The result was a major railroad boom throughout the mountain counties. In all regions, main lines were extended and branch lines were quickly added to provide direct access to the needed materials. In western Pennsylvania, southeastern Ohio, southern West Virginia, eastern Kentucky, eastern Tennessee, northern Georgia, and northern Alabama, construction took place at a rapid rate. These and similar routes, including one in western North Carolina, also provided access to massive hardwood forests found in the highland region.[19] Quite often these initiatives took the companies into largely rural areas that could not provide the kind of social or structural infrastructure necessary to harvest the sought-after materials. At the same time, local people often did not have the requisite skills or industrial discipline to provide the workforce necessary to start and expand production.

The need for what the industrialists thought was an appropriate group of workers led to a significant number of innovations in this area. Until the postwar period, the vast majority of mountain people had lived as farmers, like many generations of their ancestors. The railroad placed mountain farmers in competition in local and national markets with farmers from the rich plains of the Midwest, greatly reducing their earning power. Thus, the industrialists were able to attract many local workers from the ranks of erstwhile farmers. At the same time, the businessmen wanted to create a diverse working population that would find cooperation difficult, eliminating the possibility that workers would join labor unions. The entrepreneurs sent recruiters into the rural Deep South, where they enticed African Americans to join their workforce. They also sent agents to the ports of entry on the East Coast to encourage central and eastern Europeans to accept industrial jobs in Appalachia.[20] Because these new workers often spoke little or no English and were often Roman Catholic or Orthodox in religious affiliation, they shared few religious or cultural traditions with the largely Protestant native workers.

The addition of African American workers from the Deep South ensured that the black population would remain approximately 10 percent of the entire region. No longer confined as slaves to agricultural and mining positions, they obtained jobs in many parts of the economy. Men often found places in the growing industrial sector, and women were offered work in the service sector. Young and old alike availed themselves of the opportunity to gain as much education as possible. Those who had been free before the war often took leadership roles in politics and the church, but their advancement was slowed by the persistent racism of the white Appalachian population. Informal, and increasingly legal, segregation came to restrict the rights of black Appalachians. These measures were enforced by economic coercion and violence, including the expanding blight of lynching. Kyle Osborn reminds us that in spite of this generally racist atmosphere, some mountain whites adopted more conciliatory attitudes. He cites the case of William G. Brownlow, whose racial attitudes evolved as African American men proved themselves to be good soldiers and were instrumental as voters in preserving Reconstruction gains. Some African Americans in the region made unexpected breakthroughs in the face of tremendous obstacles, including baseball player Sol White of Wheeling and other professional athletes in the Ohio State minor baseball league.[21]

Valuable natural resources were often located in previously ignored locations, which forced businessmen to make a further policy innovation: they began to build company towns to house workers and their families. These communities differed greatly in size and quality of life provided. Some offered little more than shelter and sufficient supplies to sustain life; others offered amenities designed to attract and keep workers, including comprehensive company stores, adequate housing, recreational opportunities, educational facilities, and houses of worship. In many of the towns, the workers were isolated from the outside world because the company controlled the railroad, which was the only means of transportation. These camps often proved to be a successful means for the company to recover most of the salaries they paid, through housing rental and purchases at the company store.[22] Even though this arrangement brought the workers in close proximity to one another, the social strains that existed among the groups made forming unions difficult.

Other workers were not enticed to the coal fields but instead came there under extreme coercion. Starting at the end of Reconstruction and extending for more than two decades afterward, southern states faced grave financial challenges. The continuation of violence spawned by the war and the hostile feelings between community members from opposing armies led to an upsurge in arrests, convictions, and incarcerations. At the same time, many communities inside and outside the mountains found that criminalizing certain behaviors provided them with what they considered to be adequate racial control. The result was that a large number of African American men were jailed for extended periods. Unfortunately for inadequate state treasuries, this large dependent population had to be housed, clothed, and fed. State budgets could not absorb the extra costs, so several states soon adopted the alternative of leasing convicts to businesses. The corporation would agree to house, feed, clothe, and teach a skill to the convicts and would pay the state a fee for the use of these workers. In Georgia, Alabama, and Tennessee, many of these convicts were used in the mountain counties to mine coal. In North Carolina, the state leased the convicts to a railroad company, and they assisted with the construction of the main rail line into the mountain region.[23]

While this arrangement seemed ideal from the perspective of the state and the industrialists, there was considerable opposition to the practice. The convicts themselves and humanitarian critics of the practice targeted the dangerous working conditions in the mines and on the rails. Mining was an inherently unhealthy profession, but the lack of supervision and the companies' desire to keep costs as low as possible made the convicts' situation even more perilous. Free black and white miners were concerned because the presence of their convict competitors ensured that wages in the mines would remain low. Work on the railroad proved to be just as dangerous as mining; more than 100 convicts died constructing tunnels on the Old Fort escarpment. Public pressure began to build in each state to end this barbaric system. Karin Shapiro and others have done comprehensive studies of this campaign to eliminate contracted convict labor, which was ultimately successful.

Many women and children also joined the public workforce in Appalachia during this period. The mountain region provides many fast-moving streams—the main source of power for mills—and therefore became a center of textile production. This factory production quickly provided large amounts of cloth at relatively low prices, driving individual craftspeople out of the market and forcing them into production lines working fifty or more hours a week for a small salary. This pittance was not enough to support a family in a company town, with the result that multiple members of the same family were often driven to work in the same mills. Many children in the region were forced to forgo education to earn enough money for their families to eat.[24]

This movement of women into the textile mills was part of a broader change in gender relations in the mountains in this period. Unlike elite and middle-class women of the plantation South and urban North, antebellum Appalachian women had not been part of the "Cult of True Womanhood."

Most of them lived on farms and before Reconstruction had worked full days as field hands, craftspeople, cooks, weavers, and washers. A substantial number were independent proprietors of farms and small businesses before and during the Civil War; the war's tragic death toll caused those numbers to remain high. Some seized increasing educational opportunities to train as teachers; others sought and obtained "public work" positions as factory workers, clerks, and domestics. These public jobs entailed significant risks for women. As Keith S. Hébert documents, African American women who worked as domestics were often subjected to violent attacks and rapes by their employers and assaults and humiliation by groups like the Ku Klux Klan.

Some women, such as Rebecca Latimer Felton of north Georgia, were pioneers who delineated entirely new patterns of life for themselves. In this period, Felton became the campaign manager for her husband's independent campaigns for Congress. Later, she would become a power in the Democratic Party, and she would be appointed to the U.S. Senate in the early 1920s—the first woman to hold that position. These developments created anxiety among many male mountaineers. One result was that many of them sold the subsoil mineral rights to their property to pay off their debts and retain the semblance of male dominance.[25] While the growing number of women seeking work outside the home was a change, the number of women working probably changed little from the earlier period.

In western Pennsylvania, southeastern Ohio, and West Virginia, the production of glass products became an important part of the local economy. Very much like weavers, craftsmen who were glass blowers had to adjust to industrial innovations. Like coal miners, many glass workers were European immigrants. In this case, companies sought highly skilled workers, particularly from Belgium, who commanded relatively high wages and had been unionized in their home countries. As was the case in the coal counties, the entrepreneurs in the glass industry were political leaders in the communities and states where their businesses were located. Many glass manufacturers, like the owners of coal concerns, lived outside of Appalachia and often did not reinvest their substantial earnings back into the region. In West Virginia cities like Moundsville, Clarksburg, and Fairmont, broad-based economies failed to develop, despite the presence of substantial capital resources in glass production.[26] This was often the case in single-industry towns in the mountains, both north and south of the Ohio River.

The timber industry demonstrated equally disturbing patterns of misuse of resources and failure to reinvest in the region. The railroads that made coal a significant force in the region's economy could also be used to transport millions of feet of logs and finished wood products. The growing U.S. economy needed a wide variety of wood products during these decades. The rapid expansion of the nation's population required a great deal of new housing and business structures of all kinds, many of them built primarily with wood. Wood was also still a primary fuel for many families and businesses, and it was essential for the ties and bridges in the railroad-building binge that took place during these years. As with other industries at the time, innovation drove consumption of this resource. The modernization of the American economy needed a great deal of inexpensive paper to record its achievements. The development of a chemical process that turned wood pulp into paper—particularly newspaper—created a tremendous demand for wood that could be cut and processed in the mountain counties.[27]

The rapid growth of industry gave rise to another significant by-product of the late nineteenth century in Appalachia: abuse of natural resources and the environment. The attitudes that shaped these policies had been present since the preindustrial phase of Appalachian history. Farms throughout the region had used slash-and-burn cultivation methods since the time of European settlement. Donald Davis has examined the shaping of the Appalachian environment as far back as the pre-European period, when American Indians used fire to shape the ecology of the land they inhabited. It is clear that the environmental effects of industrial practices were as much a question of scale as of a change in policy. The rapid expansion of the coal industry meant that much more of the economically unusable overburden was stored in unstable ponds and piles that limited growth in the immediate area of the mine. These unstable holdings often leaked or slid into water sources, rendering the water unsuitable for all life downstream. Paper mills, glass plants, furniture factories, and textile mills dumped most of their refuse—often including dangerous chemicals—into the region's waterways. As destructive as these processes were over a wide area, communities that lived in the immediate vicinity of copper mines were in greater danger. The extraction process, which included the use of toxic chemicals, destroyed all plant life for miles in every direction.[28]

Perhaps the lumber companies' most devastating policy was to clear-cut all the timber available to them. Ron Lewis has documented the results of this practice in illuminating detail. By the turn of the century, at least three-fourths of the immense Appalachian forest had been cut, and most of it had not been replanted. This was a catastrophe for the companies, because they had few resources to exploit, but the results were even worse for the residents of the mountain counties. The clear-cut landscape was unsightly, which deprived the region of the possibility of developing a service section of the economy around tourism. In addition, the destruction of tree cover led to significant erosion of the soil and greatly increased runoff of rain and devastating floods. This misuse of the region's resources would not be fully addressed until the innovative federal programs of the New Deal era that would lead to large-scale reforestation of the region.[29]

These massive alterations in the region's environment and economy forced other significant changes upon the Appalachian population that threatened its traditional ways of living. Many poor landowners and land-less families had been able to subsist during the antebellum period because most land was used in common. Needy families had been able to hunt on land owned by others or to let their livestock graze in the woods, eating the abundant nuts and other vegetation available. This way of life was threatened by the rapid deforestation of the region. In addition, the desire of some companies and landowners to obtain exclusive use of their lands led to creation of restrictive state laws known collectively as "fence laws," which ended the practice of considering all forested property as part of the commons. Many farmers were forced to go into debt, and the landless were forced off the land entirely. Robert Weise demonstrates in his study of Floyd County, Kentucky, that this debt burden encouraged many land owners to sell the subsoil rights to minerals in an effort to retain ownership of the surface land.[30]

This increasing emphasis on land ownership and exclusive use of the resources on or beneath the earth created tension in many mountain communities. As Altina Waller has demonstrated, this competition for resources was one of the central causes of the family violence between the Hatfields and the McCoys. Other family controversies, like the Rowan County War, were products of political battles that were often rooted in the struggle to control natural resources in the region. Increasingly, people forced off the land and into the industrial labor force entered into hostilities with business owners who lived outside the community. These conflicts often were fought by people who had avoided economic dependency as much as possible before industrialization and now found themselves to be "wage slaves."[31]

This well-documented violence became part of the Appalachian stereo-type that was widely circulated during this period. While there were several strands woven into the mountaineer image, most scholars trace widespread popular recognition of the stereotype to novelists and short-story writers, including Mary Noailles Murfree and John Fox Jr. Murfree, a resident of Middle Tennessee who vacationed in East Tennessee, was the first popular writer to rely heavily on a complete description of the people and the region. Her mountain people spoke in a distinct and unconventional dialect that indicated they were poorly educated. They were also financially challenged, poorly housed, and poorly dressed; they attended unconventional worship services and often were intoxicated and violent. In addition, the landscape was threatening, and the mountains cut their inhabitants off from the ben-eficial impact of middle-class society. Fox's mountain people suffered from most of the same afflictions as Murfree's. In addition, they were forced to wrestle with the blighting impact of rapid industrialization.[32]

These depictions of the mountaineer—named the "hillbilly" by a con-temporary New York reporter—were disseminated to the broader American public by a number of other sources. The most effective of these perpetra-tors were the nation's daily newspapers. Spurred on by technological inno-vations—including a much larger printing press that could print many more pages at one time—the papers were in a constant search for news. The development of a new chemical process that made cheap newsprint out of wood pulp encouraged large print runs, low prices, and greatly expanded circulation. The publishers had much more space to fill and sought to sell advertisements for as much of this space as possible. Sensational news sto-ries seemed to provide the ideal way to achieve all of their objectives. The development of national press pools ensured that lurid developments from all parts of the nation reached urban audiences. Unfortunately for Appa-lachia, it was at this opportune moment that widespread family violence became manifest in the region. The Hatfields, Tollivers, McCoys, and other highland families seemed to confirm all of the negative features of the new Appalachian stereotypes.[33]

All of this publicity about the needy, seemingly premodern popula-tion in the Appalachian Mountains encouraged many groups and individu-als to try to assist the stereotypical hillbillies. Ironically, these efforts only reinforced the stereotypical image of the mountain people in the public eye. Educators were among those seeking to address the challenges faced by the rural Appalachian poor. While some educators sought to combat widespread illiteracy at the local level, Berea College became the symbol of educational outreach to the mountains. Starting in 1890, Berea's president, William G. Frost, moved the college away from its founding commitment to biracial education and instead emphasized improving the lives of mountain youth. Calling the highlanders "Our Contemporary Ancestors," Frost maintained that geographical isolation explained virtually all of the supposed failures of these people. Frost said the Appalachians did in fact have a viable and worthy culture, but it was simply outdated. All that was needed was a rapid expansion of contemporary educational opportunities. Berea's mission was not only to educate its own students but also to train as many teachers as possible to carry on this work in high schools and grammar schools. Soon Alice Lloyd College, Warren Wilson College, Mars Hill College, and Berry College followed the same strategy.[34]

Berea and these other institutions were dependent upon outside sources of funding, which further confirmed the Appalachian stereotype in the popular mind. Appealing to philanthropists and ordinary donors, these organizations relied on the stereotype to legitimize their appeals. These campaigns proved to be very fruitful, and other colleges and universities soon borrowed this strategy to reach donors. In time, many graduates of these Appalachian colleges began to return to the region, holding these same preconceived ideas and preaching the same message. Before long, an image that had been developed in fictional literature was hailed as legitimate by recognized academic and professional authorities.

Much the same process occurred in the fields of medicine and social work. In both cases, the new professionals faced a culture that had developed informal practices with many generations of tradition behind them. This was particularly the case with childbirth. Rural mountain culture had identified older women—often known as "granny midwives"—who assisted with dozens of births in their lifetimes. Their broad experience made them quite competent to handle normal births and to recognize complications in delivery. Female middle-class reformers and doctors trained in medical schools worked diligently to replace the traditional midwives with scientifically trained midwives and doctors. Increasingly, children were born in hospitals instead of their homes. To accomplish this dramatic change in practice, the new professionals stigmatized the traditional midwives as isolated, ignorant, and incompetent.[35] This characterization reached a broad audience and further reinforced Appalachian stereotypes.

The new religious professionals further contributed to negative images of the Appalachian people. Novelists and newspaper reporters had noted that religious services featured strongly emotional sermons, seemingly un-structured liturgies, and unfamiliar hymns. At the same time, outside reli-gious observers noted that the proportion of church membership was smaller in the mountain counties than in the country as a whole. In addition, those Appalachians who did become church members often joined small commu-nity congregations with no national ties or were part of seemingly obscure and suspect groups like the Old Regular Baptists. One exception to this general picture, according to Mary Ella Engel, was John Hamilton Mor-gan's Mormon mission to north Georgia. The Mormons recognized the financial challenges that the mountain people faced, but Morgan and his colleagues concentrated on winning converts and defending themselves from violent opposition. Thus, the "facts" appeared to indicate that the ste-reotype of the highlanders as unchurched was true.[36]

As was the case with the other elements of the hillbilly image, this portrait was based on misunderstanding and misinformation. The widely scattered population of rural Appalachia made the new professionalism of urban congregations very difficult to follow. Many of the clergy in the mountain churches were selected because of their character and religious commitment rather than their attainment of formal religious education. To outsiders, these preachers appeared to be ignorant, and their services seemed primitive. Outside observers also failed to note that Appalachian congregations had very high standards for admission to church member-ship. The requirements included not only a personal experience of conver-sion but also a demonstrable change in the convert's attitude and activities. The result was that most people formally joined the church as mature adults after waiting a long probationary period.

The failure to understand Appalachian religious traditions encouraged outsiders to emphasize the perceived limitations of the mountaineers. Cit-ing the stereotype, Protestant and Roman Catholic home mission societ-ies appealed to the American public for initiatives to reach the mountain people. Often using offensive images of poverty and violence to strengthen their appeals, the national churches promised to rehabilitate the spiritual and material life of the rural Appalachian population. This affirmation of the hillbilly image by a seemingly disinterested source only served to fasten the stereotype onto the region with greater strength.

Ironically, mountain life—which the stereotype depicted as static—was undergoing dramatic changes, many of which are described throughout this volume. The industrial and transportation revolutions in the mountain counties were accompanied by the rapid growth of urban populations. Pittsburgh was the only true metropolitan area in the region, but cities like Spartanburg, Knoxville, Birmingham, Portsmouth, Johnstown, Huntington, Asheville, Altoona, Chattanooga, Roanoke, Marietta, Charleston, Wheeling, Greenville, and the counties near Cincinnati and Atlanta experienced rapid population growth. The people who lived in these places were increasingly part of the new middle class in the United States. Their inconvenient presence was usually ignored by those creating and using the regional stereotype.

Part of the reason that the stereotype endured was its seeming confirmation in the region's political system. Many of the most sensational episodes of regional violence took place on election day, especially when candidates provided copious amounts of alcoholic beverages to stimulate voter turnout. Further, mountain partisans appeared to be unreasoning adherents of political parties, with their party loyalty established by family tradition or in response to incidents that took place during the Civil War. They seemed to retain that commitment even when hopelessly outnumbered, like Democrats in the Second Congressional District in East Tennessee or Republicans in Fannin County, Georgia, and Winston County, Alabama. Further, their political independence appeared to be compromised by the presence of many political machines in both parties. All of these "facts" appeared to confirm the absence of political values shared by large numbers of Americans who would create the Progressive movement soon after 1900.

As was the case with mountain religion, this seemingly unchanging political scene was in fact rapidly changing throughout this time period. After the controversies and disruptions of Reconstruction, which challenged old ways of seeking votes, political organizations in all parts of Appalachia, both Republican and Democrat, tried to find structures and policies that would strengthen them. Democratic platforms embraced local control, low taxes, and small governments, and they clearly advocated white domination in race relations. In this volume, Paul Yandle explodes the myth of the Ku Klux Klan as a defensive organization of former Confederates resisting federal encroachments; instead, he asserts that the Klan was the terrorist arm of the Democratic Party and that it was crushed by the U.S. Army. For many Democrats in former Confederate states and Kentucky, the myth of the "Lost Cause" was the potent cement that held the party together. As Anne E. Marshall demonstrates in her chapter, this memory retains great power down to the present day, despite efforts to repress it for more than a century.

Most Republicans found these positions unacceptable. They supported political rights for African Americans as well as government expenditures on infrastructure and high tariffs on imported goods—the latter policies strongly supported by big business. Randall S. Gooden shows how a growing bipartisan consensus regarding the growing importance of industrialization undercut the virulent partisanship of Reconstruction. Moderate Republicans and Democrats ended restrictions on African Americans and former Confederates. Republicans also backed pensions for Union army veterans and identified with the Union war effort; the Grand Army of the Republic, a Union army veterans group in Fannin County, Georgia, named itself the William T. Sherman post.[37] This unified Unionist heritage, as Keith S. Hébert demonstrates in detail, was a construct and not reality. It was created to limit racial animosities that developed before, during, and after the war.

Local political machines proved to be strong organizations that could contest elections effectively. Using state and federal patronage to reward their followers, these machines fought each other in bitter contests. Despite their apparent strength, political bosses and organizations soon faced internal dissension and revolt because of rapidly changing economic and cultural conditions. Economic depressions in the 1880s and 1890s created more independently minded political movements in some Democratic states. The Readjusters in Virginia and the Populists in Alabama, Georgia, Tennessee, and North Carolina challenged the Democratic machines in contests that often led to unexpected Republican and independent victories. Republican leaders in Ohio, Pennsylvania, Tennessee, and West Virginia—as well as their Democratic counterparts—lost control of their party's organizations to the increasingly powerful industrialists in their regions. H. Clay Evans, Henry G. Davis, Stephen B. Elkins, and others seized control of existing organizations and used them for their own purposes. Ken Fones-Wolf provides a sophisticated reading of this change in West Virginia, where the industrialists triumphed over determined opposition. He shows how business leaders in both parties were forced to adapt their programs and compromise on some issues with opponents in their own parties. Despite these compromises, the old political bosses discovered that they could not compete with businessmen with vast financial resources.[38]

These changes in the Appalachian political landscape clearly refuted the regional stereotype. Rather than the mountain counties being the location of a static culture, politics demonstrated a clear connection between the highlands and the rest of the nation. Civil War memories, depressions, farmers' distress, and controversial legislation influenced voters all across the nation at the same time. Mountain politicians became influential national figures—President Andrew Johnson, for example—and debated the same issues that their counterparts across the nation did. The mountain counties experienced the Civil War, Reconstruction, urbanization, and industrialization along with the rest of the United States, and developments in Appalachian public life paralleled those of other Americans too.

The essays in this volume have added important new information and analyses to our understanding of the region and its past. As John C. Inscoe clearly shows, however, observers at the time were selective in deciding which characteristics defined the region and its inhabitants. People as different as William G. Frost, Emma Bell Miles, John Fox Jr., Horace Kephart, and John C. Campbell viewed the impact of the Civil War in very different ways and offered varied assessments of its impact on the mountain South. More than three decades ago, scholars at the Cratis D. Williams Symposium at Appalachian State University offered a similarly diverse set of assessments of the region.[39.] While the topics under discussion now are different, we can hope that these essays launch another broad-based inquiry into the region, as that meeting did. It seems likely that these scholarly investigations are a sign of a healthy respect for the Appalachian past and hope for a robust future.

Notes

1. See William L. Barney, *The Making of a Confederate: Walter Lenoir's Civil War* (New York: Oxford University Press, 2008); Martin Crawford, *Ashe County's Civil War: Community and Society in the Appalachian South* (Charlottesville: University Press of Virginia, 2001); William C. Davis and Meredith L. Swentor, *Bluegrass Confederate: The Headquarters Diary of Edward O. Guerrant* (Baton Rouge: Louisiana State University Press, 1999); Noel C. Fisher, *War at Every Door: Partisan Politics and Guerrilla Violence in East Tennessee, 1860–1869* (Chapel Hill: University of North Carolina Press, 1997); John D. Fowler, *Mountaineers in Gray: The Nineteenth Tennessee Volunteer Infantry Regiment, C.S.A.* (Knoxville: University of Tennessee Press, 2004); E. Stanly Godbold and Mattie U. Russell, *Confederate Colonel and Cherokee Chief: The Life of William Holland Thomas* (Knoxville: University of Tennessee Press, 1990); W. Todd Groce, *Mountain Rebels: East Tennessee Confederates and the Civil War, 1860–1870* (Knoxville: University of Tennessee

Press, 1999); John C. Inscoe and Robert C. Kenzer, eds., *Enemies of the Country: New Perspectives on Unionists in the Civil War South* (Athens: University of Georgia Press, 2001); John C. Inscoe and Gordon B. McKinney, *The Heart of Confederate Appalachia: Western North Carolina in the Civil War* (Chapel Hill: University of North Carolina Press, 2000); Robert Tracy McKenzie, *Lincolnites and Rebels: A Divided Town in the American Civil War* (New York: Oxford University Press, 2006); Gordon B. McKinney, *Zeb Vance: North Carolina's Civil War Governor and Gilded Age Political Leader* (Chapel Hill: University of North Carolina Press, 2004); Brian D. McKnight, *Contested Borderland: The Civil War in Appalachian Kentucky and Virginia* (Lexington: University Press of Kentucky, 2006); Kenneth W. Noe and Shannon H. Wilson, eds., *The Civil War in Appalachia: Collected Essays* (Knoxville: University of Tennessee Press, 1997); Sean Michael O'Brien, *Mountain Partisans: Guerrilla Warfare in the Southern Appalachians, 1861–1865* (Westport, CT: Praeger, 1999); Phillip Shaw Paludan, *Victims: A True Story of the Civil War* (Knoxville: University of Tennessee Press, 1981); Jonathan Dean Sarris, *A Separate Civil War: Communities in Conflict in the Mountain South* (Charlottesville: University of Virginia Press, 2006); Daniel E. Sutherland, ed., *A Very Violent Rebel: The Civil War Diary of Ellen Renshaw House* (Knoxville: University of Tennessee Press, 1996).

2. Zebulon B. Vance to James A. Seddon, February 25, 1863, in U.S. War Department, *War of the Rebellion: A Compilation of the Official Records of the Union and Confederate Armies*, ser. 4, vol. 2 (Washington, DC: U.S. Government Printing Office, 1900), 1061–62; McKinney, *Zeb Vance,* 144–45. For another interpretation of this destruction, see Paul E. Pashoff, "Measure of War: A Quantitative Examination of the Civil War's Destructiveness in the Confederacy," *Civil War History* 54 (March 2008): 35–62.

3. For discussion of this development in an eastern Kentucky county, see Robert S. Weise, *Grasping at Independence: Debt, Male Authority, and Mineral Rights in Appalachian Kentucky, 1850–1915* (Knoxville: University of Tennessee Press, 2001).

4. Crawford, *Ashe County's Civil War,* 118–19.

5. Paludan, *Victims.*

6. Kenneth W. Noe, "Exterminating Savages: The Union Army and Mountain Guerrillas in Southern West Virginia, 1861–1862," in *The Civil War in Appalachia,* 104–30; Fisher, *War at Every Door,* 41–153.

7. Sarris, *A Separate Civil War.*

8. Inscoe and McKinney, *The Heart of Confederate Appalachia,* 137.

9. Forest Conkin and John W. Wittig, "Religious Warfare in the Southern Highlands: Brownlow Versus Ross," *Journal of East Tennessee History* 58 (1991): 33–50; Richard Alan Humphrey, "The Civil War and Church Schism in Southern Appalachia," *Appalachian Heritage* 9 (Summer 1981): 334–47.

10. Eric Foner, *Reconstruction: America's Unfinished Revolution, 1863–1877* (New York: Harper & Row, 1988), 176–227; W. Scott Poole, *Never Surrender:*

Confederate Memory and Conservatism in the South Carolina Upcountry (Athens: University of Georgia Press, 2004), 20–79.

11. Gordon B. McKinney, *Southern Mountain Republicans, 1865–1900: Politics and the Appalachian Community* (Chapel Hill: University of North Carolina Press, 1978), 30–61; Foner, *Reconstruction, 233–39.*

12. Foner, *Reconstruction, 228–459.*

13. McKinney, *Southern Mountain Republicans, 30–47; Louisville (KY) Courier-Journal,* November 26, 1868.

14. McKinney, *Southern Mountain Republicans, 36–42.*

15. Foner, *Reconstruction, 212, 326–27, 374, 542.*

16. John Bodnar, *Steelton: Immigration and Industrialization, 1870–1940* (Pittsburgh: University of Pittsburgh Press, 1977).

17. William M. Hahn to H. Clay Evans, April 29, 1891, scrapbook, vol. 50, Henry Clay Evans Papers, Chattanooga Public Library; *Chattanooga Republican,* October 18, 1891.

18. W. David Lewis, "The Emergence of Birmingham as a Case Study of Continuity between the Antebellum Planter Class and Industrialization of the New South," *Agricultural History* 68 (Spring 1994): 62–79; Henry M. McKiven Jr., *Iron and Steel: Class, Race, and Community in Birmingham, Alabama, 1875–1920* (Chapel Hill: University of North Carolina Press, 1995).

19. John T. Lambie, *From Mine to Market: The History of Coal Transportation on the Norfolk and Western Railway* (New York: New York University Press, 1954); Ronald D Eller, *Miners, Millhands, and Mountaineers: Industrialization of the Appalachian South, 1880–1930* (Knoxville: University of Tennessee Press, 1982); Ronald L. Lewis, *Transforming the Appalachian Countryside: Railroads, Deforestation, and Social Change in West Virginia, 1880–1920* (Chapel Hill: University of North Carolina Press, 1998).

20. Crandal A. Shifflett, *Coal Towns: Life, Work, and Culture in Company Towns in Southern Appalachia, 1880–1960* (Knoxville: University of Tennessee Press, 1991); Kenneth R. Bailey, "A Judicious Mixture: Negroes and Immigrants in the West Virginia Mines, 1880–1917," *West Virginia History* 34 (January 1973): 141–61; Ronald L. Lewis, "From Peasant to Proletarian: The Migration of Southern Blacks to the Central Appalachian Coalfields," *Journal of Southern History* 55 (February 1989): 77–102; Margaret Ripley Wolfe, "Aliens in Southern Appalachia: Catholics in Coal Camps," *Appalachian Heritage* 6 (Winter 1978): 43–56.

21. Ann Field Alexander, "Like an Evil Wind: The Roanoke Riot of 1893 and the Lynching of Thomas Smith," *Virginia Magazine of History and Biography* 100 (April 1992): 173–206; W. Fitzhugh Brundage, "Racial Violence, Lynchings, and Modernization in the Mountain South," in *Appalachians and Race: The Mountain South from Slavery to Segregation,* ed. John C. Inscoe (Lexington: University Press of Kentucky, 2001), 302–16; Gordon B. McKinney, "Negro Professional Baseball Players in the Upper South in the Gilded Age," *Journal of Sport History* 3 (Winter 1976): 273–80; Michael D. Webb, "'God Bless You All—I Am Innocent': Sheriff

Joseph F. Shipp, Chattanooga, Tennessee, and the Lynching of Ed Johnson," *Tennessee Historical Quarterly* 58 (Summer 1999): 156–79.

22. Shifflett, *Coal Towns;* Douglass Flamming, *Creating the Modern South: Millhands and Managers in Dalton, Georgia, 1884–1984* (Chapel Hill: University of North Carolina Press, 1992).

23. Karin Shapiro, *A New South Rebellion: The Battle against Convict Labor in the Tennessee Coalfields, 1871–1896* (Chapel Hill: University of North Carolina Press, 1998); Robert David Ward and William Warren Rogers, *Convicts, Coal, and the Banner Mine Tragedy* (Tuscaloosa: University of Alabama Press, 1965); A. C. Hutson, "The Overthrow of the Convict Lease System in Tennessee," *East Tennessee Historical Society's Publications* 51 (1979): 92–113; Gordon B. McKinney, "Zeb Vance and the Construction of the Western North Carolina Railroad," *Appalachian Journal* 29 (Fall 2001–Spring 2002): 58–67.

24. Randall L. Patton, "E. T. Barwick and the Rise of Northwest Georgia's Carpet Industry," *Atlanta History* 42 (Winter 1999): 5–18; Frances S. Hensley, "Women in the Industrial Work Force in West Virginia, 1880–1945," *West Virginia History* 44 (1990): 115–24.

25. Jacquelyn D. Hall, "Disorderly Women: Gender and Labor Militancy in the Appalachian South," *Journal of American History* 73 (September 1986): 354–82; Gordon B. McKinney, "Women's Role in Civil War Western North Carolina," *North Carolina Historical Review* 69 (January 1992): 37–56; Lillian J. Waugh and Judith G. Stitzel, "Anything but Cordial: Coeducation and West Virginia University's Early Women," *West Virginia History* 49 (1990): 69–80; Robert Weise, "Property, Gender, and the Sale of Mineral Rights in Pre-industrial Eastern Kentucky," *Journal of the Appalachian Studies Association* 7 (1995): 79–90; Lee Ann Whites, "Rebecca Latimer Felton and the Wife's Farm: The Class and Racial Politics of Gender Reform," *Georgia Historical Quarterly* 76 (Summer 1992): 354–72.

26. Ken Fones-Wolf, *Glass Towns: Industry, Labor, and Political Economy in Appalachia, 1890–1930s* (Urbana: University of Illinois Press, 2007).

27. Lewis, *Transforming the Appalachian Countryside;* Daniel S. Pierce, *The Great Smokies: From Natural Habitat to National Park* (Knoxville: University of Tennessee Press, 2000); Robert S. Lambert, "Logging the Great Smokies, 1880–1930," *Tennessee Historical Quarterly* 20 (December 1961): 350–63.

28. Donald Edward Davis, *Where There Are Mountains: An Environmental History of the Southern Appalachians* (Athens: University of Georgia Press, 2000); David C. Hsiung, "Geographical Determinism and Possibilism: Interpretations of the Appalachian Environment and Culture in the Last Century," *Journal of the Appalachian Studies Association* 4 (1992): 14–23.

29. Lewis, *Transforming the Appalachian Countryside.*

30. Weise, *Grasping at Independence;* Alan J. Banks, "Land and Capital in Eastern Kentucky, 1890–1915," *Appalachian Journal* 8 (Autumn 1980): 8–18; Mary Beth Pudup, "The Limits of Subsistence: Agriculture and Industry in Central Appalachia," *Agricultural History* 64 (1990): 61–89; Paul J. Weingarten, Dwight

B. Billings, and Kathleen M. Blee, "Agriculture in Preindustrial Appalachia: Subsistence Farm in Beech Creek, 1850–1880," *Journal of the Appalachian Studies Association* 1 (1989): 70–80; Shawn E. Kantor and J. Morgan Kousser, "Common Sense or Commonwealth? The Fence Law and Institutional Change in the Postbellum South," *Journal of Southern History* 59 (May 1993): 201–42; Mathew R. Walpole, "The Closing of the Open Range in Watauga County, N.C.," *Appalachian Journal* 16 (Summer 1989): 320–35.

31. Altina Waller, *Feud: Hatfields, McCoys and Social Change in Appalachia, 1860–1900* (Chapel Hill: University of North Carolina Press, 1988); William Lynwood Montell, *Killings: Folk Justice in the Upper South* (Lexington: University Press of Kentucky, 1986).

32. Henry D. Shapiro, *Appalachia on Our Mind: The Southern Mountains and Mountaineers in the American Consciousness, 1870–1920* (Chapel Hill: University of North Carolina Press, 1978); Mary N. Murfree, *The Prophet of the Great Smoky Mountains* (Boston: Houghton Mifflin, 1885); John Fox Jr., *The Little Shepherd of Kingdom Come* (Lexington: University Press of Kentucky, 1987); John Fox Jr., *The Trail of the Lonesome Pine* (Lexington: University Press of Kentucky, 1984); Rodger Cunningham, "Signs of Civilization: *The Trail of the Lonesome Pine* as Colonial Narrative," *Journal of the Appalachian Studies Association* 2 (1990): 21–46; Marilyn De Eulis, "Primitivism and Exoticism in John Fox's Early Work," *Appalachian Journal* 4 (Winter 1977): 133–43; Marjorie Pryse, "Exploring Contact: Regionalism and the Outsider Standpoint in Mary Noailles Murfree's Appalachia," *Legacy* 17, no. 2 (2000): 199–212; Cratis D. Williams, "The Shaping of the Fictional Legend of the Southern Mountaineer" and "Charles Egbert Craddock and the Southern Mountain in Fiction," *Appalachian Journal* 3 (Winter 1976): 100–162.

33. Waller, *Feud*, 166, 207, 209, 214, 221–22, 238.

34. Richard Sears, *A Utopian Experiment in Kentucky: Integration and Social Equality at Berea, 1866–1904* (Westport, CT: Greenwood University Press, 1996); P. David Searles, *A College for Appalachia: Alice Lloyd on Caney Creek* (Lexington: University Press of Kentucky, 1995); Jonathan M. Atkins, "Philanthropy in the Mountains: Martha Berry and the Early Years of the Berry Schools," *Georgia Historical Quarterly* 82 (Winter 1998): 856–76; Mark Banker, "Warren Wilson College: From Mountain Mission to Multicultural Community," *American Presbyterians* 73 (Summer 1995): 111–23; Shannon H. Wilson, "Window on the Mountains: Berea's Appalachia, 1870–1930," *Filson Club History Quarterly* 64 (July 1990): 384–400.

35. Sandra Lee Barney, *Authorized to Heal: Gender, Class, and the Transformation of Medicine in Central Appalachia, 1880–1930* (Chapel Hill: University of North Carolina Press, 2000); Nancy S. Dye, "Mary Breckinridge, the Frontier Nursing Service and the Introduction of Nurse-Midwifery in the United States," *Bulletin of the History of Medicine* 57 (Winter 1983): 485–507.

36. Loyal Jones, *Faith and Meaning in the Southern Uplands* (Urbana: University of Illinois Press, 1999); Deborah Vansau McCauley, *Appalachian Mountain*

Religion: A History (Urbana: University of Illinois Press); Robert Hartman, "Origins of the Mountain Preacher," *Appalachian Heritage* 9 (Winter 1981): 55–69.

37. McKinney, *Southern Mountain Republicans;* McKinney, *Zeb Vance.*

38. McKinney, *Southern Mountain Republicans,* 142–82; Samuel L. Webb, *Two-Party Politics in the One-Party South: Alabama's Hill Country, 1874–1920* (Tuscaloosa: University of Alabama Press, 1997); Thomas T. Tull, "The Shift to Republicanism: William L. Wilson and the Election of 1894," *West Virginia History* 37 (October 1975): 17–33.

39. J. W. Williamson, ed., *An Appalachian Symposium: Essay Written in Honor of Cratis D. Williams* (Boone, NC: Appalachian State University Press, 1977).

Chapter 1

A New Frontier

Historians, Appalachian History, and the Aftermath of the Civil War

Andrew L. Slap

John C. Inscoe, one of the deans of Appalachian history, commented in 2002 that "curiously, the Civil War era has been among the last to attract the full-fledged attention of Appalachian scholars." While historians belatedly studied the Civil War in the mountain South, Inscoe observed that "Reconstruction remains one of the least examined eras" in the region's history. The field of Reconstruction—or, even more broadly, postwar— Appalachia started auspiciously in 1978 with Gordon B. McKinney's *Southern Mountain Republicans, 1865–1900.* McKinney sought to test the validity of Appalachian stereotypes by analyzing why the region was the sole center of Republican strength in the Democratic-dominated post–Civil War South. Exploring the region's political, social, and economic history, he found that anti-Confederate sentiment fueled the Republican Party's growth immediately after the war, and only the skillfulness of mountain politicians allowed regional Republican Party organizations to survive the national party's embrace of African American civil rights during Reconstruction. Many of the new books on Civil War Appalachia end with a short chapter on the postwar period, and a few historians have published articles specifically on Reconstruction Appalachia, but unfortunately this has mainly been a case of a scholar writing a pathbreaking book and no one following after it. In 2002 Kenneth W. Noe could still write that "McKinney's now two-decades-old *Southern Mountain Republicans* remains the last word on regional Reconstruction."[1]

The dearth of work on Reconstruction-era Appalachia is particularly problematic given the nature of the region's scholarship as a whole. Scholars of the mountain South have concentrated on explaining its persistent poverty and debunking the region's long-standing stereotypes. The first wave of Appalachian historians, in the 1970s, argued that the region's industrialization (which lasted approximately from 1880 to 1920) caused the poverty that afflicted Appalachia throughout the twentieth century. Another group of historians has since contended that the sources of Appalachian poverty can be found before 1860 and the Civil War. The crucial decades between the periods covered by these two dominant interpretations of Appalachian poverty have received scant attention, and understanding the interval between 1865 and the mid-1880s may help answer this central question in Appalachian history.

The decades immediately after the Civil War are likewise vital for analyzing the region's stereotypes, for it was during this period that the idea of Appalachia was first constructed. While Appalachian scholars still debate the provenance of particular stereotypes, they do agree that the region has been, and continues to be, portrayed as a primitive, isolated frontier homogenously populated with white Anglo-Saxons who are lazy and prone to violent feuding and making moonshine, but who were loyal to the Union during the Civil War. "More often than not," John Inscoe writes, "those studying the region have a strong attachment to place and commitment to those living there, both of which drive the passion with which scholars seek to overturn the stereotypes and promote a real understanding of the region." In addition, many of the stereotypes are directly related to the region's poverty, so it is important to understand how and why the stereotypes were created, as well as their degree of validity. For instance, the degree to which Appalachia was isolated is one of the more contentious debates, and this issue is key to analyzing the region's poverty and its stereotypes. The history of Appalachia during Reconstruction, one of the most transformative periods in United States history, is important in its own right; but, perhaps more significantly, studying Reconstruction can also help refocus persistent debates by chronologically connecting the major fields of Appalachian scholarship.[2]

While Appalachianists have been overlooking Reconstruction, historians of Reconstruction have disregarded Appalachia. Examining Reconstruction in Appalachia will not only give new insights into the period but also may help the field of Reconstruction emerge from its two decades of stagnation following the 1988 publication of Eric Foner's grand synthesis of the era, *Reconstruction: America's Unfinished Revolution, 1863–1877*, which "represents the culmination of the Revisionist revolution: its final form so to speak," as one leading historian concluded. The Revisionist revolution began in the middle of the twentieth century and sought to overturn the Dunning School, the first academic interpretation of Reconstruction, which originated with Professor William A. Dunning at Columbia University at the beginning of the century. The Dunning School's fundamental premise was the incapacity of African Americans, which meant that Reconstruction was doomed to failure because it sought to promote African American rights and equality. While some scholars challenged the Dunning School from the start, most notably W. E. B. DuBois in *Black Reconstruction in America,* it was not until the 1940s that a large number of historians sympathetic to African Americans and Republicans formed the Revisionist interpretation. By the time of the civil rights movement in the 1960s, the premise of the Dunning School had been completely reversed, and Reconstruction was seen as a success, laying the groundwork for a second social revolution a century later. Disillusionment with the limitations of the civil rights movement, however, helped lead to the rise of the post-Revisionists in the 1970s and 1980s, who contended that Reconstruction had been a failure because it was too conservative. Foner's synthesis managed simultaneously to put the final nail in the coffin of the Dunning School while reconciling the Revisionists and post-Revisionists by acknowledging Reconstruction's accomplishments and its limitations, all of which created a huge vacuum in the field. In the twenty years since, historians such as Heather Cox Richardson have been stretching the traditional geographic and chronological boundaries of the era in an attempt to more fully understand it, while historians such as David W. Blight have analyzed how Americans remembered the Civil War in the decades afterward.[3]

Much of the growing work on the construction and uses of Civil War memory in the last few decades has focused on the postwar South. Historians such as Gaines M. Foster, Gary W. Gallagher, and Charles Reagan Wilson have analyzed how white southerners constructed the "Lost Cause," a myth asserting in part that the war was about state rights and not slavery. This myth held that slavery was a benevolent institution in a superior society that the North only overcame through greater numbers. White southerners used the Lost Cause to find meaning and purpose after defeat, to keep the region politically united, and to help themselves adjust to the economic and social changes associated with the emergence of the New South. The study of the Lost Cause has led historians to look at such factors as the development of civic religion, representations of history in popular culture, and the influence of historical associations, but the major works on the Lost Cause rarely include Appalachia, a region that is often excluded from analysis of the South. Meanwhile, Appalachian historians have traditionally focused on the myth of Appalachia's Unionism and have neglected the importance of the Lost Cause in the region. Some historians, such as William L. Barney in the recent *The Making of a Confederate: Walter Lenoir's Civil War,* have begun to study the intersection of the Lost Cause and Appalachia, but much more needs to be done to integrate these two fields of study.[4]

The authors of the essays in this volume are using many of the methods and ideas developed in the study of Reconstruction and Civil War memory to study postwar Appalachia. Because the authors in this volume seek to integrate Appalachian history, Reconstruction, and memory of the Civil War, understanding the historiographical and methodological evolution of these is essential. This introductory essay will forgo repeating the well-known drama surrounding the history of Reconstruction and the Lost Cause, concentrating on the much more neglected evolution of Appalachian historiography.

The idea of Appalachia was first created during Reconstruction. The "local color" genre of writing, with its focus on the culture, land, and dialect of a particular region, dominated American literature from the Civil War to the end of the nineteenth century, and local-color writers often turned their attention to the mountain South, regularly depicting it as a backward frontier that was culturally and economically behind the rest of the nation. Will Wallace Harney set the tone in one of the most famous early local-color pieces, an 1873 article about his travels through eastern Kentucky. The very title, "A Strange Land and Peculiar People," embodies the local-color movement's construction of Appalachia as an alien place. Harney described how "the natives of this region are characterized by marked peculiarities of the anatomical frame" and had unusual speech patterns. Other writers presented a similar image of Appalachia in the decades immediately after the Civil War; according to historian Henry D. Shapiro, "the cumulative effect of the publication of the numerous descriptive sketches and short stories of local color which used Appalachia as a subject was the establishment of a conventional view of the mountain region as an area untouched by the progressive and unifying forces that seemed to be at work elsewhere in the United States." Rebecca Harding Davis was also a local-color writer whose stories evolved from an exposé of the iron industry in West Virginia to an examination of divisions within communities during the Civil War to stories that incorporated mountain stereotypes and sectional reunion in the mid-1870s in western North Carolina.[5]

William Goodell Frost, the Yale-educated president of Berea College in Kentucky, codified and gave a scholarly sheen to the local-color writers' conception of Appalachia in 1899, describing the region's residents as "our contemporary ancestors," an "anachronism" who were surviving remnants of the white frontiersmen who had first settled America. He insisted that since "Appalachian America has received no foreign immigration, it now contains a larger proportion of 'Sons' and 'Daughters' of the Revolution than any other part of our country." One result of this anachronism, according to Frost, was that "the feeling of toleration and justification of slavery, with all the subtleties of state rights and 'South against North,' which grew up after the Revolution did not penetrate the mountains." The preserved Revolutionary heritage and antipathy toward slavery, he argued, made "Appalachian America clave to the old flag" and, "with its old-fashioned loyalty," support the Union during the Civil War. Thus, while primitiveness made Appalachia different from the rest of the nation, the supposed absence of slavery and presence of a monolithic Unionism made it different from the rest of the South.[6]

By the turn of the twentieth century, novelists began using the otherness of Appalachia as a literary device to add dramatic tension, in the process reinforcing the developing image of Appalachia. John Fox Jr., probably the most famous and influential Appalachian novelist, used many Appalachian stereotypes in his popular novels. For instance, in his 1903 novel *The Little Shepherd of Kingdom Come,* he depicted a southern mountain boy's first meeting with an African American upon moving to a nearby valley. Though the character becomes accustomed to African Americans and slavery as a teen in Kentucky's Bluegrass region, when the Civil War breaks out he chooses to fight for the Union. The novel thus perpetuates the idea that Appalachians were ignorant of slavery and monolithically supported the Union during the Civil War. Five years later, Fox wrote the best-selling *The Trail of the Lonesome Pine,* a contemporary novel about outsider John Hale coming to the Cumberland Mountains of Kentucky and Virginia just as the area started to industrialize. Hale becomes involved in a romance with a local woman and tries to transform her from a mountain girl to a sophisticated lady, an allegory for what others were trying to do to Appalachia as a whole. The novel, with its description of feuds and other stereotypes, highlights Appalachia's isolation and primitive otherness compared to modern America.

The sparse scholarly work done on Appalachia in the first half of the twentieth century attracted few historians and strengthened the power of existing stereotypes by treating the region as an isolated folk culture. For example, reformer John C. Campbell's influential 1921 book *The Southern Highlander and His Homeland* argues that the people of Appalachia needed to be uplifted and their folk arts preserved. According to the editors of *Appalachia in the Making,* "The early treatment of preindustrial Appalachia as an isolated folk culture had at least two important scholarly consequences." On the positive side, it led to a tradition of ethnographic studies of rural Appalachia that are still indispensable, but unfortunately it also reinforced the idea of "Appalachians as a 'people without history,' thus making the study of the region the proper professional domain of anthropology and ethnography rather than history."[7]

Renewed attention to poverty in the 1960s made the supposed peculiarity of Appalachia problematic rather than quaint. In his 1962 book *The Other America,* Michael Harrington helped to launch the War on Poverty, arguing that many poor people were invisible because they looked so much like other Americans. Appalachians were different, though, according to Harrington: tourists and outlanders saw the natural beauty of the region while failing to see the poverty, which was off the beaten path. When social scientists and reformers did look at Appalachia, one of the poorest areas of the United States, the generations-old stereotypes of Appalachia fit perfectly with the new theory of the culture of poverty, allowing outsiders to blame the region's poverty on its inhabitants' culture.

While trying to convince people to help lift Appalachians out of poverty, missionary Jack E. Wells repeated many of the standard regional stereotypes in his 1965 *Yesterday's People,* a title eerily similar to Frost's "Our Contemporary Ancestors" more than six decades earlier. Wells asserts that "mountain people do both think and hope for many things—but in a different way from middle class people." Harry M. Caudill explains in the book's foreword that a combination of historical circumstances created both Appalachia's peculiar culture and its poverty, starting with the first settlers in the colonial era, who moved to the region to avoid restraint. "They were stubborn, opinionated, and sometimes cruel. People have to have these qualities in order to survive on the tooth-and-talon frontier," he explains; "the mountain walls sheltered their strengths, their quirks, and their shortcomings from the rest of the world. They turned aside subsequent streams of human migration. In a century of isolation Appalachian subculture was born." The continued acceptance of Appalachia as an isolated, primitive culture often led reformers and social scientists to use modernization theory, which argued that the way to eradicate poverty in the region was to adapt Appalachian culture to modern society.[8]

Caudill, though, represented a transition from culture of poverty theory to dependency and modernization theory to explain Appalachian poverty. While Caudill portrayed Appalachians as a benighted people prone to feuding, he primarily blamed outside economic forces for the region's poverty in his 1963 polemic *Night Comes to the Cumberlands*, about eastern Kentucky. Outsiders looking for coal duped the natives into selling their rights for almost nothing, and "the countryside was then systematically plundered in what constitutes one of the ugliest eras of exploitation in American history," he wrote. Borrowing from Third World dependency theory, Appalachian scholars began arguing that the region's poverty was not caused by its isolation from the rest of America but by the way it was connected with America. This became known as the colonial model or the inner colonial model. Significantly, this model explained the region's poverty without blaming its inhabitants, as did the culture of poverty theory. As Kenneth Noe puts it, "When combined with the foundations and methods of the 'new social history,' new-Marxist labor studies, a commitment to interdisciplinary approaches, and often an underlying anger and pride of place that grew from mountain roots and sixties activism, the colonial model metamorphosed far beyond Caudill's thesis into a movement that eventually came to be called Appalachian Revisionism." Noe succinctly describes the Revisionist argument: "Into an Arcadian, Jeffersonian, preindustrial paradise of yeoman farming and relative equality, celebrated but rarely defined in any detail, had come ruthless outside industrialists seeking profits at all costs. The genesis of the industrial era was abrupt and violent."[9]

The academic study of Appalachian history began in the 1970s as part of the interdisciplinary Appalachian Revisionism. Ronald D Eller provided the symbolic call to arms with his 1977 essay "Toward a New History of the Appalachian South," criticizing the continued scholarly acceptance of Appalachians "as a vanishing frontier and its people as frontiersmen, suspended and isolated, while the rest of the country moves across the twentieth century." Intellectual historians like Cratis D. Williams and Henry D. Shapiro began specifically investigating the creation of Appalachia as a concept to rationalize its colonial status. Shapiro's 1978 *Appalachia on Our Mind: The Southern Mountains and Mountaineers in the American Consciousness,* still standard in the field, persuasively shows how outsiders created the concept of Appalachia as primitive other during the last decades of the nineteenth century, at first to provide a contrast to modernizing America and then to justify Appalachia's exploitation into the early twentieth century. Others have expanded on Shapiro's thesis, notably Allen Batteau, who in 1990 argued that the "invention" of Appalachia actually had little to do with the southern mountains and their people but instead served the various needs of northeastern urban elites. Most Appalachian Revisionists naturally concentrated on the industrialization that occurred during the same time period, with its clear-cutting of old-growth forests and insatiable demand for coal. A prominent example is John Alexander Williams, who anticipated Eller with his 1976 *West Virginia and the Captains of Industry.* Williams examined the connections between the new state's political and business leaders during the Gilded Age and argued that the creation of new political institutions coincided with the emergence of a new industrial economy to result in "a phenomenon best described as a colonial political economy."[10]

Eller signified the importance of the turn of the twentieth century to Appalachian history with the 1982 publication of one of the most influential historical works of Appalachian Revisionism, *Miners, Millhands, and Mountaineers: Industrialization of the Appalachian South, 1880–1930.* Decades after its publication, historians still refer to this book as "the crowning achievement of this prodigiously creative period in Appalachian studies" and "a quantum leap forward." Eller used the colonial economic modernization models of Appalachia that were popular with social scientists, but he put them into a historical context, attempting to "describe the economic and social revolution that swept the mountains at the turn of the century, creating modern Appalachia." He contended that the extractive timber and mining industries in the decades around the turn of the century robbed Appalachia of its natural resources and destroyed its traditional society without fully modernizing it. Eller viewed preindustrial Appalachia as an arcadia where hardy frontiersmen lived in tight-knit communities isolated from the rest of the nation. "Few other areas of the United States more closely exemplified Thomas Jefferson's vision of a democratic society," insists Eller. Only the intrusion of outside forces like industrialization destroyed this utopian traditional Appalachian society. David E. Whisnant expanded the Revisionists' colonial model deep into the twentieth century with his 1980 book *Modernizing the Mountaineer: People, Power, and Planning in Appalachia*, contending that federal programs from the New Deal through the Great Society constituted instances of outsiders perpetuating Appalachian poverty, which began with industrialization at the turn of the century.[11]

While many of the first Revisionist works covered all of Appalachia and made broad generalizations, the next set of historians focused on local studies that still characterize the field today. Many of these historians also disliked the helpless victimhood of Appalachians implied by the original Revisionist model of outsiders ruthlessly exploiting the region. Historians such as David Corbin and Crandall Shifflett suggested that Appalachians were not duped or forced into entering the vortex of social and economic changes engulfing the region around the turn of the twentieth century. For instance, after comparing the living conditions in West Virginia and southwest Virginia mining camps to those in the area's poor rural communities, Shifflett argues that in many cases Appalachians consciously and rationally chose to become coal miners to improve their material conditions. Tom Lee likewise recently contends in a study of northeast Tennessee that Appalachians themselves bore some responsibility for their situation, finding that the "power of Appalachia's elite over the people of the region is key to understanding Appalachia's history" because "the power of the urban elite to affect rural Appalachia not only continued after the elite aided the initial entry of industry into Appalachia in the nineteenth century, but expanded as the urban elite refined tools for managing the urban environment" during the first half of the twentieth century.[12]

Many historians also began attacking the stereotypes of turn-of-the-century Appalachia that the first Revisionists had accepted. Joe William Trotter, Ronald L. Lewis, and others showed that far from being a homogenously white region, Appalachia had a long (if limited) history of racial and ethnic diversity. Wilbur R. Miller has likewise demonstrated that the moonshine stereotype was in large part created during the late nineteenth century. Altina Waller's excellent study of the infamous feud of the Hatfields and the McCoys attacks the feuding stereotype that had been adopted by the culture of poverty theory. Waller meticulously reconstructs the Tug Valley, where the families lived, to show that their feud was actually an internal conflict among Appalachians over whether the Tug Valley would modernize and who would control the process. The supposed feud and the stereotype of Appalachians' primitive violence was only later used as an excuse for outsiders to exert control over the region so they could exploit the Tug Valley's rich coal resources. Waller thus tweaks the original Revisionism by giving Appalachians more agency and including in her study an examination of the time before Appalachia's transformative industrial period. Still, Waller's work fits within the larger Revisionist school. According to Waller, "before the building of the railroad in 1889, the Tug Valley home of the Hatfields and McCoys was rural and isolated"; she argues that "the pejorative feud was used by the dominant culture as a politically useful category to explain violence of mountain dwellers as well as excuse the violence incurred in their subjection."[13]

One of the sharpest critiques of the original Revisionists was that their idyllic portrayal of preindustrial Appalachia actually reinforced the existing stereotypes of the region as an isolated, primitive, homogenous society. Building on nearly two decades of work in the field, Ronald L. Lewis provided a nuanced reinterpretation of the Revisionist school in his excellent 1998 *Transforming the Appalachian Countryside: Railroads, Deforestation, and Social Change in West Virginia, 1880–1920*. Like earlier Revisionists, Lewis saw the late nineteenth century as a period that witnessed "the transformation of Appalachia from a rural-agricultural society dependent on virgin forest, to a twentieth-century society denuded of the forest and fully enmeshed in capitalism and the markets." Significantly, though, he did not see preindustrial Appalachia as some golden age. According to Lewis, "The primeval forests harbored wild animals, hostile natives, and a dark immensity in which one might get lost and never be found," and he sums up early Appalachians' attitude toward the forest with a quote from Francis Parkman: the forest was "an enemy to be overcome by any means, fair or foul." Lewis incisively contends that the first Revisionist scholars "juxtaposed the modern industrial Appalachia of poverty and dependency with the preindustrial countryside where self-sufficient farm families enjoyed a life of relative comfort and egalitarian independence. The result of this dichotomous approach has been merely to reverse the normative value placed on preindustrial Appalachia, leaving the conception itself unchallenged."

For Lewis it was not a transition from a utopian traditional past to the evils of capitalism, but from a difficult life living off the land to industrial armageddon.[14]

Three decades of historical work have refined the original Revisionism into something that might be called Neo-Revisionism. This new interpretation allows Appalachians some agency in the transformation of their society, dispels some of the region's stereotypes, and eliminates the idea of a preindustrial arcadia. "Modern scholars of Appalachia typically reject the uniform application of this great polarity between preindustrial and industrial Appalachia or the cataclysmic transition of a region previously untouched by capital," Lewis explains. Despite its many refinements, however, Neo-Revisionism still focuses on the wrenching social and economic changes that started in the late nineteenth century to explain Appalachia's persistent poverty. In accordance with its focus on the late nineteenth century as the turning point in Appalachian history, Neo-Revisionism tends to see Appalachia before industrialization as relatively isolated from the rest of the nation. Lewis still considers the turn of the twentieth century the decisive era in Appalachian history, asserting that "the market revolution transformed the relations of the backcountry and pulled subsistent farmers into the market economy." The Neo-Revisionists have added depth and complexity to the original Appalachian Revisionism, but they still accept many of its main tenets.[15]

The greatest challenge to the Appalachian Revisionism has come not from Neo-Revisionists but from a host of historians examining Appalachian history from colonial times through the Civil War. Like their Revisionist colleagues, these historians are primarily interested in exploring the region's stereotypes and the causes of its persistent poverty. Historians studying early Appalachia, however, naturally do not consider the turn of the twentieth century the breaking point in Appalachian history, and they dispute the Revisionist depiction of an isolated preindustrial Appalachia. Most historians of early Appalachia argue that the region was significantly integrated into the rest of the nation prior to the late nineteenth century and was not an internal colony, and that the causes for poverty can often be found well before industrialization.[16]

Robert Mitchell's seminal *Commercialism and the Frontier* (1997) shows how market forces were at work in the earliest settlement of Virginia's Shenandoah Valley, a discovery that other historians replicated for other regions, particularly East Tennessee. In 1988 Durwood Dunn questioned the isolation of one of the supposedly most isolated parts of Appalachia, Cades Cove. He argued that isolation is always relative and that by the time of the Civil War, the cove's residents had "frequent exposure to new ideas and attitudes" and "easy access to regional markets for their crops and live-stock." David C. Hsiung's provocative 1997 work on East Tennessee during the late eighteenth century challenges two traditional paradigms of Appalachian studies. First, he argues that the region was more integrated into market activity during the Revolutionary era than previously thought. Because of this commercial activity, "Town residents living in East Tennessee's more accessible valleys held broader world views than" those in the mountains. Second, while most historians have considered the concept of Appalachia an external imposition that started in the late nineteenth century, Hsiung contends that the efforts of local elites in East Tennessee to stigmatize their more isolated neighbors who opposed economic development resulted in Appalachians themselves constructing some Appalachian stereotypes at an early date. This trend of finding commercial activity and connections to other parts of the country during the earliest stages of European settlement shows no sign of slowing. Kevin T. Barksdale's 2008 book on the State of Franklin explores the political and social effects of an expanding regional economy in East Tennessee during the Revolutionary period.[17]

In a direct attack on the Revisionists, historians started using Immanuel Wallerstein's world systems theory in the 1980s to argue that the region was already in economic decline well before the Civil War. Wallerstein's world systems theory rejects modernization theory's emphasis on cultural isolation and primitiveness causing poverty, but it also dismisses the colonial model favored by the Revisionists. Wallerstein conceived of capitalism as a world system evolving over centuries, with all parts of the world enmeshed at different stages. Core areas, flush with capital and commerce, exploited peripheries for raw materials and cheap labor. In a wide-ranging study covering all of Appalachia over two centuries, Paul Salstrom insists that "rather than 'colonial,' the word 'peripheral' best describes Appalachia's status, and that designation fits as far back as white settlement goes." He argues that large families and soil exhaustion started Appalachia's economic decline in the 1840s, which was only exacerbated by such phenomena as industrialization and New Deal programs. "With the adoption of the 'center-periphery' model," asserts Salstrom, "the previous rationales for demanding a 'decolonization' of Appalachia have become anachronistic. Without denying that the 1970s model of 'intercolonialism' has contrib-

uted to our understanding . . . we must now probe further. We must search
not for political conspiracies but for economic laws." Sociologist Wilma
A. Dunaway, in her 1996 book *The First American Frontier: Transition to
Capitalism in Southern Appalachia, 1700–1860,* was likewise controversial in using world systems theory to contend that Appalachia's consistent
exploitation as a capitalist periphery from 1700 to 1860 helps explain its
poverty. She argues that antebellum "Southern Appalachia never made the
transition to the kind of capitalism that characterized the core," and thus
that "the basis for its future growth—its land and mineral resources—had
been degraded, squandered, or hoarded in response to periodic changes
in commodity demanded by the core." Unlike Salstrom and Dunaway's
broader studies, sociologists Dwight B. Billings and Kathleen M. Blee's
2001 longitudinal study of Clay County, Kentucky, during the nineteenth
century uses world system theory. Explicitly rejecting both the culture of
poverty and internal colonial explanations of poverty, they insisted that
Clay County, far from being isolated, had always been a part of the world
capitalist system. It was the nature of the region's connection to the world
capitalist system as a periphery, that caused poverty in Clay County and
the rest of Appalachia, not isolation.[18]

Historians examining Appalachia in the decades immediately before
the Civil War have focused on demonstrating that the region was economically and culturally part of the South. Robert Tracy McKenzie's 1994 *One
South or Many?* uses a comparative analysis of Tennessee during the Civil
War era to suggest "the possibility that recent scholarship both oversimpli-
fies distinctions between plantation and nonplantation regions and exag-
gerates the socioeconomic heterogeneity of the Old South." Though not
using the world systems theory model like scholars such as Salstrom and
Dunaway, McKenzie similarly concludes that East Tennessee was in economic decline as early as the 1840s. The same year McKenzie published his
study, Kenneth W. Noe more explicitly rejected the Revisionist insistence
that Appalachia was isolated and premodern before the 1880s, explaining
that "the problem with Eller's interpretation is that all the factors pointed
to as post-1880 Appalachian modernization . . . were active in southwest
Virginia and other parts of the southern mountains well before the Civil
War." Noe's analysis of railroad development in southwest Virginia shows
not only that the area was economically connected to the rest of the South
and already in the process of modernizing by the time of the Civil War, but
also that "residents unloaded their ideology as well as their goods off the

train." Noe's findings reinforce the newer tendency "to describe the region not as an isolated Jeffersonian paradise soon to be lost but rather reaffirm its warts-and-all southernness."[19]

Slavery and race relations, of course, were the antebellum South's biggest warts. Noe discovered how slavery expanded along with the railroad into southwest Virginia, so that by 1861 that part of Appalachia was politically linked to Richmond. The pathbreaking work on slavery and Appalachia was John C. Inscoe's 1989 *Mountain Masters, Slavery, and the Sectional Crisis in Western North Carolina,* which demonstrates that the idea of a racially innocent and homogenous Appalachia, free of both blacks and slavery, was a myth. He shows that the mountain elite, almost without exception, were slave owners who were commercially linked to the lower South. Though he considered mountain slavery to be different from that in the lower South, Inscoe still found that in western North Carolina "the majority of citizens and their leaders were very much within that mainstream of southern sentiment throughout the sectional crisis." Wilma A. Dunaway has since challenged some of Inscoe's characterizations of mountain slavery, particularly whether it was less harsh than lowland slavery, but if anything her work only reemphasizes the importance of slavery in the Appalachian South. Inscoe has spent much of his career exposing the dual myths that Appalachia "was basically free of slaves" and that, as a consequence, Appalachia was predominantly Unionist during the Civil War. The central point of his 2008 collection of essays, *Race, War, and Remembrance in the Appalachian South,* is that "southern highlanders were also southerners—sometimes foremost, sometimes more secondarily—and their actions and attitudes were often dictated as much or more by their identity with that larger regional entity."[20]

The degree of Appalachia's isolation versus its southernness is one of the fiercest debates among the region's Civil War historians. One of the difficulties is that all recent work has focused on particular sections of Appalachia, and it is difficult to compare them and find generalizations. Ralph Mann's comparative analysis of four different communities in Tazewell County, Virginia, before the Civil War demonstrates the problems of identifying a typical Appalachian community in even one county, let alone the entire mountain South. Not surprisingly, John Inscoe and Gordon McKinney contend in their joint study of western North Carolina that a "large portion of the planters, yeoman farmers, artisans, merchants, and professionals were already integrated into the market economy of the South," and

Martin Crawford even argues that the residents of Ashe County in western North Carolina were increasingly "extending their economic and cultural horizons beyond the confines of neighborhood or county border . . . to those of regional and national society." W. Todd Groce finds a similar situation in East Tennessee, where he argues the coming of the railroad made the region's economy "increasingly interdependent with that of Virginia and the lower South." Interestingly, though, another historian of Civil War East Tennessee, Noel C. Fisher, has recently complained about the current literature's "somewhat strained attempt to demonstrate that the southern Appalachia regions were, in fact, Southern—integrated into the Southern economy, in harmony with Southern politics and institutions, and attuned to Southern interests and grievances." Not limiting his analysis to East Tennessee, he takes particular issue with the work of Inscoe, McKinney, Noe, and Groce. Fisher describes in his own research how "East Tennessee's geographical isolation, its separate sense of identity, and its history created a different set of loyalties and divided much of East Tennessee from the rest of the state and the South." John D. Fowler likewise asserts in his study of East Tennessee Confederates that the region was a "product of its geographic isolation" and "had little in common with the slave-based plantation economy that dominated most of the rest of the South." Altina Waller argues that residents of the Tug Valley, on the border of Virginia and Kentucky, were even more isolated, for they "perceived themselves as different from and perhaps even in active opposition to the economic, religious, and political configurations, not only of the United States and the South, but also their own counties."[21]

Some Civil War historians have tried to find a middle ground between isolation and southernness for Appalachia. Tracey McKenzie contends that when residents of Civil War–era Knoxville did "evaluate and respond to national events, they did so first and foremost through the medium of local institutions and in a manner shaped by local circumstances." Jonathan Dean Sarris likewise asserts that "localism was a pervasive force in the mountains, underlying most of the choices north Georgians made" and that "the mountain guerrillas described in his book were largely illiterate, pragmatic, ruthless people who fought not for 'cause and comrade' but for local power and influence." The degree of Appalachia's isolation or integration is an important question, both for understanding the region during the Civil War era and for answering larger question's concerning Appalachia's persistent poverty and stereotyped isolation.[22]

Regardless of whether they consider Appalachia to be southern or not, Civil War historians studying the region agree that Appalachia was not a Unionist stronghold; rather, it was a mixture of pro-Union and pro-Confederate sentiments. The recent emphasis on destroying the old myth of a Unionist mountain South can be seen in recent book titles: *Mountaineers in Gray, Mountain Rebels, The Heart of Confederate Appalachia,* and *Lincolnites and Rebels.* A general consensus has also emerged about why Appalachians decided to side with either the Union or the Confederacy. Altina Waller hypothesized in 1988 that Unionist Appalachians were motivated by their "entanglement, both economically and culturally, with the dominant planter economy," but the last two decades of research has actually shown the opposite. Residents of towns had more connections with the South and were more likely to support the Confederacy. McKenzie finds Knoxville split between the camps, while the surrounding countryside was predominantly Unionist, a pattern that Fowler and Groce document throughout East Tennessee. Fowler also discovered that slaveholders disproportionately served in the area's Confederate regiment. This corresponds with Crawford's account of western North Carolina's Ashe County, where "the typical Unionist came from a poor, nonslaveholding tenant or small landowning household located away from the county's main commercial and political centers." The borderland between eastern Kentucky and southwest Virginia, including one of the counties Waller studied, seems to be an exception to this model, for according to Brian D. McKnight, slavery in this area "appears to have exercised minimal influence over the decision of the mountaineers to join the Southern cause."[23]

The myth of a savage Appalachia, naturally prone to violent feuds, has been another primary target of recent scholarship. Appalachians' divided loyalties and the lack of consistent government control of the region created a toxic situation during the Civil War that often led to violent guerrilla warfare in parts of the mountain South. One of the first scholarly books about the Civil War in Appalachia was a study of the Shelton Laurel massacre in the mountains of North Carolina, where thirteen prisoners were executed, a choice of topic that implicitly validated the stereotype of feuding Appalachians. No matter what part of wartime Appalachia is examined, it seems as though almost every book recounts horrific acts of violence. For example, Fisher describes men, women, and children being tortured and hanged in East Tennessee. By 1864 in western North Carolina, according to Inscoe and McKinney, "civilians found themselves victimized by increased abuse and terrorism from roving bands of bushwhackers or deserters, which were subject to no obvious control or authority." Atrocities also occurred in northeastern Georgia, according to Jonathan Sarris: "By the war's final months, few ethical barriers to brutality remained, and violence became a casual, causeless affair." Immediately after the war in East Tennessee, according to both Fowler and Groce, former Confederates were subject to a systematic campaign of terror and intimidation. Historians, though, are at pains to demonstrate that the violence was not natural to mountain residents, as the stereotype now holds. Fisher connects much of the violence in East Tennessee to larger political and military concerns. Sarris emphatically argues that though "north Georgians participated in extralegal violence and bloody massacres during the Civil War . . . their behavior stemmed not from cultural retardation or innate savagery but from a series of identifiable events that gradually turned highlanders against each other in the most violent ways."[24]

The violence in Appalachia during the Civil War and its immediate aftermath, of course, did more than just create a stereotype, for it devastated communities throughout the region and had long-lasting effects. Civil War historians have begun to explore some of the conflict's long-term effects on Appalachia, usually in their book's last chapter. In East Tennessee, according to Fisher and others, Unionists drove Confederate sympathizers out and turned the region into a Republican bastion for years to come. For north Georgians, Sarris explains, the war "did not end in 1865; it simply shifted theaters—from the battlefield to the minds and memories of the participants." Crawford finds that the conflict severely strained local communities in western North Carolina's Ashe County, while Inscoe and McKinney contend that the war essentially destroyed the antebellum communities of western North Carolina. This reshaping of antebellum communities helped prepare the region for the advent of the railroad and industrialization in the 1880s, according to Inscoe and McKinney: "By destroying the viability of the more traditional community system, the Civil War eased the way for the modernization of western North Carolina." Ideas about how the Civil War affected Appalachia are mainly hypotheses, though, because so little work has been done on the decades immediately after the conflict.[25]

While the Civil War may have divided the nation, Reconstruction still divides Appalachian scholarship. In broad terms, Revisionist historians consider pre-1880s Appalachia to be isolated and preindustrial before

outside capitalist forces invaded. The process of industrialization then led
to persistent poverty and the creation of many of the stereotypes of the
region, including violent feuding. Historians studying the mountain South
before 1865, though, generally consider the idea of the region's isolation a
stereotype that needs dispelling. For these historians, Appalachia was significantly integrated into the South, if not the nation, and it was already on
the path to both modernization and poverty well before the first shot was
fired at Fort Sumter. The essays in this volume are an effort to start exploring in depth the Civil War's aftermath in Appalachia, both to understand
those crucial years and to engage in larger debates about the region. It is
perhaps appropriate, though unplanned, that these essays often come to
different conclusions.

The next four essays focus on violence and politics in Reconstruction
Appalachia. All four essays analyze the continuing conflict in the region
after the war, but they have extremely different interpretations of its meaning. Keith S. Hébert argues that localism, not larger issues of Reconstruction
and race, drove the Ku Klux Klan in northeast Georgia. Reconstruction-era
Klan violence, according to Hébert, was just one example of the prolonged
nineteenth-century conflict between local and outside forces that eventually doomed the region to colonization. T. R. C. Hutton, meanwhile,
thinks that localism has been stressed too much in evaluating postwar violence in eastern Kentucky, for which he directly assails the Revisionists. He
contends that eastern Kentucky Appalachians, both black and white, were
similar to other southerners during Reconstruction in being motivated by
national and racial issues to commit acts of violence. Because Kentucky
never seceded or faced an official reconstruction, however, Hutton theo-
rizes that outside observers chose to attribute the postwar violence to a lack
of civilization, despite its being driven by crucial issues of power alloca-
tion—issues faced by all former Confederate states.

Steve Nash interestingly finds that in at least part of one former Confederate state, western North Carolina, race was not the decisive issue. He
insists that it was a combination of national and local issues centering on
the political restoration of southern states to the Union that forced moderate white mountaineers in western North Carolina to abandon their previous anti-Confederate coalition, thus paving the way for Congressional
Reconstruction and the rise of the Republican Party in the mountains.
While Nash looks at the beginning of Reconstruction in North Carolina,
Paul Yandle shows how residents of western North Carolina later became

part of a statewide effort to end Reconstruction that would have rever-
berations for decades to come. He focuses on how the Republicans' failure
to expel three state legislators accused of Ku Klux Klan activity from the
North Carolina General Assembly in 1871 and 1872 was a precursor to
what African Americans would face in the early twentieth century.

The degree of Appalachia's isolation during Reconstruction is also
examined in an essay on William "Parson" Brownlow's changing racial
rhetoric, and in a study of a Mormon missionary. Kyle Osborn demonstrates how Brownlow, a prominent East Tennessee Whig, quickly reacted
to political and constitutional changes at the state and national levels, such
as emancipation and suffrage, by changing his public attitudes toward African Americans. Mary Ella Engel likewise discusses Appalachia's connections to broader American society in her study of a Mormon missionary in
northwest Georgia who successfully convinced Appalachians to migrate to
the West. To some degree, Appalachians' willingness to relocate westward
demonstrates the social and economic upheaval of post-Reconstruction
Georgia, but the establishment of the settlement in Colorado also places
Appalachian Georgians within broader nineteenth-century movements seeking communitarian solutions in social and religious experiments in the
West.

Randall S. Gooden and Ken Fones-Wolf focus on a more traditional
Appalachian question: the intersection of economics and politics in West
Virginia. Gooden argues that different economic interests combined with
rifts between Unionists over the treatment of former Confederates to create
a new political coalition in the state during Reconstruction. According to
Gooden, the new coalition shaped the state's politics for decades, including the conflict over West Virginia's small African American population
and reform of the state's constitution in 1872. Fones-Wolf uses borderland
theory to analyze how West Virginia's leaders decided to identify themselves within the context of the United States, politically and economically.
Fones-Wolf examines how West Virginia, a border state born of Civil War–
era sectionalism, straddled southern and northern notions of economic
development in the nation's transformative postwar period. Increasingly, he
finds, it was issues of economic development, and not divisions over southern identity, that shaped West Virginia's political divisions.

Issues of economic development also figure prominently in two essays
on how Appalachians constructed their memory of the Civil War in the
decades after the conflict. Robert M. Sandow brings an unusual perspective

to the study of Appalachia by looking at the rarely examined northern part of the region. Ronald Lewis and others have shown that many of the businessmen involved with southern Appalachia's postwar extractive industries, such as timber and coal mining, got their start in Pennsylvania, the area on which Sandow focuses his work. Sandow demonstrates how industrial capitalism and extractive industries were already undermining traditional society in northern Appalachia during the antebellum period, prefiguring the whirlwind that would engulf the mountain South after the Civil War and inclining many residents of Pennsylvanian Appalachia to oppose the Civil War for local reasons. In the decade immediately after the Civil War, Pennsylvania Appalachians drew on their memories of their wartime resistance in protesting the postwar economic development of their region. Tom Lee finds just the opposite in East Tennessee, an area that was also internally divided during the Civil War. In the immediate postwar period, according to Lee, East Tennessee leaders focused on the region's ties to the American Revolution to allow both Union and Confederate supporters to claim a common heritage of patriotism and nationalism, a myth that would simultaneously mediate internal conflicts and appeal to northern industrialists. In addition, Lee shows that throughout the later nineteenth century leaders in East Tennessee consciously obfuscated the region's internal Civil War divisions and helped foster a myth of monolithic Unionism to attract northern capital.

The last two essays demonstrate the continuing importance of the construction of the Civil War well into the twentieth century. While the Civil War had a huge impact on the mountain South, John C. Inscoe finds that by the turn of the twentieth century, many writers and scholars increasingly ignored the region's role in the conflict and only used simplistic explanations of wartime loyalty to explain their characters and subjects. He contends that many of these early-twentieth-century Appalachian writers marginalized the region's important Civil War past to sell the "otherness" of the mountain South to northern philanthropists and organizations. In a study of Civil War memory in eastern Kentucky, Anne E. Marshall shows how stereotypes can be used to construct different myths. The stereotype of an all-white Appalachia was first used in the late nineteenth century to shape a Unionist myth for the divided region, but in the twentieth century the same stereotype was instrumental in creating a mythical Confederate past for the Union state. Marshall traces the development of these evolving myths since the end of the Civil War and argues that only at the beginning of the twenty-first century has Appalachia started to escape the myth of racial innocence.

In 1997 Kenneth W. Noe and Shannon H. Wilson published the much-needed *The Civil War in Appalachia: Collected Essays,* a seminal anthology that produced a new wave of scholarship embracing new trends in Appalachian and Civil War historiography. It is hoped that this volume can come close to replicating that success. Similar to *The Civil War in Appalachia,* the essays in this volume do not paint a coherent portrait of the Civil War's aftermath in Appalachia. They suggest that in some places, Appalachia was more integrated with the rest of the nation than was previously thought; in other areas, Appalachia was more isolated than the conventional wisdom has had it. There were places where people sought outside capital, and places where they resisted development. The variation in descriptions of Appalachia reflects the chaos and upheaval of Reconstruction, one of the most difficult periods of American history; it may also demonstrate the difficulty of defining Appalachia.[26]

Notes

1. John C. Inscoe, "The Discovery of Appalachia: Regional Revisionism as Scholarly Renaissance," in *A Companion to the American South,* ed. John B. Boles, 377–78 (Malden, MA: Blackwell Publishers, 2002); Gordon B. McKinney, *Southern Mountain Republicans, 1865–1900: Politics and the Appalachian Community* (Chapel Hill: University of North Carolina Press, 1978); Kenneth W. Noe, "Appalachia before Mr. Peabody: Some Recent Literature on the Southern Mountain Region," *Virginia Magazine of History and Biography* 110, no. 1 (2002): 32. Some of the articles specifically on Appalachia during Reconstruction include: Paul D. Escott, "Clinton A. Cilley, Yankee War Hero in the Postwar South: A Study in the Compatibility of Regional Values," *North Carolina Historical Review* 68 (October 1991): 404–26; Benjamin H. Severance, "Loyalty's Political Vanguard: The Union League of Maryville, Tennessee, 1867–1869," *Journal of East Tennessee History* 71 (1999): 25–46; Bruce Stewart, "'When Darkness Reigns Then Is the Hour to Strike': Moonshining, Federal Liquor Taxation, and Klan Violence in Western North Carolina, 1868–1872," *North Carolina Historical Review* 80 (October 2003): 453–74; Bruce Stewart, "Attacking 'Red-Legged Grasshoppers': Moonshiners, Violence, and the Politics of Federal Liquor Taxation in Western North Carolina, 1865–1876," *Appalachian Journal* 32 (Fall 2004): 26–48. Wilbur R. Miller deals with some aspects of Reconstruction in *Revenuers and Moonshiners: Enforcing Federal Liquor Law in the Mountain South, 1865–1900* (Chapel Hill: University Press of North Carolina, 1991). McKinney deals with Reconstruction politics again in *Zeb Vance: North Carolina's Civil War Gover-*

nor and Gilded Age Political Leader (Chapel Hill: University of North Carolina Press, 2004).

2. Inscoe, "The Discovery of Appalachia," 383. Three of the best historiographical treatments of Appalachia are the introduction to *Appalachia in the Making: The Mountain South in the Nineteenth Century,* ed. Mary Beth Pudup, Dwight B. Billings, and Altina Waller, 1–24 (Chapel Hill: University of North Carolina Press, 1995); Inscoe, "The Discovery of Appalachia"; and Noe, "Appalachia before Mr. Peabody."

3. Eric Foner, *Reconstruction: America's Unfinished Revolution, 1863–1877* (New York: Harper & Row, 1988); Michael Perman, "Eric Foner's Reconstruction: A Finished Revolution," *Reviews in American History* 17 (March 1989), 74; Heather Cox Richardson, *The Death of Reconstruction: Race, Labor, and Politics in the Post–Civil War North, 1865–1901* (Cambridge, MA: Harvard University Press, 2001); Heather Cox Richardson, *West from Appomattox: The Reconstruction of America after the Civil War* (New Haven, CT: Yale University Press, 2007); and David W. Blight, *Race and Reunion: The Civil War in American Memory* (Cambridge, MA: Harvard University Press, 2001). A good starting point to learn about both the past and the future of Reconstruction history is Thomas J. Brown, ed., *Reconstructions: New Perspectives on the Postbellum United States* (New York: Oxford University Press, 2006).

4. The literature on the Lost Cause is immense. Among the classic works are Thomas L. Connelly, *The Marble Man: Robert E. Lee and His Image in American Society* (New York: Knopf, 1977); Charles Reagan Wilson, *Baptized in Blood: The Religion of the Lost Cause, 1865–1920* (Athens: University of Georgia Press, 1983); Mark E. Neely Jr., Harold Holzer, and Gabor S. Boritt, *The Confederate Image: Prints of the Lost Cause* (Chapel Hill: University of North Carolina Press, 1987); and Gaines M. Foster, *Ghosts of the Confederacy: Defeat, the Lost Cause and the Emergence of the New South, 1865–1913* (New York: Oxford University Press, 1988). Gary W. Gallagher has written and edited numerous works on the Lost Cause in the last decade, including *The Myth of the Lost Cause and Civil War History* (Bloomington: Indiana University Press, 2000), coedited with Alan T. Nolan; *Lee and His Generals in War and Memory* (Baton Rouge: Louisiana State University Press, 2004); and *Causes Won, Lost, and Forgotten: How Hollywood and Popular Art Shape What We Know about the Civil War* (Chapel Hill: University of North Carolina Press, 2008). Some of Gallagher's students have been doing the most cutting-edge work on the Lost Cause, including William A. Blair, *Cities of the Dead: Contesting the Memory of the Civil War in the South, 1865–1914* (Chapel Hill: University of North Carolina Press, 2004), and Caroline E. Janney, *Burying the Dead but Not the Past: Ladies' Memorial Associations and the Lost Cause* (Chapel Hill: University of North Carolina Press, 2008). Work on the Lost Cause in Appalachia has been more sparse. One of the few books in this area is William L. Barney, *The Making of a Confederate: Walter Lenoir's Civil War* (New York: Oxford University Press, 2008). Many of the works on Civil War Appalachia devote a few

pages to the subject, some of the most notable being John C. Inscoe and Gordon B. McKinney, *The Heart of Confederate Appalachia: Western North Carolina in the Civil War* (Chapel Hill: University of North Carolina Press, 2000), and Jonathan Dean Sarris, *A Separate Civil War: Communities in Conflict in the Mountain South* (Charlottesville: University of Virginia Press, 2006). Among the few articles specifically on the Lost Cause in Appalachia are Rod Andrew Jr., "Martial Spirit, Christian Virtue, and the Lost Cause: Military Education at North Georgia College, 1871–1915," *Georgia Historical Quarterly* 79 (Fall 1996): 486–505, and Richard D. Starnes, "'The Stirring Strains of Dixie': The Civil War and Southern Identity in Haywood County, North Carolina," *North Carolina Historical Review* 74 (July 1997): 238–59.

5. Will Wallace Harney, "A Strange Land and Peculiar People," *Lippincott's Magazine* 12 (October 1873): 431; Henry D. Shapiro, *Appalachia on Our Mind: The Southern Mountains in the American Consciousness, 1870–1920* (Chapel Hill: University of North Carolina Press, 1978): 5; Kenneth W. Noe, "'Deadened Color and Colder Horror': Rebecca Harding Davis and the Myth of Unionist Appalachia," in *Back Talk from Appalachia: Confronting Stereotypes,* ed. Dwight D. Billings, Gurney Norman, and Katherine Ledford (Lexington: University Press of Kentucky, 2000), 67–84.

6. William Goodell Frost, "Our Contemporary Ancestors in the Southern Mountains," *Atlantic Monthly* (March 1899): 311, 313–14.

7. Introduction, *Appalachia in the Making,* 4–8.

8. Jack E. Weller, *Yesterday's People: Life in Contemporary Appalachia* (Lexington: University Press of Kentucky, 1965), 3, xvi; *Appalachia in the Making,* 5–7.

9. Henry M. Caudill, *Night Comes to the Cumberlands: A Biography of a Depressed Area* (Boston: Brown & Little, 1963), back cover; Noe, "Appalachia before Mr. Peabody," 11; Helen M. Lewis, Linda Johnson, and Donald Askin, eds., *Colonialism in Modern America: The Appalachia Case* (Boone, NC: Appalachia Consortium Press, 1978).

10. Ronald D Eller, "Toward a New History of the Appalachian South," in "A Guide to Appalachian Studies," ed. Stephen L. Fisher, J. W. Williamson, and Juanita Lewis, special issue, *Appalachian Journal* 5 (Autumn 1977), 75; Cratis D. Williams, "The Southern Mountaineer in Fact and Fiction" (PhD diss., New York University, 1961); Shapiro, *Appalachia on Our Mind,* 5; Allen W. Batteau, *The Invention of Appalachia* (Tucson: University of Arizona Press, 1990); John Alexander William, *West Virginia and the Captains of Industry* (Morgantown: West Virginia University Library, 1976), 1; Inscoe, "The Discovery of Appalachia," 378. There is a rich literature on the creation of Appalachia as an idea. For some examples, see David E. Whisnant, *All That is Native and Fine: The Politics of Culture in an American Region* (Chapel Hill: University of North Carolina Press, 1983); Jane S. Becker, *Selling Tradition: Appalachia and the Construction of an American Folk, 1930–1940* (Chapel Hill: University of North Carolina Press, 1998); and Billings, Norman, and Ledford, *Back Talk from Appalachia.*

11. *Appalachia in the Making*, 8–9; Inscoe, "The Discovery of Appalachia," 378; Ronald D Eller, *Miners, Millhands, and Mountaineers: Industrialization of the Appalachian South, 1880–1930* (Knoxville: University of Tennessee Press, 1982), xxiv, 3; David E. Whisnant, *Modernizing the Mountaineer: People, Power, and Planning in Appalachia* (Boone, NC: Appalachia Consortium Press, 1980; Knoxville: University of Tennessee Press, 1994); Noe, "Appalachia before Mr. Peabody," 11.

12. David Corbin, *Life, Work, and Rebellion in the Coal Fields: The Southern West Virginia Miners, 1880–1922* (Urbana: University of Illinois Press, 1981); Crandall A. Shifflett, *Coal Towns: Life, Work, and Culture in Company Towns of Southern Appalachia, 1880–1960* (Knoxville: University of Tennessee Press, 1991); Tom Lee, *The Tennessee-Virginia Tri-cities: Urbanization in Appalachia, 1900–1950* (Knoxville: University of Tennessee Press, 2005), xiv.

13. Ronald L. Lewis, *Black Coal Miners in America: Race, Class, and Community Conflict, 1780–1980* (Lexington: University Press of Kentucky, 1987); Joe William Trotter Jr., *Coal, Class, and Color: Blacks in Appalachia, 1915–1932* (Urbana: University of Illinois Press, 1990); Wilbur R. Miller, *Revenuers and Moonshiners: Enforcing Federal Liquor Law in the Mountain South, 1865–1900* (Chapel Hill: University of North Carolina Press, 1991); Altina L. Waller, *Feud: Hatfields, McCoys, and Social Change in Appalachia, 1860–1900* (Chapel Hill: University of North Carolina Press, 1988), 106; Altina L. Waller, "Feuding in Appalachia: Evolution of a Cultural Stereotype," in *Appalachia in the Making*, 370.

14. Ronald L. Lewis, *Transforming the Appalachian Countryside: Railroads, Deforestation, and Social Change in West Virginia, 1880–1920* (Chapel Hill: University of North Carolina Press, 1998), 3, 50.

15. Lewis, *Transforming the Appalachian Countryside*, 50, 8.

16. Robert D. Mitchell, *Commercialism and the Frontier: Perspectives on the Early Shenandoah Valley* (Charlottesville: University of Virginia Press, 1977).

17. Robert D. Mitchell, *Commercialism and the Frontier: Perspectives on the Early Shenandoah Valley* (Charlottesville: University of Virginia Press, 1977); Durwood Dunn, *Cade's Cove: The Life and Death of a Southern Appalachian Community, 1818–1937* (Knoxville: University of Tennessee Press, 1988), 115, 143; David C. Hsiung, *Two Worlds in the Tennessee Mountains: Exploring the Origins of Appalachian Stereotypes* (Lexington: University Press of Kentucky, 1994), 19; Kevin T. Barksdale, *The Lost State of Franklin: America's First Secession* (Lexington: University Press of Kentucky, 2008).

18. Paul Salstrom, "Appalachia's Path toward Dependency, 1840–1940" (PhD diss., Brandeis University, 1988), 3–4; Paul Salstrom, *Appalachia's Path to Dependency: Rethinking a Region's Economic History, 1730–1940* (Lexington: University Press of Kentucky, 1997); Wilma A. Dunaway, *The First American Frontier: Transition to Capitalism in Southern Appalachia, 1700–1860* (Chapel Hill: University of North Carolina Press, 1996), 320, 322; Dwight B. Billings and Kathleen M. Blee, *The Road to Poverty: The Making of Wealth and Hardship in Appalachia* (New York: Cambridge University Press, 2001).

19. Robert Tracy McKenzie, *One South or Many? Plantation Belt and Upcountry in Civil War–Era Tennessee* (Cambridge, MA: Cambridge University Press, 1994), 193; Kenneth W. Noe, *Southwest Virginia's Railroad: Modernization and the Sectional Crisis in the Civil War Era* (Urbana: University of Illinois Press, 1994), 5, 7. For variations of "Southernness" even within a section of Appalachia, see Meredith Anne Grant, "Internal Dissent: East Tennessee's Civil War: 1849–1865" (master's thesis, East Tennessee State University, 2008).

20. Noe, *Southwest Virginia's Railroad,* 84; John C. Inscoe, *Mountain Masters, Slavery, and the Sectional Crisis in Western North Carolina* (Knoxville: University of Tennessee Press, 1989), 9; Wilma A. Dunaway, *Slavery in the American Mountain South* (Cambridge, MA: Cambridge University Press, 2003); John C. Inscoe, *Race, War, and Remembrance in the Appalachian South* (Lexington: University Press of Kentucky, 2008), 2, 7. See also John C. Inscoe, ed., *Appalachia and Race: The Mountain South from Slavery to Segregation* (Lexington: University Press of Kentucky, 2001). Kyle Osborn argues that an analysis of Civil War–era rhetoric suggests that race attitudes in East Tennessee were not significantly different from those of the South in general, in "'Bondage or Barbarism': Parson Brownlow and the Rhetoric of Racism in East Tennessee, 1845–1867" (master's thesis, East Tennessee State University, 2007).

21. Ralph Mann, "Diversity in the Antebellum Appalachian South: Four Farm Communities in Tazewell County, Virginia," in *Appalachia in the Making*, 132–62. See also Ralph Mann, "Mountain, Land, and Kin Networks: Burkes Garden, Virginia, in the 1840s and 1850s," *Journal of Southern History* 58 (August 1992): 59–66; Inscoe and McKinney, *Heart of Confederate Appalachia*, 282; Martin Crawford, *Ashe County's Civil War: Community and Society in the Appalachian South* (Charlottesville: University Press of Virginia, 2001), 10; W. Todd Groce, *Mountain Rebels: East Tennessee Confederates and the Civil War, 1860–1870* (Knoxville: University of Tennessee Press, 1999), 18; Noel Fisher, "Feelin' Mighty Southern: Recent Scholarship on Southern Appalachia in the Civil War," *Civil War History* 47 (December 2001): 345; Noel C. Fisher, *War at Every Door: Partisan Politics and Guerrilla Violence in East Tennessee, 1860–1869* (Chapel Hill: University of North Carolina Press, 1997), 183; John D. Fowler, *Mountaineers in Gray: The Nineteenth Tennessee Volunteer Infantry Regiment, C.S.A.* (Knoxville: University of Tennessee Press, 2004), 14; Waller, *Feud,* 33.

22. Robert Tracy McKenzie, *Lincolnites and Rebels: A Divided Town in the American Civil War* (New York: Oxford University Press, 2006), 26; Sarris, *A Separate Civil War,* 184, 3.

23. McKenzie, *Lincolnites and Rebels,* 6; Fowler, *Mountaineers in Gray,* 20, 26; Groce, *Mountain Rebels,* 70; Crawford, *Ashe County's Civil War,* 132; Waller, *Feud,* 31; Brian D. McKnight, *Contested Borderland: The Civil War in Appalachian Kentucky and Virginia* (Lexington: University Press of Kentucky, 2006), 17.

24. Kenneth W. Noe and Shannon H. Wilson, eds., *The Civil War in Appalachia: Collected Essays* (Knoxville: University of Tennessee Press, 1997), xiv; Phil-

lip Shaw Paludan, *Victims: A True Story of the Civil War* (Knoxville: University of Tennessee Press, 1981), 62; Fisher, *War at Every Door,* 88–89; Inscoe and McKinney, *The Heart of Confederate Appalachia,* 238; Sarris, *A Separate Civil War,* 102, 184; Groce, *Mountain Rebels,* 154; Fowler, *Mountaineers in Gray,* 189. One exception to the attacks on the myth of the savage Appalachian is Brian D. McKnight. He is agnostic about Appalachian violence in general, but he insists that in the part of Kentucky he examined, "a violent tradition did exist" (McKnight, *Contested Borderland,* 15). Ralph Mann produced one of the early scholarly works on guerrilla warfare in Appalachia, "Guerrilla Warfare and Gender Roles: Sandy Basin, Virginia as a Test Case," *Appalachian Studies Association* 5 (1993): 59–66.

25. Fisher, *War at Every Door;* Groce, *Mountain Rebels,* 154; Fowler, *Mountaineers in Gray,* 189; Sarris, *A Separate Civil War,* 144, 102, 184; Crawford, *Ashe County's Civil War,* 172; Inscoe and McKinney, *The Heart of Confederate Appalachia,* 285.

26. Noe and Wilson, eds., *The Civil War in Appalachia.*

Chapter 2

Reconstruction-era Violence in North Georgia

The Mossy Creek Ku Klux Klan's Defense of Local Autonomy

Keith S. Hébert

The Mossy Creek Ku Klux Klan formed shortly after the Republican Party's strong second-place showing in White and Habersham counties during the 1868 Georgia gubernatorial election. From the summer of 1868 through the November presidential election, the KKK unleashed a wave of intimidation and violence designed to reduce further the political power of the region's Republican minority. In White County, the Klan's tactics produced immediate political gains, as the Democratic Party received an additional 258-vote majority.[1]

Politics influenced the founding of the Mossy Creek Ku Klux Klan, but by the end of 1868 the organization had shifted its focus toward resisting revenuers sent to enforce the federal liquor tax, whose actions had threatened local autonomy in the region.[2] Contextualizing Klan-related violence within the larger narrative of Appalachia's tenuous relationship with the outside world—and particularly with the federal government—adds new dimensions to our understanding of the complex cultural and socioeconomic factors behind the group's brutality. The behavior of the Mossy Creek KKK sheds new light on the Reconstruction-era Klan's place within Appalachian history. Localism, rather than politics, led to the White County Klan's escalation of violence. Their actions were responses to the federal government's efforts to increase its postwar presence throughout the north

Georgia mountains. The conflict between north Georgia distillers and revenuers ultimately instigated the moonshine wars. Their activities between 1868 and 1872 represented another phase of a prolonged conflict that began prior to the Civil War and extended beyond Reconstruction, leading the region along a path toward colonization. The Reconstruction-era KKK in White County, Georgia, was an anomaly in comparison to similar organizations in the state because of the distinctiveness of its members and the unique motivations behind its violence.[3]

The Mossy Creek Klan's brutality was influenced initially by a widespread counterrevolutionary movement, but a close examination of the group's members and terrorism reveals its grassroots evolution. Most existing accounts of the Reconstruction-era KKK interpret the organization's activities as representative of a counterrevolutionary conspiracy enacted by southern white conservatives (Democrats) to undermine the Republican Party and to infringe upon the civil liberties of freedpeople. This interpretation depicts local Klan chapters as part of a much larger state and regional network commanded from the top down by influential conservatives.[4] Another explanation stresses the independent, autonomous nature of Klan violence. From this point of view, local Klan groups evolved as a grassroots movement or cultural backlash rather than as part of an extensive conspiratorial network. Specific concerns ranged from acts of retribution committed against wartime Unionists to bands of white men forming to protect the continued unmolested production and sale of whiskey. White County's experience suggests that a synthesis of these two prevalent interpretations best explains the area's Klan behavior.[5]

The history of the Ku Klux Klan in Appalachia contrasts sharply with romantic images of the region that formed during Reconstruction. The mythical notion of a distinctive land filled with a noble people who "had fought for the Union though their homes were in the heart of slave territory" and "who owned the land but did not own slaves" ignores the mountain Klan. While numerous scholars have debunked the myth of Appalachian unionism, the dynamics of Klan violence and membership have received less attention. Existing scholarship has not examined the possible links between the Reconstruction-era Klan and the region's relationship with the outside world.[6]

The Mossy Creek Klan's efforts to protect local distillers from federal law enforcement agents led to the murder of a deputy marshal and a brutal attack upon a black family. On the morning of Wednesday, November

9, 1870, freedwoman Mary Brown watched as five armed men—Bailey Smith, Frank Henderson, Tom Oakes, Albert Henderson, and Henry Henderson—left her employer's house on horseback and headed toward federal deputy marshal John Cason's neighboring farm. When she asked her employer, Mrs. Henderson, where they were headed, the elderly woman told Brown they were going to kill deputy marshal Cason. A few minutes later, another band of men stopped by the house. One of these men, Isaac Oakes, asked Mrs. Henderson, "How long have the boys been gone?"

"Not more than out of sight," she replied.

"I don't want them to do that shooting today," he declared as he and the others started toward Cason's farm.[7]

Within an hour of the departure of the second band of riders, Brown heard gunshots from the direction of Cason's home. A few minutes later, she stumbled upon two white men in a cornfield, Bailey Smith and Frank Hancock, whose faces were smeared with lamp oil. The men had just returned from Cason's home, where they had mortally shot him in the head as he stood on his front porch. They had smeared lamp oil on their faces in an effort to conceal their identities and create the illusion that black men had murdered Cason, but Mary Brown knew the two men well. "The reason I knew Smith," Brown later testified, "was that I worked for him the day before that." As she passed the poorly disguised men, Smith told his accomplice, "That's Mary Brown."[8]

For the next few months, the members of the Mossy Creek Ku Klux Klan attempted to intimidate Mary Brown and her family. They wanted Brown to leave the county before she could report what she had seen, but she refused to leave. Consequently, the Klan visited her home on several occasions, shouting threatening messages from outside but never entering the house. For months, the identity of Cason's murderers remained a mystery. Brown kept quiet until deputy marshal George Holcombe, who had secondhand knowledge of her story, approached her. He convinced her to testify to a grand jury that would indict Cason's killers. Holcombe's visit to the Brown house attracted the attention of Klansmen and led to renewed violence.[9]

Dew saturated the ground during the predawn hours of an unseasonably cold May morning in 1871 when a band of forty members of the Mossy Creek Ku Klux Klan came upon the home of Joe and Mary Brown. During the next hour, the Mossy Creek Klan committed the most violent acts of physical and psychological abuse in their group's short history. Although they were targeting a black family, race was of secondary importance in the attack, given the terrorist group's preoccupation with undermining federal efforts to detain suspected moonshiners. The mounting dispute between distillers and federal agents left in its wake a number of collateral victims, including the Browns.[10]

Joe Brown was a forty-one-year-old freedman born in Virginia and sold at auction along with his mother before the age of two. For nearly two decades, Brown worked as a slave on a small farm in White County, where he remained until the war ended. In the fall of 1869, Brown paid $120 for a fifty-acre farm located eight miles from the town of Cleveland. At the time, a local white man also wanted to buy the property but could not come up with an adequate payment before the owner, an aging widow, sold it to Brown. During two previous elections, Brown had voted Republican. While Brown's purchase of real estate and his support for the Radicals attracted the ire of some white men, the Klan had never disturbed him prior to his wife's involvement in the federal investigation of Cason's murder.[11]

The freedpeople inside the Brown home remained asleep as the Klansmen filed into the swept front yard. Inside the one-room hewed-log house with Brown were his two young sons, Alfred and Augustus; his wife, Mary; his mother-in-law, Caroline Benson; his daughter, Mary; his unidentified niece; his sister-in-law, Rachel Arnold; and Mary Neal, a houseguest. Joe, Mary, and the four children slept on a bed located in the center of the single room. The remaining women slept on the floor near the fireplace.[12]

Joe Brown awoke to the sound of a Klansman's voice shouting: "Boys, surround the house." The freedman stumbled from bed, falling onto the wooden floor. Rays of light from several torches carried by the Klansmen shined through chinks in the log walls. Before Brown could regain his footing, the white men had surrounded the house and kicked in the front and rear doors. The attackers entered the house and ordered Brown to stoke the dimly lit fire burning in the home's fireplace. As the fire flared up to illuminate the house, the Klansmen saw Mary lying motionless in the bed, hiding beneath the covers, awake but silent. Two disguised white men, Coleman Alley and Isaac Oakes, grabbed her by the arms, pulled her from the bed, and roughly tossed her onto the floor. After forcing the remaining women and children out of bed, the vigilantes ordered the group into the yard. An unidentified man told them to build a fire. Joe Brown later testified that he "would not have known one of them if they had not made up a big fire."[13]

During the attack, the Klansmen's disguises failed to hide their identities. Most of the white men used a paper-thin strip of cloth to cover their faces. As the men leaned over to spit tobacco juice on the ground, the flimsy masks pulled away, revealing their identities. Joe Brown later described the costumes as "false faces, with little red dots on them."[14] The freedman described an uncoordinated group whose members seemed unsure of who was in charge. According to Brown, only a few of the Klansmen arrived on the property on horseback. Some of the men rode double; most of the band traveled by foot at a leisurely pace behind the mounted vanguard. Only a handful of the white men were armed with an assorted array of weapons ranging from antique hunting rifles and Colt revolvers to large sticks.[15]

Brown's depictions of the motley crew of Klansmen bore little resemblance to any highly organized group that may have been linked to a developed statewide terrorist network. Those who observed the night riding in White County had trouble identifying the band's leaders or distinguishing longtime Klan members from new recruits. In fact, as an ex-Klansmen later testified, a large number of the men who participated in night raids in White County were not longtime conspirators but rather new associates recruited in a fashion more commonly associated with less organized forms of collective violence, such as vigilantism and lynch mobs. Many of the Mossy Creek Klan followers who participated in this particular night raid had little connection to the group's earlier 1868 violence.[16]

For the next hour, the band of Mossy Creek Klansmen viciously attacked every member of the Brown household. Initially, they focused their attention solely upon Joe and Mary Brown. The Klan, Joe recalled, "just stripped me stark naked." Mary watched from a few feet away, restrained by two men, as Coleman Alley and Isaac Oakes, among others, began whipping her husband's exposed body with his own long, slender hickory fishing poles, which he had stored on the front porch. Joe fell to the ground in pain. As he prayed for the beating to stop, a disguised white man firmly thrust his boot against the side of Brown's head, pushing his face into the ground and nearly suffocating him. Meanwhile, two other white men grabbed a couple of hoes that had been left in the yard. When Brown temporarily lifted his head from beneath his attacker's boot, the two men struck him with the hoes, causing the wooden handle of one of the hoes to shatter from the blow. Joe reported that his assailants "wore out three fishing poles on me" before the whipping stopped.[17]

Somehow, Joe Brown remained conscious during the attack. After the disguised men finished whipping him, their leader, Duke Palmer, placed a chain around the battered freedman's neck and "dragged him about a great deal" before tossing one end of the chain over the limb of a nearby tree and pulling Joe off the ground. As Joe struggled to breathe while suspended a few inches from the ground, the white men turned their attention toward his wife. They demanded that she reveal the details of what she had seen in the cornfield following Cason's murder. The commotion impaired her ability to hear her attacker's questions. She told them: "Hold on! I cannot talk to about forty of you; give me time, and I will talk." Palmer replied: "We are not going to hold on at all; we are going to kill you." Mary Brown recognized his voice and knew it was Duke Palmer despite his white oil-cloth disguise. Several men then threw her to the ground face first. A group of younger Klansmen pulled her away from Palmer and "then tore off her clothes. They did not pull them off, but just jibbeted them off, like paper." She then received approximately twenty-five lashes. When the whipping stopped, Coleman Alley stuck a pistol to her forehead and demanded that she reveal what she had seen. As Alley cocked the pistol, Duke Palmer and Isaac Oakes came forward and ordered the gunman to stop. Only then did the battered freedwoman reveal that she had seen Bailey Smith and Frank Hancock—Cason's murderers—fleeing from Cason's farm.[18]

The Klansmen jerked her off the ground by her hair and yanked her across the yard as her naked form scraped the ground. Mary was then forced to hug her nude husband, who was still suspended by a chain around his neck. As the men jeered at the sight of the bloodied couple's embrace, they placed the chain around her neck too, pushing the couple together as they proceeded with a "mock" lynching.[19]

A group of young Klansmen then turned their attention toward Mary Neal, Caroline Benson, Rachel Arnold, and the children. "They had a show of us all there," reported Caroline Benson. They made the three women and one female child line up in a row along the road in front of the Brown house. The young white men, recalled Benson, "had us all stripped there, and laughed and made great sport. Some of them just squealed the same as if they were stable horses just brought out. You never saw such ill-behaved men." A few of the men exposed their genitals to the freedwomen and added further insult by making lewd sexual gestures. A group of Klan members then used hickory switches to whip the nude women, paying particular attention to striking their bare breasts repeatedly.[20]

The Mossy Creek Ku Klux Klan finally left the Brown house about one hour after their initial arrival. They left behind an abundance of physical wounds and emotional scars that would remain with their victims for the remainder of their lives. Joe Brown suffered a leg injury during the attack that permanently inhibited his normal gait, and Mary Brown's neck had a permanent scar where her attackers had strangled her with a chain. Several of the victims testified that the sound of the Klansmen striking their bodies with fishing poles and hickory switches remained with them long after the incident ended.[21] A few hours after the Mossy Creek Klan left the Brown household, Mary Brown limped into the town of Cleveland to report the attack. Andrew Merrit, the county sheriff and a Klan member, predictably ignored the complaint. When local authorities seemed unwilling to act, Brown turned to the federal deputy marshal for assistance. George McCollum responded by requesting that a squad of federal soldiers be stationed on Cason's farm, a location within close proximity to the Brown house. Lt. Frank B. Taylor, a native of New York and a Union veteran, commanded the detachment. After the arrival of federal troops, Klan violence tapered off.[22]

The Mossy Creek Ku Klux Klan's reaction to the increased federal presence during Reconstruction was similar to the reactions of other white mountaineers during the late nineteenth century who acted in opposition to industrialists who used local elites and corrupt state and national politicians to colonize the region. The Klan's violent tactics frequently differed from other forms of resistance, but the two groups often shared common adversaries. Enforcement of the federal liquor tax disrupted existing commercial and entrepreneurial practices, such as the production of whiskey.[23]

Since the arrival of the first white settlers in north Georgia in the late eighteenth century, scores of mountaineers had operated whiskey distilleries. The ranks of the region's distillers included the rich and the poor. For example, Godfrey Barnsley, a wealthy cotton factor who moved to Cass County from Savannah during the early 1830s, gloated to his urban friends that his orchards produced the finest peach liquor in the world. Barnsley learned how to create peach whiskey from a poor Scots-Irish tenant farmer who lived on his property. During the antebellum period, distillers developed a reputation in the region as skilled craftsmen whose activities were of a commercial nature and were in keeping with the demands of their consumers. Prohibition advocates certainly existed in the region, but their numbers were limited.[24]

The first government-enforced restrictions that affected mountain distillers came during the Civil War, when Gov. Joseph E. Brown helped enact a series of laws prohibiting distilleries from producing corn liquor, in an effort to reserve the state's limited food supply for soldiers and destitute families. The upcountry governor's policy alienated many among his core constituency, adding to the mounting dissatisfaction with Confederate and state governments that spread across the region, especially following the passage of the 1862 conscription acts. Meanwhile, the U.S. Congress had reenacted the federal tax on distilled spirits, to help fund the war. Across the country, the federal government took few steps to enforce the tax, but in north Georgia a number of federal marshals began aggressively enforcing the measure after the war as a way to prosecute suspected Klansmen.[25]

The Ku Klux Klan first appeared in Georgia in the spring of 1868, when John B. Gordon, Dudley DuBose, and other leading conservatives, intent upon restoring the Democratic Party to power, created a loosely organized statewide network. The Klan murdered Republican organizer George Ashburn in Columbus on March 31, 1868, initiating a wave of violence that reached its zenith during the 1868 presidential election before declining sharply following the restoration of Democratic control in the state by late 1871. In Georgia, the Klan was most active in counties with an African American majority large enough to influence elections and in areas without sizeable numbers of white Republicans. The Mossy Creek Klan, however, emerged in a locale with few freedpeople and where Republicans accounted for more than 40 percent of the white population. In White County, the federal liquor tax, which threatened the autonomy of whiskey distillers, bridged the divide between "the rebel element" and many white Republicans.[26]

During Reconstruction, north Georgians could legally produce alcohol, but the sale of that product was now subject to a $2-per-gallon tax collected by the Bureau of Internal Revenue. The tax threatened to diminish the profits of local producers, leading many to hide their operations and sales activities. While enforcement varied across the nation and throughout the state of Georgia, in northeast Georgia federal officials began aggressively enforcing the law following the passage of the Second Enforcement Act in 1871. The bureau, however, lacked the manpower necessary to collect the tax. Consequently, they solicited help from U.S. marshals, who then appointed dozens of deputy marshals to work in the region.[27]

Deputy marshals depended upon informants to help them identify, arrest, and prosecute liquor tax violators. Freedman Silas Hutchens provided a deputy marshal with information in 1870 that drew attention to the activities of distiller Frank Hancock. Shortly thereafter, Hutchens discovered a letter pinned to his door: the note's message warned him to leave the county or die. Hutchens chose to ignore the threat, probably in part because vigilantes such as the Klan had been relatively quiet in the area since the 1868 presidential election. He awoke a few nights later to discover a group of disguised men standing over his bed. After the white men whipped him for nearly an hour, they again ordered him to leave the county. This time Hutchens fled to Clay County, North Carolina. Without his testimony, the deputy marshal lacked enough evidence to detain Hancock.[28]

Deputy marshals also depended upon the services of friends, family members, and neighbors to help them capture suspected distillers. A federal marshal selected brothers Daniel and George McCollum to serve as deputy marshals in 1869. Daniel's brother-in-law, George Holcombe, informed them that Duke Palmer, a local merchant, had been distributing whiskey produced by Bailey Smith. Holcombe also revealed the names of several other distillers. Within days, Holcombe and the McCollums arrested "some parties who had been engaged in illicit distilling." Several months later, two poorly disguised men "bushwhacked" Holcombe along an isolated road while he was en route to testify in court against several distillers, and they shot him in the leg. Holcombe survived the attack, but the incident escalated tensions between federal agents and illegal distillers in the region. For the first time in the county, distillers had assailed a white man for cooperating with a federal agent.[29]

The Klan's association with distillers attracted a number of members into the organization whose backgrounds and motivations differed from those of other Klansmen in other parts of the state. The struggle between white men who represented federal authority in the region and those who supported the interests of distillers gave rise to some odd alliances. During the Civil War, hostilities had erupted between the county's pro-Confederate and Unionist households, and those divisions remained after the war, directly influencing political affiliations. By 1870, however, the addition of the federal liquor tax to the equation caused some of these disputants to switch sides. For example, George Holcombe had voluntarily enlisted in the Confederate army, had favored secession, and—until 1870—had voted Democratic. He told a congressional investigation that he had "always been a Democrat . . . a secessionist and a rebel soldier but renounced democracy when they tried to run it by the Ku-Kluk organization." Daniel and George McCollum also underwent a similar conversion. Conversely, according to a federal soldier stationed in the county, some wartime Unionists had joined the Klan to oppose black suffrage and support local distillers. Those white men now belonged to an organization whose leaders, such as Andrew Jackson Comer and Duke Palmer, had persecuted Unionists during the war. The rise of the Klan combined with the increased federal presence in the region to permanently alter allegiances that a few years earlier had appeared to be unbreakable.[30]

Most Unionists refrained from joining the Ku Klux Klan, however, and Unionists in general remained a target of Klan intimidation because of their Republican ties and advocacy for an increased federal presence in the region. John Cason had opposed secession and had refused to serve in the Confederate army; he became a deputy marshal following the attack upon his neighbor George Holcombe in 1870. Cason despised distillers because of their local association with the Mossy Creek Klan. Following Cason's appointment, he and the McCollums rode to the home of "moonshiner" Bailey Smith to arrest him for allegedly violating federal liquor laws and for reportedly taking part in the attack upon Silas Hutchens. Smith learned of the deputies' impending visit and eluded the party by hiding in some neighboring woods.[31]

The deputies' efforts to apprehend Smith attracted the attention of the Mossy Creek Klan leaders. Reportedly, two Klansmen harbored Smith in their homes. One evening, Cason returned to his farm to discover brothers and Klan leaders Duke and Noah Palmer awaiting his arrival. Duke threatened to kill the deputy marshal if he did not leave the county within the next two weeks. During the following fortnight, the Klan delivered similar messages to three other deputy marshals.[32]

Federal agents believed that a large number of the region's Klansmen were distillers. George Holcombe reported that the KKK sheltered illegal distillers and ran "off men whose property they want[ed as] . . . part of their business." Lt. Frank Taylor claimed that the White County justice of the peace "ran a distillery quite openly" and "made threats that [he] had organized a Ku-Klux there . . . on purpose to prevent the breaking up of the still. And one part of the [KKK] oath . . . was to drive out and wage war against the United States revenue officers who should come up there to break up the distilling." Based upon an examination of the Klan's roster, it was likely that the organization would have faded away following the 1868 presidential election had it not been for the increased federal presence in the area. The Klan was reacting to a problem that had emerged in their immediate vicinity that required an escalation of violence to resolve.[33]

Deputy marshals also believed that the majority of local Klansmen, in addition to being moonshiners, were poor, illiterate ex-Confederates. Of the twenty white men whom local victims and witnesses identified as suspected Mossy Creek Klan members during 1871 congressional hearings, nineteen can be located in the U.S. manuscript census in either the 1860 or 1870 returns. Bailey Smith failed to appear in the Georgia returns but was listed in the 1880 enumeration for Smith County, Texas. The census returns help determine the age, occupation, literacy, wealth, and household affiliation of suspected Klansmen while suggesting possible kin connections. In White County, the typical Klansman was a twenty-four-year-old wage laborer who owned no real property and less than $100 in personal property. Approximately 30 percent of the local Klan members could not read or write. For example, twenty-one-year-old illiterate farm laborer Miles Meadows lived with his parents. Likewise, Charles Potts—who, at age thirty-three, was one of the oldest members of the group—was an illiterate sharecropper with no real or personal property. Allegedly, Potts and Meadows helped Smith operate a still and sold whiskey in town. The desire of poor whites to defend local distillers from federal agents extended across class lines, as many volunteered their service in defense of yeoman distillers. The arrival of federal agents sent to disrupt the local alcohol trade turned the dissension that typified relations among white males during the Civil War into a relatively unified front fighting against federal intrusions.[34]

Federal agents also suspected that many Klansmen had served in the same Confederate military companies during the Civil War, but agents offered no substantial proof of this beyond commenting that they "marched as soldiers do, and seemed to have some kind of drill and organization." Most of the twenty Klan suspects had neither served in the Confederate military nor the State Guard (although, oddly, one of the accused had fought in a Union regiment formed in East Tennessee). For example, Frank Comer and James Alley were only eight years old when the war began, and Miles Meadows and Isaac Tomlin were only ten. Henry Alley was also too young to have fought until the last months of the war, while Washington Brock—one of the men accused of ambushing Holcombe—was seven years old in 1861. Some members were old enough to have fought in the war but, for unknown reasons, never enlisted. Klan leader Duke Palmer, for example, was twenty-seven years old in 1861 but never served in the

Confederate army, despite his known secessionist views. Coleman Alley and Charles Potts also avoided enlistment. James Potts claimed an exemption during the war, providing the enumerator with no specific reason why a healthy twenty-six-year-old male was not subject to conscription. Isaac Oakes—who, according to Holcombe, was a main figure in the White County Klan—also never served in either the Confederate army or the State Guard. The federal attack upon local liquor producers provoked a desire to defend the region from outsiders that did not exist during the Civil War. Men who had been unwilling to take up arms to defend the Confederacy now volunteered to defeat revenuers because the threat posed by federal agents proved to be of greater local importance.[35]

Only a handful of the identified members of the Mossy Creek Klan served in the Confederate army. Of those who did perform some military duty, Bailey Smith and Bill Smith both deserted their regiments. Andrew Jackson Comer worked as an enrolling agent for the State Guard. Frank Hancock, a suspected distiller, enlisted in the "Currahee Rangers," the Twenty-fourth Georgia Infantry Regiment. And finally, Noah Palmer served in the Sixteenth Georgia Infantry Regiment—in the same company as two future federal deputy marshals. No other member of the KKK in White County served in the Confederate army or State Guard. Contrary to the beliefs of federal agents, the Mossy Creek Klan's roster included few Confederate veterans.[36]

While veterans seemed sparse among the Mossy Creek Klan's members, men who shared varying networks of kinship were commonplace. For example, brothers Henry, Frank, and Albert Henderson belonged to the Klan. Likewise, Klan leader Duke Palmer and his brother recruited most of the county's members. Brothers Henry and James Alley participated in an attack upon a black family in a group that included at least two father-and-son pairs. Freedpeople identified Coleman Alley, age fifty-six, and his sons, Henry and James Alley, as Klansmen. Similarly, Andrew Jackson Comer and his son, Frank Comer, rode with the Klan. In all, a majority of Mossy Creek Klan members had at least one family member who also belonged to the Mossy Creek Klan. These findings, drawn from congressional hearing testimonies, validate the beliefs held by federal officials in the region that the Klansmen were quite literally a band of brothers.[37]

A close analysis of the reconstructed membership rolls of the Mossy Creek Ku Klux Klan sheds light upon the nature and composition of Reconstruction-era organized violence in north Georgia. Young, illiterate adult males with no real property or prior military service constituted a majority of Klan suspects. The Mossy Creek Klan's leaders, however, differed sharply from the bulk of their followers. Duke Palmer, Noah Palmer, and Andrew Jackson Comer owned significant amounts of property stemming from their successful business ventures. While the disparity in wealth among Klan members might not be surprising, the fact that a majority of Klansmen were poor reveals much about the organization's appeal among the region's lower classes, as well as the character of some of the area's most active distillers. Of the twenty men suspected of having ties to the Klan, federal officials also identified half of them as federal liquor tax violators.[38]

The sample of Klan membership documented in White County seems to reflect broader geographic patterns. Of the 268 suspected Klan members found in north Georgia, approximately 80 percent (215) owned no property, and another 45 percent (120) never learned to read. The average age of a Klansman in north Georgia was twenty-two years old. The vast majority of Klan members identified themselves as farm laborers in either the 1870 or 1880 federal census. Though more research is needed to substantiate any claim that Confederate veterans were a sizeable minority within the Reconstruction-era KKK in north Georgia, initial findings suggest that less than 30 percent of the region's alleged Klansmen who had been eligible to serve in the Confederate army or State Guard between 1861 and 1865 ever enlisted (K. S. Hébert, unpublished data).

While Mossy Creek Klan members shared common ground with other north Georgia Klansmen, the influence that alcohol production had upon their violent agenda distinguished them from other Klan organizations. Contemporaries commented that Klan chapters in Cherokee and Floyd counties had some connection with distillers, but only in White County did the Klan's desire to protect distillers from federal agents become the group's raison d'etre.[39] By the winter of 1870, the Mossy Creek Klan—with Democratic Party domination in the region assured—shifted the focus of its violence toward federal agents responsible for prosecuting liquor tax violators. The campaign to shelter distillers and oust federal agents from the county produced a brand of violence that was more intense than earlier acts committed against Republican supporters. Whereas Republicans presented only a minor threat to the county's conservative majority, the escalating intrusions of the federal government directly endangered local autonomy.[40]

One month after the attack upon the Brown family, federal agents arrested suspected Klansman and distiller Robert Kenimer for liquor tax violations. In exchange for amnesty, he identified Cason's murderers as well as a number of Klansmen and distillers. Following Kenimer's capture, Cason's murderers, Frank Hancock and Bailey Smith, fled the county. While Kenimer never confessed to taking part in the attack upon the Brown household, his knowledge of that incident casts serious doubt upon his proclamations of innocence. Nevertheless, the recalcitrant ex-Klansman provided federal agents with invaluable information that further reinforced the belief that the terrorist organization had been committing acts of violence to protect distillers.[41]

Five months after the Mossy Creek Ku Klux Klan attacked the Brown house, Joe Brown, Mary Brown, Rachel Arnold, and Caroline Benson accompanied George Holcombe, Frank Taylor, and Robert Kenimer to Atlanta, where they testified before a congressional committee investigating KKK violence in Georgia. Many of the state's preeminent conservative leaders, such as John B. Gordon, Joseph E. Brown, and Augustus R. Wright, had appeared before members of this same body in hearings held in Washington. At the Atlanta hearing, the congressmen asked each witness to recount his or her memory of the incident. The congressmen subsequently asked a number of leading questions about whether or not Klansmen in the area were illegal distillers and if they were Democratic Party supporters or Confederate veterans. Prior to their departure from White County, Duke Palmer warned Mary Brown that if she went to Atlanta and testified, she had better stay there. Determined to seek some semblance of justice and prodded by federal agents eager to display the region's violence before a highly politicized audience, Mary Brown made the long trip to the state capital.[42]

On the surface, the testimony gathered by the congressional hearings was biased and revealed only one side's assertions about the Klan. Nonetheless, the congressional testimony recorded a scattering of names believed to be members of the KKK as reported by their victims, observers, federal agents, and ex-Klansmen. In White County, the hearings recorded the names of half of the county's suspected twenty Klan members. The inclusion of Robert Kenimer's testimony lends additional credence to the hearing's findings. While he testified to avoid prosecution, his account provides an insider's perspective that corroborates the stories of the Mossy Creek Klan's victims and prosecutors. Federal agents may have coached Kenimer's testimony, but the fact that Holcombe and Taylor's own account includes a number of minor inconsistencies that contradict their informant's description of events suggests that their stories lacked careful coordination.[43]

When Robert Kenimer joined the Mossy Creek Ku Klux Klan in 1868, that organization was part of a regional network of politically and racially motivated terrorists aiming to undermine the Republican Party. In White County, however, neither the Republican Party nor freedmen voters presented a real threat to the Democratic Party. Following the 1868 presidential election, the local Klan turned its attention toward impeding the enforcement of federal liquor laws. The group included a significant number of men involved in the distillation and distribution of moonshine and merchants who traded locally produced whiskey. Poor whites, young adults, and men who had never served in the Confederate military made up the overwhelming majority of the Klan's members. The men attacked federal agents and witnesses who provided revenuers with information during a series of exceptionally violent and sometimes deadly assaults that constituted the moonshine war's opening salvos.

While the Mossy Creek Klan shared much in common with Klan groups in other southern regions, the manner in which whiskey production motivated their violence distinguishes them from similar organizations located outside of southern Appalachia or other subregions where the production of alcohol was not a significant component of the local economy. Matters of economics, culture, and race motivated the local Klan's campaign. Economically, the federal liquor tax posed a threat to profits gained from the sale of alcohol. Meanwhile, federal efforts to enforce the tax portended increased government involvement in the daily lives of the region's white inhabitants. The White County Klan achieved some temporary success. The men involved in the murder of John Cason escaped justice, and alcohol production in the area continued. However, the Klan's tactics attracted additional attention from the Bureau of Internal Revenue and the Justice Department, which erased the group's Reconstruction-era victories in the following decades. The Mossy Creek Klan's resistance was a harbinger of the region's unsuccessful efforts to maintain local autonomy in the face of external forces.

Notes

1. "Klan Outrages," *Daily News and Herald* (Savannah, GA), May 1, 1868; "The Southern Colored Vote," *Georgia Weekly Telegraph* (Macon), November 13, 1868. White County, Georgia, is located on the eastern edge of the Appalachian

Mountain chain, approximately eighty miles northeast of Atlanta. The county was created in 1857 from a portion of Habersham County and was named in honor of state legislator David White. Cleveland is the county seat. For an account of the Republican Party's failed efforts to garner support from mountain whites during Reconstruction, see: Gordon B. McKinney, *Southern Mountain Republicans, 1865–1900: Politics and the Appalachian Community* (Chapel Hill: University of North Carolina Press, 1978). In 1868 Georgia was one of only two ex-Confederate states to provide a majority vote in favor of Democratic presidential candidate Horatio Seymour. A history of Reconstruction in White County can be gathered from the following sources: House Select Committee on Reconstruction, *Condition of Affairs in Georgia,* 40th Cong., 3rd sess., 1868–1869; U.S. Joint Select Committee to Inquire into the Condition of Affairs in the Late Insurrectionary States, *Affairs in Insurrectionary States,* part 7, Georgia, vols. 1–2, 42nd Cong., 2nd sess., 1871; "Registered Letters Received," Bureau of Refugees, Freedmen, and Abandoned Lands (microfilm), M 798, National Archives and Records Administration, southeast region, Morrow, Georgia (hereafter cited as BRFAL microfilm); "Reports Relating to Operations and to Murders and Outrages, 1865–1868," BRFAL microfilm; "Field Office Reports," BRFAL microfilm. Reconstruction-era Democrats and some contemporary scholars have questioned the validity of this congressional testimony because of its leading questions and highly politicized nature, and because of payments made to witnesses in exchange for their statements. While it is true that freedpeople earned compensation for their testimony, the risks associated with their statements far outweighed the limited monetary compensation they received. In several instances, freedpeople who testified were later beaten or killed by Klan members specifically because they had provided the federal government with sworn statements. The congressional records should be read with a critical eye, but they nonetheless remain invaluable primary resources that shed light upon Klan violence.

2. Prior to the work of Bruce E. Stewart, the linkages in Appalachia between moonshiners and Ku Klux Klan violence had been mentioned but not fully explored. Stewart, "'When Darkness Reigns, Then Is the Hour to Strike': Moonshining, Federal Liquor Taxation, and Klan Violence in Western North Carolina," *North Carolina Historical Review* 80, no. 4 (2003): 453–74. The works of Allen Trelease and Wilbur R. Miller mention the connection but offer no further analysis. Allen W. Trelease, *White Terror: The Ku Klux Klan Conspiracy and Southern Reconstruction* (Baton Rouge: Louisiana State University Press, 1971), xlviii, 185, 189, 190, 239, 282, 305, 331, 340–41, 345, 357; Wilbur R. Miller, *Revenuers and Moonshiners: Enforcing Federal Liquor Laws in the Mountain South, 1865–1900* (Chapel Hill: University of North Carolina Press, 1991), 43–44, 53–54. William F. Holmes examined the connection between moonshine and collective violence in Georgia from 1889 to 1895 but did not explore a possible connection between the Reconstruction-era Klan and the subsequent moonshine wars. Holmes, "Moonshining and Collective Violence, Georgia, 1889–1895," *Journal of American History* 67 (December 1980): 589–611.

3. For an account of the moonshine wars in north Georgia and Appalachia, see: Robert Scott Davis Jr., "The North Georgia Moonshine War of 1876–77," *North Georgia Journal* 4 (Spring 1989): 41–46; Davis, "Whitecapping in Late Nineteenth Century Georgia," in *From the Old South to the New: Essays on the Transitional South,* ed. Walter J. Fraser and Winfred B. Moore (Charlottesville, VA: University of Virginia Press, 1981), 123–24; Holmes, "Moonshining and Collective Violence," 596; John Alexander Williams, *Appalachia: A History* (Chapel Hill: University of North Carolina Press, 2002), 187–91.

4. While the Klan undoubtedly formed for the reasons mentioned above, the Mossy Creek Klan's motivations changed following the 1868 election and differed from the motivations of other Klan organizations due to the influence of local and regional factors. Scholars must consider the timing and location of Klan violence in order to fit an array of localized distinctions into larger patterns. Mark Wetherington, *Plain Folk's Fight: The Civil War and Reconstruction in Piney Woods Georgia* (Chapel Hill: University of North Carolina Press, 2005), 272. Wetherington provides the following description of the Piney Woods Georgia Klan: "Conservative white men of high social standing formed the symbolic core of a counterrevolutionary movement that drew on virtually every meaningful tradition—Confederate memory, paternalism, racism, religion, ritual, and secessionism—to remind plain folk that violence against blacks and Republicans was legitimate and fulfilled the white community's expectations." For similar depictions, see: George Rable, *There Was No Peace: The Role of Violence in the Politics of Reconstruction* (Athens: University of Georgia Press, 1984), 15; George C. Wright, *Racial Violence in Kentucky, 1865–1940: Lynchings, Mob Rule, and "Legal Lynchings"* (Baton Rouge: Louisiana State University Press, 1990), 39–43; Lisa Cardyn, "Sexualized Racism/Gendered Violence: Outraging the Body Politic in the Reconstruction South," *Michigan Law Review* 100 (February 2002): 675–867; Heather Cox Richardson, *The Death of Reconstruction: Race, Labor, and Politics in the Post–Civil War North, 1865–1901* (Cambridge, MA: Harvard University Press, 2001), 91; Kathleen Gorman, "'This Man Felker Is a Man of Pretty Good Standing': A Reconstruction Klansman in Walton County," *Georgia Historical Quarterly* 81 (Winter 1997): 897–914; Xi Wang, *The Trial of Democracy: Black Suffrage and Northern Republicans, 1860–1910* (Athens: University of Georgia Press, 1997), 54; Richard Zuczek, "The Last Campaign of the Civil War: South Carolina and the Revolution of 1876," *Civil War History* 42 (March 1996): 18–31; William Gillette, *Retreat from Reconstruction, 1869–1879* (Baton Rouge: Louisiana State University Press, 1979), chapter 2; Trelease, *White Terror,* xlviii, 185, 189, 190, 239, 282, 305, 331, 340–41, 345, 357; Eric Foner, *Reconstruction: America's Unfinished Revolution, 1863–77* (New York: HarperCollins, 1988), 184–85; William G. Brown, "The Ku Klux Movement," *Atlantic Monthly* 87 (May 1901), 634–44; Sheldon Hackney, "Southern Violence," in *Violence in America: Historical and Comparative Perspectives,* ed. Hugh Davis Graham and Ted Robert Gurr (Beverly Hills, CA: Sage Publications, 1979), 407; Otto H. Olsen, "The Ku Klux Klan: A Study of Reconstruction Politics and Pro-

paganda," *North Carolina Historical Review* 39 (Summer 1962), 340–42; John Hope Franklin, *Reconstruction: After the Civil War* (Chicago: University of Chicago Press, 1961), 119–20.

5. Stewart, "'When Darkness Reigns,'" 453; Michael Fitzgerald, *A Splendid Failure: Postwar Reconstruction in the American South* (Chicago: Ivan R. Dee, 2007), 62–71; Paul A. Cimbala, *Under the Guardianship of the Nation: The Freedmen's Bureau and the Reconstruction of Georgia, 1865–1870* (Athens: University of Georgia Press, 1997), 74; Michael Perman, "Counter Reconstruction: The Role of Violence in Southern Redemption," in *The Facts of Reconstruction: Essays in Honor of John Hope Franklin,* ed. Eric Anderson (Baton Rouge: Louisiana State University Press, 1991), 121–40; Wyn Craig Wade, *The Fiery Cross: The Ku Klux Klan in America* (New York: Oxford University Press, 1987); Jonathan M. Weiner, *Social Origins of the New South: Alabama, 1860–1885* (Baton Rouge: Louisiana State University Press, 1978); Gordon B. McKinney, "The Klan in the Southern Mountains: The Lusk-Shotwell Controversy," *Appalachian Journal* 8 (Winter 1981), 89–104.

6. Quoted material from: Shannon H. Wilson, "Lincoln's Sons and Daughters: Berea College, Lincoln Memorial University, and the Myth of Unionist Appalachia, 1866–1910," in *The Civil War in Appalachia: Collected Essays,* ed. Kenneth W. Noe and Shannon H. Wilson (Knoxville: University of Tennessee Press, 1997), 243. See also Henry Shapiro, *Appalachia on Our Mind: The Southern Mountains and Mountaineers in the American Consciousness, 1870–1920* (Chapel Hill: University of North Carolina Press, 1978), 18; Allen Batteau, *The Invention of Appalachia* (Tucson: University of Arizona Press, 1990), 57–58; Shannon H. Wilson, "Window on the Mountains: Berea's Appalachia, 1870–1930," *Filson Club History Quarterly* 64 (July 1990), 384–400; Kenneth W. Noe, "Toward a Myth of Unionist Appalachia, 1865–1883," *Journal of the Appalachian Studies Association* 6 (Spring 1994), 73–80; Nina Silber, *Romance and Reunion: Northerners and the South, 1865–1900* (Chapel Hill: University of North Carolina Press, 1993), 124–58.

7. Testimony of Mary Brown, *Condition of Affairs in Georgia,* 375–76; testimony of George Holcombe, *Condition of Affairs in Georgia,* 496–97. Brown's testimony incorrectly reports that Cason was murdered on Sunday, October 30, 1870. During her testimony she became confused and switched the date of her initial encounter with members of the KKK with the date of Cason's murder. George Holcombe's testimony and corroborating documents located in U.S. Department of Justice files identify Wednesday, November 9, 1870, as the correct date of Cason's murder.

8. Testimony of Lt. F. B. Taylor, *Condition of Affairs in Georgia,* 503–4; testimony of Mary Brown, *Condition of Affairs in Georgia,* 375–76.

9. Testimony of George Holcombe, *Condition of Affairs in Georgia,* 496–500.

10. Testimony of Joe Brown, *Condition of Affairs in Georgia,* 501; Trelease, *White Terror,* 331.

11. Joe Brown, Deed of Land Purchase, Land Records, book A:156, Clerk of Superior Court Records, White County, Cleveland, Georgia.

12. Testimony of Mary Brown, *Condition of Affairs in Georgia,* 376; Trelease, *White Terror,* 331.

13. Testimony of Joe Brown, *Condition of Affairs in Georgia,* 501.

14. Trelease, *White Terror,* 331.

15. Testimony of Mary Brown, *Condition of Affairs in Georgia,* 376; testimony of Joe Brown, *Condition of Affairs in Georgia,* 501–3; Trelease, *White Terror,* 331.

16. Testimony of R. T. Kenimer, *Condition of Affairs in Georgia,* 908–13.

17. Ibid.

18. Testimony of Joe Brown, *Condition of Affairs in Georgia,* 502; testimony of Mary Brown, *Condition of Affairs in Georgia,* 375; testimony of Caroline Benson, *Condition of Affairs in Georgia,* 387; Trelease, *White Terror,* 331.

19. Testimony of Joe Brown, *Condition of Affairs in Georgia,* 501–3.

20. Testimony of Caroline Benson, *Condition of Affairs in Georgia,* 387; testimony of Rachel Arnold, *Condition of Affairs in Georgia,* 389.

21. Testimony of Joe Brown, *Condition of Affairs in Georgia,* 501–3; testimony of Mary Brown, *Condition of Affairs in Georgia,* 377; Joe Brown, *Ninth Census of the United States,* 1870, White County, Georgia, RG 29, M 593, National Archives and Records Administration, southeast region, Morrow, Georgia (hereafter NARA); Trelease, *White Terror,* 331.

22. Testimony of R. T. Kenimer, *Condition of Affairs in Georgia,* 908–13; testimony of George Holcombe, *Condition of Affairs in Georgia,* 496–500; testimony of Lt. F. B. Taylor, *Condition of Affairs in Georgia,* 503–4.

23. Kenneth W. Noe, "Appalachia before Mr. Peabody," *Virginia Magazine of History and Biography* 110 (Spring 2002): 5. For examples of Revisionist scholarship that depicts the colonization of southern Appalachia and examines the region's response to losses in local autonomy, see: Harry M. Caudill, *Night Comes to the Cumberlands: A Biography of a Depressed Area* (Boston: Jesse Stuart Foundation, 1963); Stephen L. Fisher, ed., *Fighting Back in Appalachia: Traditions of Resistance and Change* (Philadelphia: Temple University Press, 1993); David Alan Corbin, *Life, Work, and Rebellion in the Coal Fields: The Southern West Virginia Miners, 1880–1922* (Urbana: University of Illinois Press, 1981); Ronald D Eller, *Miners, Millhands, and Mountaineers: Industrialization of the Appalachian South, 1880–1930* (Knoxville: University of Tennessee Press, 1982); David E. Whisnant, *All That Is Native and Fine: The Politics of Culture in an American Region* (Chapel Hill: University of North Carolina Press, 1983).

24. Plantation journal, series 3, subseries 3.1, M 1521, George Scarborough Barnsley Papers, Southern Historical Collection, University of North Carolina at Chapel Hill Library; Charles W. Howard to Godfrey Barnsley, June 1857, series 1, box 1, folder 6, correspondence, 1826–1955, Godfrey Barnsley Papers, 1822–1980, Manuscript, Archives, and Rare Book Library, Emory University; Wilbur R. Miller, *Revenuers and Moonshiners: Enforcing Federal Liquor Laws in the Moun-*

tain South, 1865–1900 (Chapel Hill: University of North Carolina Press, 1991), 43–44, 53–54.

25. Jonathan Dean Sarris, *A Separate Civil War: Communities in Conflict in the Mountain South* (Charlottesville: University of Virginia Press, 2006), chapter 4; Keith S. Bohannon, "The Northeast Georgia Mountains during the Secession Crisis and Civil War" (PhD diss., University of North Carolina at Chapel Hill, 2001), 202; Joseph H. Parks, *Joseph E. Brown of Georgia* (Baton Rouge: Louisiana State University Press, 1977), 157; Paul D. Escott, "The Context of Freedom: Georgia's Slaves during the Civil War," *Georgia Historical Quarterly* 58 (Spring 1974): 79–81.

26. Kenneth Coleman, ed., *A History of Georgia*, 2nd ed. (Athens: University of Georgia Press, 1991), 214; Wetherington, *Plain Folk's Fight*, 272, 275; Wade, *The Fiery Cross*, 31–53; Steven Hahn, *The Roots of Southern Populism: Yeoman Farmers and the Transformation of the Georgia Upcountry, 1850–1890* (New York: Oxford University Press, 1983), 212–13.

27. Records of the Internal Revenue Service, Georgia: 1866–1873, RG 58, reels 1–2, National Archives and Records Administration, southeast region, Morrow, Georgia (hereafter cited as Records of the Internal Revenue Service); Internal Revenue Service Assessment Lists for Georgia: 1865–1866, White County, RG 58, M762, National Archives and Records Administration, southeast region, Morrow, Georgia. The $2 tax was later reduced to a 50-cents-per-gallon tax in 1868. Stewart, "'When Darkness Reigns,'" 461; Tun Yuan Hu, *The Liquor Tax in the United States, 1791–1947* (New York: Columbia University Press, 1950), 50; Everette Swinney, "Enforcing the Fifteenth Amendment, 1870–1877," *Journal of Southern History* 28, no. 2 (1962): 203; William W. Davis, "The Federal Enforcement Acts," *Studies in Southern History and Politics: Inscribed to William A. Dunning* (New York: General Books, 1914), 205; Frederick S. Calhoun, *The Lawmen: United States Marshals and Their Deputies, 1798–1989* (Washington, DC: Smithsonian Institution, 1989), 350; Jess Carr, *The Second Oldest Profession: An Informal History of Moonshining in America* (Englewood Cliffs, NJ: Prentice-Hall, 1972), introduction; Joseph Earl Dabney, *Mountain Spirits: A Chronicle of Corn Whiskey from King James's Ulster Plantation to America's Appalachians and the Moonshine Life* (New York: Bright Mountain Books, 1974), 250.

28. Testimony of Lt. F. B. Taylor, *Condition of Affairs in Georgia*, 510. Silas Hutchens was a freedman who lived in White County; Bailey Smith accused Hutchens of revealing information to deputy marshals about the Klansman's violation of federal liquor laws.

29. Testimony of George Holcombe, *Condition of Affairs in Georgia*, 499; Records of the Internal Revenue Service, RG 58, reel 1:154.

30. Testimony of George Holcombe, *Condition of Affairs in Georgia*, 499; testimony of Lt. F. B. Taylor, *Condition of Affairs in Georgia*, 503–4. Clearly, a vast majority of Klan members were Democratic Party supporters, although the White County Klan likely had several ex-Republicans as members. For a discussion of

mountaineer resistance to Republican Party efforts to extend civil liberties to African Americans, see McKinney, *Southern Mountain Republicans.*

31. Testimony of George Holcombe, *Condition of Affairs in Georgia,* 499; testimony of Lt. F. B. Taylor, *Condition of Affairs in Georgia,* 503–4; Records of the Internal Revenue Service, RG 58, reel 1:165.

32. Testimony of George Holcombe, *Condition of Affairs in Georgia,* 499; testimony of Lt. F. B. Taylor, *Condition of Affairs in Georgia,* 503–4; Records of the Internal Revenue Service, RG 58 M 1.

33. Testimony of George Holcombe, *Condition of Affairs in Georgia,* 499; testimony of Lt. F. B. Taylor, *Condition of Affairs in Georgia,* 503–4; Records of the Internal Revenue Service, RG 58 M 1.

34. Testimony of George Holcombe, *Condition of Affairs in Georgia,* 496–500; Bailey M. Smith, *Ninth Census of the United States,* 1870, Smith County, Texas, RG 29, M 593, NARA; Charles Potts, *Ninth Census of the United States,* 1870, White County, Georgia, RG 29, M 593, NARA; Miles Meadows, *Ninth Census of the United States,* 1870, Habersham County, Georgia, RG 29, M 593, NARA; Frank Comer, *Ninth Census of the United States,* 1870, White County, Georgia, RG 29, M 593, NARA. Frank Comer's father, Andrew Jackson Comer, was a successful merchant who served as an enrolling officer for the state militia during the Civil War. Sarris, *A Separate Civil War,* chapter 4; Bohannon, "The Northeast Georgia Mountains," 202.

35. Steven Hahn, *A Nation Under Our Feet: Black Political Struggles in the Rural South from Slavery to the Great Migration* (Cambridge, MA: Belknap Press, 2003), 268. Hahn asserts that the Ku Klux Klan primarily comprised ex-Confederate soldiers. Testimony of George Holcombe, *Condition of Affairs in Georgia,* 496–500; testimony of Lt. F. B. Taylor, *Condition of Affairs in Georgia,* 503–4; Washington Brock, *Ninth Census of the United States,* 1870, White County, Georgia, RG 29, M 593, NARA; Nancy J. Cornell, *1864 Census for Re-Organizing the Georgia Militia* (Baltimore: Genealogical Publishing Co., 2000), 672.

36. Frank Comer, *Ninth Census of the United States,* 1870, White County, Georgia, RG 29, M 593, NARA; Charles Potts, *Ninth Census of the United States,* 1870, White County, Georgia, RG 29, M 593, NARA; Miles Meadows, *Ninth Census of the United States,* 1870, Habersham County, Georgia, RG 29, M 593, NARA; Cornell, *1864 Census,* 672; Testimony of George Holcombe, *Condition of Affairs in Georgia,* 499.

37. Frank Comer, *Ninth Census of the United States,* 1870, White County, Georgia, RG 29, M 593, NARA; Charles Potts, *Ninth Census of the United States,* 1870, White County, Georgia, RG 29, M 593, NARA; Miles Meadows, *Ninth Census of the United States,* 1870, Habersham County, Georgia, RG 29, M 593, NARA; Cornell, *1864 Census,* 672; testimony of George Holcombe, *Condition of Affairs in Georgia,* 499.

38. Testimony of George Holcombe, *Condition of Affairs in Georgia,* 499.

39. Cherokee and Floyd counties are located southwest of White County, in

the foothills of the Appalachian Mountains. Freedpeople represented a larger percentage of the total population in those counties than in White County.

40. Testimony of George Holcombe, *Condition of Affairs in Georgia*, 496–500; testimony of Lt. F. B. Taylor, *Condition of Affairs in Georgia*, 503–4.

41. Testimony of R. T. Kenimer, *Condition of Affairs in Georgia*, 908–13.

42. Testimony of Mary Brown, *Condition of Affairs in Georgia*, 377.

43. Testimony of R. T. Kenimer, *Condition of Affairs in Georgia*, 908–13; testimony of George Holcombe, *Condition of Affairs in Georgia*, 496–500; testimony of Lt. F. B. Taylor, *Condition of Affairs in Georgia*, 503–4; Walter L. Fleming, "The Ku Klux Testimony Relating to Alabama," *Gulf States Historical Magazine* 2 (November 1903), 155–60.

Chapter 3

UnReconstructed Appalachia

The Persistence of War in Appalachia

T. R. C. Hutton

In September 1874 an interracial gang of sixteen men rode into the small county seat of Jackson, Kentucky, and forcibly took possession of the courthouse. They were led by William Strong, a local farmer who had been one of eastern Kentucky's most influential Unionists during the Civil War, thereby securing a reputation for theft and terrorism against civilians. After returning from cavalry service in 1863, Strong's war had primarily been fought in his home territory, an isolated, sparsely populated mountain county that, unlike many others in eastern Kentucky, had maintained a staunch pro-Confederate majority. Although he was temporarily successful in brutally promoting the Union cause, by the 1870s the Democrats who had moved the county in a pro-Confederate direction had regained control. Strong's courthouse insurrection was only one of numerous bold postwar attempts to enforce Union victory in a county where pro-Confederate government had never been effectively removed from power. Four years later he was involved in a fracas outside of the same courthouse but this time with far deadlier results: three men, one of them a recently elected county judge, were killed during a standoff between Strong's men and Confederate veterans.

His struggle against his home county made long-lasting enemies but gained Strong the support of local society's lowest social and economic echelons. In 1894, after employing his allegedly inherent belligerence toward preventing surveys of land occupied by squatters, Strong was labeled the "feudal hero" of the landless population, a title that exemplified the seemingly medieval nature of his position (or at least the manner in which his detractors characterized it).[1] A few years later, after his death from an unknown assassin's bullet, Kentucky's most widely circulated newspaper eulogized him as the last of the "Red Strings," a label directly associated with the memory of the Civil War. But within the same article, "feudal chieftain," a description with a far different meaning, was applied as well.[2] Placed in opposition, these names reveal not only the unique political authority established by Strong's military leadership but also the tenuous efforts of observers to *depoliticize* him and his past.[3] Was he to be deemed a product of relatively recent events or a vestige of a far more distant past?

Ultimately, it was to be the latter. By the time of his death, Strong, his allies, and his enemies were not widely remembered as combatants in a larger national struggle but rather uncivilized fighters taking part in killings with motivations strictly endogenous to their immediate community: "feudists." The only operative difference between his courthouse seizure and contemporary events farther south was that the former took place in a state outside the jurisdiction of Reconstruction. Strong's martial and political affiliations, however, were obscured by his supposed mountain primevality. Placed in this context, he was less Union guerrilla than apolitical brute.

This essay examines a single Kentucky county, Breathitt County, a small section of the South untouched by federal Reconstruction efforts during the 1860s and 1870s despite being embroiled in the same social and political conflicts suffered by the South at large. Breathitt County, a discreet space of an unseceded (but, in many ways, decidedly Southern) state, was geographically and politically wedged uncomfortably between North and South, a condition that one could apply to much of southern Appalachia during the Civil War. But although it shared similar terrain to parts of neighbors to the south, eastern Kentucky was in many way unlike these state's mountainous regions. As one of the most sparsely populated areas of the upper South with little economic development at the beginning of the Civil War, there was no new shock of modernization to tie it to the state at large, as the railroad did in southwestern Virginia (resulting in the latter's consistent loyalty to the Confederacy).[4] Nor did eastern Kentucky's Unionist majority find a leader who could articulate their dissent, as eastern Tennessee Unionists found in William Brownlow.[5] No factor arose before or during the war to knit together the interests of Kentucky's mountain counties. As a result, the counties themselves were established as bodies through which scattered beliefs in union or disunion were expressed.[6] Given this remarkable lack of centrality, it is little wonder that William Strong would express his postwar anger by attacking his own home county's courthouse, a building that had come to have far greater significance during and since the war than when it was originally built.

While the actions of Strong and his wartime opponents were motivated by the war's legacy, observers from outside Breathitt County would come to dissociate the county's subsequent cycle of violence from its actual origins, creating in its place the commonly accepted image of intrinsic violence (i.e., feuding) among the "mountain whites." This image was a primary component of the creation of what anthropologist Mary K. Anglin has called "the fiction known as 'Appalachia,'" a fiction that was useful for diminishing or obscuring the Civil War's actual legacy in the eastern portion of the Bluegrass State.[7] The mountain feud (or the Kentucky feud) is a supposedly discernible social phenomenon that, for decades, captured the attention and imagination of local-color writers, journalists, and sociologists. Only in recent decades have scholars begun to approach nineteenth-century eastern Kentucky's feud phenomenon as something other than sui generis products of mountain isolation and degeneracy.[8]

For the most part, however, these accounts of feud violence have dealt solely with the standard Revisionist narrative of Appalachian history, the region's economic integration into the American economy, and the tensions and conflicts this integration created. While these economic motifs are important in understanding the history of the region, it is equally important to remember that the mountain South had been fully *politically* integrated within the United States since the early days of white settlement, and to consider the possibility that "feuds" had a larger connection to exogenous impetuses for violence. With this in mind, it might also be suitable to place feud violence within another larger narrative, that of the Civil War and Reconstruction. Breathitt County, a place that seemed to play host to multiple "feuds" over the course of decades following the war, reveals itself as the best possible case study for exploring this possibility.

Places like Breathitt County have remained relatively untouched within the context of Reconstruction, for relatively obvious reasons.[9] The mass of Reconstruction history has understandably been dedicated to questions of black citizenship, enfranchisement, and the resultant white resistance, so that the period's narrative has been dominated by the Deep South. Kentucky never officially seceded and was accordingly not subject to federal efforts toward reincorporation into the Union. Moreover, as a section of the South with a tiny African American minority, this area of central Appalachia seemingly did not suffer from the conflicts that seemed to inevitably accompany the granting of citizenship to a formerly enslaved population. With the Freedmen's Bureau, federal troops, and "carpetbagger" politicians out of the picture, the Appalachian Kentucky experience during this time does not outwardly appear familiar. Had the disputes that ran rampant across the South after the Civil War been solely about questions of race, extremely white places like Breathitt County should, theoretically, have maintained peaceful relations amongst their citizenries. However, the employment of violence—both revolutionary and counterrevolutionary—shows that southern communities left untouched by outside forces were still subject to internal conflict and a sporadic extension of the war for years after 1865.

A small but diverse number of publications have recognized Kentucky's political peculiarity during the 1860s and 1870s.[10] In comparison to the other unseceded border South states (Delaware, Maryland, and Missouri) Kentucky was by far the most divided in its internal wartime loyalties.[11] Although Kentucky never seceded, it was never exclusively loyal to the Union (as demonstrated by its early attempt at neutrality) and ultimately contributed large numbers of Confederate volunteers until the South's defeat in 1865. As the war progressed, the Confiscation Acts, the presidential suspension of habeas corpus, the manumission and arming of African Americans in the Union army, and other federal actions disillusioned loyal white Kentuckians and increased sympathy for the Southern cause. After the war, the state was not subject to presidential or Congressional Reconstruction (although the habeas corpus suspension continued long after the war by presidential proclamation, as it did in the rebellious states), leaving the war-torn state without significant federal oversight.[12] Attacks on African Americans and former Unionists were carried out with relatively little punitive action by state authorities. In one historian's phrasing, the state seemingly "seceded in 1865."[13] Recognizing that conditions in Kentucky were on par with the states that were subject to federal occupation, Sen. Charles Sumner of Massachusetts advocated placing Kentucky under federal military authority.[14]

For reasons both constitutional and political, Sumner's suggestion was never enacted. Unlike other states of the upper South that had remained in the Union, most notably West Virginia and Missouri, the Republican Party was unable to form a majority in the Kentucky state legislature during the war.[15] In 1865 the Democratic majority immediately restored political and civil rights to Confederate veterans and sympathizers, a measure that contributed to an increasingly conservative, antifederal turn in the state's political character after the war. In addition, the constitutional power afforded to the central state government was particularly lacking in situations of civil disorder. Consequently, lynching, riots, and politically motivated mur-ders continued in the state well into the 1870s, particularly after the Ku Klux Klan's emergence in the state in 1869. White southern resistance to the changes brought about by the Civil War was as virulent in Kentucky as it was in the Deep South, as Charles Sumner recognized. But as an unreconstructed state, Kentucky did not have the necessary infrastructure to impede, much less prevent, the resulting violence.[16] A recent history of Reconstruction-era Tennessee points to its Unionist government's coercive "force politics" as an indicator of what a broader, "more forceful military-style Reconstruction" might have looked like had it been attempted throughout the rebellious states.[17] In contrast, during the same years Tennessee's northern neighbor may well have resembled what a larger South would have looked like had it been left completely to its own wits after defeat.

For this reason, incidents that bore some resemblance to Strong's attempted insurrection were common in Kentucky during the 1870s. Local animosities between former Unionists and Confederates contributed to one of the worst records of violence during the years of Reconstruction. Even before incarnations of the Ku Klux Klan appeared in the state in 1869, other "regulator" groups of varying political allegiances appeared as well. Paramilitary groups composed primarily of Confederate veterans terrorized Unionists and freedpeople in the Bluegrass region and western Kentucky until the early 1870s.[18] These organized groups emerged alongside a statewide increase in documented lynchings, most of which were racially motivated.[19] But violence was a tool of suppression for both sides of the conflict; even in areas with broad Southern sympathies, Confederate veterans were also subject to harassment, forced exile, or murder perpetrated by pro-Union partisans.[20] In the eastern third of the state (an area with few African Americans and somewhat more consistent Unionist loyalty), armed "Loyal Leagues" intimidated local Democrats during elections.[21]

Such crimes were significantly less likely to be prevented or punished in the mountain counties for a number of reasons. Primarily, when simultaneously faced with violence in more developed, racially mixed parts of the state (particularly the densely populated Bluegrass) and the sparsely populated mountain counties, the state's Reconstruction-era governors preferred to err on the side of enforcing the law in the more developed regions. Violence in the mountains was less likely to involve racial antagonism and was therefore less likely to attract negative attention from the federal government or the northern press. Secondarily, local law enforcement was less effective in these counties because violent actions were often carried out by, or at the behest of, local political leaders. What appeared to be apolitical vigilante-style violence was actually the enforcement of local state policies.[22] Finally, the symbiosis between state and local government played a considerable role. Most southern historians' interpretations of Reconstruction have generally failed to consider governments below the state level as viable subjects, leaving a familiar (and often taken for granted) institution unexamined: the county.[23] County courts held far more authority over the maintenance of law and order than did the state capital. The question of whether governors and legislators chose to disregard the memory of the war had little to do with the actions of judges, law enforcement officials, and private citizens whose political and factional identities had been forged during the war and whose actions generally played out almost strictly on the county level.[24] Such local policies paralleled the conservative "Southern rights" position favored by a majority of white Kentuckians and, from a white conservative perspective, were more effective than legislation or law enforcement carried out by other legal means.[25] Essentially, allowing mass violence in the most rural counties assisted the maintenance of the conservative status quo without attracting unwanted notice from outside the state.

But the subject of violence could not be entirely ignored. For the sake of averting federal meddling in the state's affairs, even the most conservative white Kentuckians had no choice but to publicly condemn it. The most suitable method for doing so was to devalue its political implications. For years the Democratic press denied that anything resembling the "true" Ku Klux Klan existed in the state. Violent acts, even those carried out by groups rather than individuals, were interpreted as the work of criminals rather than political or military partisans.[26] For an observer like *Louisville (KY) Courier-Journal* editor Henry Watterson, a former lieutenant for one Nathan Bedford Forrest, his best case in point was the Ku Klux

Klan. While the South Carolina and Tennessee manifestations of the Klan came about through resistance to northern tyranny (and had clear links to the southern Democratic Party), according to Watterson, the Kentucky Klan "was not an outgrowth of civil war. Neither was it made up of ex-Confederate soldiers. . . . One-third bully and two-thirds whisky, a thorough coward and scoundrel, it disgraced the name of KuKlux when it assumed it."[27] Thus, the state's predominant Democratic organ, and the leader of the "New Departure" could simultaneously decry ku kluxing while denying that Kentucky's continuing cycle of violence had any political implications.[28] Even Kentucky's most prominent Union/Republican newspaper, a publication usually in the habit of connecting all things harmful and disorderly to the Democratic Party, attributed white intraracial bloodshed to "heated blood, family difficulties, old grudges, intoxication, and inborn malevolence" rather than organized reaction to postwar change.[29] Republicans, even those who saw a clear need for federal intervention, knew that such an action could only hurt their already weakened standings at the polls.[30] As long as such outrages remained in the hinterlands, it was easy work for the state's urban press to report violence apolitically for interested outsiders.

Although the state's mountainous section had a marked Unionist majority, the Democratic Party, led by Confederate veterans, thrived in some eastern Kentucky counties and often did so using aggressive methods. As was the case in much of the South, the party built its platform upon local sovereignty and resistance to federal authority. The remoteness of the mountains made consolidation of renewed federal authority difficult, particularly in counties that retained pro-Southern majorities. Even though racial politics had little direct impact on local government, mountain Democrats joined their compatriots in condemning the effects of "radicalism" in the state.[31] The antifederal bias extended beyond the bounds of party platform; less than a year after the war's end, Democrats in Floyd, Morgan, and Wolfe counties (three heavily Democratic contiguous counties that had served as an island of Confederate support during the war) organized to forcibly expel federal revenue agents.[32]

Moreover, unlike Democrats in other parts of the state, Democratic leaders in the eastern counties did not attempt to hide their association with vigilante groups and openly used them as a means of enforcing party policy and intimidating local voters. Estill County's state senator and local Democratic Party boss served as the head of a multicounty Ku Klux Klan klavern in the early 1870s.[33] A Breathitt County town constable—one of the county's leading Democrats, who joined the Klan in the 1870s and soon became the local chapter's "vice president"—laconically recalled years later that membership "gave a man great power over his neighbor."[34] The constable's nonchalance belied the Klan's actual brutality; in the fall of 1870, nineteen men—all of whom were Union veterans or Republicans— were killed in Klan attacks in Breathitt and three surrounding counties.[35] Eastern Kentucky's record of violence during these years was probably no worse than in much of the rest of the state and nowhere near as bad as contemporaneous atrocities in South Carolina and Louisiana. But, hidden by the relative isolation of mountainous terrain, these incidents received little attention and continued unabated with no interference from state or federal oversight for years. The seminal history of the nineteenth-century manifestation of the Ku Klux Klan notes that the group lasted longer in Kentucky than in any other state.[36] Indeed, with the turn of the century looming, gangs still claiming the title continued to be violently active in eastern Kentucky, albeit on a smaller, more secretive scale than thirty years earlier.[37]

It is difficult to determine whether Klan factions in eastern Kentucky were related to the larger organization that was far more influential in the Deep South. For that matter, it is equally difficult to connect eastern Kentucky's Loyal League to the larger fraternal organization populated by freedmen and white Unionists that was also more active farther south. Nonetheless, the fact that organizations in the Kentucky mountains assumed those names demonstrates that white mountaineers saw parallels between their own local conflicts and the larger struggle between conservative southern whites and the encroachment of black enfranchisement and federal authority—the "master cleavage" of contemporary southern politics.[38] Mountain whites who had chosen to take part in the Civil War supposedly did so for reasons that had a direct bearing on their own local existence: property, kinship ties, and local political affiliations.[39] Even among "bushwhackers," who supposedly held few or no formal ties to official federal and Confederate forces, local issues became conflated with national issues such as racial politics and the conflict between state and federal power. As a result, mountaineers continued to understand the rifts caused in their local communities in light of these same conflations after the war was over.

William "Captain Bill" Strong was an exemplar of this postwar state of affairs. Having left the Fourteenth Kentucky Cavalry in 1864 to return home to lead a company in the Three Forks Battalion, Strong and his local supporters managed to temporarily dictate Breathitt County's political direction in favor of the Union.[40] The county's staunchly pro-Confederate elites had established Jackson, the county seat, as one of eastern Kentucky's two most active Confederate mustering grounds early in the war.[41] Confederate recruitment had caused a drain on the county's number of men of fighting age, leaving behind families that may have had publicly known political leanings favoring the Confederate cause but were, for the most part, willing to remain inactive. Working with allies from neighboring counties that were more heavily Unionist, as well as Breathitt County's landless and African American people, Strong harassed, threatened, and killed any of the county's male population that he saw as an obstacle to the Union cause, regardless of their direct affiliation with the Confederate military. In 1863 only forty-seven men were willing to vote for the Democratic gubernatorial candidate, giving Breathitt County an overwhelming majority in favor of Union candidate Thomas Bramlette.[42] The absence of a large segment of the male population and Strong's bullying tactics provided Breathitt County's only gubernatorial defection from the Democratic Party in the nineteenth century. Decades later, a local historian described this as the beginning of Strong's campaign to "rid the county of all but Republicans," a campaign that outlasted the war by many years.[43] His notoriety matched that of "home guard" units all over Kentucky.[44]

Perhaps only by virtue of his local Union leadership, Strong was able to subvert his pro-Confederate home county's governmental legitimacy.[45] In the process, he also became a "special protector" for the local black population.[46] In the process of fighting the war, Strong developed an alliance with black Kentuckians in his vicinity, an alliance that may have been conveyed by his own family's slaves. Nearly a decade after the war's end, "Nigger Dick" Strong, a freedman said to have once been owned by Strong's father, was seen armed in Strong's company.[47] Strong also developed alliances with Breathitt County's poorer white farmers, particularly those who illegally occupied property owned by Jeremiah W. South, the man who had petitioned for the county's formation years earlier, guided its political development, and eventually led it toward support for the Confederacy.[48] The formation of this "Red String" organization, operating outside the oversight of higher authorities (and only tenuously beneath that of the state of Kentucky), was both a response to the perceived threat of Unionism and a challenge to private property.[49]

Two men who were violent associates of Strong for years after the war, Henderson Kilburn and Hiram Freeman, are among a small number of people who can be identified as consistent Red String devotees. Historical records reveal little about Kilburn other than that he was a landless farmer at the beginning of the war (possibly on South's acreage) whose wartime experience exemplifies the ambivalence many poor whites felt toward both sides of the war effort.[50] Kilburn initially joined the Confederate Fifth Kentucky Infantry but deserted after less than two months. He eventually joined the Unionist Fourteenth Kentucky Cavalry and later returned to Breathitt County in early 1865 to join the Three Forks Battalion.[51] As a bushwhacker assassin during and after the war, Kilburn was said to be Strong's "chief lieutenant" and "right hand, right foot, and right eye."[52]

Hiram Freeman, the racially mixed son of a manumitted male slave, moved to Breathitt County after escaping indentured servitude in 1838.[53] Freeman used his biracial heritage to negotiate multiple (or perhaps overlapping) racial identities. Although he was listed as mulatto on the 1860 census, Freeman and at least one of his sons—all of whom were listed as white on the same document, as was Freeman's wife—were able to join the otherwise all-white Fourteenth Kentucky Cavalry.[54] Though Freeman was not as brutal as Kilburn, he was remembered as "among the worst" of Strong's Union allies.[55] Freeman and two of his sons were said to have "terrorized the county" in the years after the war.[56] Strong's association with these men and the populations that they each represented probably originated as a wartime marriage of convenience. He himself was the offspring of landed slaveowners.[57] But the longevity of his association with these groups suggests that Strong's wartime experience had an effect upon his ideological outlook.

Strong's political socialization remains blurry, but the war clearly established him as a leader among Breathitt County's black and white poor in a manner rarely seen during the war.[58] Operating in and around a pro-Confederate county ensconced within a Union state, Strong was able to use the ensuing confusion of legitimacy to negotiate a transformation of his military leadership into the subaltern "chieftain" status for which he was later known. But as much sway as he may have held during the war, Strong could not prevent the return of "a more determined democratic element" within Breathitt County's court, a change that coincided with the local emergence of the Ku Klux Klan.[59] Their attacks on other Unionists, and the return to electoral power of the men who had brought Breathitt County into the Confederate fold, only hardened his resolve.

But resistance was preceded by a measure of acquiescence, or at least acceptance of the county court as a still-viable institution, despite its being Democrat controlled. In the late 1860s Strong was the target of litigation for his war record. Aside from terrorizing families that he saw as political or martial enemies, one of his other wartime tactics had been to commandeer property, usually livestock, from farmers with purported Confederate sympathies. Postwar lawsuits against Strong and his allies for the loss of property were unsuccessful because Strong always testified that his wartime acquisitions were carried out for the purpose of "suppressing the late rebellion." While county positions like sheriff and county judge were firmly under Democratic control by 1867, Breathitt County's circuit trials were often presided over by Republican judges elected by Republican majorities in surrounding counties within the same judicial district, who acknowledged Strong's invocation of Unionist loyalty as just cause to have the lawsuits transferred to federal courts in Louisville.[60] Strong was also willing to attend court when it suited his purposes more directly. When an old Confederate adversary was tried for murder in 1873, Strong and seven other Union veterans were called as witnesses for the prosecution. In opposition, five Confederate veterans acted as witnesses for the defense (the trial resulted in an acquittal).[61]

For years, Strong functioned in a bizarre legal and political equilibrium, aided by a circuit court controlled by his political allies but at the mercy of a county court under the authority of his enemies. Unsurprisingly, he was not above using physical intimidation during his court trials, a tactic that was not without some success. After assaulting one of his plaintiffs in the confiscation lawsuit, Strong was summarily sued for $500 on the grounds of assault and battery. One of the jurors on the case confessed later that he had persuaded the jury (including one unnamed "strong Rebel" who advocated imposition of the full fine) to reduce the fine to $100 for fear of further threats from Strong. The juror defended his reduction as a way to "soften the enemy rather than hardening him," considering that, even two years after the end of official hostilities, "the war spirit was high and . . . it was pretty hard to enforce the civil law." The usually irascible defendant seemed to be somewhat willing to play along; after the trial, Strong "treated" the jury at the local grocery store, which also served as a tavern.[62]

This did not mean that Strong's standing in the community was fully restored. Outside of the county court, many of Strong's enemies were unwilling to compartmentalize their wartime and peacetime roles. At the time of the trial Strong was said to have a $500 bounty placed upon him by Jeremiah South, who blamed Strong for his loss of two sons during the war.[63] At the same time he also had conflicts with former allies. At an unspecified time in the latter days of the war, Strong ran afoul of fellow Unionists over the apportionment of confiscated livestock. While captured hogs, oxen, and horses were officially to be used to "suppress the late rebellion," in Strong's war there was a thin line between duty and material gain.[64] In 1867 Strong's father, William Strong Sr., sued his son's former allies for compensation for wartime confiscations (Strong Sr., a slave owner, was apparently considered pro-Confederate, unlike his son).[65] The ensuing conflict was acted out in the circuit court as well as on the field of battle, the latter without apparent interference from local legal authorities.[66] Attesting to the way in which the war had intermingled personal and property conflicts with political identity, a local historian described the men's defection from Strong as "turn[ing] democratic."[67] As a result, at least three members of the Amis family were killed, after which the rest of the family migrated to Missouri.[68] The memory of what became known as the "Strong-Amis feud" was used by local Democrats for years afterward to throw his Unionist credentials into question, thereby portraying him as nothing more than an apolitical outlaw or "feudist," a social type that was to gain widespread use in the decades following the war as a label for those who committed white intraracial violence.

Shortly after his break with the Amis family, Strong was attacked by an unknown knife-wielding assailant while spending the night in a hotel.[69] It had become clear that Strong was no longer able to act with the impunity he had displayed during his litigation. Nevertheless, he did not retreat from the ties he had formed with Breathitt County's squatter population and the county's small number of African Americans. With his influence among Breathitt County's unruly poor, Strong's Democratic adversaries reluctantly recognized him as a formidable power broker, and he was consulted for political endorsements for years.[70] But tensions between the two segments of the population increased in 1872 after Strong's first cousin, Edward Strong, acting in his capacity as county judge, sold a large segment of the county's "wild lands" to a land speculation firm. Well aware that their livelihoods were endangered by the purchase of adjacent lands, both legitimate smallholders and squatters would not allow the area to be claimed by outside parties. The land's inhabitants formed an armed squad and confronted the surveyors shortly after the sale was made. Although the squatters were unable to prevent the sale, their demonstration of armed force delayed further surveying of the area around Quicksand Creek for years.[71] The following year, "republicans of the war element" burned Breathitt County's courthouse, possibly in order to destroy extant land grants, thereby preventing further speculations on unimproved land in the county.[72] William Strong was accused of the arson but was never indicted. Even though he remained able to negotiate a safe position between Breathitt County's poor and landed, Strong was at the center of a roiling class conflict fueled dually by the expectation of an approaching railroad and an element of suppressed tension left over from the war. It was only now that the incongruity between national Union victory nearly a decade earlier and Democratic persistence in Breathitt County began to appear as a danger.

William Strong's attempt to forcefully capture the newly rebuilt courthouse in 1874, his first public act of violence in years, was carried out in reaction to the unpunished murder of a black man, William Hargis, by a white man. With the support of Freeman, Kilburn, Freeman's sons William and Daniel, "Nigger Dick" Strong, and ten other unnamed associates of both races, Strong attempted a coup d'état, taking possession of the courthouse and supposedly the entire town of Jackson.[73] Strangely, Strong seems to have encountered little resistance. His party staged the uprising by force of arms, but there is no evidence that they killed or injured anyone in Jackson; nor does it seem that anyone was ever punished for killing Hargis, by Strong or by legitimate authorities.

The relatively anticlimactic rebellion did not go completely unnoticed. In mid-September rumors spread between Frankfort and Louisville that a "party of 200 desperados" had barricaded themselves in and around the Breathitt County courthouse.[74] Unknown parties contacted Gov. Preston H. Leslie with a request to send members of the militia to reestablish order in the county. Having been accused of hesitation in dealing with Klan violence in the recent past, and alarmed by the exaggerated reports, Leslie dispatched a militia company to Breathitt County and requested that Republican district judge William H. Randall suspend his current court dates in order to schedule a special court session in Jackson that would allow no case continuances.[75] After false reports that the company had been attacked, Leslie anticipated further requests from Breathitt and sent four more companies. By the end of September more members of the state militia had been sent to Breathitt County than to any of the Bluegrass counties that had requested intervention the previous month.[76]

By the time of the militia's arrival, Strong and his men had relinquished control of the town and subsequently allowed themselves to be disarmed.[77] Beside the fact that they were far outnumbered by the militia, Strong and the Freemans were probably less reluctant to give up their arms knowing that the court was to be handed over to Randall. As a Republican with a strong civil-rights background, Randall appeared as an ally to the county's Republican partisans, both black and white.[78] Strong himself was not arrested for his attempted insurrection, and the Freemans, although indicted by a county magistrate for delinquent murder accusations, were dismissed from trial due to a lack of witnesses for the prosecution.[79] Randall's leniency to the Strong party may have been reported to the state government, for shortly after the beginning of the special court session Randall was instructed by Governor Leslie to turn the court over to Breathitt County's Democratic county judge James Back. In November, Back indicted Strong and the Freemans for carrying concealed weapons, but all four men were acquitted.[80] Back did not attempt to reverse any of Randall's rulings, nor did he further pursue Strong and the Freemans for their earlier crime. Randall's dismissal altered Leslie's original plans for the special court session. After Back was given control of the court, both criminal and civil cases were carried over to future court sessions, against Leslie's instructions.[81]

The confluence of personal grievances, class division, and racial violence endangered the political and social balance in Breathitt County during the later years of Reconstruction. Jurisprudence in the county, carried out by men who had a greater stake in maintaining control of local government than in enforcing a peaceful social order, was consequently highly politicized. William Strong's attempt to carry out what appeared to be a purely symbolic act of insurrection demonstrated his refusal to recognize Democratic authority in his home county. Local Democrats, particularly those in control of the county court, saw leniency showed to him by a Republican with superior judicial authority as a threat to their autonomy and their local hegemony, both of which had motivated them to support the Confederacy the previous decade. The threat to local legitimacy established by the war a decade earlier had reemerged.

Strong and his cousin Edward were again embroiled in a deadly political conflict in 1878 when a disputed criminal trial and an equally tumultuous election for county judge prompted a return of the state militia and a far greater degree of attention on Breathitt County from the national media. Although the county had not suffered from any major violence since 1874, tensions had been simmering since Edward Strong's sale of land to outside speculators, an action that forced him out of office the following year. His cousin, secure in the knowledge that he could count on Republican authorities from outside the county for protection, maintained his old alliances but chose not to take further action against the county's Democrats until a newcomer to the county successfully challenged the local Democratic cabal for the position of county judge. John W. Burnett, a young lawyer from Virginia, moved to the county in 1875, joining the local bar organization and making friends with the sheriff and other Jackson residents. In 1878 Burnett decided to use his popularity in a bid for county judge. Although Burnett was a Democrat, as a political neophyte with no preexistent ties to the county he was an interloper within the local political scene, and the more stalwart Democrats nominated Edward Strong.

The weeks leading up to the August election were fraught with threats of violence; a third candidate chose to withdraw after being intimidated by unnamed parties. Shortly before the election a fellow Democrat (and a Klan member) had warned Edward Strong that "any man who is elected in [Breathitt] county and will not take sides with the lawless will be killed by them."[82] "The lawless," Strong and the Red String, were still a political force to be reckoned with, both as a threat to civil order and as a considerable voting bloc. Seeing his chance, William Strong readily endorsed Burnett after rejecting his cousin's request for support, giving Burnett a narrow win thanks in part to the squatters who had been angered years earlier by Edward Strong's land sale.[83] Burnett's resultant eight-vote victory over Edward Strong represented the first electoral challenge to local Democratic rule in the county since the Civil War.[84]

Burnett's term in office was complicated by personal conflicts that eventually expanded into Breathitt County's largest instance of mob violence ever. Even though Burnett had a reputation for brashness—he was rumored to have come to Breathitt County to escape punishment for killing a man in a duel in Virginia—in the three years since his relocation to Kentucky he had managed to remain personally aloof from the county's internecine political conflicts. Before his election as judge, Burnett had been deputized by the sheriff in the arrest of a farmer named Jerry Little. Burnett was said to have acted with particular brutality in carrying out the arrest, and he had earned the enmity of the Little's extended family. When Little's uncle, Jason Little, was arrested months later for murdering his wife, Burnett had him transferred to the city jail in Lexington, more than one hundred miles away. After being narrowly elected with the support of a controversial quasi bandit like William Strong, local Democrats interpreted Burnett's arrest and removal of Jason Little as a politically motivated affront. When Little was returned to Jackson for trial in late November, a mob of Confederate veterans massed outside of the jail in an apparent threat to forcibly release Little. The mob was confronted by William Strong, the Freemans, and approximately a dozen of their supporters. The ensuing showdown resulted in the shooting deaths of Daniel Freeman and Tom Little, a cousin of Jason Little whom William Strong later said had threatened to lead "two hundred Kuklux" from neighboring Wolfe County.[85] The following day as Burnett was walking to the courthouse to convene court with William Randall, he was shot and killed by one of the Confederate veterans, prompting Randall to flee the county.

A county judge's assassination was enough to persuade Gov. James McCreary to grudgingly dispatch the state militia to Jackson, as Governor Leslie had done four years earlier, but still only at the request of Judge Randall, after his escape from the county; McCreary had initially dismissed the reports of rioting in Jackson as exaggerations. As had been the case before, the governor was constitutionally required to await Randall's request before dispatching the state militia. McCreary had other considerations at hand regarding the use of the militia that his predecessor had not been obliged to deal with—considerations that made him hesitant to dispatch militia units far away from the Bluegrass cities. The previous year, Louisville had been the scene for one of the Great Railroad Strike's larger manifestations, bringing commerce to a halt and resulting in massive property damage (as well as a disturbing new cooperation between working-class whites and blacks).[86] Klan and regulator violence had generally ebbed in the closing years of Reconstruction, and Kentuckians were reluctant to believe that violence born of the war could still menace the state. With the rural disorders of Reconstruction resistance apparently at an end, the Bluegrass and urban middle class now recognized that threats to civic order in the state would now be more likely to come from the cities rather than the countryside.[87] In contrast, Breathitt County did not appear to urban Kentuckians as a continuation of old problems with violence and disorder, but rather an unfortunate distraction from newer ones. Nevertheless, these same economic considerations also depended upon good relations with northern business interests. Conscious of criticism from the northern press, and equally conscious of the ramifications of a public official's violent death,

Governor McCreary reluctantly dispatched the state militia to Jackson in early December.[88]

Soon after the militia's arrival in Jackson, Judge Randall returned, and court was reconvened, only to have proceedings interrupted by political maneuverings. After Randall officiated during the conviction of the wife-murderer, the Republican judge was sworn off the bench and replaced by a Louisville probate judge to try the "conspirators" in Burnett's murder. Randall's party affiliation, compounded by his flight from the county a month earlier, made him too controversial a figure to try the remaining cases. The probate judge convicted Alfred Gambrel for Burnett's murder while Wallace Maguire, the only one of Strong's allies to be put on trial, was convicted for the killing of Tom Little.[89] John Aikman, the ringleader of the Democratic mob that had rushed the jailhouse, had fled the county on the advice of a Klan collaborator but was later captured and sentenced for conspiring to murder Burnett (his killing of Daniel Freeman the previous day was apparently ignored).[90] Before Aikman's capture, letters from him were printed in Kentucky's predominant Bourbon Democrat paper, accusing William Strong of using the chaotic situation in the county for material gain.[91] Both he and Gambrel were eventually pardoned through the intercession of the influential South family, who recognized Aikman's role in attempting to uphold Democratic control over the Breathitt County court.[92] Still, although the continuity of violence showed clear correlations with recent incidents in other areas of Kentucky and the South (namely, the reassertion of conservative Democratic regimes utilizing counterrevolutionary violence), Breathitt County's troubles were judged to be the outcome of "an imperfect organization [resulting] from the practical isolation of the people, the unlettered authorities, and the absence of schools and moral example," as well as the lack of contact with "more advanced communities."[93]

In his message to the Kentucky General Assembly late in 1879, Governor McCreary declared the success of the state government in pacifying Breathitt County, stating that "no county is more orderly or peaceable than Breathitt."[94] McCreary's pronouncement of success failed to acknowledge that since the militia's withdrawal from Jackson the previous winter, the log building used as Breathitt County's jailhouse had been destroyed by a mob, and a Confederate veteran had been killed in ambush while working in his field.[95] Over the next few years Henderson Kilburn supposedly killed nine men in a similar "bushwhacker" manner. This new tactic prompted the first major reprisal from Strong's enemies. In 1884 Kilburn and Ben Strong (possibly another former slave of the Strong family or a descendant thereof) were arrested for the murder of a purported Klansman. After their arrest both men were forcibly extracted from the jail by Klansmen and hanged from the Breathitt County courthouse's bell tower.[96] A Methodist evangelist, having recently arrived in Jackson to minister to what he had been told was a benighted, bestial population, assured himself that their deaths had reflected "the sentiment of the county" and "a better, healthier public sentiment." Moreover, even though he was evidently unsure of their identities, he suspected that "these regulators are of *the better class*" (italics mine).[97] Even though rumors circulated that he would avenge Kilburn's and Ben Strong's deaths, William Strong instead sent a messenger requesting that their bodies be sent to him so that they could be "both buried in the same grave on his farm among their friends."[98]

The lynching of the landless white and the African American in front of the courthouse in Jackson indicated not only that their deaths were the will of the majority of the county's population, but also that the Klansmen had acted in the interest of law and order, a law and order determined by the wealthier landowners who headed the local Democratic Party as well as the local Ku Klux Klan. Just as William Strong's capture of the courthouse ten years earlier had represented the Red Strings' attempt to reaffirm their ostensible wartime victory in Breathitt County, the hangings of Red String members in front of the same courthouse demonstrated that their efforts were in violation of the local commonweal. Strong, Kilburn, and their affiliates had remained free from prosecution for their crimes for years because of juries' fears of reprisal. The murder of Judge Burnett and the lynchings nearly six years later showed that local Democrats had come to the realization that extralegal violence was necessary for the maintenance of the status quo. The violence seemed to prove effective: the lynching of Ben Strong and his most merciless compatriot marked the end of William Strong's more aggressive efforts against Breathitt County's Democratic elites. Until the time of his 1897 assassination, Strong remained the county's squatters' "chieftain" and presumably that of the dwindling black population as well. However, he would no longer attempt insurrections, act as an enforcer during elections, or order the deaths of his political enemies. His influence was still feared, however. His murder was apparently in response to his denouncement of a new incarnation of the Ku Klux Klan that emerged in Breathitt County in the 1890s.[99]

Because Breathitt County, and Kentucky as a whole, had never been subject to federal reconstruction, "redemption" of the locality by conservative forces was never deemed necessary in the sense that it had been in the Deep South. Moreover, the Democratic hegemony over Breathitt County, imposed and protected through violence, was politically advantageous to Kentucky's state government; hence, state interference in local matters was limited to a two-month imposition of martial law in 1878 and 1879 (the 1884 lynching was ignored by the state government).[100] The suppression of the county's landless population was also advantageous, in this case economically, for the landowning Democrats of Breathitt County as well as for a Bluegrass population ready to invest in the untapped timber and coal resources publicized during the state militia's two visits to the county. The squatter and the black man not only represented a threat to the public good but also resistance to commercial progress. As was the case in many other parts of the post-Reconstruction South, where conventional political methods were unsuccessful in creating a conservative consensus, the creation of a Democrat-directed New South required violence for its implementation.[101]

The past three decades have produced a wealth of monographs broadly chronicling the American Civil War as it was fought and suffered in Appalachia.[102] But relatively little has been observed about the region in the years after the war, an omission that leaves much to be written about the way in which some communities succeeded or failed to establish a postwar peace. The record of violence in Breathitt County, Kentucky, in the 1870s fits uneasily into the more familiar narrative of Reconstruction history, but it should be examined more closely for that very reason. A place such as Breathitt County reveals a narrative that combines elements that are both strange and familiar to scholars of Reconstruction, events that perhaps could only have taken place in a border state so internally ravaged, yet also distortedly reflecting larger efforts for or against change elsewhere in the South. For instance, it was the tenuous, and ultimately failed, union between freedpeople and poor whites that suffused the aspirations of many southerners while simultaneously causing anxiety among conservative elites.[103] This attempt certainly took place in the county, albeit in miniature form, but had even less of a chance to affect local ballot boxes than did similar efforts farther south.

The counterrevolutionary brutality employed by the county's Democrats was matched, and sometimes surpassed, by the revolutionary brutality employed by the interracial Red String, giving Breathitt County the appearance of a place in which violence was absolutely reciprocal and used between actors of equal means; hence the media's usage of the apolitical "feud" nomenclature to describe this violence and later incidents in other eastern Kentucky counties.[104] As factional violence began to appear elsewhere in the section in the 1880s, the term "feud" proliferated as a name for violence in Kentucky (particularly eastern Kentucky and, by extension, southern Appalachia as a whole), conjuring images of a distant antiquity rather than the depravity recently experienced all over the South.[105] Horace Kephart, the early twentieth century's most widely regarded authority on southern Appalachia, declared these "blood feuds" to be "simply a horrible survival of medievalism."[106]

By utilizing this language, with its implied allusions to a premodern past, observers from both the North and the South could dismiss the modern political implications of death and destruction in the South's mountainous hinterlands. The press also minimized the racial significance of the county's disputes. One newspaper went as far as to explain that "there is no distinction between races up in that country," a contention thrown into doubt by John Aikman's reported announcement that he intended to "take a dead nigger" immediately before shooting Daniel Freeman.[107] Rather than admitting the role of outside forces in disrupting the county's social order, the national press blamed the violence on lack of civilization brought on by spatial isolation, an isolation that had somehow failed to separate the county, physically or politically, from the ruin of the war in the previous decade.[108] Ultimately, the image of the bestial mountaineer was more palatable, and more politically advantageous, than the unrepentant Southern rebel in the eyes of an American public that preferred to believe that the South had truly been reconstructed.

Notes

The writing of this article was made possible by the Gordon Family Fellowship, provided through the Vanderbilt University Graduate School. The author would also like to acknowledge the helpful critiques of this article, and of other writings leading up to it, provided by Richard Blackett, Tim Boyd, David Carlton, Peter Kuryla, and Sam McSeveney.

1. *Hazel Green (KY) Herald,* May 10, 1894.

2. *Louisville (KY) Courier-Journal,* May 10, 1897.

3. I use the term *depoliticization* in a manner different from that in which it is often used. Typically, the act of depoliticization involves removing political (usually partisan) influence from an institution or organization. Instead, I use it

to mean the removal of political agency from an individual or group with the purposes of portraying their actions as something other than working toward rational ends. In short, to depoliticize is to make one appear irrational and unknowing of the outcomes or purposes of one's own actions, particularly violent actions.

4. Kenneth W. Noe, *Southwest Virginia's Railroad: Modernization and the Sectional Crisis* (Urbana and Chicago: University of Illinois Press, 1994).

5. Robert Tracie McKenzie, *Lincolnites and Rebels: A Divided Town in the American Civil War* (Oxford and New York: Oxford University Press, 2006), 63–70, 115, 128, 148, 190, 207–8.

6. My contention regarding the importance of county government in Civil War–era Appalachia is not wholly original. Martin Crawford's *Ashe County's Civil War: Community and Society in the Appalachian South* (Charlottesville and London: University Press of Virginia, 2001) demonstrates the strengths and weaknesses of Southern counties with regard to steering communities toward, or away from, state majorities. However, Breathitt County, Kentucky, presents a very different situation from Ashe County, North Carolina, during the Civil War. For various reasons, the latter was both a pocket of Unionist resistance as well as a space of Southern loyalty, depending upon relationships within families and communities, and was perhaps little different from many other mountain counties within the seceded states. Had Ashe County been fully Unionist, its citizens could have defended their actions by affirming loyalty to the prewar Union. But Breathitt County presents a case in which county leaders were able to persuade an apparent majority of their county's white male population to resist the majority of Kentuckians and the Union of which they were a part by supporting the Confederacy (this done while being almost surrounded geographically by some of Kentucky's staunchest hotbeds of mountain Unionism). In other words, Unionism within the Confederate states is a familiar theme, while the concept of Confederate loyalty within an unseceded state is a far different situation that deserves further exploration.

7. Quote from Mary K. Anglin, "A Question of Loyalty: National and Regional Identity in Narratives of Appalachia," *Anthropological Quarterly* 65 (July 1992): 105–16 (106q).

8. Dwight Billings and Kathleen Blee, *The Road to Poverty: The Making of Wealth and Hardship in Appalachia* (Cambridge: Cambridge University Press, 2000), particularly chapter 8; Billings and Blee, "Violence and Local State Formation: A Longitudinal Case Study of Appalachian Feuding," *Law & Society Review* 30 (1996): 671–705; Keith F. Otterbein, "Five Feuds: An Analysis of Homicides in Eastern Kentucky in the Nineteenth Century," *American Anthropologist* 102 (Summer 2000): 231–43; Altina Waller, "Feuding in Appalachia: Evolution of a Cultural Stereotype," in Dwight Billings, Mary Beth Pudup, and Altina Waller, eds., *Appalachia in the Making: The Mountain South in the Nineteenth Century*, 347–76 (Chapel Hill: University of North Carolina Press, 1995); Waller, *Feud: Hatfields, McCoys, and Social Change in Appalachia, 1860–1900* (Chapel Hill: University of

North Carolina Press, 1988); James Klotter, "Feuds in Appalachia: An Overview," *Filson Club Historical Quarterly* 56 (July 1982): 290–317; Gordon McKinney, "Industrialization and Violence in Appalachia in the 1890s," *Appalachian Journal* 4 (1977): 131–44. See also Henry D. Shapiro, *Appalachia on Our Mind: The Southern Mountains and Mountaineers in the American Consciousness, 1870–1920* (Chapel Hill: University of North Carolina Press, 1978), 63. All of these can be placed within the "Revisionist" school of Appalachian history; thus, they look at feuding primarily as a stereotypical construction created by "outsiders" to justify the exploitive economic and cultural incorporation of the Appalachian region into the larger United States. But none of these sources delve into the fairly evident connections between such incidents of violence and the Civil War or the postwar record of violence connected to enforcement of, and resistance to, the policies of Reconstruction. Considering that the use of the word "feud" gained popularity during these years to describe white intraracial violence, the possibility of connections should be considered. I agree with Waller that the "feud" nomenclature is significant in its politically motivated usage, but I differ with her in that I consider the connections to Reconstruction violence as a product of not only "outsider" interpretation but of brute reality. Moreover, a close reading of interpretations of feud violence by the *New York Times* and the *Louisville Courier-Journal* (the two newspapers Waller incorporates in "Feuding in Appalachia: Evolution of a Cultural Stereotype") do not reveal a metropolitan consensus but rather a partisan dispute between, respectively, a Northern Republican viewpoint and a Southern Democratic viewpoint, based upon the discursive rupture created by Reconstruction-era state and federal policies (in addition, I also use other newspapers of varying political alignments). The war, and the ruptures it created, cannot go unmentioned when addressing a place as internally divided as southern Appalachia during this period. For the contextualization of conflicts termed as blood feuds within Civil War environments (and the problems inherent in dissociating civil wars from ensuing postwar violence), see Stathis Kalyvas, *The Logic of Violence in Civil War* (Cambridge, MA: Cambridge University Press, 2006), 21, 71, 99.

9. Two important exceptions are Gordon McKinney's *Southern Mountain Republicans* and Wilma Dunaway's *The African American Family in Slavery and Emancipation*. However, because the former is a relatively traditional (but groundbreaking) political history and the latter is strictly a social history of the region's freedpeople, neither of these books fully addresses the failure of white political consensus within Appalachian localities and the resultant factional violence; Dunaway, *The African American Family in Slavery and Emancipation* (Cambridge, MA: Cambridge University Press, 2003); McKinney, *Southern Mountain Republicans, 1865–1900: Politics and the Appalachian Community* (Chapel Hill: University of North Carolina Press, 1978).

10. As a product of the "Dunning School" of southern history, Merton Coulter's *The Civil War and Readjustment in Kentucky* (Chapel Hill: University of North Carolina Press, 1926) approvingly establishes postbellum Kentucky as an essen-

tially pro-South (and by extension, antiemancipation and anti–black suffrage) state despite its having remained in the Union. Ross Webb's Revisionist *Kentucky in the Reconstruction Era* (Lexington: University Press of Kentucky, 1979) explains the state's lack of cooperation with postwar federal policies as resistance to unwelcome federal authority rather than genuine adherence to the Lost Cause. Thomas Connelly ["Neo-Confederatism or Power Vacuum: Postwar Kentucky Politics Reappraised," *Register of the Kentucky Historical Society* 64 (October 1966): 257–69] also downplays the importance of race and the memory of the Confederacy in the years following the war; after 1865 Kentuckians were supposedly more caught up in sectional competition over internal resources and railroad construction than in issues relating to the recent war. By the mid-1870s the "New Departure" school of political thought, favored by the state's development-minded Democrats, had led the state into an era of relative prosperity unmatched by the rest of the South due to greater cooperation with northern interests. In Connelly's interpretation, as a state Kentucky was therefore detached from the ravages of Reconstruction disorder. Considering Coulter's overt Confederate sympathies, both Webb's and Connelly's revisions are understandable. However, more recent local studies portray a postwar white Kentucky every bit as conservative and "neo-Confederate" as Coulter portrayed it; see Richard C. Wright, *Racial Violence in Kentucky, 1865–1940: Lynchings, Mob Rule, and "Legal Lynchings"* (Baton Rouge: Louisiana State University Press, 1990); J. Michael Rhyne, "'We are Mobed and Beat': Regulator Violence against Free Black Households in Kentucky's Bluegrass Region, 1865–1867," and J. Michael Crane, "'The Rebels Are Bold, Defiant, and Unscrupulous in Their Dementions of All Men': Social Violence in Daviess County, Kentucky, 1861–1868," *Ohio Valley History* 2 (Spring 2002): 17–29, 30–42.

11. William Freehling, *The South vs. the South: How Anti-Confederate Southerners Shaped the Course of the Civil War* (New York and Oxford: Oxford University Press, 2001), 52.

12. *(Frankfort) Kentucky Tri-Weekly Yeoman*, December 2, 1865.

13. Coulter, *Civil War and Readjustment*, 334.

14. *Cincinnati (OH) Commercial*, May 31, 1867.

15. Like Kentucky, Maryland also emerged from the war under the control of the Democratic Party. But because Maryland had not experienced anything approaching the same level of internal strife as Kentucky, conservative control over the state government did not come with the same implications and the same potential for a continuation of violence; James Klotter and Hamilton Tapp, *Kentucky: Decades of Discord, 1865–1900* (Frankfort, KY: Kentucky Historical Society, 1977), 10–14; Richard O. Curry, ed., *Radicalism, Racism, and Party Realignment: The Border States during Reconstruction* (Baltimore: Johns Hopkins Press, 1969).

16. Wright, *Racial Violence in Kentucky*, 19; Robert Ireland, *Little Kingdoms: The Counties of Kentucky, 1850–1891* (Lexington: University Press of Kentucky, 1977), 85–89.

17. Ben H. Severance, *Tennessee's Radical Army: The State Guard and Its Role*

in Reconstruction, 1867–1869 (Knoxville: University of Tennessee Press, 2005), xiii, xvi.

18. Coulter, *Civil War and Readjustment*, 359, 361; *The Nation* 3, no. 70 (November 1, 1866).

19. Wright, *Racial Violence in Kentucky*, 307–11. See also Rhyne, "'We Are Mobed and Beat,'" and Crane, "'The Rebels Are Bold, Defiant, and Unscrupulous.'"

20. *(Frankfort) Kentucky Tri-Weekly Yeoman*, January 2, 1866.

21. *(Frankfort) Kentucky Tri-Weekly Yeoman*, March 17 1871.

22. Ireland, *Little Kingdoms*, 73–76. In this instance the term "state" is used not in the sense in which Kentucky was a state within the American union of states. Rather, it is used in the sense in which sociologist Max Weber used the term: to describe an organization or body that holds a "monopoly of legitimate use of physical force within a given territory," or, more generally, the institution through which allocations of power are mediated. Due to the remarkable decentralization of government and jurisprudence in Kentucky, the individual counties, rather than the capital in Frankfort, constituted true "states" in that sense of the word. However, unless otherwise indicated, "the state" as used in this essay refers to Kentucky as a whole; H. H. Gerth and C. Wright Mills, eds., *From Max Weber: Essays in Sociology* (New York: Oxford University Press, 1958), 78–79. For a concise treatise on violence as a political device, see Julie Skurski and Fernando Coronil, "Introduction: States of Violence and the Violence of States," in *States of Violence*, ed. Julie Skurski and Fernando Coronil (Lansing: University of Michigan Press, 2006), 1–27, particularly 3.

23. Slavery and the ensuing antebellum debate over states' rights have influenced historians of the era to focus almost exclusively upon either state government or the plantation as the nineteenth-century South's most significant institutions. As a result, the institution that the white male Southerner regarded "as having much and perhaps paramount importance among the governments to which he was subject" has been somewhat acknowledged but generally overlooked as the chief arbiter of issues both public and private. Although the decisions of individuals and families affected the state's wartime trajectory, so too did local government. Surprisingly, prior to the work of Robert Ireland cited in note 16 above, there was only one intensive study of the significance of county government in the Civil War era: Charles S. Sydnor, *The Development of Southern Sectionalism, 1819–1848* (Baton Rouge: Louisiana State University Press, 1948), 33–53. While the former only alludes to the possibility, the latter insists that the primacy of county government was more pronounced in Kentucky than in any other state (although no histories of county government in other states have arisen to challenge this assertion).

24. Coulter gave considerable attention to the state's postwar violence but attributed "ku kluxing," "feuding," and other similar incidents to "weakened respect for state authority" rather than describing them as attempts to effect or suppress political change. In reaction to Coulter's clear neo-Confederate sympa-

thies, liberal historians of later generations downplayed Kentucky's postwar conservatism; in the process, however, they neglected to focus on violence; Coulter, *Civil War and Readjustment,* 365. The tendency to view violence as simply an outcome of a lack of social order does not acknowledge the functional nature of violent acts in causing or preventing political change. For a concise treatise on violence as a political device, see Skurski and Coronil, "Introduction: States of Violence and the Violence of States."

25. Ireland, *Little Kingdoms,* 60–72.

26. Coulter, *Civil War and Readjustment,* 361; *Louisville (KY) Courier-Journal,* August 13, 1870.

27. *Louisville (KY) Courier-Journal,* March 14, 1870; December 2, 1870.

28. Watterson's opposition to the "Bourbons" of his party was partially based upon his moderate views on race. However, as a conservative often mistaken for a progressive by white editors farther south, Watterson often preferred that the less said about race the better, especially before the cessation of Reconstruction; C. Vann Woodward, *Origins of the New South: 1877–1913* (Baton Rouge: Louisiana State University Press, 1951), 6; Carl R. Osthaus, *Partisans of the Southern Press: Editorial Spokesmen of the Nineteenth Century* (Lexington: University Press of Kentucky, 1994), 152–54.

29. *Louisville (KY) Commercial,* June 15, 1870.

30. The position and ultimate importance of the emerging Republican Party in Kentucky was questionable even as late as the 1870s, because the party's only core of support was in the state's poorest and least politically influential region: the mountainous east. Eastern Kentucky had been widely considered the most consistently pro-Union section of the state and was accordingly the most fertile territory for Republican politicians in the 1860s and 1870s. Compared to other mountain sections of southern states, however, the Republican Party in Kentucky was relatively unsuccessful. As a result, local parties became increasingly isolated from the national party, especially after the passage of the Fifteenth Amendment in 1870. Conversely, this isolation acted as a preservative for Republican enclaves. Because Republicans were never able to control state government in Kentucky, as they could in the reconstructed states, they managed to survive the later years of Congressional Reconstruction without causing significant resentment among voters. Even the passage of the 1875 Civil Rights Act (the action that caused the most massive retreats of white voters from the southern Republican Party) did not do fatal damage to the party in mountain counties because voters dissociated their own local affiliates from the national "radicals"; McKinney, *Southern Mountain Republicans, 1865–1900* (Chapel Hill: University of North Carolina Press, 1979), 50–56; Klotter and Tapp, *Kentucky,* 14.

31. *(Frankfort) Kentucky Tri-Weekly Yeoman,* January 12, 1867.

32. Brian D. McKnight, *Contested Borderland: The Civil War in Appalachian Kentucky and Virginia* (Lexington: University Press of Kentucky, 2006), 229.

33. *Louisville (KY) Courier-Journal,* July 23–25, 1871.

34. G. W. Noble, *Behold He Cometh in the Clouds: A Religious Treatise from Inspiration and Illumination with Life and Adventures of the Author* (Hazel Green, KY: Spencer Cooper, printer, 1912), 179.

35. *Louisville (KY) Commercial,* December 28, 1870.

36. Allen W. Trelease, *White Terror: The Ku Klux Klan Conspiracy and Southern Reconstruction* (Westport, CT: Greenwood Press, 1971), 89.

37. *Hazel Green (KY) Herald,* May 20, 1897; *Louisville (KY) Courier-Journal,* May 10, 1897; *New York Times,* September 13, 1897.

38. The iconography of the Ku Klux Klan became ubiquitous in the southern states, even after the organization had ceased to be a factor in political terrorism. It was not uncommon for white southerners to take on the costume of the Klan when engaging in collective violence that did not involve enforcement of Democratic power or white supremacy. For instance, see William F. Holmes, "Moonshining and Collective Violence, 1889–1895," *Journal of American History* 67 (December 1980): 592–93. The phrase "master cleavage" is borrowed from Bill Berkeley, *The Graves Are Not Yet Full: Race, Tribe, and Power in the Heart of Africa* (New York: Basic Books, 2001), 151.

39. James McPherson has demonstrated that, while soldiers on both sides of the Civil War initially chose to participate in battle for a myriad of reasons, their participation had a politicizing effect, prompting many soldiers to negotiate between their individual or communal motivations and the war's larger calling; James McPherson, *For Cause and Comrades: Why Men Fought in the Civil War* (New York: Oxford University Press, 1997). But historians who have specifically addressed Civil War–era Appalachia from the early 1980s until the present have tended to downplay ideological connections between the larger war and local fighting in the mountain fastnesses. Phillip Shaw Paludan, *Victims: A True Story of the Civil War* (Knoxville: University of Tennessee Press, 1981), 28–30; Jonathan Dean Sarris, *A Separate Civil War: Communities in Conflict in the Mountain South* (Charlottesville: University of Virginia Press, 2006), 2–3. As of yet, there have been no scholarly attempts to reconcile these differing interpretations.

40. The Three Forks Battalion was one of ten battalions within the "First Regiment of Capital Guards," authorized in May 1864 by secretary of war Edwin Stanton to suppress the state's internal "guerrilla evil" once major invasions from the South had trailed off. Although a local account that was generally sympathetic to Strong's enemies suggests that he had deserted the Fourteenth Kentucky Cavalry, records show that Strong was given officially authorized leave from the unit. His official connection to the Three Forks Battalion bears this out as well; G. W. Noble, *Behold He Cometh in the Clouds,* 23; *Kentucky Adjutant General's Report* (Frankfort, KY: State Journal Company, 1915), 388–89; Charles C. Wells, ed., *1890 Special Veterans' Census for Eastern Kentucky* (Baltimore: Gateway Press, 2000), 52.

41. *Kentucky Adjutant General's Report,* 210–13.

42. From the time of its creation in 1839, Breathitt County exhibited an

unyielding loyalty to the Democratic Party despite being carved out of three counties that were just as consistently dedicated to the Whig party (and later to the Republican Party). The 1863 Union Party victory in the county presents a stark contrast and demonstrates the remarkable influence that local manifestations of the war had upon elections. Only 95 men out of a total of 142 voters cast their votes in favor of Democrat Thomas Bramlette, a fraction of the usual voter turnout in the county but more than enough to give the Union candidate a considerable majority. Over the next two years of the war the small number of extant returns suggest that Democratic votes were virtually forbidden from being cast; *Tribune Almanac and Political Register* (New York: Greeley & McElrath, 1856–1902), *1838*, 28; *1840*, 25–26; *1841*, 23–24; *1843*, 46; *1844*, 56; *1845*, 51; *1846*, 48; *1848*, 46; *1849*, 55; *1850*, 48; *1852*, 47; *1853*, 43; *1854*, 47; *1856*, 47; *1857*, 52; *1858*, 59; *1859*, 56; *1862*, 60; *1864*, 59; *1867*, 57. Ernest Collins, "Political Behavior in Breathitt, Knott, Perry and Leslie Counties" (master's thesis, University of Kentucky, 1940), 63.

43. E. L. Noble, *Bloody Breathitt* (Jackson, KY: Jackson Times Printing Company, 1936), 2:18.

44. As a member of the Three Forks Battalion during the latter half of the war, William Strong was technically not a home guard. However, the use of that phrase to describe him and his allies is every bit as telling as the later "Red String" appellation, mainly because of the notoriety that went along with the former label. Confederate Lt. William Guerrant, assigned to track down William Strong, equated "home guards" with "bushwhackers," the nineteenth century's most damning epithet for wartime irregulars. Home guards were militia units originally formed "as a wholly defensive measure" to protect individual communities against incursions from invading armies, either Southern or Northern (although it was implicitly understood that even in the neutrality months home guards were implicitly expected to provide Union support). The various home guards that were established throughout the state in 1861, or rather the very idiom "home guard," came to mean something far different from their intended purposes and meanings. Although the home guards were mandated and armed by the state government from early in the war, they were not under the state's direct authority, as was the Three Forks Battalion. After Kentucky's official joining of the Union, state oversight over the numerous county-based home guards came to an end, leaving the opportunity for preexisting units to act according to their own interests. Segments of the home guard, particularly those in and around Frankfort, began acting outside of what many Kentuckians considered their true mandate. Many Kentuckians in the state's rural areas came to view the home guard as a band of guerrillas bent upon brigandage rather than military victory and as an aberration from the internal partisan lines that they came to accept as routine within a border state. Months after the war's end, Gov. Thomas Bramlette publicly proclaimed the home guards' formation a deplorable failure. After the war, "home guard" was simply an imprecise pejorative for men who had taken advantage of the war's chaos for the sake

of personal gain and love of havoc, despised by Unionists and Confederates alike for sullying an otherwise mutually noble cause. The home guard's wartime record in Kentucky, its tacit interchangeability with the Three Forks Battalion, and its "guerrilla" tactics provide useful ways to understand the relationship between local conflicts as seen in and around Breathitt County and the war at large. But even if Strong was technically not a home guard, he became one in function if not by official designation. Strong's command approximated a home guard more than it did a segment of the Capital Guard for a number of reasons, not least of which was its political autonomy and malleability. The decentralized authority and small numbers characteristic of Kentucky's home-guard units made their purposes and actions malleable to the wishes of individual commanders, like Strong, and the insular concerns of the communities. Early in the war home guard organization was so apolitical that some groups were shared by pro-Unionists and pro-Confederates (although the latter soon withdrew). In terms of how they actually operated, the home guards were more political than they were military. As has been the case with militia-related groups in many civil war settings, the most active home guards focused upon local state-building and attempts to reallocate local rule rather than on defending their respective territories from invaders. Given the prevailing Confederatism of the county's majority, Strong's activities during the war's latter half dealt more with attempts to weaken local state power and influence Breathitt County's politics in favor of the Union. For the history of Kentucky's Civil War–era home guard, see *Kentucky Senate Journal, Special Called Session, 1861*, 24; Works Progress Administration, *Military History of Kentucky, Chronologically Arranged* (Frankfort, KY: Kentucky State Journal, 1939), 166, 240; Coulter, *Civil War and Readjustment*, 87, 147. For Governor Bramlette's denouncement of the home guards, see *Lexington (KY) Observer and Reporter*, December 9, 1865. For Strong being referred to as such, and the linguistic significance of "bushwhacker," see William Davis and Meredith Swentnor, eds., *Bluegrass Confederate: The Headquarters Diary of Edward O. Guerrant* (Baton Rouge: Louisiana State University Press, 1999), 245, 252; Robert Mackey, *The Uncivil War: Irregular Warfare in the Upper South, 1861–1865* (Oklahoma City: University of Oklahoma Press, 2004), 6–10. For the distinctions of practice that make wartime militias more political than military in nature and practice, see Kalyvas, *The Logic of Violence*, 107–9.

45. Strong's complex position as the enforcer of Unionist policy in a Confederate county contained within a neutral, and later officially pro-Union, state can best be described by Alfredo Schulte-Bockholt's concept of "*oligopolies* [his italics] of violence." In contrast to classical sociologist Max Weber's idea of a successful state's monopoly of legitimate violence, an oligopoly of violence is created when more than one minority body within a territory can lay some claim to the legitimized use of violence. As a military officer, Strong's use of deadly violence was fully recognized as such by a minority within Breathitt County for their own purposes, while his mandate from the state government had to, at the very least, be acknowledged by his opponents. The result was a disruption of Breathitt County's

government as a fully legitimate political body; Alfredo Schulte-Bockholt, *The Politics of Organized Crime and the Organized Crime of Politics: A Study in Criminal Power* (Lanham, MD: Lexington Books, 2006), 201–4.

46. Workers of the Writers' Program of the Works Projects Administration in the State of Kentucky, *In the Land of Breathitt* (Northport, NY: Bacon, Percy & Daggett, 1941), 59 (hereafter WPA, *In the Land of Breathitt*).

47. *Louisville (KY) Courier-Journal*, October 6, 1874.

48. Jeremiah Weldon South was often referred to as the "father of Breathitt County" for having petitioned for its creation in 1839, serving as a justice of the peace and legislator in its service and owning a tremendous expanse of land within the county. From the 1850s until the 1870s he served as the superintendent of the state penitentiary and, by virtue of the appointment and the monopoly of free labor it represented, became one of Kentucky's most influential Democrats; *Louisville (KY) Courier-Journal*, July 27, 1877; February 10, 1880. Edward L. Ayers, *Vengeance and Justice: Crime and Punishment in the 19th-Century American South* (New York: Oxford University Press, 1984), 195; Lowell H. Harrison, ed., *Kentucky's Governors, 1792–1985* (Lexington: University Press of Kentucky, 1985), 65; Robert Gunn Crawford, "A History of the Kentucky Penitentiary System, 1856–1937" (PhD diss., University of Kentucky, 1955), 29.

49. *Louisville (KY) Courier Journal*, May 10, 1897; *New York Times*, May 10, 1897; September 13, 1897; interview with Harlan Strong, 1978, Appalachian Oral History Project of Alice Lloyd College, Appalachian State University, Emory and Henry College, and Lees Junior College, no. 279, 20–21. The Red String or "Heroes of America" was a secretive organization of southern Unionists said to have acted as spies and saboteurs during the war, primarily in Virginia and North Carolina. For years after the war the term was later used to describe "regulators" who enforced local Republican policy just as the Ku Klux Klan did for southern Democrats. The local identification of William Strong and his adherents as Red Strings indicates that the term was used outside of the former Confederacy and that "Red String" was a commonly recognized term for the southern Unionist "underground." This identification with the organization as late as Strong's death suggests a decades-long continuity of political fracture lasting from the Civil War until the last years of the nineteenth century. For characterizations of Strong as a "Red String," see *Louisville (KY) Courier-Journal*, December 5, 1878; May 10, 1897; May 12, 1897. For more general descriptions of the group's larger activities during the Civil War and Reconstruction (particularly in North Carolina), see the *New York Times*, April 29, 1867, March 11, 1871, and January 31, 1882; Wayne K. Durrill, "Political Legitimacy and Local Courts: 'Politicks at Such a Rage' in a Southern Community during Reconstruction," *Journal of Southern History* 70, no. 3 (August 2004): 577–602; William T. Auman and David D. Scarboro, "The Heroes of America in Civil War North Carolina," *North Carolina Historical Review* 58 (October 1981): 327–63; Kenneth W. Noe, "Red String Scare: Civil War Southwest Virginia and the Heroes of America," *North Carolina Historical Review* 59 (July 1992): 301–22.

50. *Breathitt County Tax Books,* 1861, Kentucky Historical Society, Frankfort, KY.

51. Kilburn and McIntosh Family Files, Breathitt County Library, Jackson, KY.

52. *Louisville (KY) Courier-Journal,* October 9, 1874; Noble, *Bloody Breathitt,* 2:56, 82.

53. Among the nineteenth-century Kentucky county's most coercive constitutional powers was the ability to assign orphaned minors into forced apprenticeships, a practice that was used most often with free blacks. In 1836 Freeman and his brother were bonded to a relative of William Strong's in order to "learn the art and mystery of farming." His infant sister was bonded to another Clay County citizen to be trained as a seamstress. In 1838 Freeman successfully challenged his and his siblings' bonds of apprenticeship on the grounds that the facts of their original bonds were erroneous; *Freeman vs. Strong and Others,* April 20, 1838, Appeal from Circuit Court, Clay County, Records of the Court of Appeals of Kentucky, Kentucky Department of Libraries and Archives Public Records Division, Frankfort, KY (hereafter KDLA); Manual Ray Spencer, "The Descendants of Joseph Spencer" (Independence, KY: self-published, 1996), 325.

54. *Breathitt County Census,* 1860, 1870, KDLA; *Kentucky Adjutant General's Report,* 388.

55. Noble, *Behold He Cometh in the Clouds,* 55.

56. *Louisville (KY) Courier-Journal,* October 9, 1874.

57. Census records show that in 1870 Strong had the fourth-most-valuable tract of land in the county's Crockettsville precinct; *Breathitt County Census, 1870,* KDLA.

58. Aside from bringing about death and destruction, civil wars are also politically subversive, calling into question the legitimacy of local government and allowing opportunities for the unseen establishment of political power (in James Scott's phrasing) "beyond the visible end of the spectrum"; quoted from James C. Scott, *Domination and the Arts of Resistance: Hidden Transcripts* (New Haven, CT: Yale University Press, 1990), 183.

59. Quote from Noble, *Bloody Breathitt,* 2:26–27; *The Tribune Almanac and Political Register, 1869,* 83; *1870,* 60; *1871,* 65; *1872,* 71; *1873,* 60; *1875,* 91.

60. *Wm. M. Combs agst. Capt. William Strong, Wiley Amis and other defendants, 1867–1869; Wm. M. Combs agst. Hiram Freeman and Jason Little, 1867–1869,* Breathitt County Circuit Court Records (KDLA).

61. *Commonwealth of Kentucky agst. John Aikman* (?), June 12, 1873, box 4, bundle 1, Breathitt County Circuit Court Minutes (KDLA).

62. Noble, *Behold He Cometh in the Clouds,* 82–84.

63. South had removed to the Bluegrass years earlier but had left his sons in Breathitt County to see to the family's land speculation and act as unofficial overseers of county government. It was Barry South who had organized the first Confederate recruitment efforts in Breathitt County; Strong Family Papers, 111, Breathitt County Public Library; *The War of the Rebellion: A Compilation of the Official Records of the Union and Confederate Armies:* series 1, vol. 32, 1892: 433,

687; *Kentucky Adjutant General's Report: Confederate Kentucky Volunteers, 1861–1865* (Frankfort, KY: State Journal Company, 1915), 210–13.

64. Noble, *Bloody Breathitt*, 2:17–18.

65. *William Strong Sr. vs. Wilson Callahan & comp.*, May 15, 1867, Breathitt County Circuit Court Records (KDLA).

66. Interview with Edward Callahan Strong, July 21, 1898, *John Jay Dickey Diary*, 2424–25, reel 3, Special Collections, King Library, University of Kentucky.

67. Noble, *Bloody Breathitt*, 2:7.

68. *(Frankfort) Kentucky Weekly Yeoman*, December 22, 1878; *Louisville (KY) Courier-Journal*, January 16, 1879; interview with John Aikman, July 20, 1898; *John Jay Dickey Diary*, 2412–13, reel 3, Special Collections, King Library, University of Kentucky.

69. Noble, *Behold He Cometh in the Clouds*, 84.

70. *Louisville (KY) Courier-Journal*, January 16, 1879.

71. Noble, *Behold He Cometh in the Clouds*, 177.

72. Noble, *Bloody Breathitt*, 2:26.

73. *Louisville (KY) Courier-Journal*, September 28, 1874; *New York Times*, December 7, 1878.

74. *Louisville (KY) Courier-Journal*, September 19, 1874.

75. *New York Times*, September 28, 1874.

76. *Louisville (KY) Courier-Journal*, September 16, 1874; September 19, 1874; Wright, *Racial Violence in Kentucky*, 31.

77. *Louisville (KY) Courier-Journal*, September 28, 1874; September 29, 1874; *New York Times*, December 7, 1878; Francis Terry Ingmire, ed., *Breathitt County, Kentucky Death Records, 1852–1858, 1874–1878* (St. Louis: Ingmire, 1983), 18.

78. James Larry Hood, "For the Union: Kentucky's Unconditional Unionist Congressmen and the Development of the Republican Party in Kentucky, 1863–1865," *Register of the Kentucky Historical Society* 76 (July 1978): 204–5, 208–12, 214–15; Victor B. Howard, *Black Liberation in Kentucky: Emancipation and Freedom, 1862–1884* (Lexington: University Press of Kentucky, 1983), 56–57, 147.

79. *Louisville (KY) Courier-Journal*, October 9, 1874.

80. *Comm. of Kentucky agst. Hiram Freeman*, November 19–21, 1874, *Breathitt County Circuit Court Records*, box 4, bundle 1 (KDLA).

81. *Louisville (KY) Courier-Journal*, September 28, 1874; October 6, 1874.

82. Noble, *Behold He Cometh in the Clouds*, 177.

83. *Louisville (KY) Courier-Journal*, January 16, 1879.

84. *Louisville (KY) Courier-Journal*, November 30, December 1, 1878; *Louisville (KY) Commercial*, December 8, 1878.

85. WPA, *In the Land of Breathitt*, 64–65; *Louisville (KY) Courier-Journal*, January 16, 1879.

86. Bill L. Weaver, "Louisville's Labor Disturbance, July, 1877," *Filson Club Historical Quarterly* 48 (April 1974): 179–83. As a result, Kentucky's militia law

was quickly revised later in the year, giving the governor authority to assemble males between the ages of eighteen and forty-five for immediate service in times of disorder. In the interest of maintaining an atmosphere of state's rights, the law restricted all military activities of the state to this new State Guard. Early in 1878, also in reaction to the previous year's strike, the "Louisville Legion," an urban militia unit that had not been mustered since the close of the Mexican War, was revived. Bearing in mind the political ambiguity that the State Guard and home guard represented during the war, the Legion was captained by both Confederate and Union veterans (although the former outnumbered the latter four to one); Federal Writers' Project of the Works Project Administration for the State of Kentucky, *Military History of Kentucky Chronologically Arranged* (Frankfort, KY: State Journal Press, 1939), 257.

87. It was deemed important that Kentucky, as an economically progressive southern state, use its military to protect its urban commercial interests from further labor disruptions. Kentucky's transition from military patrols of its hinterlands to a more urban-based military presence parallels the federal government's pivotal post-Reconstruction transition from using military coercion as a tool for solving "the Southern question" to protecting northern capitalist interests through strikebreaking. For the larger trend of military redirection away from the rural South to the urban North and Midwest, see Eric Foner, *Reconstruction: America's Unfinished Revolution* (New York: Harper & Row, 1988).

88. *Cincinnati (OH) Daily Gazette,* September 25, 1874; *New York Times,* September 28, 1874.

89. *Louisville (KY) Commercial,* February 1, February 24, 1879.

90. Noble, *Behold He Cometh in the Clouds,* 186.

91. *(Frankfort) Kentucky Weekly Yeoman,* February 6, 1879.

92. Noble, *Bloody Breathitt,* 2:34.

93. *Appleton's Annual Cyclopaedia and Register of Important Events* (New York: D. Appleton & Co., 1862–1902), *1879:* 540–41.

94. Klotter and Tapp, *Kentucky,* 499.

95. *Washington Post,* March 21, 1879; *New York Times,* May 27, 1879.

96. Interview with Harlan Strong, 18–19.

97. *John Jay Dickey Diary,* entry for April 9, 1884, 285–86, reel 3; WPA, *In the Land of Breathitt,* 74–75. A highly erroneous account of a mob attack on the Breathitt County jailhouse was printed in the *New York Times,* April 25, 1884.

98. *John Jay Dickey Diary,* entry for April 10, 1884, reel 3, 286–87.

99. *Louisville (KY) Courier-Journal,* May 10, May 12, 1897.

100. Wright, *Racial Violence in Kentucky,* 69.

101. The use of violence in the formation of the New South's political structure, and the domination of the Deep South in most monographs on Reconstruction and Redemption, are both described in Kenneth Barnes, *Who Killed John Clayton? Political Violence and the Emergence of the New South, 1861–1893* (Durham, NC: Duke University Press, 1998), 5.

102. Jonathan Dean Sarris, *A Separate Civil War: Communities in Conflict in the Mountain South* (Charlottesville: University of Virginia Press, 2006); Robert Tracy McKenzie, *Lincolnites and Rebels: A Divided Town in the American Civil War* (New York: Oxford University Press, 2006); Brian D. McKnight, *Contested Borderland: The Civil War in Appalachian Kentucky and Virginia* (Lexington: University Press of Kentucky, 2006); Gordon B. McKinney, "The Civil War and Reconstruction," in *High Mountains Rising: Appalachia in Time and Place,* ed. Richard A. Straw and H. Tyler Blethen, 46–58 (Urbana: University of Illinois Press, 2004); John W. Shaffer, *Clash of Loyalties: A Border County in the Civil War* (Morgantown: West Virginia University Press, 2003); Martin Crawford, *Ashe County's Civil War: Community and Society in the Appalachian South* (Charlottesville: University of Virginia Press, 2001); Susan G. Hall, *Appalachian Ohio and the Civil War, 1862–1863* (Jefferson, NC: McFarland, 2000); John C. Inscoe and Gordon B. McKinney, *The Heart of Confederate Appalachia: Western North Carolina in the Civil War* (Chapel Hill: University of North Carolina Press, 2000); Sean Michael O'Brien, *Mountain Partisans: Guerrilla Warfare in the Southern Appalachians, 1861–1865* (Westport, CT: Praeger Press, 1999); Kenneth W. Noe and Shannon H. Wilson, eds., *The Civil War in Appalachia: Collected Essays* (Knoxville: University of Tennessee Press, 1997); Noel C. Fisher, *War at Every Door: Partisan Politics and Guerilla Violence in East Tennessee, 1860–1869* (Chapel Hill: University of North Carolina Press, 1997); William R. Trotter, *Bushwhackers: The Civil War in North Carolina (The Mountains)* (Winston-Salem, NC: J. F. Blair, 1991); Phillip Shaw Paludan, *Victims: A True Story of the Civil War* (Knoxville: University of Tennessee Press, 1981).

103. For another instance in which land access became intermingled with interracial political cooperation, see Steven Hahn, "Hunting, Fishing and Foraging: Common Rights and Class Relations in the Postbellum South," *Radical History Review* 26 (October 1982): 55–57.

104. The significance of counterrevolutionary violence in contrast to revolutionary violence within the context of Reconstruction is addressed in Foner, *Reconstruction,* 425.

105. Between 1874 and 1895 the *Louisville (KY) Courier-Journal,* Kentucky's most widely read newspaper, reported forty-one violent conflicts identified as "feuds" in thirty-one different Kentucky counties throughout the state. Waller, "Feuding in Appalachia," 353, 354, 357–58. For the cultural resonance that "feud narratives" had among nineteenth-century readers, and their utility in separating past from present, see Jeffrey Guy Johnson, "Feud, Society, Family: Feud Narrative in the United States, 1865–1910" (PhD diss., Harvard University, 2000), 24–53.

106. Horace Kephart, *Our Southern Highlanders* (New York: Outing Publishing, 1913), 357.

107. *New York Herald,* November 30, 1878.

108. Viewed from an international perspective, this is a common phenomenon because of the "systematic slippage between political ideas as understood in the

city and as practiced in the village." But urban bias may also be combined with political bias when, as was the case with Breathitt County, urban chroniclers of varying political stripes can agree that the violence being reported is best separated as far as possible from its causes; James C. Scott, *The Moral Economy of the Peasant: Rebellion and Subsistence in Southeast Asia* (New Haven, CT: Yale University Press, 1976), 4; see also Kalyvas, *The Logic of Violence,* 35–43.

Chapter 4

"The Other War Was but the Beginning"

The Politics of Loyalty in Western North Carolina, 1865–1867

Steven E. Nash

"You have been a happy people in the old North State," mused Mira Brown of Columbia, Tennessee, in a letter to a western North Carolina relative during the summer of 1865. There was no trace of humor or irony in those words. Blue- and gray-clad armies had fought over her middle Tennessee community for four years during the American Civil War, inflicting hardship and suffering upon all segments of society. She worried she might never recover from the ordeal, which made her grief condescending at times. Only those directly touched by the regular armies, she implied to her friends and family in the North Carolina mountains, truly understood the horrors of war. Brown felt certain that the military occupation, racial turmoil, and loss of property that she experienced was the *real* war and that western North Carolina's experience was different. Believing herself a member of an exclusive club united by Yankee-induced suffering, she blatantly ignored the economic privations, internal divisions, and guerrilla violence experienced in western North Carolina, not to mention the regular military incursions during the war's final months. None of this mattered to the war-weary Brown, who claimed that "you have all been very much blessed in North Carolina; you dont [*sic*] know a thing about distress and trouble."[1]

The Civil War brought privation, loss of life, and governmental power to western Carolinians' doorsteps to an unprecedented degree. Conscription officers, tax collectors, and soldiers became commonplace in the region during the war. White mountaineers greeted the Richmond government's policies with more of an attitude of exasperation than the defiant opposition that many later observers read into their responses. When the Richmond government inaugurated the first draft of the war in April 1862, its exemption for white men on farms with twenty or more slaves led to a spike in desertion and violence.[2] Wilkes and Caldwell counties endured terrible irregular violence, which hit such a fevered pitch in 1864 that many Confederate sympathizers refused to sleep, out of fear. In the more remote counties of Ashe, Watauga, and Madison, a pattern of reciprocal violence developed. The infamous massacre of thirteen alleged Unionists along Shelton Laurel in Madison County by the Sixty-fourth North Carolina Infantry Regiment grew out of partisan raids that included a Unionist raid on the county seat of Marshall in January 1863. The murder of a Confederate supporter plunged a community along the Watauga and Ashe County border into disarray. Few mountain guerrillas achieved the infamy of Unionist Keith Blalock, whose band patrolled the region around Grandfather Mountain. Even Blalock conformed to this reciprocal pattern; his most fervent attacks on local Confederates followed the murder of his stepfather by regular Southern soldiers.[3]

Historians have largely neglected Reconstruction in the mountain South. Such oversight fits within the prevailing historical interpretation of Reconstruction, which emphasizes emancipation and its aftershocks. Eric Foner's synthesis, *Reconstruction: America's Unfinished Revolution, 1863–77*, concentrates on the conflict and negotiation over freedom in the postwar South. The relative absence of African Americans in southern Appalachia, therefore, made the region's neglect by Reconstruction scholars a logical consequence of that interpretive trend. Even scholars who have addressed Reconstruction in the mountain South have often focused on emancipation and racial issues. Although race was a powerful force in western North Carolinians' lives, as well as in the United States's reunion, it was not the decisive issue in the political battles that immediately followed the war. All whites, Unionist and Confederate, agreed that black mountaineers' status should change as little as possible.[4]

Given the preponderance of whites and the bitter wartime divisions in the region, the mountain sections of the former Confederacy focused on another major aspect of Reconstruction: the political restoration of the

Southern states to the Union. This issue proved no less thorny than the adjustment from slave to free labor, and in the Appalachian South, where according to Phillip S. Paludan, mountaineers wore their loyalties like targets over their hearts, loyalty was as important as the color of one's skin. The violence, rancor, and communal fissures refused to simply fade away, and new political factions renewed the struggle (albeit in political form) between Unionists and Confederates over the meaning of loyalty, Unionism, and local political power. Confederate defeat did not neatly end the war throughout the South. Southern Appalachia's civil war had been messy and intensely personal. A close examination of the postwar conflict between a white Unionist-led anti-Confederate faction and a stunned Conservative Party, which had led the state through the war, reveals that postwar politics in western North Carolina was no less chaotic. The battle between the anti-Confederates and the Conservatives seriously damaged an antebellum political culture that had privileged local ties. In this postwar world, local control was worth fighting desperately for, and if an alliance with outside forces was the only way to obtain it, mountain Unionists would eventually take that unprecedented step. Standing in the calm between the storm recently passed and the one on the darkening horizon, one mountain politician, Leander Sams Gash, concluded that "the other war was but the beginning."[5]

Lingering tensions from western North Carolina's brutal and personalized Civil War enhanced the sense of dislocation that accompanied the redrawing of political lines in the war's wake. Politics had always acted as a lifeline between the rugged mountain region and North Carolina's central and eastern counties. Confederate defeat left only the Conservative Party, composed mostly of former Union-Whigs who accepted secession only when it became reality, as the state's only regular political organization. Even that party, however, was relatively new to the state's political neighborhood. Formed in 1862, the Conservatives gained an immediate victory when Zebulon B. Vance, a Buncombe County native and colonel of the Twenty-sixth North Carolina Infantry, ascended to the governorship that year. His election marked a turning point in the war for North Carolinians, many of whom viewed Vance as the moderate or possibly even the antiwar alternative. With Vance's 1862 victory and his reelection in 1864, these former Whigs came to dominate that party.[6]

The Conservative Party that emerged out of the war, though, was not the same party it was in 1862. Frustration with central Confederate poli-

Zebulon B. Vance's election as governor of North Carolina in 1862 marked a turning point in the war for North Carolinians and the ascendancy of the Conservative Party in the state. He remained a political power for decades, being reelected governor in 1864 and 1876 before being elected to the U.S. Senate in 1878. (North Carolina Department of Archives and History)

cies and war weariness splintered the Conservative ranks by the war's third year, with some members joining outspoken newspaper editor William W. Holden's peace movement. Other Conservatives stuck with Governor Vance, who steadfastly vowed to fight the war to its conclusion. Once the war ended, however, the Conservatives turned back the clock to their previous conditional Unionism of the secession crisis. Faced with a frustrated and exhausted population, Conservatives distanced themselves from the war effort.[7] Secession had forced Unionist-Whigs to choose between the union and their state, and they had felt that refusal to serve their state would shame them and their families. They distanced themselves from the unpopular conscription and anti–civil liberty policies of Jefferson Davis's administration. Well-educated and experienced in state politics, they dominated most professional classes and social groups, and they emerged from the war eager to restore the antebellum status quo and with much of their landed wealth intact. Neither had the war fully destroyed their Whiggish roots; Conservatives promoted many of the same issues that Whigs had previously championed: law and order, guarantee of due process of law, and the preservation of tradition.[8] One Conservative, Allen T. Davidson, a delegate to the state secession convention and a Confederate congressman, gave clear expression to this claimed continuity between 1861 and 1865. According to Davidson, there were two groups: the secessionists, or "Destructives," and the "Conservatives" who "had always been for the Union and was for the most cautious and deliberate measures."[9]

Many Unionists undoubtedly scratched their heads in disbelief at Davidson's description of himself and his Conservative colleagues as having been "always" for the Union. William W. Holden fell before the Vance political juggernaut in the 1864 gubernatorial election, but after President Andrew Johnson appointed him provisional governor on May 29, 1865, the editor moved to legitimize his peace faction and challenge Conservative rule. Holden's leadership of the Conservative Party's peace faction garnered him significant influence in western North Carolina. He needed that strength to hold together a diverse opposition group best labeled "anti-Confederate." According to historian Otto H. Olsen, North Carolina's anti-Confederates incorporated "prewar opponents of secession, consistent Unionists and wartime peace advocates, reform-minded yeomen and artisans, upper-class moderates and realists, regional representatives seeking some shift in state policy and power, and whites especially receptive to some degree of racial equality, nationalism, or the principles of free labor capitalism." Each of these disparate elements shared an acceptance of federal demands as the surest means of achieving a speedy reunification. Each of these classes of citizens lived in western North Carolina, but the mountain counties' strong Unionist contingent enhanced its power in the west.[10]

Charged with reorganizing the state government, the new provisional governor searched the state for men suitable for local office. In particular, he leaned heavily upon the recommendations of "respectable" lawyers, merchants, and successful farmers who had expressed at least ambivalence toward the war. For the western counties, Holden solicited names from three men: Augustus Merrimon, Ceburne Harris, and Calvin Cowles. In Buncombe County, Augustus Merrimon, a former Whig turned Conservative lawyer, struggled to prosecute the Confederate officers responsible for the Shelton Laurel massacre and opposed some of the Richmond government's excesses during the war. Harris was a large landholder near Chimney Rock in Rutherford County, who had served as a lieutenant colonel in the Confederate Home Guard during the war, became disillusioned with the war as it dragged on, and joined his brother-in-law, known Unionist George W. Logan, in the peace movement. Calvin Cowles of Wilkes County was a merchant and Holden's future son-in-law. Each man briefed Holden on conditions in his portion of the west and suggested local officials, yet none of them held formal office of their own.[11]

Complaints reached the governor's desk soon after the ink dried on his new magistrates' bonds of office. Events in Buncombe County proved typical of events in western North Carolina. One of those magistrates, William Pickens, a sixty-two-year-old farmer from Flat Creek in Buncombe County, expressed his outrage in letters to Holden in mid-August 1865. "Some considerable confution [sic] have & will be Experienced on the Subject of disloyal magistrates in the Co. of Buncombe," Pickens informed Holden. This was a grave concern for Pickens and other Unionists, who, after four years of Confederate rule, desired a greater political role for themselves as a reward for their sacrifice. He fumed that "Reason & good Sense dictate to us those who Abandoned this Union for which we Fought cannot Reconstruct it." From what he knew of his fellow Buncombe County provisional justices, their wartime allegiances offered little encouragement to a Unionist. In particular, Pickens singled out Augustus Merrimon. Whereas Davidson and Merrimon saw no contradiction in restoring conditional Unionists to power after the war, such a policy was tantamount to treason for Pickens. A number of men such as Merrimon "claim to be Loyal now but have been willing Aiders & Abeters [sic] of the Rebellion." Pickens informed the governor that during the war Merrimon prosecuted Unionists, even those who read Holden's *North Carolina Standard,* so that the prosecutor could "walk by the Iron Cage in Asheville Jaild [sic], & taunt Loyal prisners Saying it is good Enough for Lincoln men. . . . Such we understand to be the conduct," groused Pickens, "of Marymon [sic] the Loyal."[12]

Although modern eyes may read such a contest as mere semantics, it mattered a great deal to western North Carolinians. Once the war ended, Conservatives rushed to reaffirm their Unionist credentials. For Holden, this was not a problem. His agent in Wilkes County, Calvin Cowles, reminded critics that Holden was "not simply the Governor of a party but of the whole people & that it would hinder a speedy return to prosperity if the strings were drawn too tight."[13] To mountain Unionists, the real issue was how loyal one needs be to govern. Buncombe justice of the peace William Pickens implored Holden to define loyalty as "original" rather than the product of a "new Birth, by virtue of the Amnesty Oath." He was appalled that an oath rendered former Confederates equal to Unionists who "Faught [sic] that Tigar Secession from his first Angry growl, I who Refused to bow my head in Submition to the Requisitions, of Confederate Authorities, & yield my comonition as a Justice of the peace, of which Several of us were proud to believe that when Uncle Sam Returned we would Honerably Resume & Act in our devotion to our countrys good." To Pickens, sacrifice and struggle proved one's loyalty and right to govern.[14]

The Unionists' challenge was to cull political support from all classes of

Newspaper editor William W. Holden led a split in North Carolina's Conservative Party during the Civil War, running as the peace movement's candidate against Gov. Zebulon Vance. He eventually became a Republican after the war and was elected governor in 1868. As governor Holden actively fought the Ku Klux Klan, which led to his impeachment. (North Carolina Department of Archives and History)

white mountain society under a broad political umbrella capable of defeating the Conservatives. Wartime suffering had led many lower-class whites
to resent the war, and the anti-Confederates counted upon their support
once the war ended. Alexander H. Jones, a consistent Unionist from Hendersonville, reprinted a wartime pamphlet that decried "these cotton lords
of creation, who own fifty, a hundred, or perhaps five hundred slaves"
and who "look upon a white man who has to labor for an honest living as
no better than one of their negroes."[15] In order to succeed, however, anti-
Confederate leaders knew they needed to combine the support of "respectable" white men with this lower-class base or else remain saddled with the
perception of having betrayed their state and section. They hoped to win the
support of the more conservative members of Holden's peace movement, such
as Leander Sams Gash, who were unsure of the future and indisputably part
of the upper echelon of western North Carolina's white society. An old-line
Whig, Gash supported Vance as governor in 1862, but he grew frustrated
with the Civil War and began advocating for peace in 1863. With the aid of
this respectable white male swing vote, the western anti-Confederates could
potentially seize a greater share of local political offices.[16]

The petitions for presidential amnesty pouring into Holden's office
gave him reason for optimism regarding his gains among wealthy former
Confederates in the west. Ladson Arthur Mills of Rutherford County was
indisputably a man of means. Prior to the war he had served in both houses
of the state legislature as a Democrat because he "honestly believed the
best interests of the whole country would be best protected and promoted
by the success" of that party. As staunch a Confederate as he was, Mills
noted, "the battle has been fought and the South has lost the wager," and he
and his fellow Confederates were "morally bound to recognize the supreme
authority of the United States." Men like Mills swore that they now considered the matter settled and wished "to render the [U.S.] authorities . . .
a cheerful and hearty support."[17] Other potential anti-Confederates spoke
of the overwhelming riptide of secession that pulled many lukewarm supporters—even some outright opponents—toward disunion. In Transylvania County, John C. Duckworth admitted that the excitement of the
times overwhelmed him. As Confederate policies and the "impropriety of
the rebelion [sic]" mounted, Duckworth testified that he returned to the
"union party and has promptly acted with it ever since."[18]

In the short term, at least, these men felt obligated to abide by northern
terms. A supporter in Salisbury wrote Holden in mid-August that he had

had a long political discussion with men from Alexander and Iredell counties, whom he found to be "thoroughly devoted to our cause." These men had suffered insults and abuse from Confederates during the war, and they were eager to lead the state in a new direction. Holden's friend was actually surprised by the level of support for the governor that he had encountered during his travels. Everyone he met seemed "highly pleased with your government and yourself." Most importantly for Holden, much of that support came from the upper crust of white society. "If such is the praise of the 'betters,'" he wrote the governor, "what must be the satisfaction of the large class of substrata with whom one does not meet on Rail Roads!" Success seemed to be coming the anti-Confederates' way.[19]

Mountain Conservatives held a far less sanguine view of the future. Former Confederates dreaded possible confiscation of their property, disfranchisement, and other harsh treatment from revenge-minded Unionists and distant policymakers. Walter Lenoir, who had lost his leg in service to the Confederacy, found his future prospects daunting enough due to his status as a widower and amputee; he feared that the summer quiet on his Haywood County property masked a "devilish element" within western North Carolina. Lower-class white men, whom he deemed "worthless," ached to settle old scores, and, in Walter's opinion, waited for the reopening of local courts in order "to bring suits for damage." Poorer Unionists "supposed that every rebel in the land is liable for damages for sustaining the war in behalf of the South." As a member of a prominent family from Caldwell County, Lenoir had a lot to lose should his nightmare become reality. Events in neighboring East Tennessee, where Walter believed that William G. Brownlow had created "a living purgatory," did little to facilitate hope. One local candidate for the coming state constitutional convention, Walter feared, was of the Brownlow stripe. He hoped that his brother's father-in-law, W. G. B. Garrett, whom he deemed "a much more moderate man," would thwart the "disciples of the Brownlow school of politics" in Haywood County.[20]

Following the president's instructions, North Carolinians across the state went to the polls in September 1865 to select delegates to revise the state constitution. The convention was a particularly enlightening political moment because it was the first time since the war that North Carolinians went to the polls in an organized political contest. Conservatives tried to stymie the convention by not voting and therefore denying it the quorum necessary to convene, but Conservative apathy created a tremendous anti-Confederate opportunity instead. Voters supported a convention, and it opened on October 2. Among western North Carolina's delegates were three prominent Union men. Tod R. Caldwell of Burke supported the peace movement, and George W. Logan of Rutherford represented that peace faction in the Confederate Congress. Alexander H. Jones of Henderson preached resistance to the Confederacy in his community, and he had served in the Union army. A second representative from Rutherford County, Ceburn L. Harris, assisted Holden in the reorganization of his county's local government after the war. The remainder of the delegation spread across the ideological spectrum, with most falling into the anti-Confederate category. Not all delegates were anti-Confederates, however; James R. Love, a former Confederate officer and member of a prominent land and slaveholding family, represented the traditional Democratic Party stronghold of Jackson County.[21]

Secession was the first issue discussed, and after much debate the delegates reached a compromise rescinding the ordinance. With secession repealed, the members turned to emancipation. During the roll call vote, William Baker voiced his disapproval, but the delegate from Ashe and Alleghany counties got in line once he realized he was a definite minority.[22] Mountain representatives overwhelmingly supported the repeal of secession, the repudiation of the debt, and slavery's abolition, which they understood as President Johnson's preconditions to reunion. Mountain delegates played prominent roles in accomplishing these goals. Caldwell County representative Rufus L. Patterson and George W. Logan served on the committee that drafted the ordinance to rescind secession, and Reverend L. L. Stewart from Buncombe County helped draft the initial resolution abolishing slavery (see table 4.1).[23]

Once the convention approved secession's revocation and emancipation, the delegates decided to put these issues before the people for popular confirmation. Western Carolinians overwhelmingly approved emancipation and the nullification of secession. Abolition's electoral victory hid the complexity of the contest in the western counties, even though there appeared to be little correlation between slave population and results. Each of the largest slaveholding counties approved the ordinances by strong majorities. Some interesting patterns emerge after wartime loyalties are factored into the equation. Black freedom received much less than a ringing endorsement in Unionist Cherokee County, where emancipation received a mere sixteen-vote edge. Most surprising was the Unionist stronghold of Wilkes

Table 4.1. Results of Referendum Election to Abolish Slavery and Rescind Secession in Western North Carolina Counties, 1865

County	Abolition		Rescind Seccession	
	For	Against	For	Against
Alleghany	48	6	133	1
Ashe	361	5	134	4
Buncombe	435	42	434	18
Burke	396	2	398	0
Caldwell	194	3	204	8
Cherokee and Clay	53	37	297	5
Haywood	261	18	243	18
Henderson and Transylvania	558	0	563	0
Jackson	117	8	102	1
Macon	52	34	67	15
Madison	278	0	278	0
McDowell	197	9	196	5
Rutherford and Polk	658	11	635	11
Watauga	144	9	215	6
Wilkes	705	302	N/A	N/A
Yancey and Mitchell	274	0	274	0
Total	4,731	486	4,173	102
Percentage	90.7	9.3	97.6	2.4
State total	18,527	3,696	19,977	1,940

Sources: *Raleigh (NC) Daily Standard*, December 28, 1865, 3; R. D. W. Connor, ed., *A Manual of North Carolina Issued by the North Carolina Historical Commission for the Use of Members of the General Assembly Session 1913* (Raleigh, NC: E. M. Uzzell & Co., 1913), 1013–15.

County, whose residents approved the measure by more than four hundred votes. In the process, however, Wilkes voters tallied nearly one-tenth of the entire state's negative vote (see table 4.1). It is unclear whether Unionists in these counties believed their loyalty exempted them from emancipation or whether they simply resented African American freedom. Most mountaineers expressed their disapproval—or apathy—by not participating at all. Only 5,175 western residents participated in the referendum, as opposed to the 10,711 ballots cast in the 1864 gubernatorial election. The number of voters was less than half of those who had participated in 1864, so it was hard to view these totals as a popular mandate. The passage of emancipation showed mountaineers' acceptance, not necessarily their approval.[24]

Fresh from the convention, the two political factions transitioned into campaigns for state legislators, national representatives, and governor. In the forty-ninth state senatorial district, one anti-Confederate candidate, W. W. Rollins, published a broadside detailing his position on the issues of the day. Rollins undoubtedly elicited a variety of reactions. Having risen to the rank of captain in the Twenty-ninth North Carolina Infantry, he deserted the Confederate army and joined the Union's Third North Carolina Mounted Infantry. Committed Conservatives and Unionists probably judged Rollins solely on that basis. Moderates may have weighed his policies in their decision. One thing is clear: Rollins placed great importance upon loyalty. He opened his appeal to the voters by putting the onus for the war squarely on the Conservatives' shoulders. Neither he nor people like him, he claimed, were responsible for the war. When he had been at home or even after he went to the Federal lines, Rollins argued, he advocated for North Carolina's best interests. "Had it not been for the selfishness of your commanders," he added, "the struggle would have passed away and western North Carolina have never felt the realities of the war." For that reason, he agreed with the president's Reconstruction policy, which Rollins interpreted as "protect the masses and punish the leaders."[25]

Regarding the future of the former slaves, appropriations for internal improvements, and repudiation of the state's war debt, Rollins expounded relatively typical anti-Confederate ideas. There was no equivocation in his belief that the United States and western Carolina were "to be a *white man's government* . . . and that it would be dangerous to the white race to elevate the freedman to be his political equal." Like many white mountain southerners, Rollins was adamant that the best response to emancipation was the freedpeople's colonization to Africa. Colonization complemented his stance on the region's development. In his estimation, repudiating the war debt freed up that money for the state to finance the mountain section's future instead. If that were to happen, Rollins felt that "in less than two years the iron horse [rail road] would be a welcome visitor to our mountain village." The final piece of Rollins's plan was immigration. Bringing outsiders with "capital and enterprise" to develop the region's resources would facilitate African Americans' removal. "As white immigration comes in," he hypothesized, "the colored population will naturally recede before it, which will continue until an outlet will be an absolute necessity, and the idea of colonization will be renewed."[26]

The gubernatorial contest pitted provisional governor Holden against Conservative Party candidate Jonathan Worth, with the meaning of Unionism and loyalty in the new postwar order at stake. Holden's leading role in the wartime peace movement appealed to anti-Confederates, but he did not possess a monopoly on wartime dissent. Worth possessed his own brand of Unionism, for as wartime state treasurer he had the credentials of a loyal Confederate, but he had also cooperated with Holden's peace movement during the war. This made Worth a nearly perfect compromise candidate, with connections and ties to both the former conditional Unionist Whigs and the anti-Confederates. Still, the Conservatives had to be careful. Lingering animosity from the mountain region's brutal partisan violence made the restoration of the wartime leadership unpalatable to western anti-Confederates, who voted against the Conservatives as much as they did for Holden. Speaking for many mountain Unionists, Alexander H. Jones insisted it was illogical to reinstate former Confederate leaders "who plied their vocations to this end [disunion] while holding offices in the Government of the United States prior to the war."[27]

When the election finally came on November 9, 1865, the anti-Confederates in the mountains achieved a pyrrhic victory. The mountainous Seventh Congressional District favored Henderson County Unionist Alexander H. Jones for Congress, and Holden carried most mountain counties in his bid for governor. The state as a whole, however, gave Worth a decisive overall victory (see table 4.2).[28] Although Worth's victory revealed the Conservatives' resurgent strength across North Carolina, Holden's 65.6 percent of the western counties' vote confirmed the strength of the anti-Confederates in the state's mountain counties. Western anti-Confederates had favored both Holden and Jones; the latter was both the only man elected to Congress in the state who could take the ironclad loyalty oath to the United States and the only mountain resident sent to Washington. Despite Worth's victory, the election proved the anti-Confederates a force to be reckoned with in the mountains. During the 1864 gubernatorial campaign, Holden polled 2,612 votes in the mountains. One year later, he won 6,557 mountaineers' votes. While it is impossible to tell how many of those voters were former Democrats, Whigs, or men resigned to Holden's election, his totals suggest the growing strength of the Unionist-led anti-Confederate faction in the west.[29]

Stymied within the state, many western Unionists, who constituted the ideological core of the anti-Confederate faction, looked to the North and the federal government to offset the Conservatives' gains. Worth's defeat in the mountains also intensified local Conservatives' redefinition of loy-

Table 4.2. Gubernatorial Election Results in Western North Carolina Counties, 1865

County	Jonathan Worth (Conservative)	William Holden (Anti-Confederate)
Alleghany	39	261
Ashe	284	472
Buncombe	424	568
Burke	218	434
Caldwell	238	251
Cherokee and Clay	241	305
Haywood	282	302
Henderson and Transylvania	240	658
Jackson	167	276
Macon	188	99
Madison	29	456
McDowell	258	270
Rutherford and Polk	136	558
Watauga	287	211
Wilkes	283	883
Yancey and Mitchell	119	553
Total	3,433	6,557
Percentage	34.4	65.6
State total	31,616	25,704

Sources: *Raleigh (NC) Daily Standard*, December 28, 1865, 2; Connor, *A Manual of North Carolina*, 999–1000.

alty. Anti-Confederates' wartime opposition to the Confederacy and their willingness to cooperate with Congress convinced Conservatives that the most ardent Unionists possessed bad character and were undeserving of respect. A prewar political culture that stressed local relationships and a sort of patron-client relationship between the wealthier mountaineers and their poorer white neighbors broke down, as Unionists rallied lower-class support and looked outward for help. No longer willing to work with the former governing elite, the mountain Unionists looked for new patrons. The logical choice was William W. Holden, but when he failed, mountain Unionists appealed to national figures such as Andrew Johnson, Thaddeus Stevens, and others whom they hoped might prove sympathetic.[30]

That shift in the political culture of western North Carolina ultimately took a heavy toll on the anti-Confederate coalition. The moderate men, previously willing to abide by Northern terms and oppose the restoration of the wartime leadership, drifted toward the Conservatives as the Unionists adopted tactics more in keeping with the Republican Party. No individual better embodies this transformation than Leander Sams Gash, who, like most anti-Confederates, felt that the war's outcome demanded both internal reform and cooperation with the North. From the forty-ninth state senatorial district, the first-term senator was frustrated by his fellow citizens' halting acceptance of the war's consequences. Although "our people" seemed slow to learn how profoundly the war had changed their world, the western legislator hoped that "we may learn it the better by its being so hard to beat in to us." The state legislature followed national and regional affairs closely, and Gash personally felt that unless North Carolinians acknowledged that they must grant concessions to the North, including the right of African Americans to testify in court, the result would be devastating. In early February 1866, he wrote his wife that the federal officials in the state had issued the order forbidding North Carolina's adoption of a vagrancy law like that enacted in other southern states. A similar fate would befall North Carolina's black codes, Gash felt, "unless we permit them to testify where their colour is concerned."[31]

The escalation of the conflict between President Johnson and the Republican-controlled Congress weakened moderate anti-Confederates' willingness to cooperate with the North. Upon his return to Raleigh in February 1866, Gash followed closely the fate of the national Freedmen's Bureau extension bill, designed to extend for another year the life of an organization created to supervise and facilitate the South's transition from slave labor to free labor. Suspense hung over the state legislature in the days leading up to the president's official response to the bill. Such tension revealed a growing concern about a Congress he felt likely "to pass some very radical measures . . . in the way of Freedmen and Freedmens rights granting them perfect equality before the law." When news arrived that Johnson had vetoed it late that month, the Conservatives cheered the president's action.[32]

So did Gash. The president's veto promised the removal of a major thorn in Conservatives' sides and an obstacle to unfettered home rule, and it was, as Gash wrote his wife, the realization of "our fondest hopes." North Carolina's mountain Conservatives increasingly understood Johnson as an ally in the restoration of the antebellum political culture that emphasized the power of wealthy, economically diverse elite white men. Mountain masters dominated antebellum politics and hoped to regain their "rightful" place after the war. Understood in that context, Johnson's veto was a powerful opening act in what Gash believed would be a "regular Political war." Gash's shift was as much of a response to local affairs as to national affairs. He believed that radicalism had infected "what we call our union friends," who, he believed, dreamed of the state's return "to a Territorial condition thereby secureing to them certain offices that they could never reach if left to the people." Gash was typically opposed to violence, but he admitted that, in this instance, "such men ought to be kept where they could do no harm." By early March 1866, his drift away from the Unionists had begun.[33]

Mountain Unionists felt the sting of the Conservatives' resurgence acutely. Despite several shared political beliefs, especially regarding internal improvements, Unionists found little mercy from the resurgent Conservatives. Marion Roberts, a Union veteran from Buncombe County, informed Thaddeus Stevens in May 1866 that the former Confederates heaped "the most inhumane treatment and unpardonable insults" upon mountain Unionists, who exercised "a great deal of magnanimity and respect towards the Confederate Soldiers and Citizens of this Country." Eight white Henderson County women went to the Freedmen's Bureau agent in Asheville at the end of the month, seeking protection. Although designed to help former slaves and white southerners adjust to a world without slavery, the Asheville agent represented their nearest access to federal power. They informed him that Confederate sympathizers had burned their homes and threatened their lives because their husbands had fought for the Union. Agent P. E. Murphy was a sympathetic, but powerless, friend. Without a military force at his disposal, "I cannot give them that protection I would like," Murphy told his superiors. He sent letters chastising the offending parties, but Murphy was not naive. Without troops to back him, he felt little confidence in his ability to preserve order.[34]

Residents of Buncombe and Burke counties at least had a federal presence nearby; the more remote northwestern counties took matters into their own hands. Just as they had during the war, Unionists banded together in order to protect and promote their interests. Union men in Wilkes County's Trap Hill community again took up arms that summer. Roughly 100 anti-Confederates in Alleghany County formed a cavalry company in order to assert their local authority. Meanwhile, a Conservative light horse company roamed the county "blustering and Cutting up Generally" and "Defying Any Union man to interfere." The local police captain informed the com-

UNION BUSHWHACKERS ATTACKING REBEL CAVALRY.

The guerrilla warfare that occurred in the mountains of North Carolina during the Civil War left lasting divisions in the region, which complicated Reconstruction. (from Junius Henry Browne, *Four Years in Secessia,* 1865)

manding general in Raleigh that these horsemen constituted "the worst kind of raiders and murderers during the war." Their defiance boded ill for the future. "They refuse to Muster under the stars and stripes," the unsettled policeman reported, "and say they are Rebels yet."[35]

The "Heroes of America" or "Red Strings," as they were known, a secret wartime organization that originated in North Carolina's Piedmont "Quaker Belt," reorganized to defend Unionists in northwestern North Carolina. Gen. John C. Robinson, commanding the state, sent Maj. Francis Wolcott to investigate conditions in the northwest late in the summer of 1866. Wolcott rode on horseback through Rowan, Alleghany, Surry, Ashe, and Wilkes counties, finding Red Strings in each county. "Its members were with hardly an exception men loyal to the Government," he informed Robinson, "and a large majority of them of the poorer Classes of people." For all intents and purposes, the Heroes aroused little concern in Wolcott. Conservatives, on the other hand, were deeply alarmed. Former Confederates spoke of arming to resist this secret organization, and Wolcott heard several pro-Confederate ministers denounce the Red Strings in their sermons and threaten its members with expulsion from their congregations.

Conservatives felt threatened by the Red Strings' vows to support the U.S. Constitution, warn each other of approaching danger, and bring those who wronged their fellow Heroes to justice. When the Gap Civil community in Alleghany County elected a Unionist as captain of their reconstituted militia, Conservative residents angrily formed their own militia. Wolcott felt certain that these former Confederate cavalrymen, if unchecked, would soon precipitate violence.[36]

Conditions in the northwestern counties had a profound impact on state affairs. Governor Worth concluded that "the secret organization commonly called 'Red Strings' is being generally revised in this state to favor the Radical Congress and frustrate the policy of the President."[37] This issue became an obsession for Worth, who was convinced that state Unionists would use affairs in western North Carolina to restore military control over the state. The Red Strings evoked a visceral disdain from Conservatives, who charged that this organization shielded "bad men" who "only joined the society to cloak their acts of wrong and violence" during the war. This alliance between local Unionists, who many Conservatives perceived as traitors to their state, and violent guerrillas underscored the anti-Confederates' continued disloyalty. Early in the summer of 1866, Judge Merrimon categorized the Red Strings as a lawless element consisting mostly of deserters and vengeful Unionists siding with the northern Radical Republicans.[38]

Northwestern Red String organizations mobilized Union men in body, while in Henderson County Unionist leaders attempted to mobilize them in spirit. Unionists issued a call for a mass meeting to vent their frustration. Like the Red Strings, Henderson County Unionists recognized that they had lost the postwar power struggles at the local and state levels. A letter to Alexander H. Jones's *Henderson (NC) Pioneer* sarcastically noted in September 1866 that Conservatives lived by one governing principle: "Give us (who have spent five years in trying to destroy the Government) the reins of Government and the keys to the public crib, then we will sing Union . . . all over the land." Since loyalty was the core of the Unionists' claims for respect and power within the region, they resented that they had "saved the country from anarchy and eternal ruin; but everything that adheres to this party now, is called radical." Such frustration was eerily familiar. During the secession crisis, disunionists and their allies painted Unionists as "submissionists" unworthy of respect. After the war, they again branded their opponents as dangerous and undeserving of respect. Backed into a political corner, the Unionists in Henderson County embraced the radical label as their own. "I care not what they call me," one Unionist opined in a letter to the editor, who also exhorted "the Radicals, or Republicans, or true Union men, stand together and watch, and when the time comes move. . . . True Union men, do not be deceived by the honeyed words, or fine party names of this intriguing, wire-working, liberty-destroying party." The alliance between northern Republicans and southern Unionists seemed all but formalized by this point in western North Carolina.[39]

Both sides realized the high stakes heading into the elections. Frustrated in their efforts to gain political control, the anti-Confederate *Rutherford (NC) Star* proclaimed Worth "the great stumbling block to restoration" and expressed the hope that he would refrain from seeking reelection to an office "he cannot fill to the advantage of the State." Alexander H. Jones's *Pioneer* reprinted these sentiments approvingly in heavily Unionist Henderson County. The part of the *Star*'s editorial that undoubtedly pleased Jones the most was its criticism of the former Unionist-Whigs. Both Jones and the anti-Confederates in Rutherford resented the resumption of power by Worth's party of "*Secessionists* and *latter day Saints.*" These men embodied the fears William Pickens expressed when reorganizing county governments in 1865; Conservatives who espoused conditional Unionist positions had reverted to their secession crisis Unionism, and the public—especially in the central and eastern counties—had put them back in office. Hardcore Unionists denounced these men whose "thirst for office is so great that all sense of duty to the people and the State has fled before their eyes." Such men lived by the "motto *rule or ruin,* and it seems at present they are determined on doing both."[40]

Conservatives expressed equally strong concerns over the outcome of the coming votes on the constitution and for state officers. Augustus Merrimon confessed that the stakes were higher in this election. "If the 'radicals' succeed in the fall elections," he opined mid-summer, "we can't imagine what may result in the end." Until his state regained its place in Congress, he feared that they would continue to face continuous harassment from "radicals north & south." It proved to be the Conservatives that had reason to celebrate after the voters cast their ballots. Worth won an even more decisive victory in 1866 than he had the previous winter. He destroyed his opponent, Alfred Dockery, and nearly swept the mountain counties in the process (see table 4.3). Only four counties gave Dockery majorities as Worth captured more than 66 percent of the region's votes. The message of this election could not have been any clearer to the anti-Confederates. They

Table 4.3. Gubernatorial Election Results in Western North Carolina Counties, 1866

County	Jonathan Worth (Conservative)	Alfred Dockery (Anti-Confederate)
Alleghany	220	51
Ashe	512	199
Buncombe	582	334
Burke	577	56
Caldwell	308	44
Cherokee	299	147
Clay	129	95
Haywood	378	207
Henderson and Transylvania	423	482
Jackson	404	28
Macon	334	47
Madison	271	49
McDowell	440	108
Mitchell	116	153
Polk	172	173
Rutherford	382	648
Watauga	282	68
Wilkes	530	462
Yancey	333	83
Total	6,692	3,434
Percentage	66.1	33.9
State total	34,250	10,759

Sources: *Raleigh (NC) Daily Sentinel*, November 15, 1866, 3; Connor, *A Manual of North Carolina*, 1001–2.

were losing the support of their moderate allies and the coalition existed more as a singular expression of the Unionist presence in the mountains.[41]

The last, best hope of the state's Unionists was the Fourteenth Amendment. Anti-Confederates supported the amendment because it was the surest path to reunion. Echoing arguments from across the South and the state, mountain anti-Confederates asserted that the amendment, no matter how odious, would prove better than the future terms its rejection would prompt. Congress would impose racial equality and black suffrage upon North Carolina from above, the *Hendersonville (NC) Pioneer* warned, "unless the Howard Amendment is adopted."

Jones opined that the people needed to make clear to their leaders that their paramount hope was reunion because the Conservatives seemed to prefer remaining outside the Union. Knowing that his fellow mountaineers opposed the political equality of black men, he warned that opposition to the Fourteenth Amendment would make such a result inevitable. "Unless the people . . . vote only for such men as are willing and anxious to return to the Union," Jones warned, "we will have to stay out, until the very conditions predicted by those who will not move a peg in that direction, are forced upon the people of the State."[42]

Frustrated mountain Unionists probed for a way to secure Reconstruction on their own terms. Writing from Hendersonville on December 16, 1866, Mary Gash informed her husband that Jones's newspaper was circulating "petitions to Congress to grant us a new state up here in the Mountains." In her opinion, Jones and his fellow Unionists seemed to believe that a new state would grant reunion, but also railroads "and every thing else they want almost by maggic [sic]."[43] That was precisely Jones's intent. The Confederacy was dead, he argued, and with it went "confiscation, tithing and impressments." No longer could men be hunted "down with bloodhounds" or have their "peaceful homes" pillaged. Yet Jones asserted that the same party responsible for such wartime policies had regained power in western North Carolina. Resolution, justice, and peace for Union men were impossible under such circumstances. Only a new state where the mountain Unionists could assume power offered them peace and prosperity. "The *wise* and *prudent* plan of Congress" offered the best chances of reunion, and Jones called for all "loyal people of Western North Carolina" to sign their names in support of forming a new state. Jones concluded ominously that if a convention based on loyal men's votes could not be had to form a new state, then "the whole State [should] be reorganized on the same basis as proposed for the new," that is, loyalty.[44]

A call for a new state was the boldest and most obvious statement of Unionists' willingness to sidestep state officials in order to gain political power. Conservative state officials dug in their heels against the Unionists and the Fourteenth Amendment. Leander Sams Gash did not believe that the amendment would find much fertile ground in North Carolina. Barring a foreign conflagration, Gash believed that Congress would resort to "the most extreme radical measures." While that would certainly be a problem, the bigger threat posed by the amendment was its growing support among Unionists. His letter to his wife betrayed Gash's intensifying disdain for these men. Gash had reached his political breaking point. In his opinion, southern

Radicals were "worse than the radicals North," and he increasingly became convinced that there was a conspiracy to "annul the acts of the President and appoint Military Governors for all the rebel states."[45]

North Carolina's legislature defeated the Fourteenth Amendment resoundingly. Only one western state senator, Ceburne Harris, the Rutherford County Unionist who helped reorganize the county government for Holden in 1865, voted for it, while forty-three other state senators rejected it. Its reception in the state house of representatives was little better.[46] The amendment's defeat spelled trouble for the southern states, and Gash and his colleagues watched national news with trepidation. The passage of the Reconstruction Acts, collectively remanding the states back to near territorial status with an overseeing military presence, marked the fulfillment of their fears. For his family and constituents seeking comfort, Gash had little advice. All he could think was for the people "to go [to] work, mind their own business and let Politicks go to thunder." Congress's vindictiveness overwhelmed Gash's earlier moderation on racial matters as well. After the Reconstruction Acts, he felt it would be best to send "negroes to Congress hereafter and Keep them there until [the North] get their fill of them."[47] When the Supreme Court failed to come to the rescue of the South, Gash resigned himself to Congressional Reconstruction, much as he resigned himself to secession. For the second time in less than a decade, Gash braced himself against a "political storm of fanaticism . . . sweeping over the land."[48]

That same "fanaticism" shocked Phineas Horton of Wilkes County. He expected "at any day to hear of the over throw of the Civil government in NC." Failure to ratify the Fourteenth Amendment had put Worth's administration on notice. Rumors abounded around Raleigh that "men of high standing in this state that are . . . going to Washington to present to the radical Congress very alarming reports and petitions," Horton noted, "saying that the union men cannot have justice or be permitted to stay in NC." For Conservatives, this was the realization of their worst fears. Unionists, men whom they largely considered base and unreliable, had the ear of the Congress and seemed determined to align with the federal government at the expense of the constituted state authorities. Moderate men, who had cooperated with Holden during the war and after it as anti-Confederates, went headlong into the Conservative ranks. Their departure precipitated a shift among the Unionists as well, and Holden's mission to Washington set the stage for the formation of the state's own Republican Party.[49]

Mira Brown may have been right: western North Carolinians may not have known her "real" war, but mountain residents became increasingly embroiled in an "unreal" war of loyalties after the soldiers returned home. Wartime leaders and former political elites struggled to regain their authority in a struggle against a large Unionist population desperate to control local political affairs themselves. Loyalty mattered immensely in this postwar political conflict. It shaped the efforts to restore the state to the Union, and it undermined the antebellum political culture. Historians' focus on the plantation districts has allowed this local contest among mountain whites to slip through the cracks. This oversight has neglected to take account of the redefinition and evolution of wartime loyalties during Reconstruction. In predominantly white western North Carolina, the political restoration of the Union continued the chaotic and personal politics that defined the war. Mira Brown may not have found this style of warfare familiar; in fact, she may have found it to be worse than anything she had imagined.

Notes

1. Mira E. Brown to "My dearest Sarah," August 30, 1865, Hamilton Brown Papers, Southern Historical Collection, University of North Carolina at Chapel Hill Library (hereafter SHC). For more on the activities of regular soldiers around Columbia and Maury County, Tennessee, see Stephen V. Ash, *Middle Tennessee Society Transformed, 1860–1870: War and Peace in the Upper South* (Baton Rouge: Louisiana State University Press, 1988), 91, 132.

2. John C. Inscoe and Gordon B. McKinney, *The Heart of Confederate Appalachia: Western North Carolina in the Civil War* (Chapel Hill: University of North Carolina Press, 2000), 111–14; Martin Crawford, *Ashe County's Civil War: Community and Society in the Appalachian South* (Charlottesville: University of Virginia Press, 2001), 76–80, 90–94, 128–35.

3. Gordon B. McKinney, *Southern Mountain Republicans, 1865–1900: Politics and the Appalachian Community* (1978; repr., Knoxville: University of Tennessee Press, 1998), 158–60; Joe A. Mobley, *War Governor of the South: North Carolina's Zeb Vance in the Confederacy* (Gainesville: University of Florida Press, 2005), 42–51; Inscoe and McKinney, *Heart of Confederate Appalachia*, 108–9, 114, 116–21, 125–6; William L. Barney, *The Making of a Confederate: Walter Lenoir's Civil War* (New York: Oxford University Press, 2008), 115, 120, 133–34; Sandra L. Ballard and Leila E. Weinstein, eds., *Neighbor to Neighbor: A Memoir of Family, Community, and Civil War in Appalachian North Carolina* (Boone, NC: Center of Appalachian Studies, Appalachian State University, 2007), 73–79, 81; William R. Trotter, *Bushwhackers: The Civil War in North Carolina*, vol. 2, *The Mountains* (Winston-Salem, NC: John F. Blair, 1988), 147–55; Phillip Shaw Paludan, *Vic-

tims: A True Story of the Civil War (Knoxville: University of Tennessee Press, 1981), chapter 4. According to Paludan, some 9,000 western North Carolinians served in the Confederate army, and approximately 800 to 1,000 of those were Madison County residents who fought in the Sixty-fourth North Carolina Infantry. Many others deserted to serve in the Union forces or to return home and try to avoid the service. Paludan also notes that many felt it worthwhile to stay home and fight for the United States "when it suited them"; Paludan, *Victims,* 62–63.

4. See Eric Foner, *Reconstruction: America's Unfinished Revolution, 1863–1877* (New York: Harper & Row, 1988). For examples of scholarship dealing with postemancipation Appalachia, see John Cimprich, "Slavery's End in East Tennessee," and Jennifer Lund Smith, "Negotiating the Terms of Freedom: The Quest for Education in an African American Community in Reconstruction North Georgia," both in John C. Inscoe, ed., *Appalachians and Race: The Mountain South from Slavery to Segregation* (Lexington: University Press of Kentucky, 2001). The one region of southern Appalachia that has received fairly significant attention from Reconstruction scholars is East Tennessee. Noel Fisher's *War at Every Door: Partisan Politics and Guerrilla Violence in East Tennessee, 1860–1869* (Chapel Hill: University of North Carolina Press, 1997) explores the role of partisan violence in the struggle between Unionists and Confederates in East Tennessee, and it shows the continuity between wartime violence and Reconstruction in Appalachia. Ben H. Severance's *Tennessee's Radical Army: The State Guard and Its Role in Reconstruction, 1867–1869* (Knoxville: University of Tennessee Press, 2005) examines the role of the Republican State Guard and the "politics of force" in East Tennessee's Reconstruction. Although Severance does not explore the political battles of Presidential Reconstruction, his study also demonstrates the importance of wartime loyalties in postwar Appalachian politics. In this regard, both his work and my own are deeply indebted to McKinney, *Southern Mountain Republicans.*

5. Otto H. Olsen and Ellen Z. McGrew, eds., "Prelude to Reconstruction: The Correspondence of State Senator Leander Sams Gash, 1866–1867, Part III," *North Carolina Historical Review* 60, no. 3 (1983): 342. George Rable helped promulgate the idea that Reconstruction constituted a continuation of wartime hostilities by other means in *But There Was No Peace: The Role of Violence in the Politics of Reconstruction* (Athens: University of Georgia Press, 1984). Dan T. Carter's *When the War Was Over: The Failure of Self-Reconstruction in the South, 1865–1867* (Baton Rouge: Louisiana State University Press, 1985) has greatly influenced this study. Carter argued that all southern whites were not blinded by race after the war and that the former Whigs were particularly open-minded about the future of the former Confederacy. Finally, Phillip Shaw Paludan's *Victims* captures the raw emotion that pervaded the mountain counties during the war.

6. Marc W. Kruman, *Parties and Politics in North Carolina, 1836–1865* (Baton Rouge: Louisiana State University Press, 1983), 252, 254–55, 258. The slave schedule of the 1860 U.S. Census reveals that Zebulon Vance owned six slaves, Merrimon owned two, and the Avery family owned dozens. See *Eighth Cen-*

sus of the United States, 1860 (Washington, DC: National Archives and Records Administration, 1860), microfilm 653, reel 920.

7. Merrimon quoted in Kruman, *Parties and Politics,* 258.

8. Edward H. McGee, "North Carolina Conservatives and Reconstruction" (PhD diss., Princeton University, 1972), 106–7; Otto H. Olsen, "North Carolina: An Incongruous Presence," in Otto H. Olsen, ed., *Reconstruction and Redemption in the South* (Baton Rouge: Louisiana State University Press, 1980), 162, 169. For more on this complex calculus of loyalties, see Gordon B. McKinney, "Layers of Loyalty: Confederate Nationalism and Amnesty Letters from Western North Carolina," *Civil War History* 51 (March 2005): 5–22.

9. Allen T. Davidson, *Case Files of Applications from Former Confederates for Presidential Pardons, 1865–1867* (Washington, DC: National Archives and Records Administration, 1977), roll 38, available at http://community.berea.edu/cwaltp/ (hereafter cited as *Presidential Pardons*). Davidson owned two slaves in 1860. See *Eighth Census of the United States,* 921.

10. Otto H. Olsen and Ellen Z. McGrew, "Prelude to Reconstruction: The Correspondence of State Senator Leander Sams Gash, 1866–1867, Part I," *North Carolina Historical Review* 60, no. 1 (1983): 43–46, 58; Olsen, "North Carolina: An Incongruous Presence," 9, 160; and Otto H. Olsen and Ellen Z. McGrew, "Prelude to Reconstruction: The Correspondence of State Senator Leander Sams Gash, 1866–1867, Part II," *North Carolina Historical Review* 60, no. 2 (1983): 207.

11. Clarence W. Griffin, *History of Old Tryon and Rutherford Counties, North Carolina, 1730–1936* (Spartanburg, SC: The Reprint Company, 1977), 319–20; *Eighth Census of the United States,* 889, 913, 918. Uniting all of these men were similar backgrounds and statuses. Harris was thirty-eight years old and owned $5,450 worth of real property and $4,000 worth of personal property in 1860. A young lawyer in 1860, Merrimon owned a comparable $7,000 of real estate, and his personal property was valued at $9,100. Cowles exceeded both of them; his vast landholdings were worth roughly $20,000, while his personal estate was a comparable $5,295. None of these men suffered terribly from emancipation. Merrimon owned two slaves and Logan owned eleven slaves in 1860. Cowles owned none. See *Eighth Census of the United States,* 920, 926, 927.

12. William Pickens to W. W. Holden, August 16, 1865, W. W. Holden Governor's Papers, North Carolina Office of Archives and History (hereafter cited as NCOAH); William Pickens to W. W. Holden, August 17, 1865, W. W. Holden Governor's Papers, NCOAH. Pickens was a modest farmer. His real estate was worth $1,600 and his personal property was worth $1,400 in 1860. See *Eighth Census of the United States,* 889.

13. Calvin Cowles to W. W. Holden, September 4, 1865, W. W. Holden Governor's Papers, NCOAH.

14. William Pickens to W. W. Holden, August 16, 1865, W. W. Holden Governor's Papers, NCOAH.

15. Alexander Hamilton Jones, *Knocking at the Door. Alex. H. Jones, Member-Elect to Congress: His Course before the War, during the War, and after the War. Adventures and Escapes* (Washington, DC: McGill & Witherow, 1866), 13. Alexander Hamilton Jones (1822–1901), a Mexican War veteran born in Buncombe County, claimed he taught himself to love the Union as a child reading about George Washington and other national figures. Jones's interests as a merchant at the outbreak of war led him into politics. He helped organize Unionists in western North Carolina, and he was captured while raising a federal regiment in western North Carolina. The state's only outright Unionist elected to Congress in 1865, Jones was an influential Reconstruction politician and newspaper editor. William S. Powell, ed., *Dictionary of North Carolina Biography* (Chapel Hill: University of North Carolina Press, 1986), 3:312–13. Lower-class mountaineers resented the Conscription Act, which exempted one white male on every farm with more than twenty slaves, and lower-class white women led a handful of bread riots throughout the western counties.

16. *Eighth Census of the United States*, 901; Olsen and McGrew, "Prelude to Reconstruction, Part I," 38, 40–41. Richard Abbott addresses the southern Republicans' need for legitimacy during the postwar period. Newspaper editors and other Republicans struggled to be seen as legitimate by a populace that largely viewed them as foreign and forced upon them by the victorious North. See Abbott, *For Free Press and Equal Rights: Republican Newspapers in the Reconstruction South* (Athens: University of Georgia Press, 2004), 46–47. At the war's outset, he and his family lived comfortably in Haywood County, with Gash's real and personal property each valued at $15,000. His wife, Margaret, was the great-granddaughter of Waightstill Avery, one of the mountain section's wealthiest and most distinguished founding figures.

17. Arthur Ladson Mills, *Presidential Pardons*, roll 41. In 1860 Mills ranked as one of the mountain counties' wealthiest men, with real property valued at $40,000 and a personal estate worth $22,000. See the *Eighth Census of the United States*, 913. It is surely worth noting that the petitions for pardon sent to Andrew Johnson were designed to remove the applicants' political disabilities and that the petitioners would put the most positive spin on their loyalty. In other words, it seems logical that they would tell the hardened Unionist from East Tennessee what they thought he wanted to hear. But this does not entirely invalidate their statements of willingness to cooperate with the restored United States. In fact, the mountain petitioners seemed frank and sincere in their professions of cooperation.

18. John C. Duckworth, *Presidential Pardons*, roll 38. It appears that Duckworth stayed true to his word and to the anti-Confederate coalition assembled by Holden. The Transylvania County resident was appointed to the rank of colonel in the reorganized state militia by Governor Holden. See General Orders No. 3, State Adjutant General, September 1, 1868, Adjutant General's Office, Order Book, 1868–1871, NCOAH.

19. R. C. Badyn to William W. Holden, August 15, 1865, William Woods Holden Papers, Rare Books and Manuscripts, Perkins Library, Duke University. Although it is unclear exactly who the Mr. Carson from Alexander County was,

it may have been John M. Carson, the representative to the state legislature from Alexander in 1866.

20. W. W. Lenoir to Joseph C. Norwood, August 4, 1865, Lenoir Family Papers, SHC.

21. William Donaldson Cotton, "Appalachian North Carolina: A Political Study, 1860–1889" (PhD diss., University of North Carolina, 1954), 169; Horace W. Raper and Thornton W. Mitchell, eds., *The Papers of William Woods Holden* (Raleigh: North Carolina Division of Archives and History, 2000), 228–31; J. G. de Roulhac Hamilton, *Reconstruction in North Carolina*, vol. 58, no. 141, Studies in History, Economics and Public Law (New York: Columbia University, 1914), 120–21. The full mountain delegation was: William Baker for Ashe and Alleghany, E. M. Stephenson for Alexander, Tod Caldwell for Burke, Rev. L. L. Stewart for Buncombe, R. L. Patterson for Caldwell, G. W. Dickey for Cherokee, W. G. B. Garrett from Haywood, A. H. Jones for Henderson and Transylvania, James R. Love for Jackson, Robert M. Henry for Macon, G. W. Gahagan for Madison, Alney Burgin for McDowell, G. W. Logan and Ceburn L. Harris for Rutherford and Polk, George W. Bradley for Watauga, P. Smith and J. Q. A. Bryant for Wilkes, and G. Garland from Yancey and Mitchell. See *Journal of the Convention of the State of North Carolina at Its Session of 1865* (Raleigh, NC: Cannon and Holden, 1865), 2, 5–6, 10. Clay County was not among the counties represented, and it was probably included with Cherokee County. Only twelve of the seventeen western delegates could be conclusively found in the *Eighth Census of the United States*. Baker, Garrett, Dickey, and Bryant were not positively identified. Despite their various political backgrounds, the delegates shared comparable class standing. Based on those identified in the 1860 census, the mountain delegates owned an average of $5,550 each in real estate and $8,004 in personal property. That put them roughly between the calculated averages for identified anti-Confederates and Conservatives. Love himself owned little property, but his father owned more than forty slaves and more than $50,000 in personal property in 1860. Rufus L. Patterson was a manufacturer whose father, Samuel F. Patterson, was an equally prosperous farmer in terms of land and slaves. Rufus owned some $20,000 of real estate and $15,000 of personal property in 1860. He owned no slaves, but his father owned thirty-six. Furthermore, slaveholding was not exclusively a Conservative phenomenon; George W. Logan owned eleven slaves himself. See *Eighth Census of the United States*, 890, 897, 903, 913.

22. Hamilton, *Reconstruction in North Carolina*, 120–26; Sidney Andrews, *The South Since the War: As Shown by Fourteen Weeks of Travel and Observation in Georgia and the Carolinas* (1866; repr., New York: Arno Press and the New York Times, 1969), 156 (page citations are to the reprint edition). Baker formally registered his discontent when he signed a protest written by a Warren County delegate that decried the issues before the convention as unnecessary "to return North Carolina to her position in the Union, and relieve her people from military rule." See *Journal of the Convention of the State of North Carolina*, 92.

23. *Journal of the Convention of the State of North Carolina,* 17, 23–24, 27–29.

24. *Raleigh (NC) Daily Standard,* December 28, 1865, 3; Hamilton, *Reconstruction in North Carolina,* 125–26. Slave populations by western North Carolina county are available in John C. Inscoe, *Mountain Masters: Slavery and the Sectional Crisis in Western North Carolina* (Knoxville: University of Tennessee Press, 1989), 61.

25. W. Wallace Rollins, October 23, 1865, "To the Voters of the Senatorial District, Composed of the Counties of Transylvania, Henderson, Buncombe, Madison, Yancy, and Mitchell," Benjamin Austin Papers, Rare Books and Manuscripts, Perkins Library, Duke University; Olsen and McGrew, "Prelude to Reconstruction, Part I," 45–46 n. 11. Gash defeated Rollins in the election, 1,429 to 852. Gash defeated Rollins soundly in every county of their district except Rollins's home county of Madison, where he outpolled Gash 238 to 187.

26. Rollins, "To the Voters of the Senatorial District." Hopes for the freedpeople's colonization were not unique to Rollins. In late 1865, Leander Sams Gash shared with the state senate pleas from the grand juries of Buncombe and Transylvania counties for either the freedmen's colonization or strong regulatory laws. See Olsen and McGrew, eds., "Prelude to Reconstruction, Part I," 48–49, 52.

27. Jones, *Knocking at the Door,* 36–37.

28. Richard L. Zuber, *Jonathan Worth: A Biography of a Southern Unionist* (Chapel Hill: University of North Carolina Press, 1965), 206–8; McGee, "North Carolina Conservatives and Reconstruction," 119. Holden had hoped that the president might overrule the Conservatives' victory, but Johnson never intended the election to produce a crop of handpicked officials. Worth and the Conservatives remained victorious statewide. With the Conservatives surging into power across the state, the new state legislature considered former Confederate senator William A. Graham and Gov. Zebulon Vance for the U.S. Senate. Apathy and low voter turnout also marked the election. In Macon County, Allen T. Davidson seethed over his inability to do anything "but lick my chops" and "grit my teeth" in opposition to the anti-Confederates. Worth's defeat seemed so likely to Davidson that he concluded, "It is a foregone conclusion that Holden must be elected Gov. for the present without a fight." See Allen T. Davidson to Zebulon B. Vance, October 22, 1865, Zebulon Baird Vance Papers #3952, SHC.

29. R. D. W. Connor, ed., *A Manual of North Carolina Issued by the North Carolina Historical Commission for the Use of Members of the General Assembly Session 1913* (Raleigh, NC: E. M. Uzzell & Co., 1913), 999–1000. Of course, Congress refused to seat the Southern delegations to the Thirty-ninth Congress.

30. Inscoe, *Mountain Masters,* 126–29.

31. Olsen and McGrew, "Prelude to Reconstruction, Part I," 52–53.

32. Ibid., 58, 69, 71.

33. Ibid., 71, 75–76, 84. For Gash, this brewing political war was painfully familiar. With the Confederate war effort seemingly beyond redemption in 1864, the North Carolina legislature debated whether to act on the peace movement's calls for separate state action to stop the fighting and save men's lives. The session

was held in secret, but it was widely stated that two Conservatives, Zebulon Vance and William Graham, both former Unionist Whigs, defeated the measure. For Gash, history seemed to be repeating itself. North Carolina's fate rested once more in the hands of actors increasingly out of touch with what he felt were the interests of the people. Vance and the war Conservatives held tight to the Confederacy and determined to fight into 1865, past what Gash felt was any real possibility of success.

34. Marion Roberts to Thaddeus Stevens, May 15, 1866, in James A. Padgett, ed., "Letters to Thaddeus Stevens, Part I," *North Carolina Historical Review* 18, no. 1 (January 1941): 190; P. E. Murphy to Clinton A. Cilley, May 28, 1866, *Records of the Field Offices for the State of North Carolina, Bureau of Refugees, Freedmen, and Abandoned Lands, 1865-1872* (Washington, DC: National Archives and Records Administration, 2004), reel 4.

35. A. C. Bryan to John C. Robinson, July 10, 1866, Governor Worth's Letter Books, NCOAH.

36. Francis Wolcott to John C. Robinson, August 16, 1866, Governor Worth's Letter Books, NCOAH; William T. Auman, "The Heroes of America in Civil War North Carolina," *North Carolina Historical Review* 58, no. 4 (October 1981): 329–31, 336–38. Auman speculates that the Heroes of America may have already been active in Wilkes County as early as January 1862, but he concludes that they definitely operated in the mountain counties in 1864. Furthermore, he suggests that the Heroes of America became a sort of umbrella organization for dissenters across the state. Wartime rumors suggested that leading mountain Unionists such as Tod Caldwell and George W. Logan used the Heroes to further the peace movement in Burke and Rutherford counties and that the organization was active in Henderson County. See Auman, "The Heroes of America," 333, 342, 345, 347–48. Kenneth W. Noe's study of the Red Strings in southwest Virginia suggests that the Heroes were active in that section of Appalachia in 1863 and became a major concern for the Confederate government, who sent detectives there in 1864. See Kenneth W. Noe, "Red String Scare: Civil War Southwest Virginia and the Heroes of America," *North Carolina Historical Review* 69, no. 3 (July 1992): 316–19.

37. Worth to W. P. Caldwell, September 7, 1866, Governor Worth's Letter Books, NCOAH.

38. Augustus Merrimon to Jonathan Worth, June 7, 1866, Governor Worth's Letter Books, NCOAH; A. C. Bryan to John C. Robinson, July 10, 1866, Governor Worth's Letter Books, NCOAH; William Mason to Jonathan Worth, August 17, 1866, Governor Worth's Letter Books, NCOAH. This problem was not limited to the northwest, either. In Transylvania County, J. M. Hamlen sought Worth's permission to form a Conservative militia unit. Unionists and anti-Confederates dominated the local militia, and Hamlen felt that "the conduct of these men (one excepted) is so far from being commendable, that in forcing men of Southern Chivalry, though of undoubtable authority, to subject themselves to their authority, will result in serious consequences." See J. M. Hamlen to Jonathan Worth, February 26, 1867, Jonathan Worth Papers, Private Collection 49, NCOAH.

39. *Hendersonville (NC) Pioneer,* September 12, 1866, 3.

40. *Hendersonville (NC) Pioneer,* June 27, 1866, 2 (italics in the original).

41. Augustus Merrimon to George W. Swepson, July 7, 1866, George W. Swepson Papers, NCOAH.

42. *Hendersonville (NC) Pioneer,* October 3, 1866, 2. Southerners often referred to the Fourteenth Amendment as the "Howard Amendment" because of Michigan senator Jacob Howard's role in guiding it through the U.S. Senate.

43. Olsen and McGrew, "Prelude to Reconstruction, Part II," 238.

44. *Hendersonville (NC) Pioneer,* December 18, 1866, 1. The idea of a separate mountain state was not new. During the secession crisis, the opponents of immediate secession discussed the idea of a central Confederacy or even a state comprising the mountain sections of East Tennessee and western North Carolina. Neither proposal went beyond the discussion phase. See Inscoe, *Mountain Masters,* 235–36. Years later, however, a mass meeting in Henderson County responded positively to a proposal that essentially called for western North Carolina to secede from the rest of the state. The key issue was the restoration of the Union. "Twenty months have elapsed since the surrender," the assembly resolved, "and every effort at restoration to the Union has been defeated, mainly through the votes and rebellious temper of the Eastern portion of the State." As a result of "the uniform course and late message of our Governor, and the spirit and actions of the State Legislature, we have lost all hope of being restored to our proper relations in the United States Government." Desperate times, it seems, required desperate measures.

45. Olsen and McGrew, "Prelude to Reconstruction, Part II," 221.

46. Ibid., 235.

47. Olsen and McGrew, "Prelude to Reconstruction, Part III," 358.

48. Ibid., 360–62.

49. Phineas Horton to E. W. Jones, December 8, 1866, Edmund Walter Jones Papers, SHC.

Chapter 5

"Resistless Uprising"?

Thomas Dixon's Uncle and Western North Carolinians as Klansmen and Statesmen

Paul Yandle

It is well known that author Thomas Dixon dedicated *The Clansman,* his fictionalized account of Klan activity on the North Carolina–South Carolina border, to Leroy Mangum McAfee. McAfee was from Cleveland County, Dixon's home county, just east of North Carolina's Blue Ridge and just north of the South Carolina line. During the Klan's heyday in the early 1870s, Cleveland County had between six hundred and eight hundred members in the organization, and McAfee was one of the county's Klan leaders.[1] "A Scotch-Irish leader of the South . . . Grand Titan of the Invisible Empire Ku Klux Klan," Dixon calls McAfee on a leaf following the novel's title page. Ben Cameron, the hero of *The Clansman,* is based in part on McAfee.[2]

McAfee's largest claim to fame today comes from Dixon's brief description of him, noted in several histories of the Reconstruction period. His post–Civil War career has remained somewhat shadowy, in part because of the secrecy of his Klan activities and in part because he died before he turned thirty.[3] Nonetheless, fictionalizations of McAfee and his Klan coconspirators were once part of the prevalent view of Reconstruction in the early twentieth century because of the popularity of *The Clansman* and another Dixon novel, *The Leopard's Spots.* The two novels are the main sources for the 1915 movie *The Birth of a Nation,* and they present Cleveland County and the rest of western North Carolina as having a decisive role in ending Reconstruction in the Carolinas. In both novels Dixon tries to define upcountry and mountain identity through the Klan. *The Leopard's Spots* is set in Hambright, North Carolina, "nestled in the foothills of the Blue Ridge under the shadow of King's Mountain."[4] Most of the action in *The Clansman* takes place in fictitious Piedmont, South Carolina, which he places just south of the state border, twelve miles from Hambright.[5] *The Leopard's Spots* describes the Klan as "a spontaneous and resistless uprising of clansmen of highland origin living along the Appalachian Mountains and foothills of the South."[6] Both *The Clansman* and *The Leopard's Spots* reveal that to Dixon the main preservers of American civilization during Reconstruction came from the hills, not the piney woods or the flat, sandier tidewater soil usually associated with the plantation South.[7] According to Dixon, upcountry Carolinians tapped into their highland origins to come up with the Klan as a vigilante solution to "negro rule." In Dixon's novels, the hills produced people like his uncle, who were uniquely qualified by their heritage to put a stop to Reconstruction through Klan violence.

Did McAfee and other western North Carolinians really see the Klan as the primary means of overthrowing Reconstruction, or was it simply one of many tools upon which they relied? Scholars have alluded to McAfee's presence in the Klan as well as his work in North Carolina's 1870–1871 legislature, which impeached and removed from office Republican governor William W. Holden and set the stage for the demise of Reconstruction in North Carolina. Few, however, have done more than lightly touch upon the activities of McAfee and other western North Carolinians after Holden's removal. A look at the events that followed Holden's loss of the governorship reveals that the federal government—and many North Carolinians—tried to hold McAfee and other Klansmen in the General Assembly to account for the very Klan activities that Dixon's novels later distorted and glorified. Western North Carolina did have a major role in overthrowing Reconstruction, but the Klan constituted only a portion of that role. After the Klan rode, North Carolina's mountain and hill counties still had to help establish North Carolina as part of the post-Reconstruction "solid South" through the activities of McAfee and other western politicians in Raleigh, North Carolina's capital. Far from breezing back into control with a "resistless uprising," McAfee and other Klansmen became the focus of efforts against the Klan on the part of the federal government as well as McAfee's own colleagues in the General Assembly. In the legislature, former Klan leaders fought for legitimacy even as they fought for the agenda that would undo Reconstruction on a long-term basis. Both fights continued after Holden was gone and the Klan was largely shut down. The most important work that western North Carolinians did to end Reconstruction was performed not in hill-country raids but in North Carolina's statehouse.

McAfee and his generation of upcountry Carolinians offer a good case study of politics and southern identity in the mountain South of the nineteenth century. Appalachian politics and identity have been treated in a growing body of scholarship since the late 1970s, when Gordon McKinney first published his groundbreaking work, *Southern Mountain Republicans, 1865–1900*. Over the past decade, historians have begun to pay greater attention to the post–Civil War politics of the mountain South, building on McKinney's theme that party competition during Reconstruction made politics during the period quite contentious in the mountains.[8] In North Carolina, hill and mountain-county politicians such as McAfee fought Reconstruction bitterly at the state level. North Carolina's Conservative Democrats looked to western North Carolina to fight the Republican Party because, in the minds of Conservatives, Reconstruction was far from over in 1871.

Kicking Holden out of office, though a big step, was only the first of many. Holden's removal came as a consequence of a series of events in North Carolina in 1870, which was a particularly tumultuous election year. Holden raised a militia in response to Klan violence in several counties in the eastern and western piedmont, including Cleveland County and Gaston County, Cleveland's neighbor to the east and the home of King's Mountain. Holden's actions against the Klan helped lead to the election of a legislature controlled by Conservative Democrats, the impeachment of Holden in December 1870, and his removal from office in 1871—events fictionalized in *The Leopard's Spots*. McAfee, then a lawyer in his twenties, was among the new legislators who voted to impeach Holden.[9]

Klan activity in North Carolina, as anywhere else, is hard to pinpoint because of the organization's secrecy and the fact that victims and members were often afraid to reveal its activities.[10] The best comprehensive review of Klan activity in the late 1860s and early 1870s is still Allen Trelease's exhaustive study *White Terror*. According to Trelease, "outbreaks" of Klan violence began in late 1868 or early 1869. The first focal point of activity was in coastal plain counties. There was also an early burst of activity in piedmont Moore County. However, the worst pockets of activity were in the north-central piedmont and included Caswell County, where the worst violence in the state took place. Another bad pocket included four contiguous counties in the southwestern piedmont: Gaston, Cleveland, Rutherford, and Lincoln. In Caswell, membership in the county's two white supremacist vigilante organizations probably numbered more than 700 out of a total population of between 16,000 and 17,000. Rutherford County, on the edge of the Blue Ridge, had a total Klan membership of about 300 out of a population of just over 13,121.[11]

Activities of the Klan included arson, beatings, shootings, drowning, hangings, and mutilations. Of course, Klan members often ended up invading victims' homes in order to find them. Sometimes the Klan doubtless acted from pure racism, punishing African Americans for "impudence" or other perceived challenges to race relations. Most victims seem to have been Republicans, however, and it is clear that Klan leadership wanted to use the Klan for political purposes, though they may have lost some control of their local organizations as they grew. According to one scholar, between the fall of 1868 and the middle of 1870 there were "hundreds" of Klan attacks and at least twenty-five victims were killed in several North Carolina counties.[12]

There is probably no accurate number to give for Klan attacks, but the violence celebrated and sanitized by Dixon is paltry compared with what took place in the hill counties on the North Carolina–South Carolina border in the late 1860s and early 1870s.[13] From mountainous Polk and Rutherford counties east into Cleveland and Gaston counties in the western piedmont, the Klan whipped, slashed, destroyed, and killed, for reasons including influencing political contests and defending illegal distilling.[14] The four counties contained only part of a larger Klan network that spread into South Carolina. There, Spartanburg, Union, and York counties hugged the southern borders of North Carolina counties Polk, Rutherford, Cleveland, and Gaston. These seven counties were part of an area that had been tied together economically for decades before the Civil War, and several efforts came to the fore after the war to improve rail connections in or near them. The improvement of existing transportation networks after the war helped create an interstate corridor of violence there during Reconstruction.[15]

Klan membership grew in these border counties in the late 1860s. Upcountry South Carolinians sought out North Carolinians to help them get rid of "negro rule" in their own state, and South Carolinians reciprocated by participating in raids in upcountry North Carolina.[16] Klan activity became intense in South Carolina after 1869, when Republican governor Robert Scott approved state legislation allowing African Americans to serve in integrated militias. Because most South Carolina whites did not want to serve with African Americans, many militia units were made up of African American enlisted men who usually served under white officers. Incensed whites who had fought for the Confederacy tried to form units made up entirely of whites, but the state did not accept them. Klansmen reacted with a flurry of violence in 1870 and 1871. Klan activity peaked just before South Carolina's state election of October 1870, and the worst of the violence took place in March 1871.[17]

Klan activity saw similar peaks in North Carolina. In December 1870, just after the election in that state, it was reported from Cleveland County "that the Ku Klux outlaws are still riding every night." Some mountain whites condemned Klan activity. The Republican *Rutherford (NC) Star* reported that in early December 1870, Cleveland's Klan rode several nights in a row "committing numerous outrages" just east of the Blue Ridge. At the time, McAfee was recognized as a political figure as well as a Klan member, having just been sent to the session of the state house of representatives that voted to impeach William Holden. The *Star* complained that McAfee and G. M. Whiteside, the state senator who represented Cleveland, Rutherford, and Polk counties, were at least indirectly complicit in the Klan activities that plagued the area. "If you do not belong to the Kuklux organization yourselves, you certainly have some influence over them, and it is well known, that neither of you have ever made any attempt publicly to put a stop to their outrageous career," the paper said.[18]

As the General Assembly prepared to remove Holden from office in early 1871, other North Carolinians presented testimony about their experiences with Klan violence to a U.S. Senate committee formed to investigate the unrest. That panel's findings led to the formation of a new committee that began a wider investigation of Klan activity in the South. The Joint Select Committee to Inquire into the Conditions of Affairs in the Late Insurrectionary States began questioning additional people about Klan activity in North Carolina on June 5, 1871, in Washington, DC. A day later, the committee began taking testimony about activity in South Carolina. Later that summer three committee members traveled to South Carolina to hear testimony.[19]

Legislation added weight to the hearings. Using two of three enforcement acts passed after 1869, the federal government was able to prosecute alleged Klan members in North Carolina, South Carolina, and other states for violating federal law. North Carolina witnessed widespread arrests and federal trials of suspected Klansmen in Raleigh. Federal efforts helped curb Klan activity in North Carolina and other southern states rife with Klan activity. Scholars have debated the effectiveness of federal intervention, but if nothing else Congress did leave behind a lengthy published record of Klan activity in the former Confederacy.[20] The Select Committee gave its report on March 10, 1871, and a year later the Joint Committee published the testimony it had taken. By then it had already become apparent to many Americans just how bad the violence was in portions of the Carolinas and other areas of the South.[21]

McAfee's role with the Klan in the early 1870s is hard to discern, in part because he was never brought to account for it. As the year progressed, Klan leaders were becoming increasingly circumspect about their involvement with the organization. Plato Durham, a politician and journalist from Shelby in Cleveland County, was a Klan member along with McAfee, and he appears to have taken over leadership of the Cleveland County Klan from McAfee in 1871.[22] When forced to account for the Cleveland County Klan's actions before the Joint Committee, Durham suggested that the Klan acted merely in self-defense. According to Durham, Shelby's "Invisible Empire" council met "in January or February, when we were expecting a negro insurrection in South Carolina."[23] The "insurrection" apparently referred to the rumors that militias were going to cause trouble in York and Chester counties.[24] Durham explained that "not more than four months ago the counties of Gaston, Rutherford, and Cleveland, on the southern border of North Carolina, were expecting a raid from the negroes of South Carolina. We were armed here for three or four days. There was an insurrection in the counties of York, Chester, and the border of Union, in the State of South Carolina; and we expected at that time that the trouble would extend into our State. Our towns were guarded night and day. The people of the country were making ready to defend themselves as possible."[25] Durham, speaking only months after the main violence took place, tried to cover it up because he was afraid of arrest. His fear points to an important aspect of western North Carolina's Reconstruction history: in 1871 the federal government presented a tangible challenge to many western North Carolinians' ideas of states' rights as it pursued Klan suspects for crimes committed in North and South Carolina.[26]

The state border itself provided a reason for the large amount of Klan activity in border counties. Because murder cases and property crimes were tried at the state level, the border provided an easy escape for people who wanted to go beyond the reach of governments still under Republican influence in those two states in the early 1870s. Extradition often proved difficult. For a governor to get a resident of his state sent home from out of state to face charges required cooperation not only with the governor of that state but also among deputies and officers of both states. Even harder for a governor was getting a resident of another state brought in for trial.[27]

Much to the chagrin of Klan members, the intervention of the federal government put a damper on their ability to hide across state lines and behind sympathetic local officials. By the summer of 1871 federal officials had begun handing out indictments, and hundreds of suspected Klan members faced federal charges in several southern states, including North Carolina. As the Joint Select Committee continued its business, the federal government began trying Klan suspects in federal district court in Raleigh in September. Federal prosecutors focused on Randolph Shotwell, a Rutherford County Klan leader implicated in a June raid on white Republican James M. Justice.[28]

In Raleigh, the Conservative Democratic *Daily Sentinel* complained that the trials' location required defendants to travel from western North Carolina and that the trials had special juries selected separately from those chosen to serve the federal circuit court district where the western North Carolinian defendants lived. In one scene described by the *Daily Sentinel,* a crowd of about two hundred people was forced east for the trial. When defendants and witnesses from Cleveland and Rutherford counties stopped in Charlotte on their way to Raleigh, African Americans gathered at a railroad depot to see them off with "all kinds of jeers, taunts and insulting epithets." Gunfire was reported at the scene when one of the whites was "knocked down."[29] The *Sentinel* made the departures look as pathetic as possible, lamenting that "it was a sad and humiliating sight, to behold the aged mother following her son or sons (many of whom, no doubt, having been falsely accused,) to the distant bar of trial."[30]

By the fall of 1871 the stir had spread well into the mountains. Conservative Democratic reaction to the crackdown on the Klan made its way into the pages of the *Daily Sentinel* from the heart of the Blue Ridge. "We are having some very exciting times down in Madison county," one person wrote that year of the county, which sat on the Tennessee border. The writer complained that as whites were forced to flee Madison, one community there had to bribe its way out of trouble.[31] Mountain North Carolina was indeed the scene of a lot of exciting times. A man suspected of leading the Klan in Madison County was arrested in Tennessee, and six Klan members from nearby Yancey County were being held in Asheville, the largest North Carolina town west of the Blue Ridge. Another twenty or more from Madison County were taken east through Asheville on their way to Raleigh. In late November, Republican newspapers published renunciations of the Klan by residents of Madison and Yancey counties. Other mountain North Carolinians seem to have fled to avoid arrest. Madison County was reported to have lost a large part of its population, and the road through Madison County to the Tennessee border provided a way out for hoards of people from Madison and elsewhere. In December, according to correspondence published in the *Era,* a mob in Yancey County helped thwart an arrest of a man by a U.S. deputy marshal. Another report suggested that there were additional arrests of Madison county residents involved with the Klan. Federal marshals continued to arrest suspected Klan members in early 1872.[32]

It is hard to know what is true and what is false in partisan newspaper reports. It is easy to imagine, however, that a large number of western North Carolinians were rattled by the events of 1871. Klansmen were turning themselves in as far east as Lincoln County, which sat solidly in the western piedmont. Throughout the western piedmont and mountain counties, others renounced the Klan or trudged away from their homes to avoid arrest.[33] Despite having regained control of the state legislature by 1870, Conservative Democrats must have felt as if federal intervention had turned their world upside down. Western North Carolinians described their Klan activities to the federal government in terms that were as low-key and defensive as possible, or else they ran and hid to avoid talking to the federal government at all.[34]

As summer wore into fall, Lee McAfee joined Klan leaders keeping a low profile. In July, white Republican Klan victim James Justice testified to the Joint Select Committee that he had heard indirectly that McAfee was a Klan leader.[35] By the end of September federal officials had more to work with after one of the witnesses for the prosecution, South Carolinian Alfred Harris, testified directly that Lee McAfee had sworn him into the Klan in 1870. Harris and another member of the "Horse Creek Den," based in Spartanburg, South Carolina, testified that they had taken part in raids in North Carolina, including the raid on Justice. South Carolinians had helped the Rutherford County Klan go after Justice, and McAfee probably had a hand in at least some of the cooperation between the two states fictionalized later in *The Clansman*.[36]

Apparently McAfee and another Klan suspect, Frederick N. Strudwick, were hard to find by September. One rumor placed him in South Carolina. Strudwick, accused of leading the Klan farther east in Orange County, had avoided testifying before the Joint Select Committee for months. One newspaper reported in July that Strudwick received a summons from the committee and replied with a telegram to the committee saying he was sick and could not testify. By late September there was talk that Strudwick risked facing a contempt of Congress charge for his continued failure to testify.[37]

On September 20, a jury found Shotwell and seven other defendants guilty of conspiracy charges related to the attack on James Justice. All of the defendants received prison terms; Shotwell and another defendant, Amos Owens, were sentenced to six years hard labor and $5,000 fines. Two more trials followed in quick succession. A few days after Shotwell's conviction, three defendants pleaded guilty and two others received acquittals in a trial dealing with a May 1871 raid on Aaron Biggerstaff. Before the end of the month Amos Owens was found guilty of charges stemming from an earlier raid on Biggerstaff.[38]

During the second trial in which Owens was a defendant, McAfee was implicated when James Thompson, a resident of Rutherford County, testified that a Rutherford County Klan leader "said he got his authority from Cleveland, from McAfee." Thompson's testimony may not have been the most reliable, but it apparently gave prosecutors additional reason to want to deal with McAfee. In early November, McAfee was finally arrested, as was another prominent North Carolinian, Hamilton C. Jones. Jones and McAfee were both members of the General Assembly, scheduled to meet later that month. Jones was from Mecklenburg County, which sat on the South Carolina border just east of Gaston County. Jones's name, like McAfee's, had surfaced several times in federal testimony. He was charged with interfering with the right of African Americans to vote.[39] After his arrest McAfee was taken to Lincoln County, which shared a federal court district with Cleveland. The next day he appeared before a commissioner and had to post $5,000 bond. He apparently had lots of supporters. "During the trial a large crowd was present, and as soon as the Commissioner decided to bind Mr. McAfee over, they flocked to his side proffering their assistance to go on his bond," someone who was at the hearing reported.[40]

Fall 1871 was a stressful time in upcountry South Carolina as well. On October 12, President Grant commanded Klan members in several South Carolina counties "to retire peaceably to their homes"—a precursor under federal Klan legislation to the suspension of the writ of habeas corpus. That next move came on the 17th with a proclamation that affected nine counties. *The Clansman* presents Grant's suspension of habeas corpus and the arrest of the novel's hero, Ben Cameron, as preceding a second Klan ride to the rescue following an initial ride to disarm African Americans in South Carolina. The Klan, however, was in no position to ride to anyone's rescue in the Carolinas by late 1871. Federal action quickly broke up cooperation between North and South Carolina Klan organizations.[41]

Because North Carolinians elected legislators to serve for two sessions, the men preparing to sit in the 1871–1872 session of North Carolina's General Assembly had, with few exceptions, cast votes during Holden's impeachment and trial. By early November, however, McAfee and other Conservative Democratic lawmakers must have felt at least a bit on the defensive. By the time the General Assembly began its business in Raleigh, North Carolina's Klansmen hardly looked like conquering heroes as they turned themselves in, faced arrest, issued public renunciations of the organization, or fled the state. McAfee, Strudwick, and Jones would have to face colleagues who had their own questions about the three men's involvement in the Klan.

North Carolina had a Conservative Democratic majority in both houses and no more than a smattering of African American lawmakers.[42] Nonetheless, for a little while longer the Conservative Democratic legislature would have to fight Reconstruction at both the state and federal levels. It was still too early for North Carolina's Conservative Democrats to win a direct fight against the federal government.[43] This became clear early in the 1871–1872 session as it dealt with a series of incidents that centered on Cleveland County. During the crackdown on the Klan, several Cleveland County men found themselves facing federal arrest in connection with crimes committed in South Carolina. In early November 1871 Allen Bettis, a county official in Cleveland, was arrested in connection with a particularly brutal Klan raid in which Union League leader Tom Roundtree was shot and his throat slit by Klan members in late 1870. The killing had taken place in York County, South Carolina.[44] Apparently Bettis was a South Carolina resident when Roundtree was murdered, and he seems to have moved north of the border some time afterward. Nonetheless, Bettis was arrested in North Carolina. His arrest outraged Conservative Democrats, not only because of its interstate nature but also because the federal government had not suspended habeas corpus in Cleveland County or anywhere else in North Carolina. Adding to the anger of Conservative Democrats was a newspaper report from Shelby that a U.S. marshal shot a South Carolina man in Cleveland County.[45]

The arrests of Bettis and three other Cleveland County men further challenged any ideas held by Conservative Democrats that Klan crimes should be handled by state and local governments. Shortly after Bettis's arrest, Caldwell got a letter that appeared to have originated with Cleveland County residents, requesting him to demand Bettis's release. Lee McAfee himself went to Caldwell and spoke to him about the Bettis arrest. In the state senate, western piedmont and mountain Conservative Democrats tried to get Caldwell to challenge all four of the arrests, first with the governor of South Carolina and later with the federal government. Early in the Bettis controversy, Sen. William M. Robbins of western piedmont Rowan County reportedly complained of the Bettis arrest that "once the precedent is set, the whole field is thrown open for the exercise of despotic power. It was a melancholy fact, that all the states are fast becoming mere provinces." Robbins suggested that Caldwell should request that South Carolina's governor send "those who thus invaded it" to face trial in North Carolina.[46]

Conservatives were left unsatisfied. As Reconstruction historian Eric Foner observes, "The Ku Klux Klan Act pushed Republicans to the outer limits of constitutional change" because it allowed the federal government to charge citizens with federal crimes in acts of violence previously seen as the business of local governments. Caldwell's reply to the General Assembly on the Bettis matter suggests the new constitutional territory in which Conservative Democrats—and the rest of the nation—found themselves. "As it does not appear that the governor or other civil authorities of South Carolina had any thing to do with the arrest of said Bettis . . . but that it was done by the federal troops, I deemed it entirely useless to open any correspondence with the executive of that state upon the subject, as I feel confident that said official would not be inclined or disposed to take upon his state our cause of quarrel, if we have any, with the government of the United States," Caldwell's letter to the senate observed. Consistent with his letter, Caldwell contacted President Grant instead of South Carolina's governor.[47] Caldwell's letter and his failure to take the Bettis matter up with South Carolina cast doubt upon whether the matter could be solved at the state level.

The final word on the matter came from the outgoing U.S. attorney general, Amos Akerman, in a letter dated December 26. Akerman responded to Caldwell that the arrest of Bettis was indeed legal despite the fact that Bettis was apparently mistaken for a South Carolina resident. On the question of Bettis's residence relative to the confines of President Grant's suspension of habeas corpus, Akerman stated that the law under which Bettis was arrested was worded so that "the right to employ the military in making arrests is not limited to such district." "In the present case," Akerman observed, "the President being authorized to use the military for the suppression of the unlawful combination in South Carolina, a member of such a combination in that State is not protected from military arrest by getting over the State line."[48]

The whole matter showed how the constitutional ground was shifting beneath Klan suspects, who looked to the state border to protect them from imprisonment. More important, Conservative Democrats thought that the same shift was eroding the integrity of North Carolina. Many other whites in the state were pleased with the turn of events. The *New North State,* a Republican newspaper based in piedmont Greensboro, sided with the new constitutional state of things: "We had supposed it to be unnecessary, for the President of the United States, and those setting by his authority, to ask the consent of a State legislature before carrying into effect the statutes of the country," it concluded.[49] Despite the sarcasm seen in the *New North State*'s piece, Conservative Democrats were correct in assuming that such a situation would have been unheard of in peacetime before the Civil War.[50] With little recourse available from the federal government, Conservative Democrats sought victories at the state level.

Despite the demise of the Klan, North Carolina's Conservative Democratic press saw the western counties as having a very important role in Raleigh. Conservative Democrats working to disfranchise African Americans and force them out of political office often called upon whites in the western counties to step up and help their white counterparts in eastern counties, which had larger African American populations. In September 1871, an anonymous correspondent using the name "Caswell" wrote to the Conservative Democratic *Raleigh Daily Sentinel* that "We, who live in negro counties, must appeal to the white men of the west to save us, so far as they can, by electing judges and magistrates by the legislature." "Caswell" charged that an African American had come to the county from the North and was telling other African Americans to vote exclusively for African American candidates. "We cannot be governed by a set of ignorant negroes, who will levy all county taxes and pay none themselves," "Caswell" complained.[51] The correspondent looked to the west not for night riders but for legislators who would permanently snatch the white residents of eastern North Carolina out of the clutches of Reconstruction politicians.

The removal of Governor Holden from office demonstrated that political and constitutional victories were still possible at the state level, and it was statehouse victories that effectively ended Reconstruction in North Carolina. Part of the evidence for Conservative Democrats' strength in Raleigh could be seen in their ability to keep not only McAfee but also Jones and Strudwick in the General Assembly. At the same time that the Bettis matter occupied the General Assembly, major battles broke out over McAfee's and Strudwick's seats in the state house and Jones's seat in the state senate. Republicans, including African Americans, were unwilling to sit and watch accused Klansmen help write the state's laws without a fight. On the other hand, Conservative Democrats knew that their real power lay in Raleigh. They did not want to set the precedent of using the General Assembly as a forum to decide the fitness of Klan members to serve there. They also probably knew they had the numbers to win any battles over whether the seats could be challenged in the General Assembly. The struggle over the three men's seats typified the sectional battles over Reconstruction that coastal plain Conservative Democrats begged their counterparts in the western piedmont and mountain counties to help them wage. The greatest Conservative Democratic strength came from the western piedmont and mountain counties, and lawmakers from those counties figured prominently in the debate over whether to hear petitions calling for the investigation of the legislators or their removal from their respective houses.[52]

As part of Republican efforts against McAfee, Jones, and Strudwick, Republican newspapers published resolutions from partisan gatherings throughout western North Carolina calling for the three men's expulsion. James Justice, one of the victims of the violence that had brought Randolph Shotwell and Amos Owens to trial, joined a meeting in Hendersonville denouncing the legislators. Backed by the resolutions, Republicans in both houses made several efforts to have the three unseated or investigated. Despite the sentiments of at least some Republicans in the west, most of the efforts against McAfee, Strudwick, and Jones came from Republicans representing coastal plain counties, including New Hanover, which had a strong African American political base. A few days after the legislative session opened, George L. Mabson, an African American legislator from New Hanover, prompted debate when he presented a petition to the legislature from two residents of his home county requesting that McAfee, Jones, and Strudwick be expelled from the General Assembly.[53]

One mountain legislator heavily involved in the debate over the New Hanover petition was Edmund Jones, a Conservative Democrat from mountainous Caldwell County. Jones did not want the petition read and was able to get a roll call on the matter. James Justice, as one would expect, argued for the reading of the petition. Jones protested that it was inappropriate for petitioners to seek the removal of a lawmaker who did not represent their county. Nonetheless, the house voted to hear it.[54]

After the petition was read, speaker of the house James L. Robinson, a Conservative Democrat from North Carolina's mountain southwest, moved to reject it. Strudwick himself denounced the petition as full of lies and dared his accusers to face him in court. He, like Robinson and other Conservative Democrats, also noted (perhaps correctly) that the petition originated in Raleigh and had been spread to different areas of the state so that Republicans could endorse it and have it sent to the statehouse for partisan purposes. Samuel A. Ashe, a white member from New Hanover and one of the most prominent Conservative Democrats in the state, also spoke against the petition. It was rejected by a 56–35 vote.[55]

A day after the rejection of the New Hanover petition, the controversy continued when a house member from coastal plain Washington County asked the house to receive another petition. Again, Conservative Democratic house members were incensed. Justice spoke in favor of a reading as he had before, but the house rejected it in a roll-call vote. Edmund Jones continued his opposition, once more joining the vocal opponents of a reading. Another mountain-county legislator, Haywood County Conservative William P. Welch, went as far as arguing for the petition to be read and to hold the member who introduced it responsible for its contents.[56]

After house members rejected the first petition and refused to hear the second, the fight spread to the senate. Senator George W. Price, an African American whose district included New Hanover County, caused a furor when he brought a petition before that body calling for an investigation of "charges made against certain officers and members of this General

Assembly."[57] As the petition was being read, another senator objected and had the reading stopped. A lengthy debate followed that involved several senators. Price argued that the petitioners had a right to be heard; other senators replied that any charges leveled against legislators were a matter for the courts. One Conservative Democrat representing a western piedmont district stood out among his colleagues by arguing in favor of the petition's reading and criticizing the Klan. However, the senate voted 19–18 against its reading.[58]

The vote was close; after it, Jones, like Strudwick before him, gave a vigorous defense of himself before his colleagues. Jones and other Conservative Democrats, however, behaved in a manner that suggested where the party line lay. Jones could have tied the tally, but he did not vote in the roll call. The day after the roll call, three Conservative Democratic senators who had voted in favor of a reading asked for their votes to be changed to "no." The *Senate Journal* for that session shows the three changed votes as part of the roll call without mentioning the original 19–18 vote.[59]

The fight did not end with Mabson and Price. In early December James M. Justice himself introduced a resolution on the house floor calling for an investigation "against Lee M. McAfee and certain other officers and members of the General Assembly."[60] A motion to table an amended version of the Justice resolution passed by one vote. The *House Journal* records McAfee's vote against tabling the resolution but fails to show that McAfee held his vote until after the passage of the motion to table was assured.[61] McAfee, like Strudwick and Jones, gave a speech defending himself. A Conservative Democratic report suggests that McAfee stated he was not afraid of an investigation, but the *New North State* reported that McAfee never denied breaking a federal law or involvement in the Klan.[62]

Republicans refused to give up. The next day Justice brought before the house a petition originating in Rutherford County that dealt with the Klan membership of house and senate members, and it was rejected 61–42.[63] The day after Justice's attempt, George L. Mabson introduced yet another resolution calling for an investigation. "Petition after petition has come to us from the people, pointing out the guilty ones, as they suppose, but you refuse to hear them," Mabson insisted. "This action of the democratic party of this House will be ample proof before the people that guilt rests with some of us." Mabson read a letter from an Orange County man claiming that Strudwick was among a group of men who had invaded his house in 1869. As the *Era* reported, the resolution was sent to the judiciary committee, which reported on it several days later.[64] Thomas A. Sykes, an African American representative from the coastal plain, argued that "the time has, in my mind, fully arrived when the dignity of North Carolina should be vindicated, and bands of midnight assassins, who do all in their power to make law-abiding citizens afraid to lie down in their own dwellings, and all other fit subjects for a dungeon or prison house, should be tried, if suspected, convicted if guilty, and punished to the fullest extent of the law."[65] Despite Sykes's speech, senators tabled the resolution by a 58–40 vote.[66]

McAfee, Jones, and Strudwick remained in the 1871–1872 General Assembly, but lawmakers faced one more major battle that session. McAfee and other Conservative Democrats saw North Carolina's Reconstruction constitution as the source of many of the state's problems. Among North Carolinians, much of the Klan violence and the Conservative Democratic reaction to federal arrests and trials centered on the nature of the U.S. Constitution and of North Carolina's state constitution, which Conservatives felt had been forced upon them.[67] Conservative Democrats in the legislature had long known that if they wanted the party to regain control of state and local governments, they had to change the state constitution, which had been rewritten in 1868 during the height of Congressional Reconstruction. The 1868 constitution allowed universal manhood suffrage and structured county governments in a manner that made them more accountable to voters then they had been before the war. It also added two justices to the state supreme court.[68] The Conservative Democratic victory in the petition fight showed that they had the power to rewrite the constitution if the federal government did not interfere. During the petition debates one North Carolinian argued in a Wilmington newspaper that the success or failure of the debates was tied to a Conservative-sponsored bill to amend the state's Reconstruction constitution. The letter-writer, identified as "Republican," explained that Conservative Democrats were determined to retain as much influence as they could in the state government as the 1872 election approached.[69]

"Republican" had a point. The General Assembly had begun discussing constitutional change during the previous session, and Conservative Democrats had worked hard throughout 1871 to change the state's 1868 constitution.[70] Among the first tasks of the 1870–1871 session was pushing through a statewide referendum on a convention to be held in August 1871. In Cleveland County, Conservative Democrats worked hard to get support for the convention during the height of Klan activity in North and South Carolina. The *Rutherford Star* even speculated that the Klan was trying to intimidate potential voters into supporting a convention, specifically blaming Lee McAfee and G. M. Whiteside, the senator representing Cleveland, Rutherford, and Polk counties, for tacitly approving of Klan activities in order to affect the vote in the convention referendum.[71] Despite their unwavering efforts, Conservative Democrats were unsuccessful. While western North Carolinians in counties with a minority of African American voters were largely in favor of the convention, it was voted down statewide.[72]

After voters went against the convention in August, Conservative Democratic legislators turned to their other option: using the legislature itself to amend the Constitution piece by piece. The work of writing the amendments was left to the 1871–1872 session. Without a convention, the party's executive committee was forced to specify an agenda for the constitution as it pushed for public support on the eve of the new session.[73] The party suggested a number of sweeping changes, including some proposed by Republicans. The amendments reflected Conservative Democrats' desire to change the structure of state government, get rid of offices held by Republicans, and lighten government expenditures. Proposed amendments included making the legislature biennial and reducing the terms of the governor and several of his appointees to two years. Amid amendments proposed for the judiciary was one that would put the jurisdictions of many state courts under the control of the General Assembly and another that would cut the number of state supreme court justices. Perhaps most telling, the committee called for the replacement of the county government structure established by the 1868 constitution. Conservative Democrats wanted to give the General Assembly power to appoint county officers in order to stop voters in counties with large African American populations from choosing their own officials.[74]

On the first day of the 1871–1872 session, William Robbins, the western piedmont senator who later spoke against the Bettis arrest, introduced the legislation to amend the constitution.[75] McAfee was among those interested in stripping the power of the judiciary, members of which had written or concurred with decisions supporting the 1868 constitution. On January 5, some time after the legislation passed the senate and was sent to the house, a Conservative Democratic legislator proposed an amendment to cut the number of associate justices on the state supreme court from four to two, effective November 1876. The amendment was probably designed to weed out at least some of the Republican justices on the court. Perhaps in a bigger hurry to be done with them, McAfee suggested cutting the two positions as soon as the amendments were ratified. McAfee's timetable for eliminating the two justiceships was too speedy even for some Conservative Democrats, and his proposal failed.[76]

With Strudwick and McAfee among its supporters, the legislation passed toward the end of the session. It took the piedmont and the mountain counties to push it through. Notably, only twenty-six of the seventy-six house votes in favor of the constitution legislation came from coastal-plain legislators.[77] Other moves by the legislature that session gave evidence that Conservative Democrats were edging Republicans out of power. To the chagrin of Republicans, the Assembly repealed a law making intimidations under disguise illegal—a move probably designed to protect accused Klansmen in the piedmont from prosecution.[78] With legislation supported mainly west of the coastal plain, the General Assembly also reapportioned the state senate districts in a manner that would minimize the number of Republican districts relative to the number of Republican voters in the state, thus giving Conservative Democrats a further advantage in the election of 1872.[79]

On May 27, 1872, not long after the legislative session ended, McAfee wrote Tod Caldwell from Galveston, Texas, to resign his house seat. McAfee seems to have had plans to move to Raleigh permanently in late 1871. However, poor health may have forced him to a warmer climate. By late January 1872, McAfee was regularly missing committee work.[80] He was probably not healthy enough to work full steam with either the state government or the Klan. "We regret to learn that the Colonel intends moving out of the State," the Conservative *Wilmington Journal* offered as it announced his resignation. However, not everyone was sad to see McAfee go. The Greensboro *New North State* exulted, "Col. Lee M. McAfee, the notorious Kuklux of Cleveland county, has gone to Texas. All right!"[81]

Strudwick, McAfee and Jones all escaped trial and investigation in the General Assembly.[82] The three seemed to end up with their reputations intact—at least among Conservative Democrats. The Conservative press stood by Strudwick as it did McAfee. "The whole State owes a debt of gratitude to Mr. STRUDWICK for the bold and manly part he took in bringing the traitor Holden to justice," suggested the *Wilmington Journal* in the summer of 1872.[83] McAfee, of course, ended up being fictionalized in *The*

Clansman. However, he did not live to see the final result of any of his work; in 1873 he succumbed to tuberculosis.[84]

McAfee helped set the stage for post-Reconstruction North Carolina, but others had to follow up on the work that Conservative Democrats had begun in 1871. Because constitutional amendments had to be approved by two concurrent sessions, the amendments were forwarded to the 1872–1873 General Assembly. Moreover, because enough Republicans remained in the legislature to fight sweeping change, the amendments that actually passed during the 1871–1872 session did not go as far as Conservatives Democrats wanted.[85] After 1872, however, Conservative Democrats became less worried about federal intervention as the federal government began increasingly to back away from intervening in state matters.[86] In the summer of 1873, the Raleigh *Era* reported that the federal government was moving away from making Klan prosecutions and toward pardoning Shotwell and the other men imprisoned for Klan activity. Shotwell was pardoned by the end of that summer. A year later, Ulysses S. Grant's support for Arkansas governor Elisha Baxter, deserted by Arkansas Republicans after a highly disputed gubernatorial election, was taken as a further signal that the federal government was retreating from Reconstruction. Between 1873 and 1876, the U.S. Supreme Court began moving toward an interpretation of the Fourteenth Amendment that lessened the ability of the federal government to intervene when African Americans' rights were threatened by individuals.[87] In this atmosphere, Conservative Democrats won a state election in 1874 and were able to push again for a constitutional convention that made more drastic changes in state governance. The convention, held in 1875, finally paved the way for the state to put county governments under the control of the legislature and effectively ended African American participation in government at the county level. It made the cuts in the supreme court proposed in 1872, though they would not be effective for a few more years. The convention also wrote an amendment requiring segregated schools.[88]

The Republican Party could not remain effective much longer in North Carolina, despite its continued efforts to retain a vestige of Reconstruction in the state.[89] As North Carolina Conservative Democrats knew, white Republicans also saw African Americans' role in the emerging New South chiefly as that of laborers; and Conservative Democrats, on the verge of officially dropping "Conservative" from their party name, knew that Republicans would not stand by African Americans if it meant losing votes. In 1874 Conservative Democrats in North Carolina were able to back the state's white Republicans against the wall by tying them to the supplemental Civil Rights Bill under consideration in Washington, DC.[90] Two years later, Democrats elected Zebulon Vance to the governorship, and the 1876–1877 General Assembly completed the work of dismantling Reconstruction in North Carolina.[91]

Decades later the statehouse maneuvers of the 1870s may not have provided Lee McAfee's nephew with stories as exciting as horse rides to victory, but they were quite important in real life. In the early 1870s the end of Reconstruction did not seem a foregone conclusion to North Carolinians of any political leanings. Western North Carolinians did not organize the Klan with the full support of the state's white population, nor did they accomplish the end of Reconstruction in a matter of days. Instead, western North Carolinians who opposed Reconstruction dueled verbally with white Republicans and African Americans for years after the Klan's violence waned. The ability of Conservative Democrats to keep McAfee, Strudwick, and Jones in the General Assembly during the height of the federal government's crackdown on the Klan showed that in North Carolina, state politics were as strong a factor as both the Klan and the federal government in determining the course of Reconstruction. The Klan played a strong and violent supporting role in ending "negro rule," and the disfranchisement of African Americans was backed by the threat of vigilante violence for decades. But unlike the state government, the Klan did not hold the power to enact statutes and write constitutional amendments. In western North Carolina, the ideological progenitors of Thomas Dixon helped Democrats win the fight for white supremacy not by coming together to ride harmlessly and triumphantly to the rescue, but by wreaking havoc in the upcountry and the mountains at the same time that McAfee and other white supremacists came to the legislature to finish the Klan's work.[92]

Notes

1. Allen W. Trelease, *White Terror: The Ku Klux Conspiracy and Southern Reconstruction* (New York: Harper & Row, 1971), 340.

2. Eric Foner, *Reconstruction: America's Unfinished Revolution, 1863–1877* (New York: Harper & Row, 1988), 433; Trelease, *White Terror,* 338.

3. Trelease, *White Terror,* 338, 341, gives information about McAfee's Klan activities.

4. Thomas Dixon Jr., *The Leopard's Spots: A Romance of the White Man's Burden—1865–1900* (New York: Doubleday, Page & Company, 1905), 5.

5. Thomas Dixon Jr., *The Clansman: An Historical Romance of the Ku Klux Klan* (New York: Grosset & Dunlap, 1905), 365.

6. Dixon, *The Leopard's Spots,* 151.

7. Introduction to Michele K. Gillespie and Randal L. Hall, eds., *Thomas Dixon Jr. and the Birth of Modern America* (Baton Rouge: Louisiana State University Press, 2006), 7; Dixon, *The Leopard's Spots,* 5; Dixon, *The Clansman,* 187–88.

8. For some of the more groundbreaking works, see Gordon B. McKinney, *Southern Mountain Republicans, 1865–1900: Politics and the Appalachian Community* (Knoxville: University of Tennessee Press, 1998); Martin Crawford, *Ashe County's Civil War: Community and Society in the Appalachian South* (Charlottesville: University Press of Virginia, 2001); Jonathan Dean Sarris, *A Separate Civil War: Communities in Conflict in the Mountain South* (Charlottesville: University of Virginia Press, 2006); Richard D. Starnes, "'The Stirring Strains of Dixie': The Civil War and Southern Identity in Haywood County, North Carolina," *North Carolina Historical Review* 74 (July 1997): 237–59.

9. William C. Harris, *William Woods Holden: Firebrand of North Carolina Politics* (Baton Rouge: Louisiana State University Press, 1987), 283–84, 287–88, 290; Trelease, *White Terror,* 224.

10. Trelease, *White Terror,* 204.

11. Ibid., 189–91, 192–93, 197, 337–38, 201, 340 (quote on 191); Ninth Census (1870), vol. 1, *The Statistics of the Population of the United States, Embracing the Tables of Race, Nationality, Sex, Selected Ages, and Occupations* (Washington, DC: Government Printing Office, 1872), 52–53, table II; *A Compendium of the Ninth Census (June 1, 1870), Compiled Pursuant to a Concurrent Resolution of Congress, and Under the Direction of the Secretary of the Interior, by Francis A. Walker, Superintendent of Census* (Washington, DC: Government Printing Office, 1872), 78, table VIII. Census data from University of Virginia Library Historical Census Browser, http://fisher.lib.virginia.edu/collections/stats/histcensus/php/county.php (accessed April 17, 2009). Another scholar notes violence in Alamance County as early as 1868. See Scott Reynolds Nelson, *Iron Confederacies: Southern Railways, Klan Violence, and Reconstruction* (Chapel Hill: University of North Carolina Press, 1999), 99.

12. U.S. Congress, Senate, *Select Committee to Investigate Alleged Outrages in the Southern States: Report and Testimony,* 42nd Cong., 1st sess., 1871, S. Rept. 1, serial 1468, xix–xxi, xxii; Otto H. Olsen, *Carpetbagger's Crusade: The Life of Albion Winegar Tourgee* (Baltimore: Johns Hopkins University Press, 1965), 158 (including quote); Trelease, *White Terror,* 199–200; Nelson, *Iron Confederacies,* 97, 126; Otto H. Olsen, "North Carolina: An Incongruous Presence," in Otto H. Olsen, ed., *Reconstruction and Redemption in the South* (Baton Rouge: Louisiana State University Press, 1980), 179.

13. 42nd Cong., 1st sess., 1871, S. Rept. 1, serial 1468, xix.

14. For recent treatments of the varied intentions of the Klan in North Carolina see Nelson, *Iron Confederacies;* Bruce E. Stewart, "'When Darkness Reigns Then

Is the Hour to Strike': Moonshining, Federal Liquor Taxation, and Klan Violence in Western North Carolina, 1868–1872," *North Carolina Historical Review* 80 (October 2003): 453–74. See also Trelease, *White Terror,* xlvii–xlviii.

15. "Mountain Community and Commerce," chapter 2 in John C. Inscoe, *Mountain Masters: Slavery and the Sectional Crisis in Western North Carolina* (Knoxville: University of Tennessee Press, 1989), 25–58; Nelson, *Iron Confederacies,* 117–18, 145–46; Gordon B. McKinney, *Zeb Vance: North Carolina's Civil War Governor and Gilded Age Political Leader* (Chapel Hill: University of North Carolina Press, 2004), 333–34, 343.

16. Nelson, *Iron Confederacies,* 124; Trelease, *White Terror,* 339–40; Stewart, "'When Darkness Reigns,'" 470–71; William Donaldson Cotton, "Appalachian North Carolina: A Political Study, 1860–1889" (PhD diss., University of North Carolina, 1954), 212.

17. Nelson, *Iron Confederacies,* 126; Richard Zuczek, *State of Rebellion: Reconstruction in South Carolina* (Columbia: University of South Carolina Press, 1996), 74; Francis Butler Simkins and Robert Hilliard Woody, *South Carolina during Reconstruction* (Chapel Hill: University of North Carolina Press, 1932), 457.

18. *Rutherford (NC) Star,* December 10, 1870 (including quotes), December 17, 1870.

19. Trelease, *White Terror,* 392.

20. Foner, *Reconstruction,* 454, 457–59; Trelease, *White Terror,* 344–45, 385–87, 418; Cotton, "Appalachian North Carolina," 235–36; Lou Falkner Williams, *The Great South Carolina Ku Klux Klan Trials, 1871–1872* (Athens: University of Georgia Press, 1996), 60; Zuczek, *State of Rebellion,* 118.

21. 42nd Cong., 1st sess., 1871, S. Rept. 1, serial 1468, xxxiii–xxxiv.

22. James M. Justice, testimony in U.S. Congress, House, *Testimony Taken by the Joint Select Committee to Inquire into the Condition of Affairs in the Late Insurrectionary States,* 42nd Cong., 2nd sess., 1872, H. Rept. 22, pt. 2, serial 1530, 144; Trelease, *White Terror,* 338, 341.

23. Plato Durham, testimony in 42nd Cong., 2nd sess., 1872, H. Rept. 22, pt. 2, serial 1530, 304, 322–23, 329–30 (quote from 329).

24. Nelson, *Iron Confederacies,* 126–29; David S. Russell, testimony in 42nd Cong., 2nd sess., 1872, H. Rept. 22, pt. 5, serial 1533, 1291.

25. Durham, testimony in 42nd Cong., 2nd sess., 1872, H. Rept. 22, pt. 2, serial 1530, 312.

26. Paul D. Escott, *Many Excellent People: Power and Privilege in North Carolina, 1850–1900* (Chapel Hill: University of North Carolina Press), 164.

27. David R. Duncan, testimony in 42nd Cong., 2nd sess., 1872, H. Rept. 22, pt. 4, serial 1532, 877–79. In recent years, scholarship has focused on the impact of borders on residents who live near them. See Edward L. Ayers, *In the Presence of Mine Enemies: War in the Heart of America, 1859–1863* (New York: W.W. Norton, 2003). James H. Powe to Tod R. Caldwell, June 2, 1872, in Tod R. Caldwell Governor's Papers, North Carolina Division of Archives and History, provides an

example of the problems presented with extradition in an episode involving something as simple as a stolen mule. A more famous example is Tod Caldwell's unsuccessful attempts to get railroad swindler Milton Littlefield returned to North Carolina from Florida to face charges.

28. Foner, *Reconstruction,* 457; Trelease, *White Terror,* 342–44, 392, 395.

29. *Raleigh (NC) Daily Sentinel,* September 12, 1871, September 13, 1871 (including quote), September 15, 1871, September 22, 1871.

30. *Raleigh (NC) Daily Sentinel,* September 22, 1871.

31. A. to "Mr. Editor," n.d. in *Asheville North Carolina Citizen,* n.d., reprinted in *Raleigh (NC) Daily Sentinel,* November 6, 1871.

32. Cotton, "Appalachian North Carolina," 237, 237 n. 41; Trelease, *White Terror,* 348, 408. For a series of reports on Klan arrests and fleeing of Klan members, and letters to the editor including Klan renunciations, see *Raleigh (NC) Carolina Era,* November 16, 1871, December 7, 1871, and December 21, 1871; *Asheville (NC) Weekly Pioneer,* October 26, 1871, November 2, 1871, November 9, 1871, November 23, 1871, November 30, 1871, and December 14, 1871; Cotton, "Appalachian North Carolina," 237, 237 n. 41; *Raleigh (NC) Carolina Era,* May 16, 1872; and "Editorial Correspondence," May 7, 1872, in *Asheville (NC) Weekly Pioneer,* May 9, 1872.

33. Trelease, *White Terror,* 408; anonymous, "To the Local Editor of the Era," October 30, 1871, in *Raleigh (NC) Carolina Era,* November 9, 1871. The anonymous letter also appears under "Ku Klux in the Mountains," *Asheville (NC) Weekly Pioneer,* November 9, 1871.

34. Trelease, *White Terror,* 404, notes that the same rush out of the state happened in South Carolina with the York County Klan.

35. Justice, testimony in 42nd Cong., 2nd sess., 1872, H. Rept. 22, pt. 2, serial 1530, 144.

36. *Raleigh (NC) Daily Sentinel,* September 21, 1871; Alfred Harris, testimony in 42nd Cong., 2nd. sess., 1872, H. Rept. 22, pt. 2, serial 1530, 431, 433; Thomas Tate, testimony in 42nd Cong., 2nd. sess., 1872, H. Rept. 22, pt. 2, serial 1530, 435–36; Trelease, *White Terror* 344; Foner, *Reconstruction,* 433.

37. *Raleigh (NC) Carolina Era,* September 21, 1871; Durham, testimony in 42nd Cong., 2nd sess., 1872, H. Rept. 22, pt. 2, serial 1530, 324; *Rutherford (NC) Star,* July 22, 1871; *Raleigh (NC) Carolina Era,* September 21, 1871; *Raleigh (NC) Daily Sentinel,* September 26, 1871.

38. *Raleigh (NC) Daily Sentinel,* September 22, 1871, September 23, 1871; 42nd Cong., 2nd sess., 1872, H. Rept. 22, pt. 2, serial 1530, 453, 469–70; *Raleigh (NC) Daily Sentinel,* September 23, 1871, September 25, 1871, September 26, 1871, September 30, 1871; Trelease, *White Terror,* 341–42, 344–45; Cotton, "Appalachian North Carolina," 235–36.

39. *Raleigh (NC) Daily Sentinel,* September 27, 1871, October 3, 1871, November 4, 1871; John W. Thompson, testimony in 42nd Cong., 2nd sess., 1872, H. Rept. 22, pt. 2, serial 1530, 505–7 (quote from 506); Josiah Turner, testimony in

42nd Cong., 2nd sess., 1872, H. Rept. 22, pt. 2, serial 1530, 528. For references to McAfee see J. B. Eaves, testimony in 42nd Cong., 2nd sess., 1872, H. Rept. 22, pt. 2, serial 1530 174–75; John B. Harrell, testimony in 42nd Cong., 2nd sess., 1872, H. Rept. 22, pt. 2, serial 1530, 203; Durham, testimony in 42nd Cong., 2nd sess., 1872, H. Rept. 22, pt. 2, serial 1530, 324.

40. *Raleigh (NC) Daily Sentinel,* November 4, 1871, November 7, 1871; *Raleigh (NC) Carolina Era,* November 16, 1871 (including quote).

41. Trelease, *White Terror,* 401, 418; *Raleigh (NC) Daily Sentinel,* October 14, 1871 (including quote); "By the President of the United States of America: A Proclamation," published in *Raleigh (NC) Daily Sentinel,* November 8, 1871.

42. Elizabeth Balanoff, "Negro Legislators in the North Carolina General Assembly, July, 1868–February, 1872," *North Carolina Historical Review* 49 (January 1972): 55, appendix; Elaine Joan Nowaczyk, "The North Carolina Negro in Politics, 1865–1876" (master's thesis, University of North Carolina, 1957), 194, appendix F. Thanks are due to Steven Massengill and Earl Ijames of the North Carolina Division of Archives and History for providing access to the archives card-file collection and collection of information on African American legislators, which pointed me to these sources.

43. Escott, *Many Excellent People,* 164.

44. *Shelby Banner,* n.d., brief reprinted in *Raleigh (NC) Daily Sentinel,* November 7, 1871; Nelson, *Iron Confederacies,* 123–26; Trelease, *White Terror,* 363–64; 42nd Cong., 2nd sess., 1872, H. Rept. 22, pt. 5, serial 1533, 1544–52. Nelson places the killing in November 1870, slightly earlier than does the House Report.

45. David Schenck, testimony in 42nd Cong., 2nd sess., 1872, H. Rept. 22, pt. 2, serial 1530, 380–82, 413; *Shelby (NC) Banner,* n.d., quoted in *Raleigh (NC) Daily Sentinel,* November 25, 1871. Schenck identifies Bettis as Pettis.

46. *Raleigh (NC) Daily Sentinel,* November 30, 1871 (including quote), January 6, 1872; *Journal of the Senate of the State of North Carolina, at its Session of 1871–'72* (Raleigh, NC: Theo. N. Ramsay, State Printer and Binder, 1872), 23, 32–33, 56, 99, 151–52, 177; "Resolution to Authorize the Attorney General to Sue Out Writ of Habeas Corpus for Allen Bettis," in *Public Laws of the State of North Carolina, Passed by the General Assembly at its Session 1871–'72, Begun and Held in the City of Raleigh, on the Twentieth Day of November, 1871* (Raleigh: Theo. N. Ramsay, State Printer and Binder, 1872), 389.

47. Foner, *Reconstruction,* 455; *Raleigh (NC) Daily Sentinel,* November 30, 1871. Scholars disagree about the extent to which Republicans wanted to change the nature of the relationship between state governments and the federal government during Reconstruction. Michael Les Benedict, "Preserving the Constitution: The Conservative Bases of Reconstruction," *Journal of American History* 61 (June 1974): 65–90, argues that the postwar amendments to the Constitution as well as Reconstruction legislation (including the Force Bill) kept the antebellum federalist structure intact. Kermit L. Hall, "Political Power and Constitutional Legitimacy: The South Carolina Ku Klux Klan Trials, 1871–72," *Emory Law Journal* 33

(1984): 921–51, argues that the Klan trials reveal a distinct constitutional break with the past. Hall revisits arguments given in scholarship predating the 1960s while avoiding the racism in much of that scholarship. For an interesting twist on the use of the military during Reconstruction, see Andrew L. Slap, "'The Strong Arm of the Military Power of the United States': The Chicago Fire, the Constitution and Reconstruction," *Civil War History* 47 (June 2001): 146–63. See especially 147–48, n. 3.

48. *Raleigh (NC) Daily Sentinel,* January 6, 1872. On Akerman's resignation see Trelease, *White Terror,* 411; William S. McFeely, "Amos T. Akerman: The Lawyer and Racial Justice," in J. Morgan Kousser and James M. McPherson, eds., *Region, Race and Reconstruction: Essays in Honor of C. Vann Woodward* (New York: Oxford University Press, 1982), 410.

49. *Greensboro (NC) New North State,* December 7, 1871.

50. *Wilmington (NC) Journal,* November 17, 1871; Foner, *Reconstruction,* 454–55. Foner 455 n. 80 cites Trelease, *White Terror,* 385–91; Hall, "Political Power and Constitutional Legitimacy," 923.

51. "Caswell" to "Editors of the Sentinel," September 24, 1871, in *Raleigh (NC) Daily Sentinel,* September 30, 1871.

52. The Conservative Democratic makeup of North Carolina's mountain counties in 1871 is determined from R. D. W. Connor, ed., *A Manual of North Carolina* (Raleigh, NC: E.M. Uzzell & Co., 1913), 1016–18; *Asheville (NC) Weekly Pioneer,* August 31, 1871; Thomas E. Jeffrey, *Thomas Lanier Clingman: Fire Eater from the Carolina Mountains* (Athens: University of Georgia Press, 1998), 204–5; John Luther Bell, "Constitutions and Politics: Constitutional Revision in the South Atlantic States, 1864–1902" (PhD diss., University of North Carolina, 1969), 233, 233 n. 16; Thomas E. Jeffrey, "An Unclean Vessel: Thomas Lanier Clingman and the 'Railroad Ring,'" *North Carolina Historical Review* 74 (October 1997): 204, 386 n. 8, 413, 413 n. 9; Cotton, "Appalachian North Carolina," 252 n. 66. For a brief synopsis of the petition battle see Balanoff, "Negro Legislators," 52–53.

53. Balanoff, "Negro Legislators," 52; *Journal of the House of Representatives of the General Assembly of the State of North Carolina, at its Session of 1871–'72* (Raleigh, NC: Theo. N. Ramsay, State Printer and Binder, 1872), 41; *Raleigh (NC) Carolina Era,* November 23, 1871, December 7, 1871; *Asheville (NC) Weekly Pioneer,* November 23, 1871. For information on Mabson see North Carolina *Public Laws* 1871–1872, xii; Escott, *Many Excellent People,* 179; Nowaczyk, "The North Carolina Negro," 194, appendix F. Trelease, *White Terror,* 52, 68, 69, 203, 224, 343, provides pertinent information on McAfee, Jones, Justice, and Strudwick. According to an untitled brief in the *Wilmington (NC) Post* (semiweekly), November 26, 1871, the petition presented by Mabson was passed at a Republican gathering in Wilmington.

54. *Raleigh (NC) Daily Sentinel,* November 24, 1871.

55. *Raleigh (NC) Daily Sentinel,* November 24, 1871, November 25, 1871; *House Journal 1871–'72,* 43; Balanoff, "Negro Legislators," 52.

56. *Raleigh (NC) Daily Sentinel,* November 25, 1871.

57. Price's full name and ethnicity in Nowaczyk, "The North Carolina Negro," 194, appendix F. See also North Carolina *Public Laws* 1871–1872, vii; Escott, *Many Excellent People,* 180.

58. Balanoff, "Negro Legislators," 52; *Raleigh (NC) Carolina Era,* December 7, 1871. Identification of Linney in North Carolina *Public Laws* 1871–1872, ix.

59. *Raleigh (NC) Carolina Era,* December 7, 1871; "Proceedings of the Legislature," *Daily Carolinian,* n.d., reprinted in condensed form in *Asheville (NC) Weekly Pioneer,* December 7, 1871. The *Era* identifies the three senators as L. C. Edwards, C. T. Murphy, and W. M. Robbins. Party affiliations from Ewing, "Two Reconstruction Impeachments," *North Carolina Historical Review* (July 1938): 222, table 1, 223, table 2. *Senate Journal 1871–'72,* 19, gives coverage of the vote.

60. *House Journal 1871–'72,* 74; Balanoff, "Negro Legislators," 52–53.

61. *House Journal 1871–'72,* 78–80.

62. *Greensboro (NC) New North State,* December 7, 1871; *Wilmington (NC) Journal,* December 8, 1871.

63. *House Journal 1871–'72,* 80–82.

64. "Speech of Mr. Mabson, in the House of Representatives," *Wilmington (NC) Post* (semiweekly), December 14, 1871; *Raleigh (NC) Carolina Era,* December 14, 1871; *House Journal 1871–'72,* 89, 125.

65. "Remarks of Mr. T. A. Sykes, of Pasquotank," in *Raleigh (NC) Carolina Era,* December 28, 1871. Sykes's full name and ethnicity found in Nowaczyk, "The North Carolina Negro," 194, appendix F.

66. *House Journal 1871–'72,* 130–31.

67. Williams, *The Great South Carolina Ku Klux Klan Trials,* 60.

68. Escott, *Many Excellent People,* 142, 144; R. D. W. Connor, *North Carolina: Rebuilding an Ancient Commonwealth, 1584–1925,* vol. 2 (1929; repr., Spartanburg, SC: The Reprint Company, 1973), 299–300; J. G. de Roulhac Hamilton, *Reconstruction in North Carolina* (1914; repr., Gloucester, MA: Peter Smith, 1964), 275–76.

69. "Republican" to "Editor Post," December 5, 1871, in *Wilmington (NC) Post* (semiweekly), December 7, 1871.

70. *House Journal 1871–'72,* 190; Horace W. Raper, *William H. Holden: North Carolina's Political Enigma* (Chapel Hill: University of North Carolina Press, 1985), 204.

71. *Rutherford (NC) Star,* December 10, 1870.

72. Jeffrey, *Thomas Lanier Clingman: Fire Eater from the Carolina Mountains,* 204; John Luther Bell, "Constitutions and Politics: Constitutional Revision in the South Atlantic States, 1864–1902" (PhD diss., University of North Carolina, 1969), 225–34.

73. "The Democratic Party of North Carolina. Address of the Central Committee. To the People of North Carolina," *Raleigh (NC) Carolina Era,* November 2, 1871.

74. Ibid; Bell, "Constitutions and Politics," 235.

75. *Senate Journal 1871–'72*, 1.

76. Ibid., 131; *House Journal 1871–'72*, 217–18; *Raleigh (NC) Daily Sentinel*, January 6, 1872.

77. Cotton, "Appalachian North Carolina," 241; *House Journal 1871–'72*, 253.

78. *Greensboro (NC) New North State*, February 22, 1872.

79. *House Journal 1871–'72*, 383–84.

80. Lee M. McAfee to Tod R. Caldwell, May 27, 1872, in Tod R. Caldwell Governor's Papers, North Carolina Division of Archives and History; *Raleigh (NC) Daily Sentinel*, November 24, 1871; *House Journal 1871–'72*, 299, 301, 326, 339, 355.

81. *Wilmington (NC) Journal*, June 7, 1872; *Greensboro (NC) New North State*, May 30, 1872.

82. Hamilton, *Reconstruction in North Carolina*, 578.

83. *Wilmington (NC) Journal*, June 7, 1872.

84. Gillespie and Hall, eds., *Thomas Dixon Jr.*, 3.

85. *Raleigh (NC) Weekly Era*, June 12, 1873; Bell, "Constitutions and Politics," 236.

86. Rogers M. Smith, *Civic Ideals: Conflicting Visions of Citizenship in American History* (New Haven, CT: Yale University Press, 1997), 334.

87. *Raleigh (NC) Weekly Era*, August 7, 1873, August 21, 1873; Foner, *Reconstruction*, 528–31, 569; Bell, "Constitutions and Politics," 237.

88. Hall, "Political Power and Constitutional Legitimacy," 951.

89. "North Carolina's Future," *Elizabeth City (NC) Carolinian*, n.d., reprinted in *Greensboro (NC) New North State*, November 23, 1871. See also "Prospectus of the New North State," *Greensboro (NC) New North State*, November 23, 1871.

90. *Raleigh (NC) Daily Sentinel*, January 26, 1872; McKinney, *Southern Mountain Republicans*, 49.

91. Escott, *Many Excellent People*, 254, 260; Helen G. Edmonds, *The Negro and Fusion Politics in North Carolina, 1894–1901* (Chapel Hill: University of North Carolina Press, 1951), 148–49, 158, 171, 205, 210.

92. See Williams, *The Great South Carolina Ku Klux Klan Trials*, 146, for the end of Reconstruction after the Klan trials as it applies to South Carolina.

Chapter 6

Reconstructing Race

Parson Brownlow and the Rhetoric of Race in Postwar East Tennessee

Kyle Osborn

In April 1867 a notable letter appeared in the *Knoxville (TN) Whig*. It was a political endorsement of Tennessee governor William "Parson" Brownlow allegedly written by an African American named J. B. Thomas. In the letter, Thomas explained that before the Civil War, when he was a slave—and, inexplicably, a Democrat as well—he was convinced that "Brownlow was the worst man on earth." But the Parson's loyalty to the Union during the Civil War and his support for black suffrage during Reconstruction had lifted Thomas from his Democratic leanings. "You have fought through the struggle," Thomas told him, and now "you have the honor and confidence of every enlightened colored man" in Tennessee.[1] Thomas finished the endorsement by requesting his letter's publication in the *Whig* in order to show Tennessee's black readers that Brownlow and his Radical Party deserved the confidence of the state's African Americans. With the upcoming gubernatorial elections scheduled for that August, Brownlow's *Whig* happily granted this request.

Parson Brownlow's historical legacy, especially with respect to his governorship during Reconstruction from 1865 to 1869, stands in low regard. In many general accounts of the Civil War era, Brownlow remains overshadowed by fellow East Tennessean Andrew Johnson. When historians have specifically dealt with Brownlow, they have found few aspects worthy of praise, with his lone academic biographer, E. Merton Coulter, likening his life and political career to that of a dreadful nightmare.[2] While subse-

163

William "Parson" Brownlow was a prominent preacher and newspaper editor in ante-bellum East Tennessee. Though an advocate of slavery, Brownlow opposed secession and was forced to flee Tennessee when the state joined the Confederacy. After the war he was elected governor in 1865, and he became a divisive figure as he led Tennessee through the turbulent early postwar years before leaving for the U.S. Senate in 1869. (from Brownlow's *Sketches of the Rise, Progress, and Fall of Secession,* 1862)

quent historians dealing with Brownlow have avoided Coulter's outright disdain, they have not directly challenged his interpretation. An advocate of slavery during the antebellum years, Brownlow embraced the Republican banner during the Civil War, spearheaded the Radical Reconstruction movement in Tennessee, and oversaw the enfranchisement of the state's male African Americans and the disenfranchisement of the state's white ex-Confederates. Furthermore, Brownlow backed up his schemes with his infamous State Guard militia in order to protect his constituency during his bid for reelection in 1867. Overall, accounts of the Brownlow regime often depict his reign as an example of partisan politics at its worst, if not downright tyranny.[3]

Fittingly, historians attribute nonidealistic motivations to Brownlow's conversion from racist proslavery ideologue to radical defender of black political rights. In explaining Brownlow's support for African American suffrage, one interpretation emphasizes political expediency: Brownlow simply needed black votes to maintain political viability.[4] Another depiction points to political pressure brought by the Republicans in Washington coercing Brownlow to toe the radical line; a third interpretation highlights Brownlow's vindictive personal nature and desire for revenge against his Confederate adversaries at all costs.[5] In short, anything but genuine concern for African Americans seems to have underpinned his political transformation.

While these interpretations stand on solid historical ground, they fail to tell the entire story of Brownlow's governorship. While political expediency clearly informed his actions as governor, this hardly negates the importance of his conversion. Moreover, the emphasis placed on expediency tends to obscure the tangible benefits the Brownlow regime produced for black Tennesseans in the areas of political and civil rights. Though the reforms of the Radical government were limited when judged against modern standards, they were revolutionary for a state so recently removed from slavery.[6] Brownlow's tenure produced the enfranchisement of male African Americans, legislation designed to promote black legal rights, the passage of the Fourteenth Amendment, and the creation of the State Guard in order to protect black Tennesseans as they voted the Radical ticket.[7] While Brownlow's State Guard was criticized by his contemporaries—and subsequent historians—for being a vehicle of Radical tyranny, the organization fit well within what historian Steven Hahn calls the "paramilitary politics" of Reconstruction.[8] The State Guard proved necessary in defending African American political rights in the volatile atmosphere of postwar politics in Tennessee, especially with the eventual appearance of the Ku Klux Klan in the state.

Perhaps more significantly, avoiding an outlook of pervasive cynicism allows for a serious analysis of Brownlow's racial rhetoric itself. Easily the most influential and widely read newspaper editor in the region throughout the Civil War era, Brownlow deployed his powerful rhetoric to help reconstruct racial discourse in East Tennessee during Reconstruction. Specifically, Brownlow and his cohorts at the *Knoxville Whig* crafted an image of African Americans that sharply contrasted with the paper's long-standing racism. Before the Civil War, Brownlow depicted blacks as inherently lazy, violent, and intellectually inferior, and thus best fit for slavery. In tune with their subsequent enfranchisement during Reconstruction, Brownlow's *Whig* began molding an image of blacks that, while still shallow and degrading in ways, blunted the extreme racism found in its previous depictions. The *Whig* began to present blacks as worthy of free-labor employment, political rights, and even the respect of white voters.

Brownlow's simple desire to attract African American voters to his political banner partially explains the changed nature of his writings on race during Reconstruction. But he was also trying to convince white readers of the logic of black political rights. With the imminent return of the state's disenfranchised ex-Confederates to political viability, Brownlow's Radicals needed white support to create a biracial constituency strong enough to resist the impending resurgence of their various political enemies. In trying to bring white Tennesseans, especially the Unionists of East Tennessee, to Brownlow's banner, the *Whig* told readers that African American suffrage would not necessarily entail social equality and that black voting was necessary to uphold the Radical cause. More importantly, however, the *Whig's* reconfigured image of blacks was designed to show that African Americans were worthy of their newfound role in Tennessee politics and that they were worthy of a political alliance with white Republicans.

That Brownlow attempted this maneuver suggests he at least believed there existed some flexibility within the racial attitudes of white East Tennesseans after the war. Historians have argued that Brownlow's popularity as an editor owed in large part to his keen understanding of his region and its mountain inhabitants.[9] Thus, as Brownlow attempted to create a new image of African Americans in his rhetoric, he was pinning his political hopes on the possibility that white readers in East Tennessee were willing to accept this transformation and vote in alliance with Tennessee's blacks.

Looking back upon his editorial career while in Northern exile during the Civil War, Brownlow rightly boasted that he had wielded as much influence as "any man in East Tennessee."[10] With its fierce polemical politics and its vicious writing style, Brownlow's *Whig* may have claimed as many as 14,000 subscribers by the outbreak of the war.[11] Much of Brownlow's editorial success derived from his humble origins in southern Appalachia and his experiences communicating with the people of the region. Born to poverty in Wythe County, Virginia, Brownlow made his way to the Tennessee mountains during his youth. Upon reaching adulthood, he served ten years as a circuit-riding Methodist preacher in the southern highlands until eventually settling down in Elizabethton in 1839, establishing the *Whig,* and quickly making a name for himself in the area with his belligerent writing style. His reputation steadily grew as he moved operations to nearby Jonesboro in 1840, eventually earning himself the moniker of "Fighting Parson." This nickname proved appropriate, as Brownlow survived one assassination attempt, a bullet wound to the thigh, and a handful of beatings during his editorial career.[12] With his penchant for violence and his malicious writing, Brownlow crafted his public persona into that of a polemical folk hero, an eccentric caricature of the political editor that mountain readers found either enthralling or odious but which they seldom ignored.

Politically, Brownlow remained a devout follower of Henry Clay and the principles of the Whig Party throughout the antebellum years. He denounced the rising sectional extremism of the age, casting blame upon both Northern abolitionists and Southern fire-eaters for jeopardizing the stability of the national Union. Brownlow reluctantly supported slavery throughout the 1840s, though he refused to advocate for slavery's expansion into the western territories. This ambiguous stance was highlighted in 1850 when the *Whig* published an editorial series authored by "Civis," which depicts slavery as a necessary evil and promotes a scheme of gradual emancipation coupled with African colonization. In one editorial, Civis asks Southern readers if "just because immediate emancipation of the negroes may be neither safe nor desirable, does that prove, that it would be just and reasonable to keep them forever in a state of brutal ignorance, utterly disqualified for the enjoyment of freedom?"[13] Slaveholders, the writer demanded, should seek to "improve the moral and physical conditions of their slaves, with a view to their future emancipation and removal to a distant location."[14] These were bold words to come from a Southern press at the time.

Brownlow emerged as an uncompromising champion of slavery only in the 1850s as Southern politics grew increasingly intolerant of any hint of abolitionism.[15] Political developments during that tumultuous decade even pushed Brownlow into promoting slavery as a positive good. Forsaking the Whig party after it nominated Winfield Scott in 1852, Brownlow was left to promote various anti-Democratic state coalitions while avoiding any connection with the burgeoning Republican Party of the North. To separate himself from the Republicans and foil his Democratic foes, Brownlow argued that his conservativism provided the best way to defend slavery because it removed the most controversial aspects of sectionalism from political debate. In an attempt to provide tangible evidence of sectionalism's threat to slavery, Brownlow accused both local Democrats and national Republicans of triggering an insurrection scare that swept Tennessee during the 1856 presidential election. He claimed that the insurrection was especially provoked by the "slavery agitation extension policy" of Southern Democrats.[16] The Parson argued that the slaves had perceived a division developing among the white population as they heard the Republicans and Democrats voice their sectional hatreds, and they fittingly chose election day as the opportune time to strike. Prefiguring an argument he would later make for preserving the Union during the secession crisis, Brownlow promoted his less controversial nonexpansionist and proslavery position as the best available safeguard for preserving the South's "peculiar institution."

By the end of the decade, Brownlow emerged as one of the South's best-known defenders of slavery. In 1857, even William Lloyd Garrison's *Liberator* included a proslavery diatribe written by "the Notorious Ruffian, Parson Brownlow," and apparently Frederick Douglass offered to challenge Brownlow's views in a public debate.[17] Brownlow refused to share such a forum with an African American, but in 1858 he accepted a similar challenge from white abolitionist Abraham Pryne. At this highly publicized debate held in Philadelphia, Brownlow unapologetically proclaimed slavery a "blessing to the master, a blessing to the nonslaveholders of the South, a blessing to civilized whites in general, and a blessing to the negro slaves in particular."[18]

While Brownlow's support for slavery grew more adamant during the antebellum years, his racism remained constant. In short, Brownlow argued that Africans and their descendents could exist in either one of two ways. If enslaved by noble white Christian masters, Brownlow claimed that Africans could be made docile, moral, and industrious. If left free, Brownlow believed blacks were naturally violent, lazy, and immoral, all of which he encapsulated simply as barbarism. The clearest articulation of this sentiment in the *Whig* came not from Brownlow but from an editorial authored by South Carolina politician Waddy Thompson. He wrote that based on his observations of blacks across the world, Africans could exist in either "bondage or barbarism . . . a destiny from which the Ethiopian race has furnished no exception" at any time.[19]

Brownlow contributed his own verbosity to this theme as well. In the late 1850s he explained to readers that he no longer envisioned African colonization as a feasible solution for the problem of American slavery because, in his eyes at least, blacks in Liberia had failed to create a civilized society. He regretted this failure "because it proves beyond all doubt, what I have for years believed . . . that the African race is an inferior race—that they are incapable of self-government—and that as soon as the restraint of slavery is removed, the race retrogrades at once, to its primitive condition."[20] He fully displayed his racism during the 1858 slavery debate in Philadelphia as well, proclaiming that "slavery, only, can elevate the negro from their state of pristine barbarism." It was no wonder, he exclaimed, that many whites classified Africans "as a superior species of the monkey tribe!"[21]

With the outbreak of the secession crisis after the 1860 presidential election, Brownlow held firm to his support of slavery. In fact, the Unionist Brownlow argued against secession by warning that civil war represented a much greater threat to the stability of slavery than the mere election of Republican Abraham Lincoln.[22] Exemplifying his political influence, the Parson played a pivotal role in keeping his mountain region from embracing the Southern call for secession. Historical explanations for East Tennessee's Unionism remain tangled and complex.[23] On the one hand, the region's economy never centered around the staple agriculture that dominated throughout much of the South, and East Tennesseans therefore counted fewer slaves (accounting for only 12.5 percent of the total population in 1860) and fewer large slaveholders than was typical below the Mason and Dixon line. But as historian John Inscoe points out, these structural factors alone hardly explain the region's Unionist leanings, especially when compared to the strikingly similar demographics of its secessionist neighbor region, western North Carolina. Inscoe suggests that the key difference between these two mountain regions lay in their contrasting "self-images." While western North Carolina foresaw a bright future of economic development and progress sponsored by allies in Raleigh, East Tennesseans felt that their underdeveloped region had been surpassed by the middle and western sections of the state. They also believed that the wealthy planters who dominated the state's politics in Nashville had purposely neglected the economic interests of East Tennessee, a sentiment Brownlow often expressed through his demands for state-funded internal improvement projects.[24] These grievances on the part of East Tennesseans distinguished them from their fellow mountaineers in western North Carolina and helped underpin the region's rejection of secession. Yet while providing a biting critique of wealthy planters, East Tennessee's regional resentment entailed little sympathy for slaves or African Americans. Indeed, during the secession crisis Brownlow warned Northerners that if the Republicans moved against slavery, "there would not be a Union man among us in twenty-four hours."[25]

Outside of Unionist East Tennessee, the majority of white Tennesseans from the middle and western sections of the state supported secession after Lincoln's call for volunteers in the aftermath of Fort Sumter. With Tennessee officially included in the Confederacy by the summer of 1861, Brownlow turned his polemical talents against Confederate authorities until he was finally arrested and imprisoned later that year. In the last issue of the *Whig* to appear before his arrest, the Parson compared himself to a Christian martyr, likened his region's occupation by the Confederacy to the terror of the French Revolution, and denounced the secessionists for instigating "the most wicked, cruel, unnatural, and uncalled for war ever recorded in history."[26] Perhaps anxious to rid themselves of his presence, the Confederates handed Brownlow over to the federal army in 1862, whereupon the Parson pursued a celebrated speaking tour of the North and published an extremely popular book, known colloquially as *Parson Brownlow's Book*, to reveal the sufferings of East Tennessee's Unionists and to "expose the guilty leaders" of secession "to the scorn and contempt of all coming generations."[27]

When the Union army gained control of the Knoxville area in September 1863, Brownlow was close on its heels. One month later, the nationally prominent Parson Brownlow and his famous newspaper, now named the *Whig and Rebel Ventilator,* made their triumphant return to publication. Much had happened during the *Whig's* two-year abeyance, and Brownlow quickly made his positions on the changed political landscape clear for his readers. He had become an unapologetic supporter of Lincoln and the Republican administration in Washington. The Parson boldly declared in the inaugural issue of the *Whig and Rebel Ventilator* that "we are not here to *excuse* . . . or to censure President Lincoln." Instead "we endorse all he has done, and we find fault with him for not having done more of the same sort!" He then voiced his intention to keep up the fight against the Confederates until they "are subjugated or exterminated."[28]

Brownlow explained that he also fully supported the Emancipation Proclamation and Lincoln's controversial decision to mobilize African Americans troops into the Union Army. The Parson made it clear, however, that pragmatism informed his support for these measures. With regard to emancipation, Brownlow considered slavery's destruction a fait accompli because of the high number of black runaways. He also argued that attacking slavery helped the overall war effort against the Confederacy, writing bluntly that "the nigger is the rebellion, the rebellion is the nigger." In order to "put down one we have to get rid of the other."[29]

Brownlow also explained to East Tennessee readers that emancipation would prove economically beneficial for the region's nonaffluent whites. Slavery, he explained, made individual slaveholders wealthy, while "the effect upon the general prosperity was decidedly injurious."[30] From the 1850s and until the secession crisis, Brownlow had shied away from the notion that slavery suppressed nonslaveholding whites. He often accused Andrew Johnson, famed political defender of the white yeoman class, of being a covert abolitionist. Yet during the war, the *Whig* carried editorials arguing that slavery had been detrimental to yeoman whites "because every laboring white man, for the want of competition, is reduced to the sheer necessity of cultivating the poor and neglected land of the country."[31] Brownlow continued this theme in his 1865 inaugural address, insisting that slavery had hindered Tennessee's economic development "by the exclusion from her borders of both capital and educated labor."[32]

Pragmatism also underpinned Brownlow's initial support for the mobilization of black troops in the Union Army. He argued that if African American soldiers could help defeat the hated Confederacy, it would prove a worthwhile experiment. Showing signs of his view of blacks as inherently violent, Brownlow declared that there was nothing morally inconsistent in letting the slaveholding rebels "now be fought by the nigger, and made sick of the nigger. Had we the power we would turn loose all the beasts of the forest, the snakes and the lizards of the swamps and all the devils in hell; but we would put down the rebellion!"[33]

These racist sentiments carried over into his first months as governor in mid-1865 and informed Brownlow's original vision of the social and political makeup of Tennessee's Reconstruction. The *Whig,* under the official editorship of the governor's son, John Bell Brownlow, made clear to African American readers they should not expect the state government to provide relief or favored legislation. Instead, the paper stated that "the sober realities of nakedness, hunger, and want . . . is the best friend of the colored man," forcing African Americans to learn to fend for themselves.[34] This sentiment apparently resonated with the anxieties of many white East Tennesseans in the aftermath of the state's 1865 passage of the Thirteenth Amendment and the appearance of the Freedman's Bureau in the state.[35] White East Tennesseans showed their displeasure with these initial postwar developments and the possible political and social elevation of African Americans by destroying black schools in Knoxville, Greeneville, and Jonesboro.

Governor Brownlow even reconsidered the idea of colonization, formulating a fanciful plan to transfer Tennessee blacks to Texas. If this scheme failed to materialize, he projected a bleak future for African Americans in Tennessee. In a June 1865 editorial, Brownlow wrote that "the negroes, like the Indian tribes, will gradually become extinct," for "having no owners to care for them . . . they will cease to increase in numbers . . . while *educated labor* will take the place of *slave labor.* Idleness, starvation, and disease will remove a majority of the negroes in this generation."[36] At this early point in his governorship, Brownlow sought to increase his constituency not with African Americans, but with European immigrants who would contribute "a vast addition to our force of able-bodied laborers!" He told the state legislature that this plan provided "a far more safe and rational process of regenerating the South than any sudden and compulsory admission of blacks to the ballot-box."[37]

It quickly became apparent, however, that this vision for Tennessee's Reconstruction was proving illusory. Tennessee failed to attract European labor in the numbers that Brownlow had hoped; worse, Brownlow's new Radical Party seemed unable to garner significant support from white Tennesseans. Brownlow's gubernatorial election in March 1865 had been a virtual rump. With Confederates disqualified from the polls and the state's conservative Unionists absconding in the hopes of delegitimizing the election, Brownlow captured almost all of the mere twenty-five thousand votes that were cast.[38] In comparison, more than 146,000 Tennessee voters had participated in the 1860 presidential election. Brownlow was already despised by ex-Confederates, and his pro-Lincoln stance during the war—especially his support of emancipation—had alienated many conservative Unionists, including influential political leaders such as T. A. R. Nelson and Emerson Etheridge.[39] This opposition increased in 1866 when the Brownlow regime passed the Fourteenth Amendment in the state, in defiance of his old nemesis, Andrew Johnson. Tennessee politics during Reconstruction was therefore shaping up as an uneven battle between Brownlow's outnumbered white Radicals centered in East Tennessee and the so-called "Conservatives" who could expect the future support of the disenfranchised ex-Confederates.

Brownlow's tentative grasp on power was clearly revealed in the congressional elections of August 1865. Even with the passage of a June franchise act that barred former Confederates from the polls for five years, Conservative candidates won five of Tennessee's eight congressional districts.[40] Then in March 1866, Conservatives found victory in most of the local county elections held throughout the middle and western sections of the state.[41] Failing to attract either European immigrants or gain a solid constituency among white Tennesseans, Brownlow quickly reconfigured his political vision of Tennessee's Reconstruction. In the same speech in which Brownlow lamented the state's inability to attract European laborers, the governor tellingly noted that "the colored race have shown a greater aptitude for learning and intelligence than expected, and their good conduct and steadfast loyalty have rapidly won upon the good opinion and respect of the white race."[42] Seeing few viable alternatives, Brownlow's beleaguered Radical legislature subsequently passed a bill enfranchising male African Americans in February 1867, a move that greatly expanded the strength of the Radical Party in time for Tennessee's gubernatorial and congressional elections scheduled for that August. As the governor explained, "without their votes, the State will pass into disloyal hands."[43]

In tune with these political developments, Brownlow's rhetoric was beginning to shed its virulent racism. In part, Brownlow and his *Whig* were trying to sell black suffrage to white Unionists in the hopes of retaining their support. The *Whig* reminded its readers of the valiant service that African American soldiers performed during the Civil War. As the paper explained, after Appomattox "everybody admitted that the negro fought well, and we never hear any person say now that, AS A RACE, they are cowardly." The editorial further argues that African American soldiers had shown that blacks could remain loyal and deferential to white authority, that they "exhibited high and noble soldierly qualities," and that they had proved "obedient, well disciplined, and well drilled, when commanded by good officers."[44]

Brownlow's *Whig* also tried to explain that African American suffrage would not foster social equality between the races. The paper quoted Frederick Douglass on this point, arguing that the notion of public equality encompassing areas such as voting rights was entirely different from private equality. As Douglass asked, "Do not character, wealth and intelligence control the matter of social relations? . . . My parlor and my table are my own," Douglass insisted, "and I can choose my own friends and associates and you have the same right."[45] This editorial highlights the transformation of Brownlow's racial rhetoric. Fewer than ten years earlier, Brownlow had refused to even publicly debate Douglass over the issue of slavery. In 1867, with black suffrage a reality in Tennessee, Brownlow not only included Douglass in his paper but praised his "great good sense" as well. At other times, Brownlow's paper blatantly asked white readers to swallow their racism for the sake of the Radical ticket. To deny this course on the "simple grounds that the negro race is an inferior one to the white" was unjust and hurt the Radical Party. Brownlow explained that if "prejudice forms the element of our reason" in denying black political rights, we thus "manifest injustice to an innocent party. Will not true nobility and manliness require us to trample down our prejudice and act from noble purposes and motives?"[46]

The most dramatic innovations in Brownlow's racial rhetoric appeared in his direct appeals to Tennessee's newly enfranchised African American voters. At first glance, these efforts seem unnecessary, because the prospects of Brownlow's Conservative enemies seemed futile in 1867. With a stricter 1866 voting act in place that completely eliminated ex-Confederates from legally reaching the polls, the Conservative gubernatorial candidate, Emerson Etheridge, appeared to wage a hopeless campaign, given that Brownlow seemed destined to win most of the approximately forty thousand newly enfranchised potential black voters in the state. Still, the Parson's efforts to court the black vote during the 1867 campaign suggest that Brownlow did not consider his reelection or his monopolization of African American voters a forgone conclusion. Neither apparently did Etheridge, as the Conservatives tried to use Brownlow's proslavery past against him, publishing a pamphlet entitled "Brownlow's Opinion of Colored People, How He Loves Them and Admires Them, Their Origin, Where He Thinks they are Fit For," which reprinted some of his most vicious proslavery rhetoric from the antebellum years. In response to this Conservative challenge, Brownlow increasingly crafted a more positive image of African Americans in an attempt to attract black voters throughout the 1867 campaign.

Principally, Brownlow dropped his prediction that Tennessee's African Americans were doomed for extinction and therefore held but a marginal role in the state's Reconstruction. Experience had shown, the *Whig* explained, that "the blacks, like the whites, rather more than held their own during the war," and a "heavy decrease" of African Americans had not occurred.[47] The paper argued that Tennessee actually needed to retain its black population to achieve economic viability. In an editorial appearing in January 1867, the *Whig* described the economic hardships of neighboring Virginia while pointing to the "mass exodus of black laborers" as the cause of the state's travails. The *Whig* advised the Old Dominion to grant its African Americans the right to vote, so that the "colored men will remain at work better than they ever did before," as was about to occur in Tennessee.[48]

Breaking from the cold, laissez-faire position Brownlow had espoused during his first months as governor, the *Whig* now promoted state protection for black Tennesseans. Noting the vulnerability of the state's African Americans to white violence, the paper pleaded for either the U.S. Army or a state militia to protect them. This theme actually appeared before the advent of black suffrage and was discussed in order to justify the state legislature's passage of the Fourteenth Amendment in July 1866, a move that paved the way for Tennessee's readmission to the Union later that month. For instance, in March 1866 the *Whig* told of a white mob that had attacked a "very peaceful" African American man in Cleveland, Tennessee. The paper stated that the "shooting was done without any provocation at all on the part of the negro," showing the penchant for random violence on the part of white Conservatives.[49]

Accounts of white atrocities committed against innocent African Americans appeared repeatedly in the *Whig*. In July 1866 an editorial told of yet "another brutal murder by a rebel on the person of an unoffending colored woman" in Memphis, a city reeling from the violent race riots of the previous month that claimed the lives of forty-six African Americans. What the *Whig* found most upsetting in this case was the inability or unwillingness of the local authorities to administer justice; no jury in Memphis dared "molest the cowardly assassin of a woman."[50] In response to the Memphis riots, the Radical legislature passed the 1866 Metropolitan Police Act, which created police districts in Memphis, Nashville, and Chattanooga, giving the governor control over the personnel that would administer these districts. Critics blasted this move as being transparently partisan, as it gave Brownlow a vehicle to strengthen the Radical presence in those cities. Yet in addition to this political motive, the action was meant to protect the beleaguered African American population in those areas as well.[51]

As seen above, when reporting the violence surrounding Tennessee's Reconstruction, Brownlow and his paper reversed antebellum racial stereotypes. Blacks were now the innocent victims, while Conservative whites were cast as depraved aggressors. This reversal was highlighted by a satirical 1867 *Whig* editorial that mocked the claims of Conservatives who accused blacks of being accountable for the state's widespread postwar violence. The editorial, sarcastically titled "How a Brutal Negro Provokes a Quarrel with a White Man," tells of a violent encounter that had recently occurred on the outskirts of Knoxville. An African American farmer was working in his fields when a "white gentleman" approached and boasted of his political support for Conservative Emerson Etheridge, railing against "Brownlow and his God d—d nigger equality party." This pestering continued as the Radical farmer repeatedly tried to avoid a confrontation. But the white Conservative's pestering continued until the black farm worker finally had heard enough. He announced his support for Brownlow and declared that anyone "who voted for Etheridge was a God d—d rascal." The "unoffending" white man, as the *Whig* mockingly deemed him, then attacked the black Radical until the "brutal negro" lashed back at his attacker to the point where the white man "was anxious for peace."[52] Before the war, Brownlow often warned that free African Americans were inherently violent and posed a grave threat to the South's white population. In Reconstruction, Brownlow began depicting African Americans as peaceful and even reluctant to use violence in the face of white aggression.

The very conceptual basis of race depicted in the *Whig* also showed subtle signs of transformation, quietly deviating from the idea of race as a biological product. This dynamic was illustrated by the paper's selective incorporation of Thomas Jefferson's writings on race. In 1852 the proslavery Brownlow had quoted Jefferson discussing the supposedly innate racial distinctions of whites and blacks. In an editorial derived from Jefferson's

Notes on the State of Virginia, the future president famously argued that "the blackman requires less sleep . . . his reasoning powers are decidedly inferior. His memory is equal to the white man's, but not his imagination, which is dull in the extreme."[53] This list of supposedly biological differences continued, encompassing such features as skin color, hair texture, body shape, facial hair, and artistic ability. Yet in 1867 the *Whig* printed and endorsed Jefferson's letter to African American mathematician Benjamin Bannaker, in which Jefferson hints that racial distinctions result more from environmental conditioning than biology and that the supposed inferiority of black slaves owes "merely to the degraded condition of their existence."[54] The *Whig* explained that it included this letter specifically for those readers who "swear that the negro is not superior to the monkey."[55]

While East Tennesseans read these editorials, Brownlow continued to back up his rhetoric with force. Partially in response to the continued violence that African Americans faced across the state, Brownlow helped organize the State Guard militia, which was specifically designed to maintain order during the 1867 state elections. As historian Ben Severance has shown, this militia force was created both to expediently support Brownlow's Radical regime and to protect his black constituency.[56] Severance also points out that the State Guard largely served the role that the federal army was meant to fulfill in most of the other former Confederate states during Reconstruction. Because Tennessee was readmitted to the Union in 1866, it was not included in the Radical Reconstruction Acts of 1867 that divided the South into military districts.

Leading up to the gubernatorial election of March 1867, Brownlow's *Whig* published excerpts of letters from African Americans throughout East Tennessee pledging their support for the Radical ticket. A committee of African American voters from Loudon County wrote that they held Brownlow as "our political creator" and pledged him "our undivided support.[57] African Americans in McMinn County expressed a similar sentiment, confirming that black suffrage had been essential for the "general elevation of our race." They wished to show their "just appreciation . . . of the Radical Union Party of Tennessee who recognize as their chieftain that champion of liberty Wm. G. Brownlow."[58] With such support in hand, the *Whig* confidently predicted that "in East Tennessee the colored vote *will* be cast in solid phalanx for the Union Republicans" and Brownlow.[59]

Brownlow was indeed successful in his quest for reelection in 1867, defeating the Conservative Emerson Etheridge by more than fifty thousand votes. In fact, the election was a complete triumph for the Radicals, as the party swept all eight of the state's congressional seats in addition to the governor's chair. African American voters played a major role in this rout, with estimates holding that thirty-five to forty thousand black votes were cast, almost all for the Radical banner.[60] After the election, the *Whig* praised the "good behavior" that black Tennesseans had shown at the polls. It was amazing, the paper exclaimed, "that a race so long down-trodden, humiliated, plundered, outraged, and enslaved . . . should at their very first election . . . exercise the highest privilege of American citizens without the slightest outbreak" of violence or disorder on their part.[61]

In another editorial that recounted the recent election, the *Whig* surpassed anything it had earlier published in praising the state's African American population. In discussing the actions of the black voter, the paper stated that "he has worked well and deported himself peaceably and well in every part of the country." The editorial continued by countering Conservative charges that blacks in Tennessee had become idle and violent since their deliverance from slavery. "Our readers in East Tennessee know," Brownlow's paper declared, that "the colored people have been as industrious as they were before the war, and we think more so." It then challenged its readers to find any contradicting evidence to the paper's claim "that the negroes of East Tennessee have committed less crime and been more respectful to the white people than they were before the war," an opinion shared by "many of the best laboring white citizens" in the region. The editorial finished by proclaiming: "The history of the world has furnished no nobler example in honesty, industry and good conduct than the negro has afforded, when we reflect upon the hundreds of years he has been in chains and slavery. . . . What honest Christian man would say that this abused race does not deserve praise instead of censure, for its good conduct in its hitherto wretched conditions and brutal usage?"[62]

Despite the Radicals' triumphs in 1867, the political alliance between Brownlow's white Radicals and Tennessee blacks would be short-lived. In 1869 the aging Brownlow decided not to seek another term as governor and accepted a seat in the U.S. Senate instead. His handpicked successor, fellow East Tennessee Unionist DeWitt Senter, won the 1869 gubernatorial contest with ease and then led an unexpected political de-Radicalization of the state that included the immediate enfranchisement of the state's ex-Confederates and an 1870 poll tax that launched the white assault on African American suffrage. Though mountain Republicanism would long linger, Tennessee Radicalism had proven nothing more than a temporary aberration, and the Volunteer State was placed on the road to "redemption" with Senter's election. Brownlow would eventually be cast into the shadows of Tennessee history, to be remembered, E. Merton Coulter later explained, only in nightmares.

Following Coulter's lead, historians have taken a negative view of the Brownlow regime. Some historians have pointed to Brownlow's failed railroad schemes, which left Tennessee burdened with a "crushing debt."[63] Another historian argues that Brownlow unleashed a "campaign of terrorism and intimidation" that perpetuated the violence and vindictiveness of the Civil War.[64] Still others criticize Brownlow for treating blacks as junior political partners while failing to promote African American candidates for state offices or give them patronage appointments.[65] These criticisms, however, tell only part of the story. Brownlow's Radical regime, in addition to enfranchising the state's male African Americans, oversaw the passage of the Fourteenth Amendment, gave blacks the right to testify in courts, outlawed specific criminal punishments based on race, and offered black Tennesseans military protection through the Metropolitan Police Act and the creation of the State Guard. These measures were surely self-serving to Brownlow's political fortunes, but they cannot be dismissed merely because they were the products of political expediency. The story of Tennessee's Reconstruction stands incomplete when these positive benefits for the state's African Americans are not emphasized.

Important as these legislative actions were, Brownlow's evolving racial rhetoric held an even greater revolutionary potential. In his attempt to create a biracial constituency, Brownlow attempted to promote black suffrage to his white readers in East Tennessee. To accomplish this feat, he created an image of blacks that constituted a dramatic transformation from his racist antebellum writings. After previously depicting blacks as universally barbaric, during Reconstruction Brownlow presented African Americans as honest, industrious, peaceful, and worthy of a political alliance with East Tennessee whites. He was trying to do nothing less than remold the discourse of race in his region.

The question remains whether white East Tennesseans were prepared to follow Brownlow down this path. With an acute knowledge of East Tennessee gleaned from years of Methodist proselytizing and editorial combat, Brownlow at least thought his mountain whites were willing to participate in a political coalition with African Americans. A handful of historians examining antebellum East Tennessee have made some intriguing discoveries suggesting flexibility in the region's attitudes on race and slavery. East Tennessee had once been an abolitionist epicenter in the early nineteenth century, highlighted by the presence of antislavery editors Benjamin Lundy and Elihu Embree.[66] And while this movement quickly faded after 1820, some historians have uncovered antislavery sentiments among East Tennesseans even after 1830. Analyzing the observations of Northern abolitionist Ezekiel Birdseye, historian Durwood Dunn argues that East Tennessee's antislavery movement left a "residual effect" upon the region's culture that was noticeable as late as 1840.[67] Furthermore, Marie Tedesco and Elizabeth Fortson Arroyo have found incidents of whites and blacks interacting under terms of relative equality in antebellum East Tennessee.[68] Finally, blacks in East Tennessee proved unusually capable of obtaining land ownership during the Reconstruction years. By 1880, 18 percent of black East Tennesseans owned land, compared to the 7.9 percent of African Americans who could claim land throughout Tennessee as a whole.[69] Brownlow himself, it should be remembered, had not championed slavery as a positive good until the decade preceding the Civil War.

But even if white East Tennesseans were willing to accept blacks as political allies, Parson Brownlow's Radical regime lacked sufficient time to build a lasting biracial constituency that could foster a new conceptualization of race. The Parson's rhetoric shows how the dynamics of political power radically transformed the language of race during the brief window opened by Reconstruction. But could this development have continued? Could Southern racism have been softened, and could the nadir that American race relations reached during the late nineteenth century have been avoided? Because of the Radicals' early demise in Tennessee, as in every southern state, this question remains compelling but ultimately, and tragically, impossible to answer.

Notes

1. *Knoxville (TN) Whig,* April 17, 1867.
2. E. Merton Coulter, *William G. Brownlow: The Fighting Parson of the Southern Highlands* (Chapel Hill: University of North Carolina Press, 1937).
3. This interpretation appears in Thomas B. Alexander, *Political Reconstruction in Tennessee* (Nashville, TN: Vanderbilt University Press, 1950).
4. This is most evident in Coulter, *Fighting Parson of the Southern Highlands;* Alexander, *Political Reconstruction in Tennessee;* and James Welch Patton, *Union-*

ism and Reconstruction in Tennessee, 1860–1869 (Chapel Hill: University of North Carolina Press, 1934).

5. See Gordon B. McKinney, *Southern Mountain Republicans, 1865–1900* (Knoxville: University of Tennessee Press, 1988), 35; Noel C. Fisher, *War at Every Door: Partisan Politics and Guerrilla Warfare in East Tennessee, 1860–1869* (Chapel Hill: University of North Carolina Press, 1997), 167.

6. Eric Foner points out that the transition from slavery to political participation experienced by African Americans proves unique in a comparative analysis of nations undergoing emancipation. Eric Foner, *Reconstruction: America's Unfinished Revolution, 1863–1877* (New York: Harper & Row, 1988).

7. See Ben H. Severance, *Tennessee's Radical Army: The State Guard and Its Role in Reconstruction, 1867–1869* (Knoxville: University of Tennessee Press, 2005).

8. Steven Hahn, *A Nation under Our Feet: Black Political Struggles in the Rural South from Slavery to the Great Migration* (Cambridge, MA: Harvard University Press), 265.

9. This point is made in Robert Tracy McKenzie, "Contesting Secession: Parson Brownlow and the Rhetoric of Proslavery Unionism, 1860–1861," *Civil War History* 48, no. 4 (December 2002): 294–312.

10. As quoted in Stephen V. Ash, ed., *Secessionists and Other Scoundrels: Selections from Parson Brownlow's Book* (Baton Rouge: Louisiana State University Press, 1999), 18.

11. McKenzie, "Contesting Secession," 294–312.

12. Coulter suggests that one of these beatings left Brownlow mentally incapacitated. *Fighting Parson of the Southern Highlands*, 43.

13. *Knoxville (TN) Whig*, December 21, 1850.

14. *Knoxville (TN) Whig*, November 9, 1850.

15. See Durwood Dunn, *An Abolitionist in the Appalachian South: Ezekiel Birdseye on Slavery, Capitalism, and Separate Statehood in East Tennessee, 1841–1846* (Knoxville: University of Tennessee Press, 1997), 15; and Forrest R. Conklin, "The Public Speaking Career of William Gannaway (Parson) Brownlow" (PhD diss., Ohio University, 1967), 148. Dunn discovered Brownlow's signature on an 1834 antislavery petition. Conklin shows that Brownlow's 1834 book *Helps to the Study of Presbyterianism* depicts slavery as a necessary evil.

16. *Knoxville (TN) Whig*, January 3, 1857.

17. *Liberator*, September 25, 1857.

18. *Ought Slavery Be Perpetuated? A Debate between Rev. W. G. Brownlow and Rev. A. Pryne* (Philadelphia: J. B. Lippincott, 1858), 162.

19. *Jonesboro (TN) Whig*, July 1, 1846.

20. *Knoxville (TN) Whig*, October 10, 1857.

21. *Ought Slavery Be Perpetuated?* 98–99.

22. See McKenzie, "Contesting Secession," 294–312.

23. For a brief introduction to the historiography of East Tennessee Unionism, see Fisher, *War at Every Door*, 179–83.

24. John C. Inscoe, "The Secession Crisis and Regional Self-Image: The Contrasting Cases of Western North Carolina and East Tennessee," in John Inscoe, ed., *Race, War, and Remembrance in the Appalachian South* (Lexington: University Press of Kentucky, 2008), 103–23.

25. As quoted in Robert Tracy McKenzie, *Lincolnites and Rebels: A Divided Town in the American Civil War* (New York: Oxford University Press, 2006), 63.

26. *Knoxville (TN) Whig*, October 26, 1861.

27. As quoted in Ash, *Secessionists and Other Scoundrels*, 89.

28. *Knoxville (TN) Whig and Rebel Ventilator,* November 11, 1863.

29. *Knoxville (TN) Whig and Rebel Ventilator,* January 11, 1865.

30. *Knoxville (TN) Whig and Rebel Ventilator,* May 10, 1865.

31. *Knoxville (TN) Whig and Rebel Ventilator,* April 7, 1864.

32. As quoted in Robert H. White, ed., *Messages of the Governors of Tennessee, 1857–1869* (Nashville: Tennessee Historical Commission, 1959), 403.

33. *Knoxville (TN) Whig and Rebel Ventilator,* January 16, 1864.

34. *Knoxville (TN) Whig,* July 21, 1865.

35. See John Cimprich, "Slavery's End in East Tennessee," in John C. Inscoe, ed., *Appalachians and Race: The Mountain South from Slavery to Segregation* (Lexington: University Press of Kentucky, 2001), 194–95.

36. *Knoxville (TN) Whig,* June 28, 1865.

37. As quoted in White, *Messages of the Governors,* 466, 458.

38. This tactic on the part of the conservative Unionists is discussed in Alexander, *Political Reconstruction in Tennessee,* 39–40.

39. For a look at the divisions that had developed among Unionist leaders in East Tennessee by 1864, see McKenzie, *Lincolnites and Rebels,* 190–91.

40. Conservative Dorsey B. Thomas's election in the Sixth District was nullified on suspicion of illegal voting on the part of ex-Confederates. Radical Samuel M. Arnell was awarded this congressional seat in Thomas's place, giving the Tennessee Radicals a fourth congressman in Washington.

41. Paul H. Bergeron, Stephen V. Ash, and Jeanette Keith, *Tennesseans and Their History* (Knoxville: University of Tennessee Press, 1999), 163.

42. As quoted in White, *Messages of the Governors,* 541.

43. As quoted in Severance, *Tennessee's Radical Army,* 7.

44. *Knoxville (TN) Whig,* January 30, 1867.

45. *Knoxville (TN) Whig,* March 13, 1867.

46. *Knoxville (TN) Whig,* January 30, 1867.

47. *Knoxville (TN) Whig,* November 18, 1867.

48. *Knoxville (TN) Whig,* January 30, 1867.

49. *Knoxville (TN) Whig,* March 14, 1866.

50. *Knoxville (TN) Whig,* July 25, 1866.

51. For a critical view of the Metropolitan Act, see Alexander, *Political Reconstruction in Tennessee,* 110. For a more balanced look, see Severance, *Tennessee's Radical Army,* 15–16.

52. *Knoxville (TN) Whig,* July 30, 1867.

53. *Knoxville (TN) Whig,* May 1, 1852.

54. Winthrop Jordan argues that this letter to Bannaker ultimately showed that Jefferson remained unconvinced of black equality. Winthrop D. Jordan, *White over Black: American Attitudes toward the Negro, 1550–1812* (Baltimore: Penguin Books, 1968), 451–52.

55. *Knoxville (TN) Whig,* August 28, 1867.

56. Severance, *Tennessee's Radical Army,* xi.

57. *Knoxville (TN) Whig,* May 1, 1867.

58. *Knoxville (TN) Whig,* January 27, 1867.

59. *Knoxville (TN) Whig,* February 10, 1867.

60. Severance, *Tennessee's Radical Army,* 140.

61. *Knoxville (TN) Whig,* August 21, 1867.

62. Ibid.

63. James W. Patton, introduction to E. Merton Coulter, *William G. Brownlow: Fighting Parson of the Southern Highlands* (Knoxville: University of Tennessee Press, 1971), xii.

64. W. Todd Groce, *Mountain Rebels: East Tennessee Confederates and the Civil War, 1860–1870* (Knoxville: University of Tennessee Press, 1999), 154.

65. Hahn, *A Nation under Our Feet,* 249–50.

66. Richard B. Drake, *A History of Appalachia* (Lexington: University Press of Kentucky, 2001), 88.

67. Dunn, *An Abolitionist in the Appalachian South,* 17.

68. Marie Tedesco, "A Free Black Slave Owner in East Tennessee: The Strange Case of Adam Waterford," in John C. Inscoe, ed., *Appalachians and Race: The Mountain South from Slavery to Segregation* (Lexington: University Press of Kentucky, 2001), 133–53; Elizabeth Fortson Arroyo, "Poor Whites, Slaves, and Free Blacks in Tennessee, 1796–1861," *Tennessee Historical Quarterly* 55 (Spring 1996): 57–65.

69. These figures come from Robert Tracy McKenzie, *One South or Many? Plantation Belt and Upcountry in Civil War–Era Tennessee* (New York: Cambridge University Press, 1994), 142. McKenzie does not attribute this unusually high rate of black land ownership in East Tennessee to a lack of racism among the region's white population. Furthermore, in his study of race in nineteenth-century Appalachia, John C. Inscoe argues that Appalachian views on race and slavery were mostly "within the mainstream of attitudes and behavior elsewhere in the South." This included East Tennessee. John C. Inscoe, "Race and Racism in Nineteenth-Century Southern Appalachia: Myths, Realities, and Ambiguities," in *Appalachia in the Making: The Mountain South in the Nineteenth Century* (Chapel Hill: University of North Carolina Press, 1995): 103–31.

Chapter 7

Gathering Georgians to Zion

John Hamilton Morgan's 1876 Mission to Georgia

Mary Ella Engel

In 1975 Mormon historian Leonard Arrington stood before an Atlanta meeting of the American Historical Association to challenge interpretations that limited the history of the Church of Jesus Christ of Latter-day Saints to regional accounts of the Northeast or West. While the number of southerners to convert to Mormonism was never large, he acknowledged, the story of southern Saints "deserves recounting, both because of what it tells us about the South and what it tells us about Mormonism." This essay goes further, arguing that the story of the Southern States Mission to Georgia in the 1870s also tells us something about Appalachia.[1]

Missionaries from the Church of Jesus Christ of Latter-day Saints first traveled south in the 1830s, but it was 1843 before the first Mormon elder reached Georgia, and then only to pass through the state on his way from Alabama to North Carolina. The Church did assign four missionaries to the state in 1844 to preach the gospel and campaign on behalf of Joseph Smith's bid for the presidency, but that endeavor proved transitory, cut short by the assassination of the candidate. Still, Arrington estimates that in the church's antebellum efforts in the South, as many as 230 Mormon elders baptized at least 1,300 southern converts. Of that number, at least one thousand "and probably many more" converts left the South to join Mormon settlements. In the years just prior to the Civil War, missionary activity in the South virtually ceased, but with the abatement of sectional warfare, missionaries ventured from Utah again—and back to the South.[2]

John Morgan in middle age. (Special Collections, J. Willard Marriot Library, University of Utah)

Among the men called to serve in the Southern States Mission was John Hamilton Morgan, who traveled to Georgia in 1876 and carved a productive field of labor among the ridges and valleys of northwest Georgia. It was, he recalled, familiar terrain. As he ambled, "his mind wandered back continuously" to his Civil War experience "among those very mountains and valleys." In truth, he believed "he had been over every mile of the country through which he was walking." His proselytizing yielded impressive results. The rugged and mountainous area that extended from Rome to Chattanooga proved to be "the most profitable field the Mormon missionaries found in the South"—so profitable, in fact, that locals soon dubbed the region "Utah."[3]

As Arrington argued, an examination of Morgan's efforts promises to reveal much about the efforts of the LDS Church, but it also reveals a great deal about Appalachian Georgia. Because it places Mormon missionaries within the contested religious terrain that was Appalachia in the last decades of the nineteenth century, it complicates Appalachian religious history. Further, the success of those Mormon elders reveals something of the postwar uncertainties and anxieties suffered by poor and disheartened Georgians. Under the influence of John Morgan, hundreds of new Saints left Georgia for a better life in the new Mormon Zion—an experience that transcends regional boundaries and places nineteenth-century Appalachian Georgians within broader national movements to the West.

As 1876 drew to a close, Mormon missionary John Morgan penned a letter to the faithful in Salt Lake City. He had left his previous mission post, he reported, to travel to Georgia "in fulfillment of a desire to visit this country" and "in answer to a call to preach." A letter from Georgia prompted his relocation. He did not reveal the name or address of the southern correspondent, just the message, which was a request for "some one to come here and preach." Morgan responded immediately, borrowing money for train fare to Chattanooga, where he disembarked and set off on foot into the northwest corner of Georgia. It is not clear whether his arrival satisfied the needs of the letter writer, but the letter may have influenced his first decision, which was to carry his message to Rome in Floyd County. There he hoped to hold his first meeting, perhaps win his first converts. But as he walked toward Rome, he found his mind wandering, so when he suddenly encountered a fork in the road, it startled him from his quiet meditation. He studied his two options, momentarily confused, "uncertain as to which road . . . would lead him to Rome." As he puzzled over the problem, he realized that he had once dreamed of just such a situation.[4]

In his dream, Brigham Young stood at the very fork in the road where Morgan now vacillated. The Prophet addressed Morgan's indecision, explaining that the fork to the right would lead to Rome, his original destination; but, if Morgan took the road to the left, it would lead him to a profound spiritual discovery. At the time the dream occurred, Morgan found it confusing, as he had not yet joined the Church of Jesus Christ of Latter-day Saints. So when he shared the strange dream with his Utah landlady over breakfast, it was "more in a spirit of joking and humor than anything else." His hostess understood Morgan's mental perambulations to be something more than comical. She interpreted the dream, explaining that in the future he would be sent on a mission for the Mormon Church: "You will be going over the same road you saw in your dream and will come to that identical fork in the road. Brigham Young will not be there, but don't forget what he told you." A decade later, John Morgan remembered her advice. He faced the fork in the road and then turned left, away from Rome and toward the small settlement of Haywood Valley, where he would establish the first branch of the church in Georgia. He was, in fact, in Chattooga County, much closer to Dirt Town than Rome.[5]

"I find my dream literally fulfilled," Elder Morgan reported. In his letter, which was directed to the editor of the *Deseret News* but intended to communicate mission news to supportive Saints as well as Church Authorities, he describes the success of his Georgia labors. Though "the opposition has been bitter, as it usually is," his ten-week endeavor had produced satisfying results. "We have a good church building," he wrote, "controlled entirely by the Saints," and each Sabbath day he carried his message to new members and their families, an audience of about fifty Georgians. Further, he could report that most of that number intended to leave Georgia for the West, in order to gather with the Saints in Zion. John Morgan claimed no credit for his remarkable achievement; instead, he suggested that a greater force directed his movements. It may have been divine intervention that guided Morgan to Haywood Valley in 1876, but the road he traveled in northwest Georgia was a familiar one. As he neared that momentous and symbolic fork in the road, Morgan had been preoccupied, his mind casting back to his last passage down that same road—as a Union soldier in 1864.[6]

The Civil War carried Morgan far away from his farm home in Coles County, Illinois. He was twenty years old and filled with enthusiasm for the Northern cause when he mustered into service in September 1862 as a private in Company I of the 123rd Illinois Infantry. Private John Morgan found himself among thousands of new recruits sent to assist the Army of the Ohio as it addressed Confederate efforts in Kentucky, and he had only a month's worth of soldiering to his credit when he prepared to engage the enemy for the first time at Perryville. Though Morgan survived, fully a quarter of the green troops of the 123rd Illinois fell at Perryville, most in a mad, unorganized downhill attack against approaching Confederates. Those who survived the initial attack quickly scrambled up the hill to safety, gained the crest, and then continued to run toward the rear. In the engagement at Perryville, an inglorious commencement to Morgan's military career, the 123rd Illinois paid a terrible price: a fourth of the regiment fell there, while the remainder broke and fled.[7]

Winter of 1863 found young Morgan languishing in camp in Murfreesboro, Tennessee, the 123rd Illinois now assigned to William S. Rosecrans's Army of the Cumberland. But his correspondence suggests no waning of enthusiasm for the war, and in a letter written to his parents from camp he restates his resolve, writing, "We of the army are in for nothing but the subjugation or annihilation of the South." Morgan's ability to annihilate Southerners ratcheted up sharply in the spring of 1863 when his regiment was assigned to Col. John T. Wilder's mounted infantry brigade and equipped with Spencer repeating rifles. It was with spurs on his boots and new rifle at hand that he mounted up in June 1863 and moved out in advance of the Army of the Cumberland toward Bragg's Confederates and Chattanooga.[8]

Chattanooga was the prize, and it seemed easily won, but the machinations of both armies carried the war and John Morgan to the rough terrain of northwest Georgia. Believing the Confederates to be on the run, Morgan and the men of Wilder's "Lightning Brigade" rushed into Georgia and toward the bloody confrontation that was Chickamauga. Prior to the great battle, Wilder's men engaged Confederates several times—in Catoosa, Whitfield, and Walker counties—and by September 17 only Chickamauga Creek separated the combatants. The Battle of Chickamauga began the following day for John Morgan and Wilder's Brigade when they could only slow a Confederate advance across the creek and toward Rosecrans's main army. In the two days of fighting that followed, Wilder's men displayed enormous courage, especially when called upon to make a bold counterattack that temporarily halted the rebels in their rout of federal forces. Chickamauga was, to borrow Morgan's own wartime phrase, "all that was good and bad at once." Redeemed from their panic at Perryville, the 123rd Illinois performed nobly at Chickamauga, though both sides suffered tremendous losses, those of the federal forces for a losing cause.[9]

By the time John Morgan prepared to reenter northwest Georgia in the spring of 1864, Union prospects seemed brighter. The Confederates had been swept from their strong positions on Lookout Mountain and Missionary Ridge. Now Grant intended several offensives to pressure Confederate forces, and he charged William T. Sherman with one of them: the capture of Atlanta. For that purpose, John Morgan and the men of Wilder's Brigade remounted and moved to join the main body of the Army of the Cumberland near Dalton in northwest Georgia. In June they confronted rebels at the base of Kennesaw Mountain. In July they waded the Chattahoochee River under Confederate fire and then destroyed the King textile mills at Roswell. As Sherman slowly strangled Confederate resistance in Atlanta, the Lightning Brigade moved east and engaged in a frenzy of destruction at Stone Mountain, Oxford, Covington, and Conyers. Then, as August drew to a close, they advanced with Sherman's forces toward the last Confederate supply line at Jonesboro, and by September, Confederates evacuated the city of Atlanta. While Sherman pursued his march to Savannah and beyond, Wilder's Brigade joined Gen. James H. Wilson's raid on the Confederacy's productive capabilities in Alabama. By the time they finished their mission, the Confederacy lay in ruins.[10]

His obligation to his country satisfied, Morgan rested in Illinois only briefly before departing for New York, where he enrolled for the fall term at Eastman's Commercial College. He anticipated a career in business after a spring graduation, but his life took an unexpected turn when a Utah cattle rancher hired him to drive a herd of Texas longhorns from Missouri to Salt Lake City. Perhaps his desire for adventure remained unsatisfied, for Morgan accepted the challenge and reached Brigham Young's new Zion in time to celebrate Christmas of 1866. Though he was not a member of the Mormon Church, the growing population promised opportunities for one possessed of a college degree; also, according to his family, Morgan was "subconsciously becoming enamoured with the city and its people." Within weeks he established Morgan Commercial College and opened the doors to Salt Lake City students, among them sixteen-year-old Mellie Groesbeck, who eventually captured the headmaster's heart and became Morgan's wife. By the time they married in 1868 at the Endowment House on Temple Square, John Morgan's conversion to Mormonism was complete.[11]

His call to mission service came in the fall of 1875, when the church formally established the Southern States Mission, a new effort to win converts for the Church of Jesus Christ of Latter-day Saints. Missionaries already labored in Texas, but Church authorities called seven men—among them John Hamilton Morgan—to travel to Alabama, Arkansas, Mississippi, Tennessee, Virginia, and Georgia. By autumn of 1876, having responded to the needs of that Georgia letter writer, John Morgan found himself at that significant fork in the road and reliving the past. As he traveled southward, he studied the terrain, noting that physical devastation left by opposing armies "had not entirely disappeared." Forests, he observed, "yet retain the evidence of cruel war in broken limbs and shattered trunks," but the scarred landscape seemed appropriate to a broken people. Towns that had once been bustling and lively, he wrote, "now lie dead and lifeless, with only lone chimneys, that seem to stand sentinel over the desolation around them, a people not yet recovered from the terrible scourge of war, and looking forward with dread to the future."[12]

The bulk of Morgan's combat experience occurred in Georgia, mostly in and around the northwest counties he selected as his postwar mission field, and his determination to seek converts in the area, more than a decade later, surely reflected his familiarity with the region and its inhabitants and his own belief that the Latter-day Saints would receive a receptive audience there. His optimism proved well-founded. After the establishment of the first branch of the church in Chattooga County in 1876, he quickly organized two more branches in Floyd County. He moved to Walker County and started three branches there, near the battlefield of Chickamauga. By 1878 his efforts produced the Varnell's Station Branch, which drew converts from both Whitfield and Catoosa counties.[13]

It was Morgan's decision to restrict his missionary efforts to the Georgia mountains, and his letters suggest that he envisioned a region that stretched across the northernmost counties of Alabama and Georgia and into North Carolina. Later, bemused newspaper reporters in Atlanta would report that Mormon elders "stick to the mountainous districts," though they could not explain the phenomenon. One correspondent admitted that "no one can tell why the Mormons have devoted so much time" to the region "in which they have been working so long. They are not to be found elsewhere, but they seem to be determined upon captivating the section spoken of" in northwest Georgia.[14]

Morgan's conclusion that the southern Appalachian Mountains held unusual promise did not signify singular wisdom. As Gordon McKinney points out, the Civil War introduced many of Appalachia's future entrepreneurs and industrialists to the abundance of natural resources in the region.

Northern soldiers who fought in and around Chattanooga—among them John T. Wilder of the "Lightning Brigade"—were the first to notice the evidence of coal and iron ore in that area. Only two years after his release from military service, Wilder relocated his family from Indiana to Chattanooga, Tennessee. With two associates he organized the Roane Iron Company and dedicated the next half century to extracting East Tennessee's natural resources. Like his commanding officer, John Morgan also cast an acquisitive eye across enemy country; however, when Morgan returned to the South, it would be to exploit only the untapped *human* resources of the area. And he deliberately selected those in the mountain counties of northwest Georgia to receive his message.[15]

John Morgan's rediscovery of north Georgia coincided with America's new awareness of Appalachia as a distinct and unusual place. It was in the decades immediately following the Civil War that local-color writers began to describe the region as a "strange land" populated by "peculiar people," convincing many Americans that Appalachian society had developed in very different ways from the rest of the country. Their articles emphasized the poverty and ignorance of southern mountaineers and portrayed a way of life culturally out of step with America's new industrialization and urbanization. Over time public fascination with tales of feuding and moonshining gave way to a new perception that the rugged geography of the southern mountains hindered the development of a people likely to be the last representatives of the American frontier. Intellectuals like William Goodell Frost, president of Berea College in Kentucky, successfully framed the destitution and backwardness of Appalachian Americans as a product of their geographic isolation and argued forcefully for intervention. As the initial enthusiasm for educating southern blacks was fading after Reconstruction, idealistic Americans turned their attention to mountain whites, a group as needy and backward as the freedmen but possessing the pure Anglo-Saxon blood of America's ancestors. Though America's development had passed them by thus far, residents of the southern highlands, it was believed, only needed "education, religion, and civilization" in order to "advance with the rest of the nation." Protestant churches rushed to offer relief in the form of home mission societies and settlement houses; in fact, as Loyal Jones has pointed out, "no group in the country" prompted more concern among Christians than did the unchurched souls of Appalachia. "Never have so many missionaries been sent to save so many," he wrote, "as has been the case in Appalachia." By the mid-1880s, in the spirit of competitive Christianity that characterized those years, the Presbyterians, Methodists, Baptists, and Episcopalians turned their attention to the mountains.[16]

Considered within the context of this powerful religious impulse into the mountains, John Morgan's mission to north Georgia seems to fit neatly within a larger movement dedicated to cultural uplift and determined to propel mountain folks back into American society. The Mormon Church, however, did not intend to send a mission to Appalachia and would not—at this particular time—have supported a program that encouraged cultural assimilation. At midcentury the Church firmly set itself apart from America's dominant culture when church officials acknowledged the practice of plural marriage, or polygamy. John Morgan likewise had little interest in preparing the inhabitants of his mission field to join the nation's march into the twentieth century. Elder Morgan believed that a world of sinfulness and corruption existed beyond the boundaries of the Mormon Zion. He understood that his goal was to warn Americans of their danger and to gather believers to the West. He had already given up on America, finding "the spirit of adultery and sin everywhere." Instead, he argued for isolation, explaining to potential converts the importance of "gathering to Zion," a physical separation that symbolized spiritual separation. According to this millennial doctrine, Mormons were to remove themselves as much as possible from the sinful world and gather together with fellow church members to prepare for the return of Christ. Under the influence of the Gathering, most new Latter-day Saints left their homes to resettle in Mormon centers in the West. In the coming years, Presbyterians, Baptists, and Methodists would promote programs intended to ameliorate sinfulness, poverty, and ignorance in Georgia; Morgan offered simply to transport Georgians out of their current condition.[17]

There was ample fuel for his proselytizing zeal. Based upon his observation, the South was a vast region of lost souls, and when he examined the state of Georgia from his Chattooga County vantage point, the task ahead of him seemed daunting. In a letter to Utah, Morgan stressed the enormity of his task and the potential richness of his new mission field: "I look around and realize that, here in this State of Georgia, there are two millions and more of people only a small portion of which ever heard the gospel." Nevertheless, with all two million to choose from, Morgan deliberately selected those in the mountain counties of northwest Georgia to receive his message. Clearly his description of the state, though it implies an unchurched population, referred only to those who had not yet received the message of the Latter-day Saints. It was certainly not the case that northwest Georgians lacked the opportunity to practice religious devotion. Whitfield County boasted fifty churches, among them eighteen Methodist churches, seventeen Baptist churches, five Presbyterian churches, one Primitive Baptist church, one Christian church, one Episcopal church, one Catholic church, one Congregational church, and five churches to meet the spiritual needs of its black residents. Floyd County counted forty-nine churches, while Walker County claimed forty-four, including one Universalist congregation. Chattooga County possessed twenty-one churches, and Catoosa County reported thirteen church organizations.[18]

As a result of this denominational diversity, northwest Georgians were "torn to pieces religiously," Elder Morgan reported. He believed that Georgians suffered under the influence of an evil and powerful apostate church that ruled Babylon and corrupted the gospel of Jesus Christ through the false teachings of its "hireling priests." Thus, he accepted as his responsibility the wrestling of lost souls from the evil and greedy influence of north Georgia's spiritual representatives. The Church of Jesus Christ of Latter-day Saints, which rejected a paid ministry, saw potential corruption in the salaries paid to ministers, believing it to be money better spent in behalf of the poor. North Georgian Benjamin Echols, whose conversion to Mormonism likely shaped his memories and criticism of mountain religious life, remembered attending many different churches but being drawn to none in particular: "I couldn't get interested enough to join any one of the churches. Each one claimed that their church was the only right one to join but I could not see where any one of them was better than the others." He recalled that attending church meant traveling approximately four miles and that meetings were held on an infrequent and sporadic basis, as one circuit preacher was paid to service four churches. On Sundays when no sermon or Sunday School meeting was available, Benjamin and his friends congregated at swimming ponds or visited with neighbors, but they respected the Sabbath, which meant "no work no hunting no fishing." Echols remembered that paying the minister proved a burden, too, even for one as celebrated as Methodist circuit rider Sam Jones, who "did his first preaching in our cirket [sic] and was paid five hundred dollars a year by the four churches." Eventually, he noted, Sam Jones "could get five hundred in one day," an amount that would have enraged John Morgan.[19]

In addition to the perceived greediness of Georgia's preachers, proof of ministerial indifference lay all around him. Northwest Georgia's poverty convinced the elder that Babylon's ministers cared little for their flocks. According to his missionary journal and mission reports, Morgan expected to find northwest Georgia only partially healed from the devastation of the recent war—he had, after all, participated in causing that devastation. He anticipated that Georgia's citizens still suffered, fiscally and emotionally. Arriving, as he did, during a time of severe economic depression, Morgan made frequent references to the financial insecurity that plagued north Georgians, but he expressed shock at the discovery that north Georgians faced "poverty of the most pinching character." As he made his way across the ridges and valleys of his new mission field, he recorded his impressions and sent them back to Utah, where they were reproduced in newspapers and delivered to Salt Lake City readers.[20]

He described in near-ethnographic detail his visits to two-room homes constructed entirely of logs that were "daubed with clay, red or yellow . . . the stoop and portico slowly rotting away," window glass gone and replaced by "various articles of wearing apparel too numerous to mention." Families, he reported, subsisted on an unhealthy diet of bacon and corn bread, but they dulled their hunger with the "constant use of tobacco." When questioned about the deplorable state of affairs, Morgan continued, the "man of the house" said it seemed as though "a curse was devouring the earth," as "his wheat won't head out, his oats won't grow high enough to cut, his corn does not produce anything, his fruit is blasted and the earth refuses to yield its increase." Asked to speculate further, most north Georgians traced their current troubles back to the war. "You hear it on all sides," Morgan wrote, "'since the war.' 'Since the war' appears to be the explanation for all the evils they are subject to." Perhaps they intended only to date their troubles to the postwar period, but they may have been affixing blame to the conflict itself. More introspective (or perhaps more melancholic) farmers interpreted their postwar difficulties as indicators of divine punishment, explaining that "there is something wrong, that the people are not right, that God is displeased with them, and that there is something terrible coming."[21]

It may have been the obvious poverty of the region that convinced John Morgan to concentrate his labors in northwest Georgia. Rex Thomas Price, a historian of nineteenth-century Mormon missions, observes that elders often preferred to labor in the poorest of districts and "may not have made a real effort to reach the rich and powerful," as the Book of Mormon indicates that "God's people could be found among the humble and poor, not the rich and proud." Northwest Georgia yielded an abundance of humble and poor. The wealthiest of Morgan's Georgia converts claimed real estate and personal property valued at $5,300, but that figure represents a greater economic resource than most new Saints enjoyed. Considered as a group, the average convert reported a total net worth of less than $1,000. Most were landless, and some—like Albion Haggard of Walker County—owned absolutely nothing at all.[22]

Price argues further that Mormon scriptures expressed an anticapitalist bias, so Elder Morgan may have anticipated that northwest Georgia's yeoman farmers, with a strong tradition of community, would embrace the Latter-day Saints' message of religious and economic communalism. Only two years earlier Brigham Young had reinstituted the United Order, a program intended to return Utah's Saints to a more communal way of life, restore economic self-sufficiency, and resist integration into the national economy. Inspired by Joseph Smith's vision of a "commonwealth of communes," the United Order stressed economic cooperation and the elimination of poverty. Mormon settlements often organized into voluntary producer cooperatives, allowing members to contribute money and property to the Order and to receive a return according to the amount of capital and labor invested. In fewer cases, the Orders reflected a more complete commitment to communal life, with members relinquishing all of their property and sharing equally in the product. In either case, Young intended the Orders to replicate family, and Morgan may have understood northwest Georgians' reliance on kin and community as congenial to Mormon values.[23]

Or perhaps economic concerns would override religious considerations entirely. Church authorities acknowledged this possibility and worried that some would come to Zion for purely temporal reasons. Even Brigham Young once speculated that the willingness of converts to migrate to the new Zion could have been motivated by economic, rather than religious, interests; he speculated that "many embrace the Gospel actuated by no other motive than to have the privilege of being removed from their oppressed condition to where they will not suffer. They will embrace any doctrine under the heavens, if you will only take them from their present condition." Certainly critics of Mormonism believed this to be the case and suggested that the Church's appeal was more economic than theological. In 1879 a reporter for an Atlanta newspaper unknowingly echoed Young's conclusion in an article that explains the seductive and subversive appeal of the Mormons' communitarian message: "They . . . talk about the fertile valleys of Utah, the lavish fruits and the luxurious crops, the fine city of Salt Lake, in which every Mormon had part ownership—in short the pretty pastoral life wherein the richest valley of earth, with little work and a powerful and contented life, was offered to all comers. This picture won the fancy of many a poor farmer who had scratched for years in the scanty soil of our hills at home, and could hardly keep body and soul together, and of many a woman, young and old."[24]

The Mormon message *should* appeal especially to North Georgia's women and children, John Morgan said, as those "deprived of their natural protectors" suffered the most. He expressed surprise to see northwest Georgia's females, white and black, married or unmarried, laboring with hoes in fields of corn, cotton, and cane, reporting that "women work in the field indiscriminately with the men." Field labor prompted a relaxation of race and gender boundaries that Morgan found distasteful, such as when he witnessed a black man cradling wheat while a white woman followed closely behind in order to bind the crop. Georgia's women suffered for lack of men, Morgan believed, and Georgians believed this as well. The *Atlanta Constitution* suggested that the Civil War had robbed Georgia of the "flower of her manhood," estimating that females exceeded males by more than sixty thousand statewide. John Morgan calculated more precisely, concluding that the state possessed "26,199 more females of a marriageable age than males." They could find husbands in Zion.[25]

It is also possible that Morgan preferred Georgia's mountain districts because fewer black Georgians lived there. During the nineteenth century, Church authorities excluded blacks from the priesthood, although Southern States missionaries occasionally carried their gospel to black Americans. Elder Henry Boyle reported that he baptized three black Virginians in 1868, and in 1883 missionary Joseph Morrell visited a black woman in South Carolina in order to minister to her ailing son, though these instances seem exceptions that serve to prove the rule. John Morgan's decision to proselytize in northwest Georgia effectively eliminated blacks from potential conversion. Overall, black Georgians represented 46 percent of the state's total population, but the northernmost counties claimed a disproportionately small number of them. Of the counties in Morgan's northwest Georgia mission field—Chattooga, Floyd, Walker, Whitfield and Catoosa—Floyd County's black population was the highest at 33 percent. Its black residents dampened Morgan's enthusiasm for Rome, a city he generally admired: "The negroes are generally idle and vicious, congregating in towns and cities, where great swarms of them can be seen sunning themselves on the street corners, having become corrupted to the lowest degree, physically and morally." In Chattooga County, black residents represented only 22 percent of the total population; in Walker and Whitfield counties, 15 percent; and in Catoosa County, 14 percent. Although Floyd County's black population grew to 39 percent by 1880, the black population in other northwest counties was shrinking. By 1880 the percentage of blacks in Chattooga County dropped to 20 percent, in Whitfield County to 19 percent, in Walker County to 14 percent, and in Catoosa County to 13 percent. Despite its growing black population, Rome's favorable location eventually overcame Morgan's prejudices, and in 1878 he located his headquarters in that city. There is no record suggesting that John Morgan proselytized among northwest Georgia's black population, however, and no reason to believe that northwest Georgia's whites would have welcomed or approved of a biracial church.[26]

Antipathy toward black Georgians likely contributed to Morgan's decision to labor in the mountains, but it is clear from his correspondence that he also believed the mountain region to be healthier than counties to the south. In reports to Church authorities, he notes that "there is an abundance of mountain country that promises very fair indeed, and is in my opinion one of the healthiest sections of the Union . . . [this] portion of the South being cool and well watered as well as very healthy." Georgians also believed in the healthfulness of the region's climate and boasted that "no country under the sun has been so munificently blessed as North Georgia. . . . She has been looked to as the land of health and vigor, of mild and genial skies." In fact, one booster doubted "whether there is a section of country in the United States more desirable to live in than North Georgia." In addition to the more temperate climate, the area's abundant mineral springs offered a respite from warm Georgia summers, as well as cures for various afflictions, and attracted tourists from both the South and North. Catoosa Springs near Ringgold, described as the "Saratoga of the South," boasted more than fifty mineral springs, each with unique medicinal properties. Young women, it was reported, seemed especially drawn to a spring that promised beauty.[27]

The mountain South also offered refuge from the yellow fever, or "Yellow Jack," that cruelly visited the South each summer, especially coastal cities like New Orleans and Mobile. The wealthiest southerners fled desperately north at the first sign of the scourge, with a frenzy that Morgan likened to wartime. They are "fleeing before it," he wrote of the disease in 1878, "as they would from an army of invasion, while those who are overtaken are perishing miserably in its track." Even residents of Chattanooga evacuated in that year, leaving the city nearly deserted and under quarantine to deter visitors from farther south. But Morgan reassured the Saints in Utah that they need not fear for Georgia missionaries, as "out in this mountain country we do not apprehend any trouble, as the pure mountain air will counteract the influences of our malarial districts." Despite his assurances, illness frequently forced Southern States missionaries to return home. At a time when Church elders labored in Europe, Samoa, New Zealand, and Palestine as well as the American South, more than one-third of the missionaries forced to return home as a result of sickness served in the southern states.[28]

A conventional explanation for Morgan's self-defined field of labor rests in the assumption that residents of the mountain South espoused Unionist tendencies during the war and thus would prove more receptive to this former federal soldier. Certainly north Georgia's mountaineers rallied only slowly to the Confederate cause, and Morgan's return to Chattooga County proved congenial to him. Morgan's turn to the left and away from Rome in 1876 carried him to the farm of Thomas Barbour, on whose property he had foraged in 1864 as Wilder's Brigade moved toward Atlanta. For two days in mid-May 1864, Thomas Barbour remembered, Wilder's men made a temporary residence on his farm. They emptied his barn, removed four mules from the corral, and fed two hundred bushels of wheat to their horses before turning to the contents of Barbour's house. As evening fell, the federals tore through the farmhouse floor to gain access to the cellar, which housed five thousand pounds of bacon, Barbour claimed. The next morning, after a night that saw the partial destruction of his home, Barbour's seven head of cattle joined a small drove of confiscated livestock. But Thomas Barbour described himself as observing the proceedings with something approaching equanimity; he was, after all, "a Union man."[29]

"From the very beginning of the rebellion," he wrote, "I sympathized with the Union cause. I thought the Union was worth more to the people than all their property, negroes, and everything else." To everyone who would listen, he argued against disunion, predicting that "if the Union was broken up we were ruined." Against his wishes, both of his sons enlisted in the Confederate army, though Barbour suggested that the decision was coerced by fear of conscription. When he learned that his son John was preparing for combat in a rebel camp in Tennessee, he paid a substitute $3,000 to take the young man's place. Older son Thomas simply recalled that his father offered him "horse, bridle and saddle to find my way through the lines" and into the Union army, as well as "a lot of land" as incentive to desert. "If I was killed I would die in a good cause," he remembered his father reassuring him. Neighbor William L. Marshal claimed to have Unionist sympathies, but when he faced Confederate conscription, he also volunteered for the rebel army. Like that of Barbour's two sons, Marshal's service proved temporary, and he credited Thomas Barbour with assisting his escape to the North.[30]

Barbour's memory of Wilder's visit assisted him in successfully claiming recompense from the federal government after the war. John Morgan's recollection of his Chattooga County sojourn proved equally vivid, guiding him back some twelve years later, armed only with a Bible and the Book of Mormon. Perhaps the Union veteran and the Southern Unionist recalled that time; if so, Morgan did not record the shared memory in his journal or correspondence, but a relationship surely blossomed. In the winter of 1876 Elder Morgan and Thomas Barbour waded into Armuchee Creek, where the Georgian was baptized into the Church of Jesus Christ of Latter-day Saints. Waiting their turn in the cold waters were Barbour's two sons and his neighbor William L. Marshal.[31]

Despite this early success among Chattooga County's Union sympathizers, Morgan did not limit his proselytizing efforts to those opposed to the Confederate cause. Dillingham H. Elledge of Catoosa County served the Confederacy with distinction as captain of Company G, Thirty-sixth (Broyle's) Georgia Infantry. Elledge's neighbors Henry and Asbury Huffaker enlisted in Company G as well. But illness forced Captain Elledge to resign his position in 1863, and he was recuperating in a Whitfield County hospital when the Huffaker brothers were captured at Vicksburg. They returned to Confederate service after their parole but in 1864 were captured again in Marietta, Georgia, and consigned to another U.S. Army prison. After the war, both brothers returned to northwest Georgia, where Henry Huffaker married the daughter of Captain Elledge. All eventually embraced the Church of Jesus Christ of Latter-day Saints. Mormon conversion, like sectional loyalty, often followed lines of kin and community.[32]

The irony of the situation did not escape John Morgan, and he noted that "he was now laboring to bring into the fold of the church . . . the very men and women with whom he and the boys in blue were then contending." His journal reveals the extent to which memories of the Civil War dogged his footsteps as he traveled again the ridges and valleys of northwest Georgia. He enthusiastically shared his wartime exploits with Elder Thomas Lisonbee, who labored nearby on Sand Mountain in Alabama and conducted battlefield tours whenever Mormon elders visited him in Georgia. He visited with General and Mrs. Wilder in Chattanooga and reunited with Colonel Woods of the Fifteenth Indiana Volunteers in that same city. In more solitary moments, he escaped his missionary labors to wade Chickamauga Creek. Perhaps the intensity of his past missions informed his current one, for he attacked his proselytizing tasks with the determination and ferocity of Wilder's "Lightning Brigade," an enthusiasm that often provoked the animus of unsympathetic Georgians. In 1879 a Georgia newspaperman, who displayed no knowledge of John Morgan's martial past, evaluated Mormon successes in Georgia's mountain districts and described the missionary in terms that could have been applied to the young infantryman on earlier visits to the state: Morgan was "an extraordinary person," the reporter wrote, "brave, aggressive, shifty and eloquent. He begged no quarter and made no concessions, but went ahead preaching his faith as one inspired. Nothing could daunt him, and very few men could argue with him." Before the first year of his Georgia mission had passed, Morgan could report to Salt Lake City that "a general spirit of inquiry has sprung up throughout all this mountain country."[33]

Morgan led the first company of southern Saints west in November 1877. How much or how little Morgan's followers understood of his plans for them is not clear. Some reported themselves bound for a Mormon settlement in New Mexico, but most of the company simply followed John Morgan to an uncertain destination in the West. Possibly their lives in the postwar South had become so precarious, so unpredictable, that they were willing to tolerate further uncertainty in their lives. Or they may have simply trusted that God would make the way clear for this company of religious pilgrims. In this instance, their optimism must be inferred from their actions. After a difficult wagon journey to Scottsboro, Alabama, Morgan's Georgia Saints traveled by rail to Pueblo, Colorado, where they constructed a winter barracks, organized a cooperative community, pooled their money to purchase supplies, and prepared for a spring resumption of their journey. They completed their exodus the following year, traveling farther south to the San Luis Valley of southern Colorado, just north of the border with

New Mexico. In time, they named their new settlement "Manassa." By late 1878 Morgan could report that the southern mission had produced more than five hundred converts; of that number, half had already emigrated to the West. Church authorities officially acknowledged Morgan's success when they named him president of the entire Southern States Mission in 1878, a position he held for a decade.[34]

As the intensity and success of Morgan's efforts accelerated, so did the violence against Mormon missionaries in Georgia. In 1879 a Catoosa County mob chased Elder Charles W. Hardy from the state; three months later, the same men confronted elders Joseph Standing and Rudger Clawson on a Whitfield County road. It is not clear that the mob intended murder, but in the confrontation, Joseph Standing was killed. Fortunate to have escaped without injury, Rudger Clawson speculated that the threat to personal safety would convince the church to abandon the South, but that was not the case. John Morgan continued to bring Mormon elders into the southern states and persisted in his efforts to send southern converts to the West, despite the threats of violence and new legislation in Georgia that forbade the preaching of polygamy.[35]

Thus, when missionaries from other faiths carried competing religious beliefs into the southern Appalachian Mountains, they confronted established representatives from the Church of Jesus Christ of Latter-day Saints. Presbyterian Samuel Tyndale Wilson wrote that he had "personally and repeatedly seen the emissaries of the Mormon abomination plying their mission of perversion and seduction" among the southern mountains. Presbyterian Edward O. Guerrant, who labored in the mountains of Kentucky, Tennessee, and North Carolina in the 1880s and 1890s, reported that he encountered Mormons "in the most distant and inaccessible parts of the mountains. They have more missionaries in Kentucky (and probably in every Southern State) than all other denominations together."[36]

As president of the Southern States Mission, John Hamilton Morgan is largely responsible for the Mormon presence in the southern mountains. He labored among northwest Georgians for a decade, led the first of many expeditions to the West, and then established a home among Georgians in the Colorado colony of Manassa. Trusting him, hundreds of Georgia Saints left the state in the last decades of the nineteenth century, hoping to find true religion and a better life in the new Mormon Zion.

Notes

The author gratefully acknowledges the assistance of John Inscoe in the preparation of this essay. Additional thanks are due the Joseph Fielding Smith Institute at Brigham Young University for its generous funding of the author's research.

1. Leonard J. Arrington, "Mormon Beginnings in the American South," *Task Paper in LDS History,* no. 9 (Salt Lake City: Historical Department of the Church of Jesus Christ of Latter-day Saints, 1976).

2. Arrington, "Mormon Beginnings"; LaMar C. Berrett, "History of the Southern States Mission, 1831–1861" (master's thesis, Brigham Young University, 1960).

3. Heather M. Seferovitch, "History of the LDS Southern States Mission, 1875–1898" (master's thesis, Brigham Young University, 1996); Devon H. Nish, "A Brief History of the Southern States Mission for One Hundred Years, 1830–1930," Special Collections, box 8677.5, Harold B. Lee Library, Brigham Young University, Provo, UT; "Southern States Mission," box 5, folder 27, John Hamilton Morgan Papers, Accn. 1465, Manuscripts Division, Marriott Library, University of Utah, Salt Lake City (hereafter cited as JHM Papers); Record of Elders in the Southern States Mission, 1877–1898, Southern States Mission, Manuscript History, reel 1, Archives of the Church of Jesus Christ of Latter-day Saints, Salt Lake City; Arthur M. Richardson and Nicholas G. Morgan Sr., *The Life and Ministry of John Morgan* (privately printed, 1965), 116–20; Marshall Wingfield, "Tennessee's Mormon Massacre," *Tennessee Historical Quarterly* 17 (March 1958): 19–20; Elder John Morgan to Editor, *Deseret News,* December 4, 1876, transcript in Letters and Articles on the Missionary Labors of Pres. John Morgan, 1872–1879, vol. 1, box 1, book 1, JHM Papers.

4. John Morgan to Editor, *Deseret News,* December 4, 1876, JHM Papers; typescript of John Morgan's journal, November 1875–November 1892, entry dated October 5, 1876, JHM Papers; Richardson and Morgan, *Life and Ministry,* 116–20; Journal History of the Church, December 4, 1876, microfilm, Historical Department, Church of Jesus Christ of Latter-day Saints, Salt Lake City.

5. John Morgan to Editor, *Deseret News,* December 4, 1876, JHM Papers; Richardson and Morgan, *Life and Ministry,* 116–20.

6. John Morgan to Editor, *Deseret News,* December 4, 1876, JHM Papers; Richardson and Morgan, *Life and Ministry,* 116–20.

7. 1840 United States Census, Pike County, Kentucky, M704, 283; 1850, Decatur County, Indiana, M432, 166; 1860, Coles County, Illinois, M653, 75, National Archives and Records Administration, Washington, DC, available at www.ancestry.com; John Morgan's journal, January 4, 1876, JHM Papers; Andrew Jensen, *Latter-day Saint Biographical Encyclopedia: A Compilation of Biographical Sketches of Prominent Men and Women in the Church of Jesus Christ of Latter-day Saints* (Salt Lake City: Publishers Press, 1971), 1:204; Richardson and Morgan, *Life and Ministry,* 3–4; compiled military service file of John Hamilton Morgan,

National Archives and Records Administration (NARA), Washington, DC; statement concerning the history of the 123rd Regiment Illinois Infantry Volunteers, Civil War, from the Adjutant General's Office, War Department, June 15, 1926, box 5, folder 12, JHM Papers; United States War Department, *War of the Rebellion: A Compilation of the Official Records of the Union and Confederate Armies,* (Washington, DC: Government Printing Office, 1880–1891), series 1, vol. 16, part 1, 1023–31, 1033, 1040, 1059–64; Frederick Henry Dyer, "Regimental Histories," in *A Compendium of the War of the Rebellion* (Dayton, OH: National Historical Society, 1979), 2:1098; Janet B. Hewett, *Supplement to the Official Records of the Union and Confederate Armies,* part 2 (Wilmington, NC: Broadfoot Publishing Company, 1999), 14:580; James M. McPherson, *Battle Cry of Freedom: The Civil War Era* (New York: Ballantine Books, 1988), 409, 512–20; James M. McPherson, *Ordeal by Fire: The Civil War and Reconstruction* (New York City: McGraw-Hill, 2001), 312–13; James A. Connolly, *Three Years in the Army of the Cumberland,* ed. Paul M. Angle (Bloomington: Indiana University Press, 1959), 17–18, 21; Kenneth W. Noe, *Perryville: This Grand Havoc of Battle* (Lexington: University Press of Kentucky, 2001).

8. John Morgan to parents, January 28, 1863, transcript in Miscellaneous Typescript Letters from John Morgan, 1863–1886, box 2, folder 1, JHM Papers; War Department Statement, JHM Papers; Hewett, *Supplement to the Official Records,* part 2, 14:732–36, 563–66; McPherson, *Battle Cry of Freedom,* 558–59, 594–95; Samuel C. Williams, *General John T. Wilder: Commander of the Lightning Brigade* (Bloomington: Indiana University Press, 1936), 13–15; Robert E. Harbison, "Wilder's Brigade in the Tullahoma and Chattanooga Campaigns of the American Civil War" (master's thesis, Army Command and General Staff College, 2002), http://handle.dtic.mil/100.2/ADA406434.

9. John Morgan to parents, January 28, 1863, JHM Papers; *Official Records,* series 1, vol. 30, part 1, 40–42, 47–52, 64, 171–79, 444–49, 450, 459–60, 464; *Official Records,* series 1, vol. 30, part 3, 75, 77–78, 103, 113, 119, 124, 267–76, 493, 495–96, 512–13, 546, 568–69, 577–78, 609, 624, 836, 878, 999, 1001–2; Harbison, "Wilder's Brigade," 10, 15, 29–37, 40, 50–53, 55–58, 60–62, 68–78, 80–86, 91n., 100; Connolly, *Three Years,* 74, 94, 97, 98 n., 101, 112–16, 119, 122–23, 127; Dyer, *Compendium,* 2:1098; McPherson, *Battle Cry of Freedom,* 281, 669–74; McPherson, *Ordeal by Fire,* 361–65; Richard A. Baumgartner, *Blue Lightning: Wilder's Mounted Infantry Brigade in the Battle of Chickamauga* (Huntington, WV: Blue Acorn Press, 1997); Joseph M. Brown, *The Mountain Campaigns in Georgia; or, War Scenes on the Western & Atlantic* (Buffalo, NY: Matthews, Northrup & Co., 1890); William Henry Harrison Clark, *History in Catoosa County* (privately published, 1972), 160; John Bowers, *Chickamauga and Chattanooga: The Battles that Doomed the Confederacy* (New York: Harper Collins, 1994), 74.

10. Compiled military service file of John Hamilton Morgan, NARA; *Official Records,* series 1, vol. 38, part 1, 3, 101–2; *Official Records,* series 1, vol. 38, part 2, 745–49, 803–6, 809, 820–22, 848–49, 850–51; *Official Records,* series 1, vol.

39, part 2, 803–5, 811–15; *Official Records,* series 1, vol. 39, part 3, 574; *Official Records,* series 1, vol. 49, part 1, 402–3, 452–55; Richardson and Morgan, *Life and Ministry,* 17–18; McPherson, *Ordeal by Fire,* 365–69; McPherson, *Battle Cry of Freedom,* 676–80; Harbison, "Wilder's Brigade," 42, 46, 48–49; Clark, *History in Catoosa County,* 183; Michael D. Hitt, *Charged with Treason: Ordeal of 400 Mill Workers during Military Operations in Roswell, Georgia, 1864–1865* (Monroe, NY: Library Research Associates, 1992), 10–18, 29–30, 33.

11. Richardson and Morgan, *Life and Ministry,* 23–24, 36–44, 48–49.

12. John Morgan to Editor, *Deseret News,* December 4, 1876, JHM Papers; Record of Elders in the Southern States Mission, 1877–1898, Archives of the Church of Jesus Christ of Latter-day Saints, Salt Lake City; Nish, "A Brief History of the Southern States Mission"; Richardson and Morgan, *Life and Ministry,* 91–93, 96, 111–15; John Morgan's journal, entry dated December 27, 1875, JHM Papers; typed version of John Morgan's journal, box 4, folder 1, JHM Papers.

13. Report of Branches of the Church in Georgia, box 1, book 1, JHM Papers; Richard E. Small, *The Post Offices of Georgia, 1764–1900* (Centerville, VA: R. E. Small, 1998); Marion R. Hemperley, *Cities, Towns, and Communities of Georgia between 1847–1962* (Easley, SC: Southern Historical Press, 1980); Kenneth K. Krakow, *Georgia Place-Names: Their History and Origins* (Macon, GA: Winship Press, 1994).

14. John Morgan to Church President John Taylor, January 11, 1879, transcript in Typescript Letters from John Morgan to Church Leaders, 1878–1887, box 2, folder 3, JHM Papers; *Atlanta Constitution,* August 5, 1879.

15. Williams, *General John T. Wilder,* 13–15; Gordon B. McKinney, "The Civil War and Reconstruction," in *High Mountains Rising: Appalachia in Time and Place,* ed. Richard A. Straw and H. Tyler Blethen (Urbana: University of Illinois Press, 2004), 54; Ronald D Eller, *Miners, Millhands, and Mountaineers: Industrialization of the Appalachian South, 1880–1930* (Knoxville: University of Tennessee Press, 1982); Ronald L. Lewis, *Transforming the Appalachian Countryside: Railroads, Deforestation, and Social Change in West Virginia, 1880–1920* (Chapel Hill: University of North Carolina Press, 1998); Robert S. Weise, *Grasping at Independence: Debt, Male Authority, and Mineral Rights in Appalachian Kentucky, 1850–1915* (Knoxville: University of Tennessee Press, 2001).

16. Henry David Shapiro, *Appalachia on Our Mind: The Southern Mountains and Mountaineers in the American Consciousness, 1870–1920* (Chapel Hill: University of North Carolina Press, 1978); Allen W. Batteau, *The Invention of Appalachia* (Tucson: University of Arizona Press, 1990); Mary Beth Pudup, Dwight B. Billings, and Altina L. Waller, eds., *Appalachia in the Making: The Mountain South in the Nineteenth Century* (Chapel Hill: University of North Carolina Press, 1995), especially Billings, Pudup, and Waller, "Taking Exception with Exceptionalism: The Emergence and Transformation of Historical Studies of Appalachia," 2; John Alexander Williams, *Appalachia: A History* (Chapel Hill: University of North Carolina Press, 2002), 201; David C. Hsiung, "Stereotypes," in *High Mountains Ris-*

ing (see note 15), 104; S. Marc Sherrod, "The Southern Mountaineer, Presbyterian Home Missions, and a Synod for Appalachia," *American Presbyterians* 71, no. 1 (1993): 35; Deborah Vansau McCauley, *Appalachian Mountain Religion: A History* (Urbana: University of Illinois Press, 1995), 339; Loyal Jones, *Faith and Meaning in the Southern Uplands* (Urbana: University of Illinois Press, 1999); James C. Klotter, "The Black South and White Appalachia," *Journal of American History* 66, no. 4 (1980): 841; Nina Silber, "'What Does America Need So Much as Americans?': Race and Northern Reconciliation with Southern Appalachia, 1870–1900," in *Appalachians and Race: The Mountain South from Slavery to Segregation,* ed. John C. Inscoe (Lexington: University Press of Kentucky, 2001), 245–58.

17. Rex Thomas Price, "The Mormon Missionary of the Nineteenth Century" (PhD diss., University of Wisconsin-Madison, 1991), 240; Wallace Stegner, *The Gathering of Zion: The Story of the Mormon Trail* (Lincoln: University of Nebraska Press, 1981); Leonard J. Arrington and Davis Bitton, *The Mormon Experience: A History of the Latter-day Saints* (Urbana: University of Illinois Press, 1992), 38; William Mulder, "Mormonism's 'Gathering': An American Doctrine with a Difference," *Church History* 23, no. 3 (September 1954): 248–64.

18. John Morgan to Editor, *Deseret News,* May 30, 1878, box 1, book 1, JHM Papers; 1870 United States Census, social statistics schedules for Whitfield, Floyd, Walker, Chattooga, and Catoosa counties, Georgia; *Atlanta Constitution,* November 2, 1877.

19. John Morgan to Editor, *Deseret News,* May 17, 1877, box 1, book 1, JHM Papers; Benjamin Echols, "Reminiscences and Journal, 1946–1950," microfilm, Archives of the Church of Jesus Christ of Latter-day Saints, Salt Lake City; Price, "The Mormon Missionary," 46, 242–43, 339, 481; David B. Parker, "'Quit Your Meanness': Sam Jones's Theology for the New South," *Georgia Historical Quarterly* 77 (Winter 1993): 711–27. In his article, Parker points out that much of Sam Jones's energy after 1880 was dedicated to raising funds for the Methodist Orphan Home.

20. John Morgan to Editor, *Deseret News,* June 16, 1877, box 1, book 1, JHM Papers.

21. Ibid.

22. 1870 United States Census for Chattooga, Floyd, Walker, Catoosa, and Whitfield counties; Price, "The Mormon Missionary," 304–8, 317–18, 390, 414–15; Converts of Elder John Morgan in North Georgia during his first Mission in 1876, box 3, folder 3, JHM Papers; Conferences Established by John Morgan in the Organization of the Southern States Mission, box 3, folder 5, JHM Papers. From these documents, which cover only the years 1876–1879, I identified 116 baptized adults, male and female, and 133 young family members. Thirty-five heads-of-households were then located on the 1870 census and yielded the figures I cite in the text.

23. Price, "The Mormon Missionary," 304–8, 317–18, 390, 414–15; Arrington and Bitton, *The Mormon Experience,* 126; Leonard J. Arrington, Feramorz Y. Fox,

and Dean L. May, *Building the City of God: Community and Cooperation among the Mormons* (Salt Lake City: Deseret Book Company, 1976).

24. Arrington and Bitton, *The Mormon Experience,* 37; *Atlanta Constitution,* July 28, 1879.

25. John Morgan to Editor, *Deseret News,* January 1877, box 1, book 1, JHM Papers; John Morgan and James T. Lisonbee to Editor, *Deseret News,* June 16, 1877, box 1, book 1, JHM Papers; *Atlanta Constitution,* November 2, 1877.

26. John Morgan to Editor, *Deseret News,* March 9, 1877, Journal History of the Church, Historical Department, Church of Jesus Christ of Latter-day Saints, Salt Lake City; Price, "The Mormon Missionary," 393, 402–4, 406, 411; 1870 United States Census, population schedules for Whitfield, Floyd, Walker, Chattooga, and Catoosa counties, available at www.fisher.lib.virginia.edu; John C. Inscoe, ed., *Appalachians and Race: The Mountain South from Slavery to Segregation* (Lexington: University Press of Kentucky, 2001); John C. Inscoe, ed., *Georgia in Black and White: Explorations in the Race Relations of a Southern State, 1865–1950* (Athens: University of Georgia Press, 1994).

27. John Morgan to Church President John Taylor, January 11, 1879, box 2, folder 3, JHM Papers; *Atlanta Constitution,* June 26, 1869, July 28, 1870, August 4, 1870, July 2, 1873, and September 1, 1873; Donald E. Davis, *The Land of Ridge and Valley: A Photographic History of the Northwest Georgia Mountains* (Charleston, SC: Arcadia Publishing, 2000), 8; Kevin E. O' Donnell and Helen Hollingsworth, eds., *Seekers of Scenery: Travel Writing from Southern Appalachia, 1840–1900* (Knoxville: University of Tennessee Press, 2004).

28. John Morgan to Editors, *Salt Lake City Herald,* August 23, 1878, box 1, book 1, JHM Papers; John Morgan to Editors, *Deseret News,* October 3, 1878, box 1, book 1, JHM Papers; Richardson and Morgan, *Life and Ministry,* 189–93; Price, "The Mormon Missionary," 453–60; Khaled J. Bloom, *The Mississippi Valley's Great Yellow Fever Epidemic of 1878* (Baton Rouge: Louisiana State University Press, 1993).

29. Converts of Elder John Morgan in North Georgia during his first mission in 1876, box 3, folder 3, JHM Papers; claim of Thomas Barbour of Chattooga County, Georgia, no. 3556, Southern Claims Commission Approved Claims, 1871–1880: Georgia, microfiche M1658, NARA; Gary B. Mills, *Southern Loyalists in the Civil War: The Southern Claims Commission* (Baltimore: Genealogical Publishing Company, 1994), 31; Clark, *History in Catoosa County,* 265; Kenneth Coleman, ed., *A History of Georgia,* 2nd ed. (Athens: University of Georgia Press, 1991); William W. Freehling and Craig M. Simpson, eds., *Secession Debated: Georgia's Showdown in 1860* (New York: Oxford University Press, 1992); Mark V. Wetherington, *Plain Folk's Fight: The Civil War and Reconstruction in Piney Woods Georgia* (Chapel Hill: University of North Carolina Press, 2005).

30. Claim of Thomas Barbour of Chattooga County, NARA.

31. Barbour's testimony concerning his Union loyalty must be evaluated with some skepticism, as it was essentially self-serving. In 1871 the U.S. Congress estab-

lished a federal agency, the Southern Claims Commission, to investigate the claims of southern Union loyalists who had property taken for use by the Union Army. Chattooga County residents submitted 148 claims, 59 of which were paid. Prominent Unionist Wesley Shropshire collected the largest payment, but Thomas Barbour's smaller claim was also approved by claims examiners, and he was awarded $3,310. Interestingly, shared political loyalties did not ameliorate discord. Though Shropshire did not directly challenge Barbour's claim of wartime Unionism, he suggested that the Barbour family were opportunists. In Thomas Barbour's Southern Claims Commission file, there is a letter from Wesley Shropshire to the claims examiner. Marked "confidential," the letter challenges Thomas Barbour's claim as "exorbitant." The letter begins, "I have frequently been astonished to hear Rebels making out claims against the Government for property lost during the war But never more surprised than I was the other day to hear T. J. Barber who has just returned from Washington say that he had reduced his father's claim down to ten thousand dollars. If the old man gets the amount he will have more money than he ever was worth before." Claim of Thomas Barbour of Chattooga County, NARA; Converts of Elder John Morgan, JHM Papers.

32. Converts of Elder John Morgan, JHM Papers; Civil War Service Record for Ignatius Henry Huffaker and Isaac Huffaker, List of Confederates Captured at Vicksburg, Mississippi, July 4, 1863, M2072_1, Register of Prisoners of War Received at Military Prison, Louisville, Kentucky, M598_90, Selected Records of the War Department Relating to Confederate Prisoners of War, 1861–1865, M598_91, all available online at www.ancestry.com; Index to Compiled Service Records of Confederate Soldiers Who Served from the State of Georgia, M-226, microfilm, roll #19, Georgia State Archives; Compiled Service Records of Confederate Soldiers Who Served in Organizations from Georgia, M-266, microfilm, roll #425, Georgia State Archives; John C. Inscoe and Robert C. Kenzer, eds., *Enemies of the Country: New Perspectives on Unionists in the Civil War South* (Athens: University of Georgia Press, 2001); Kenneth W. Noe and Shannon H. Wilson, eds., *The Civil War in Appalachia: Collected Essays* (Knoxville: University of Tennessee Press, 1997); Martin Crawford, *Ashe County's Civil War: Community and Society in the Appalachian South* (Charlottesville: University of Virginia Press, 2001); John C. Inscoe and Gordon B. McKinney, *The Heart of Confederate Appalachia: Western North Carolina in the Civil War* (Chapel Hill: University of North Carolina Press, 2000).

33. John Morgan's journal, entries dated June 20, 1877, June 28, 1877, June 29, 1877, August 27, 1877, October 23, 1877, and November 10, 1877; John Morgan to Editor, *Deseret News,* September 21, 1877, box 1, book 1, JHM Papers; *Atlanta Constitution,* August 5, 1879, and October 23, 1879; typed version of John Morgan's journal, box 4, folder 2, JHM Papers.

34. Minutes of the Southern States Conference, August 9–11, 1878, box 1, book 1, JHM Papers; Diary of James T. Lisonbee, 1876–1877, box 6, folder 8, JHM Papers; Garth N. Jones, *James Thompson Lisonbee's Missionary Labors on the*

Sand Mountain of Northeastern Alabama and Northwestern Georgia: Beginning of a New Gathering in the San Luis Valley of Colorado, 1876–1878 (Provo, UT: Brigham Young University Press, 2000).

35. John Nicholson, *The Martyrdom of Joseph Standing; or, The Murder of a "Mormon" Missionary* (Salt Lake City: Deseret News Company, 1886); William Whitridge Hatch, *There Is No Law . . . A History of Mormon Civil Relations in the Southern States, 1865–1905* (New York: Vantage Press, 1968); Ken Driggs, "'There is No Law in Georgia for Mormons': The Joseph Standing Murder Case of 1879," *Georgia Historical Quarterly* 4 (Winter 1989): 747; Gene A. Sessions, "Myth, Mormonism, and Murder in the South," *South Atlantic Quarterly* 75 (Spring 1976): 213.

36. Sherrod, "The Southern Mountaineer"; Martha B. Crowe, "'A Mission in the Mountains': E. O. Guerrant and Southern Appalachia," *American Presbyterians* 68, no. 1 (1990): 46–54; Edward O. Guerrant, *The Galax Gatherers: The Gospel among the Highlanders* (Knoxville: University of Tennessee Press, 2005), 119; Samuel Tyndale Wilson, *The Southern Mountaineers* (New York: Trow Press, 1906).

Chapter 8

"Neither War nor Peace"

West Virginia's Reconstruction Experience

Randall S. Gooden

A combination of political, social, and economic circumstances made peace elusive in West Virginia at the close of the Civil War. Like other border states, West Virginia faced the difficulties of dealing with former enemies living in the same communities: one group defeated and resentful of their loss, the other victorious and suspicious of their rebellious neighbors. Strife over the status and roles of African Americans did not erupt as it did in the South; but as in the southern states, as well as other border states, West Virginia struggled with questions about the loyalty of ex-Confederates to the United States. In West Virginia, however, an extra question of loyalty existed. That was the question of whether ex-Confederates, opponents of the wartime division of Virginia, would accept the new state and its government.

Although historians have touched upon the political and social issues in postwar West Virginia, the treatment of the subject has been insufficient given the unique and complex nature of West Virginia's wartime creation and struggle for stability during Reconstruction. One of the deans of West Virginia history, Charles H. Ambler, saw Reconstruction in the state as largely a political story of Republicans versus Democrats and ex-Confederates. In his view, moderate Republicans ended disfranchisement out of fear of a reaction from their opponents.[1] Revisionist historian Richard O. Curry emphasized the role of the coalition of former Whigs and Democrats that became the postwar Democratic Party in his study of Reconstruction and its demise in West Virginia.[2] Postrevisionists, looking at West Virginia within national studies of the period, strained to explain Reconstruction in the state in terms of racial politics and "redemption" by the Democrats. For example, Eric Foner attributed the end of Reconstruction in West Virginia to hostility toward African American suffrage and the disappearance of Republican electoral majorities with the end of disfranchisement.[3] While these studies added to the understanding of the aftermath of the Civil War in West Virginia, they only filled in part of the story. West Virginia shared many traits with other states during Reconstruction, but it experienced an evolution of both the Democratic and Republican parties that was linked to the state's search for identity and stability. Part of that evolution included the forming of coalitions based upon common causes, especially economic growth and stability. The result was the end of disfranchisement and Reconstruction through changes emanating from both parties, not just through a "redemption" at the hands of the Democrats.

West Virginia's party politics originated not only in the Civil War and Reconstruction but also in the creation of the state. Conceived amid sectional differences between eastern and western Virginia that came to a head during the secession crisis of 1861, West Virginia came to life in 1863, conceived by a pro-Union element in western Virginia and delivered by the U.S. government. The party that voters chose to head West Virginia's government was a coalition of Republicans, Democrats, and former Whigs who supported the Union. In the heady days of revolution against old-guard Virginia, the Republicans came to dominate the coalition, much as their brethren, the radical Republicans, became the dominant faction in Congress. The new rulers of West Virginia set about to make reforms that had been stifled by Virginia's antebellum government and to bolster the state's economy, but a large part of their attention fell upon securing the state from its enemies, both outside and inside West Virginia.

Thus, when the war came to a close and West Virginia faced questions about the loyalty of ex-Confederates to the United States and the new state, its leaders were already well practiced at internal security. Many of the state's leaders had participated in the pro-Union government of Virginia, known as the Restored Government of Virginia, that had been organized at Wheeling in 1861 in response to the secession of Virginia's Richmond government from the Union. The Restored Government of Virginia had dealt with threats from Confederates and Confederate sympathizers as well, and the leaders that the new state inherited from the restored government brought their experiences in dealing with internal enemies with them.

When West Virginia entered the Union in 1863, its government continued to guard against enemies and potential enemies. Its approach proved more stringent than that of Virginia's restored government. The new state gave its citizens the ability to challenge the right of other citizens to vote because of questionable loyalty. Legislation required loyalty oaths of jurors, applicants for licenses, and a test oath for state officials. Additional laws allowed for the confiscation of the property of Confederates and their sympathizers, the attachment of the property of nonresident Confederates, and the voiding of any judgment, decree, or deed of trust that benefited a Confederate.

As the West Virginia legislature turned its concern to the return of nearly ten thousand Confederate soldiers to their homes in West Virginia at the end of the war in 1865, they adapted and extended wartime proscriptions to head off possible resistance from these men while also looking at new laws to control ex-Confederates. This prompted a Clarksburg newspaper to ask, "Upon what meat doth Caesar feed that he hath grown so great?"[4]

The legacy of wartime measures provided the meat for the new restrictions. One measure allowed voters to protest the right of others to vote in peacetime based on disloyalty during the war. The challenged voters had to submit to a test oath. Prosecuting attorneys compiled lists of ex-Confederates within their counties in order to impose an oath of present loyalty upon them. Another new law implemented a test oath for those involved in lawsuits, and the right to appeal court decisions was limited to those who could swear that they had never participated in the rebellion in any way.

West Virginia capped its 1865 legislation against returning Confederates with a proposed constitutional amendment that would take the rights of citizenship away from ex-Confederates. The amendment became known as the Maxwell amendment for Edwin Maxwell, the Harrison County senator who chaired the committee that drafted the measure. Ironically, although Maxwell favored banning ex-Confederates from voting, he opposed total disfranchisement.[5]

Debates over the Maxwell amendment uncovered increasing rifts between moderates and radicals in the Union party in 1865. Wartime differences had existed over states' rights, slavery, and even the process of statehood itself. As the war came to a close, the coalition that had been necessary to create West Virginia weakened as new differences over proscriptions and disfranchisement overshadowed the need for unity in crisis. An early example of this occurred when *Wheeling Intelligencer* editor Archibald Campbell, a leading radical Republican, challenged the more moderate incumbent U.S. senator Waitman T. Willey, a leading personality in the creation of West Virginia, for reelection.

Returning Confederates knew little about rifts within the Unionist coalition, but they knew about the Maxwell amendment and other proscriptive measures, and they were unsure of the conditions they would meet in the state. The editor of the *Charles Town Spirit of Jefferson* in the eastern panhandle expressed the feelings of many ex-Confederates:

> Of the past four years—with their memories and bitter griefs—
> how shall we speak? We cannot approach the household, from
> which some cherished idol has been torn, and congratulate the living that the rude hand of war, which deprived them of their loved
> ones, has been stayed, with the loss of the cause for which they fell.
> . . . Nor can we—without violence to our own feelings, and the use
> of the vilest hypocrisy—aver that we prefer the government under
> which we are henceforth to live, to that which four years of bloody
> strife were expended to establish, without success.[6]

The editor, in spite of his regret, offered the hope that ex-Confederates could find common ground with the moderates who had emerged in the Unionist coalition.[7]

Much of the hope that returning Confederates had for finding common ground with moderate Unionists was based on the principles of President Lincoln's Proclamation of Amnesty. That hope turned tenuous when Lincoln was assassinated, but ex-Confederates' fears of Johnson soon proved unwarranted. On May 29 Johnson issued a presidential proclamation that offered amnesty and pardons similar to Lincoln's.

Although ex-Confederates received presidential leniency and hoped for cordial relations with moderate Unionists, many encountered resistance from Unionists as they returned to their home counties and communities, especially in the northern part of the state. In Harrison County, for instance, Union citizens held meetings on the township level to discourage ex-Confederates from living in the county, and this grassroots movement resulted in a county meeting for the same purpose. Similar meetings occurred in other parts of the state, and these were fueled by rumors of crimes being committed by returning Confederates.[8] In Marion County,

Unionists went a step further than holding meetings and ran several ex-Confederates out of the county. The editor of the *Fairmont National* voiced the feelings that had led to these actions when he warned, "If there is any one subject on which our loyal people all agree it is that none of those leaders who left Fairmont shall ever return to take their abode with us."[9] State officials joined in discouraging the return of ex-Confederates. Governor Boreman counseled the former rebels to curb their sentiments and warned them not to expect protection from the government if they returned. While the state government offered no protection to ex-Confederates, the U.S. army commander in West Virginia, Maj. Gen. William H. Emory, took away their ability for self-defense when he ordered them not to arm themselves because of the military truce that had ended the war.[10]

The prospects of hostility and political proscriptions caused former Confederates to consider the wisdom of coming back to the state. Jonathan M. Bennett, wartime auditor general of the Virginia government in Richmond, asked a friend in his hometown of Weston for advice. "I hardly know what to say in relation to your coming here at this time," the friend replied. "Many have returned who I should think would be more obnoxious than yourself and are remaining unmolested. So that I hardly think there would be any objection to your return merely to settle up your business." He concluded, though, that "it might be more prudent to delay it for a while."[11]

A number of West Virginia ex-Confederates found encouragement of their return to the state from moderate Unionists. U.S. district judge John J. Jackson Jr. dismissed treason charges against seventeen ex-Confederates after they swore loyalty oaths. Baltimore and Ohio Railroad officials helped important clients in obtaining pardons.[12] Personal friendships, family relationships, political ties, and business associations motivated much of the support from moderate Unionists. Such demonstrations of sympathy buoyed former Confederates but drew criticism from many Unionists, including Governor Boreman.

Privately, however, even Boreman was not free from personal considerations upon the return of ex-Confederates. He wrote to his brother in Missouri regarding their nephew, Kenner B. Stephenson, a Confederate from Parkersburg: "He now begs to be permitted to come home & lead a quiet and peaceable life for the remainder of his days," Boreman confided. "On his mother's account (who in my opinion has never been a rebel) I will have to aid him to get back."[13]

Despite the reactions from staunch Unionists and the political restrictions that they authored, signs of moderation emboldened some former Confederates to take action against the atmosphere of proscription in West Virginia. In one such incident, men wearing Confederate uniforms desecrated American flags at Independence Day celebrations at Ravenswood and Sandyville, prompting General Emory to send a company of soldiers to arrest them.[14] Others protested through political and legal channels. Residents of Berkeley and Jefferson counties in the extreme eastern end of the panhandle, for example, protested the agreement between West Virginia and the Restored Government of Virginia in 1863 for the inclusion of those counties in the new state. The addition of Berkeley and Jefferson counties had been approved by voters at the time, but only pro-Union voters had participated in the referendum in the predominantly Confederate area. In 1865 ex-Confederates and their supporters took their protest to the Virginia legislature, the U.S. Congress, and eventually the Supreme Court. Meanwhile, residents of Jefferson County planned to participate in Virginia state elections, and Governor Boreman asked for the intercession of federal troops. The whole affair resurrected old arguments against the legitimacy of West Virginia at both the state and national levels and soured relations between West Virginia and Virginia's restored government, which had taken the reins of power in Richmond at the end of the war.[15] The fight over the two counties also raised the subject of the reunification of West Virginia with Virginia. Calls for the restoration of the mother state to its prewar boundaries were particularly strong in border counties. The editor of the Democratic *Wheeling Register* wrote that if "proscriptive and odious laws [are not repealed] a very large proportion of the residents of West Virginia would gladly welcome a return to the bosom of the old State."[16]

This unrest put the state on edge as Unionists and ex-Confederates alike tried to put their lives back in order after the war. As ex-Confederates tried to determine their place in the state, Unionist citizens struggled with their own problems. In one instance, former Union army major E. Herrington found that his store in Martinsburg had been targeted by a Confederate home guard unit during the war. Damages and theft made it impossible for Herrington to reopen his store, and he filed a $25,000 lawsuit against four members of the home guard.[17]

As both Unionists and ex-Confederates tried to pick up the pieces of their lives and return to a peaceful existence in 1865, the political coalition of the Union Party began to fall apart. The state election of 1865, the first such election in peacetime, clearly showed how fragile the coalition had become. The election, and the campaign leading up to it, allowed moderate or conservative Unionists to challenge Republican domination of state politics, and the protest movements of the ex-Confederates influenced those campaigns. Residents in the eastern panhandle rejected the radical nominees for circuit court judge and state senator and held an alternate Union Party convention to choose more moderate candidates. Stronger indications of the weakening coalition appeared when candidates stopped using the Union Party label. M. A. McClung, one such office-seeker, ran for the House of Delegates in Roane County as a "Constitutional Conservative Union man."[18]

The election of 1865 in West Virginia proved to be pivotal. Despite the voter test oath, substantial numbers of ex-Confederates still participated, with some even winning elections in eastern and southern portions of the state. This group included future West Virginia governor Henry M. Mathews, a former Confederate major, elected to the state senate from Greenbrier County. Governor Boreman and the state legislature took measures to keep these men from assuming office. The governor withheld commissions from elected judges and local officials who had served the Confederacy, and the legislature refused to seat ex-Confederates.[19]

The symbolic victories in the election of 1865 heartened ex-Confederates, but they alarmed state leaders. In his annual message to the legislature, Governor Boreman said that "many of the intelligent and leading participants in the Rebellion, instead of counselling observance of the law, have pursued a course of conduct that has prevented complete organization [of government]."[20] The legislature responded with a series of new proscriptions and measures to tighten old ones, including a test oath for attorneys and a voter registration law. The registration law empowered the governor to appoint three-man boards of election for each county. The boards would hold hearings on the right of any person to vote, strike disqualified people from the lists of voters, and oversee local election registrars, who would register voters and administer test oaths to suspected ex-Confederates.[21] Not everyone welcomed the new laws. Rufus Maxwell, a member of the House of Delegates, said of the legislative session, "Radicalism holds sway here with unrelenting hand, and I can't help it."[22]

The capstone for the legislature of 1866 was its sustaining vote on the Maxwell amendment, renamed the Disfranchisement Amendment, which drove opponents of disfranchisement completely away from the wartime coalition of the Union Party. The dissenters, known as the Conservative

Party, organized at Wheeling on March 1, 1866, in a move that resembled Andrew Johnson's efforts that same year to unite opponents of radical Republicanism on the national level. The Conservatives called for supporters to organize on the county level and choose delegates to a state convention. Newspapers in Wheeling, Fairmont, Clarksburg, Parkersburg, Martinsburg, and Charles Town took up the Conservative cause and helped to rally supporters. The party convention, which met in Clarksburg on April 12, included men who had been active in the creation of West Virginia, including two presidents of its constitutional convention. The new party's platform supported the administration of Andrew Johnson and the federal and state constitutions. It declared against the Freedmen's Bureau, the Civil Rights Act, higher federal taxes, harsh Reconstruction measures, and voting rights for African Americans. It did, however, recognize the right of individual states to grant other civil rights to blacks. The main plank in the Conservative Party platform opposed the disfranchisement amendment. It contended that the amendment would "prevent the reestablishment of peace, order and good government [and] drive away immigration and capital by causing constant strife and discord among the people."[23]

The Union Party wielded a powerful weapon in defending against opposition to the amendment. Officials used the new registration law to full effect in eliminating many opponents of the amendment from the voter rolls. It has been estimated that fifteen thousand men did not vote in the election because of enforcement of the registration law.[24] In addition, Unionists held mass meetings in the north central and Ohio Valley regions of the state in support of the amendment.[25] When the disfranchisement amendment passed by a vote of 22,334 to 15,302, Conservatives blamed the registration law for giving the amendment's supporters the advantage. They resorted to the courts for redress against the law, as well as the suitor's oath and attorney's oath, and won cases in circuit courts, only to have their efforts stifled in the state supreme court.[26]

While the Conservatives waged battle in the courts, they continued their political fight in August when they convened to choose nominees for the fall election, which would be the first challenge to Governor Boreman's administration. The Conservatives chose Benjamin H. Smith, U.S. district attorney for West Virginia and a longtime Whig leader in the Charleston area, as its candidate for governor. As early as July 1865, Smith had written to Jonathan M. Bennett that he "might throw in [his] might to correct some gross legal heresies which have found favor." Smith added, "Whilst I support the Union I cannot sustain a course of injustice towards anyone & will never consent that justice shall be perverted and the law administered falsely to maintain any policy or any party."[27]

The Union Party, with Boreman as its nominee, wasted no time in engaging in a personal and vindictive campaign. Boreman declared that Smith "never was [the] right sort of Union man." The governor claimed that Smith would try to abolish the state's free school system and reunite West Virginia and Virginia.[28] Boreman won reelection by a vote of 23,802 to 17,158, though Smith managed to win six largely ex-Confederate counties as well as two Ohio Valley counties. As historian Gordon McKinney pointed out, enforcement of the registration law bolstered the chances for the Union Party.[29] However, the skillful choice of statewide and congressional candidates who drew support from diverse regions and the courting of Union veterans by the nomination of former soldiers for many offices also helped the Union Party.[30] Apart from state politics, the Unionist win coincided with the general victory of radical Republicans against the aggressive challenge of President Johnson and his supporters nationwide in the 1866 elections.[31]

Despite overall Unionist victories in the election of 1866, the contest exposed voter dissatisfaction with the status quo. This included an anti-incumbent movement that resulted in a turnover of six of the state's senate seats and thirty-four of the fifty-two seats in the House of Delegates.[32] In this trend, West Virginia was not unique. Noting a similar postwar tendency in neighboring Ohio, Felice A. Bonadio wrote in *North of Reconstruction: Ohio Politics, 1865–1870* that the "great majority of Republican members had never served in the legislature before" and added that, much like West Virginia, "they were war veterans; most of them had been commissioned officers."[33]

As the new legislature convened in 1867, even Republicans were taken aback by its stance toward ex-Confederates. J. M. Hagans wrote to Senator Willey, "The tone of the Legislature is of the extreme radical stomp."[34] Governor Boreman set the tone before the legislature by telling it that ex-Confederates presented a security risk and that the Conservative Party only encouraged that risk. The governor reported that ex-Confederates and their sympathizers continued to disregard the laws, especially the registration law, in four or five counties along the borders of Kentucky and Virginia. The southeastern part of the state particularly worried Boreman, and he asked that federal troops be stationed at Union in Monroe County.[35] Troops also went to Wayne and nearby Logan in the southwestern corner of the state to protect residents from marauding ex-Confederate guerrillas. Violent resistance to the registration law in Barbour, Randolph, and Tucker counties prompted the stationing of an army unit in Philippi. Conservatives resented the presence of U.S. troops, but the state militia had not been reorganized since it mustered out at the end of the war. Besides, Boreman believed that pitting West Virginian against West Virginian might plunge the state into civil war.[36]

In spite of the perception among many West Virginians that the governor and legislature were too radical, others saw the need for forceful action. J. O. Addison, a Raleigh County physician, called for the use of federal troops to keep peace in his region of the state. Addison warned that if "the democratic party succeed[s] the sufferings of the Union people throughout this part of West Va. as well as the south would be too horrible to contemplate."[37]

When Governor Boreman began his new term in 1867, the economy received more attention than he had given it before, and he even allowed it to overshadow political considerations in some cases. This attitude reflected the changing priorities of many West Virginians. Boreman believed that the wartime forfeiture law that targeted Confederate property for confiscation discouraged investment in the state. The legislature also gave attention to the economy but did not allow it to preempt politics; it changed county seats and county boundaries and created new counties to favor Unionist business people in areas of the state with large ex-Confederate populations. The West Virginia Supreme Court of Appeals also favored Unionist business interests by invalidating land transactions that had been made in the state by the authority of Virginia's Richmond government during the war. The court also ruled that debts that had been made payable in Confederate money were void and unenforceable.[38]

The Conservatives also made the economy an issue. In an appeal to farmers and laborers, they attacked Republican plans on the national level to redeem money and bonds in gold and to contract the currency. They won the support of industrial workers in the northern panhandle, many of whom were Irish and German immigrants who traditionally identified with the Democratic Party. This association of the Conservatives in West Virginia and of Democrats as a whole with progressivism ran counter to the antebellum Democratic tradition of lawyer-dominated courthouse cliques and patrician politics in Virginia that remained rooted in the political traditions of many counties, especially in the southern and eastern counties. The paternalistic, closed-door politics of the courthouse cliques contrasted with the Republican-dominated Union Party, which sent mostly farmers to the legislature and included a sizable faction of artisans. That contrast, combined with the Union Party's emphasis upon citizen input and participation in politics through the creation of townships on the local level, the reduction of terms of office for state officials, introduction of the secret ballot, and creation of free schools, meant that the appeal of the Conservatives to the working class could go only so far.

The Unionists and Conservatives carried their strengths and weaknesses into the political season of 1868, which began as the legislature convened in January. Conservatives attempted to score political points by bringing petitions for relief from proscriptions and redress of grievances of ex-Confederates to the lawmakers. Unionists showed willingness to compromise in individual cases, but the Conservatives downplayed the compromises and emphasized the extremism of Unionists in order to set the tone for the year's election campaigns.

The political campaigns of 1868 opened in May when West Virginia Republicans met in convention. The convention signaled the end of wartime politics, as it no longer used the Union Party title and joined in national politics in the presidential election year. The convention chose state senate president William E. Stevenson, a longtime Republican, as the party's gubernatorial candidate. Stevenson's voting record in the senate showed that he was a pragmatic politician and hinted that he was open to compromise.[39]

The Conservatives, in their own name change, became the Conservative Democrats in a move to align themselves with the national Democratic Party. The party chose Parkersburg oil baron and banker Johnson N. Camden as its candidate for governor over one of the party's founders, former congressman William G. Brown of Preston County. Brown had been a leader in the statehood movement and a leading Democrat in western Virginia in antebellum times. The choice indicated a change of direction toward an economic agenda and national interests. Camden had interstate business ties and courted national Democratic leaders.[40] This change of direction for the newly named Conservative Democratic Party showed division within the ranks of the party. It became clear that a business wing of the party had emerged to overshadow the traditionalists, who associated themselves more with the cause of states' rights and state issues. They had identified with the South before and during the Civil War and were suspicious of the northern domination of the Democratic Party after the war. The traditionalists also resisted civil rights for African Americans.

Three other factions brokered power between the business wing and the traditionalist wing: the lawyer-courthouse cliques, farmers, and laborers. The lawyer-courthouse cliques relied on relationships between law firms and county officials to control regional politics. The farmers and laborers, though not as powerful as the lawyer-courthouse cliques, both concentrated on issues of taxation, money policy, and tariffs. They also protested banking policies that negatively affected them and the rail monopoly of the Baltimore and Ohio (B&O) Railroad in the state. Land law reform and transportation improvements also interested farmers, and laborers wanted improved working conditions. While farmers did not universally support the Conservative Democratic Party, their influence on the party was particularly strong in the southern and eastern sections of the state. Laborers, who had an antebellum affinity with the Democratic Party, were concentrated mostly in the northern panhandle. Despite their differences, opposition to disfranchisement held the Conservative Democrats together in 1868.

Factions also existed in the Republican Party and mostly centered on regional differences as players competed for political leadership, state patronage, and the sites for state institutions, such as the capitol, penitentiary, and agricultural college. The major regional centers of power were in the Wheeling and northern panhandle region, Upshur County, the Monongalia and Preston County region, and Parkersburg. The Republicans often neglected other regions, and party members in those places complained about the lack of attention. Without support from state party leaders they became more inclined to cooperate with local Conservative Democrats.

The 1868 gubernatorial campaign turned bitter. Republicans claimed that Camden was the candidate of the rich and suggested that he had sympathized with the Confederacy during the war. Conservative Democrats, for their part, portrayed the Pennsylvania-born Stevenson as a radical carpetbagger who would bow to northern business interests and betray states' rights in favor of federal civil rights provisions. Stevenson won the governor's race with 27,348 votes, which was 3,500 more votes than Boreman had received in 1866. Camden received 22,250 votes, which was about five thousand votes more than Smith won against Boreman. Stevenson's gains over Boreman cannot be attributed to the effects of disfranchisement in favor of Republicans, because the Conservative Democrats also showed gains. Turnout for the presidential election cannot be cited as the reason for the increase in votes over the 1866 election, because two thousand fewer votes were cast in the presidential election than in the gubernatorial race. The presidential race in West Virginia was significant because of signs that Conservative Democrats voted for Grant to give him a nine-thousand-vote margin over Horatio Seymour in the state. Without turnout for the presidential election as the reason for the increase in the gubernatorial vote between 1866 and 1868, one can only assume that the higher numbers were due to greater interest in state politics and perhaps increased identification of residents with the relatively new state.[41]

After the election of 1868, West Virginia politics entered a phase of moderation. The Republicans still controlled state government, but new faces occupied the majority of the seats in the legislature and the governor's office. The war and the splitting of Virginia were becoming more distant, and the tensions of that period concerned these men less. In this they reflected a growing tendency among their constituents to put old animosities aside to cooperate in what historian John A. Williams called the "economic aspirations that united West Virginians."[42]

The economic cooperation of this period brought together partnerships and associations that transcended state boundaries and tremendously influenced politics and government, regardless of party. One of the most prominent of such associations, that of Johnson N. Camden and Henry G. Davis, Democrats of a new generation, pointedly dispels revisionist historical theory that economic coalitions between old Whigs in the Democratic Party and Republicans led to the unraveling of Reconstruction. Indeed, Williams observed that the freedom of Camden and Davis from antebellum and wartime political associations made them "superbly, if only temporarily, fitted to part the muddy waters of West Virginia politics."[43] Camden, the Conservative Democrats' gubernatorial candidate in the recent election, had taken over the Parkersburg branch of the Northwestern Bank of Virginia in the midst of the Civil War and transformed it into the First National Bank of Parkersburg. Taking advantage of the intimate knowledge of land transactions in the area that the bank provided, Camden built up his land holdings. In spite of his Democratic politics, Camden included men of both parties in his business and social circles. Davis had come to the state in 1854 as an agent for the B&O and pursued interests in lumber, coal, and banking in what is now Mineral County. Davis, a would-be Republican, turned Democrat after he faced false charges of disloyalty and lost his right to vote for a time. He won election to the House of Delegates and then the state senate, where he chaired the powerful finance committee and gained a reputation for working with Republicans. In 1871 he replaced Waitman T. Willey as a U.S. senator. Camden and Davis respected each other's spheres of influence but cooperated on issues of mutual interest, including control of the business wing of their party.

Camden, Davis, and other business leaders in West Virginia shared banking as one of their mutual interests. The impact of banking upon the state's economy did not escape the notice of legislators, and banking policy occupied an important place on the legislative agenda. Many people in the state had relied upon branches of Virginia-based state banks, but when the Civil War ended, the branches' parent banks faced ruin in Virginia's war-torn economy. Rather than rescue the parent banks, the officers and depositors in the relatively untouched western branches took advantage of West Virginia law, which allowed them to reorganize as national banks or to invest in new national banks. This separated branch banks from weak parent banks and encouraged the formation of new banks in communities that previously had not had them. In these efforts, Conservative Democrats and ex-Confederates cooperated with Republicans. Business people, farmers, and laborers of all parties had an interest in banking, whether they sought a strong currency or a steady supply of money in the regional economy.

The most extensive economic cooperation took place in the promotion of railroads. Railroad companies and their promoters figured prominently in West Virginia politics because of the jobs, commerce, and rise in land values that would come to any region where railroads were built, and railroad politics depended on regional loyalties more than party loyalties. The state first experienced railroad politics before the Civil War when the B&O completed tracks from the Maryland border to Wheeling and built a branch, the Northwestern Railroad, from Grafton to Parkersburg. Political dealing gave the B&O tax breaks, but when West Virginia became a state, those tax privileges disappeared because of many state residents' resentment of such favoritism. That resentment increased when the railroad company appealed the loss of its favored status in the courts and ignored tax assessments. The B&O gained new enemies when it engaged in rate discrimination against local shippers and bypassed West Virginia stations with its fast freight service.[44]

Resentment of the B&O in West Virginia opened the way for competitors in northern West Virginia, including the B&O's major competitor, the Pennsylvania Railroad. The Pennsylvania schemed with Johnson N. Camden to construct several short-line railroads between oil fields and the B&O's Northwestern Railroad. By controlling oil production and shipping along the short lines, Camden and his Pennsylvania Railroad cohorts could manipulate rates on the B&O. All the while, Camden maintained good relations with the B&O in the open and fell back on those relations when the scheme failed.[45] The Pennsylvania Railroad did succeed in getting a foothold in the northern panhandle when a group of industrialists helped it complete the Pittsburgh and Steubenville Railroad through Wellsburg and a connecting line, the Panhandle Railroad, to Wheeling.[46] This rivalry between the railroad giants intensified with a movement for a north-south railroad through the state.

"[A] railroad should be built through the central portion of the state, connecting the different sections and identifying them more closely in interest, so as to make all our people realize more sensibly that they are brethren of the same commonwealth, whose pride and pleasure it should be to contribute by all means in their power to advance the prosperity and happiness of each other," Governor Boreman told legislators before he left office in 1869.[47] The governor had in mind the unifying effects and economic benefits of a north-south railroad, but even before his call, efforts to build such a railroad divided West Virginians. These divisions existed not only between the B&O and Pennsylvania railroads and their supporters but also among residents of different regions as competing plans for railroads emerged.

The most ambitious of these plans involved the West Virginia Central Railroad. Plans called for the proposed railroad to run from the Pennsylvania Railroad in the state of Pennsylvania south into West Virginia, bridge the B&O Railroad in order to avoid a junction with the Pennsylvania's rival, join with the projected terminus of the Chesapeake and Ohio (C&O) Railway in the Kanawha Valley, and then turn westward to the Ohio River. Although West Virginia's government initially supported the West Virginia Central through a land-for-stock exchange, financial problems and construction delays caused the state to withdraw its backing and give the right of way between Charleston and the Ohio River to the C&O, which was moving westward out of Virginia on its construction route. Besides suffering from the loss of state support, the West Virginia Central lost support among its own officers and board members, a group of which bargained to turn the railroad's assets over to the C&O. The West Virginia Central's secretary, Spencer Dayton, who coincidentally chaired the state senate committee that had jurisdiction over railroad charters, figured prominently in the group.[48]

While Governor Boreman's goal of building a railroad to unite the state was never achieved, the competition for railroad routes, subscriptions of money, and state charters to railroads brought together Conservative Democrats, Republicans, ex-Unionists, and ex-Confederates on behalf of their regions and business interests in ways that no deliberate political compromise could. When it came to railroads, partisan politics and wartime differences were put aside. In commenting on railroad politics in Virginia in the same era, Richard Lowe observed that Virginians cared less about railroads than about disfranchisement and race issues; by contrast, railroads affected every West Virginian, whether they were farmers, merchants, or industrialists, because rail expansion meant the opening of isolated Appalachian counties to economic potential.[49]

Another important economic issue on which members of both parties cooperated was the Virginia debt. From the earliest discussions of statehood, political leaders had been concerned about ensuring the payment of the new state's portion of Virginia's antebellum debt, and West Virginia's constitution included guarantees in that regard. When West Virginia and Virginia differed on the amount of the debt during postwar discussions, West Virginians of both parties and of different wartime loyalties lined up with one another on the basis of state loyalty. The commission that the governor appointed to represent West Virginia in debt negotiations with Virginia represented this new sense of state identity. The three-member commission included two Democrats and a Republican, and two ex-Unionists and an ex-Confederate. Thus, an issue that posed a crisis for the state's economy served as a uniting factor for West Virginians, but the debt controversy was not settled until it reached the Supreme Court in the twentieth century.[50]

The accommodation between political factions on economic issues spurred West Virginians toward accommodation on other issues and a "let-up" on political proscriptions against ex-Confederates. It was into this atmosphere that William E. Stevenson stepped in 1869 as the first new governor since statehood. Republicans began seeing ex-Confederates on individual terms rather than as a group. Proscriptions were removed or not enforced in specific cases, often based on political or economic affiliations between ex-

Confederates and Republicans. As a result, it did not take long for Republicans to begin to reflect upon disfranchisement as a whole. Historian Michael Perman provided a national context for West Virginia's "let-up" in his study of Democratic politics in Texas, Tennessee, Mississippi, and Virginia in 1869. In a "new movement," Perman wrote, Democrats in those states shifted away from confrontation with Republicans toward cooperation with moderates in order to drive wedges into state Republican organizations. Part of the Democrats' strategy included support for African American suffrage in return for the lifting of proscriptions against ex-Confederates. While the "new movement" failed in those states, a parallel move toward cooperation between Democrats and moderate Republicans in West Virginia advanced in 1869 and came to fruition in 1870. Whereas in West Virginia the movement succeeded due to bipartisan economic cooperation, the Democrats in Perman's study did not work with Republicans on economic grounds until they reorganized their efforts into a "new departure" in 1870.[51]

The "let-up" on disfranchisement in West Virginia received the endorsement of the nationally influential *New York Tribune* editor Horace Greeley in May 1869. In a letter to the *Wheeling Intelligencer,* Greeley warned Republicans of ex-Confederate reaction against disfranchisement when he wrote, "Look at Kentucky and Maryland and read your fate in theirs."[52] However, Greeley misread the experiences of West Virginia's neighboring border states. In Kentucky, the Republican Party ended disfranchisement in an effort to retain political control, and still they lost power to the Democrats in 1868.[53] For Maryland, the demise of disfranchisement came about as the result of the disintegration of the Unionist Party over racial issues, the presence of federal troops in the state, and the consequent election of Democrats to power in 1866.[54] While similarities existed among West Virginia, Kentucky, and Maryland, it was to another border state, Missouri, that West Virginia's moderate Republicans looked for inspiration.[55] Moderate Republicans in Missouri believed that they could succeed on their own political merits and did not need the artificial support of disfranchisement. However, Missouri Republicans counted on the strength of the state's twenty-three thousand African American voters, an advantage that West Virginia Republicans did not enjoy in a state with only about 3,500 African American voters.[56]

As West Virginia's leaders considered the issue of rights for ex-Confederates in 1869, the question of rights for African Americans did arise, and the two issues became linked. The Fifteenth Amendment went before the legislature for ratification that year after receiving divided support from West Virginia's congressional delegation. Legislators held mixed views on the amendment, and it proved controversial among state residents. In spite of the relatively low number of blacks in the state, racial troubles did exist, and the prospect of suffrage for African Americans heightened prejudice among some whites. In December 1869 a battle reportedly instigated by members of a secret society similar to the Ku Klux Klan, known as Gideon's Band, took place between a group of whites and a group of black salt-industry workers (and their white supporters) at Malden in the Kanawha Valley. The resultant outcry fueled calls for continued proscriptions against ex-Confederates. The *Preston County Journal* in Kingwood chided the *Wheeling Intelligencer,* which had favored the let-up. "Isn't this some of the fruits of your 'Let Up' scheme advocated so persistently last Summer and Fall?" asked the Preston County editor. "You see they don't stop at one law, but desire to 'let up' on the whole superstructure of state government."[57]

West Virginians still wrestled with the questions of rights for ex-Confederates and African Americans when the legislative election of 1869 approached. On the surface, the Republicans "waved the bloody shirt" to evoke patriotic support for the party that was responsible for saving the Union and creating the state. The Conservative Democrats campaigned against proscriptions and suffrage for African Americans. Beneath the surface, however, Republicans and Conservative Democrats worked together, particularly when they shared sectional and economic positions. Grassroots meetings led to open bipartisan cooperation. In other instances, politicians worked out secret deals. Henry G. Davis, for example, placed some of his eggs in the Republican basket when he agreed to back George Harman for state senator from the eastern panhandle in return for Harman's vote to repeal proscriptions.[58]

The Republicans continued to control the legislature after the election of 1869, but they divided into two camps. Those who supported an easing of proscriptions and the end of disfranchisement were known as "let-uppers"; hard-line Republicans who wished for proscriptions to remain in full force were known as "bitter-enders." The let-uppers controlled the House of Delegates, but the bitter-enders held the senate. The let-uppers gained an edge, however, when Governor Stevenson came down on the side of the let-up. He called for eliminating the oaths for attorneys, teachers, and plaintiffs in lawsuits, and he raised the question of whether it was time to consider the end of disfranchisement, having cited instances of its abuse.[59]

Pendleton County delegate William H. H. Flick answered the governor's question. He introduced a constitutional amendment that linked the repeal of disfranchisement with African American suffrage. Opposition came from Republicans who did not want to enfranchise blacks and others who did not want to restore rights to ex-Confederates. For the Conservative Democrats' part, they offered alternative measures ranging from allowing blacks to vote only on local railroad subscriptions to removing black suffrage from the Flick Amendment altogether. John J. Davis, a Harrison County delegate, emerged as the Conservative Democrats' own version of a bitter-ender in his opposition of voting rights for African Americans. Flick's amendment gained ground nonetheless, and versions passed both houses.

The Flick Amendment and the Fifteenth Amendment took center stage when the political season began in 1870. The Democrats, as the Conservative Democrats now called themselves, met in convention in Charleston in June, and Davis emerged as a candidate for governor through the backing of the states'-rights wing of the party. Johnson N. Camden also sought the nomination for the second time amid promises from Parkersburg-area Democrats that they would back the designation of Charleston as the permanent state capital if delegates from the Kanawha Valley supported Camden. Neither Davis nor Camden won, and the convention turned to a compromise candidate in B&O attorney John J. Jacob. Davis did win platform planks against the Flick Amendment and the Fifteenth Amendment and the consolation prize of being a candidate for Congress.[60] The Republicans also met in June and nominated William E. Stevenson for a second term as governor. The let-uppers and bitter-enders repaired their rifts long enough to endorse the Fifteenth Amendment and indirectly endorse the Flick Amendment.[61]

As the election campaigns of 1870 unfolded, it became clear that a new bipartisan association was influencing the races. Henry G. Davis told his friend, powerful Republican state senator Spencer Dayton, that the Democrats would support a strong "liberal" Republican in an effort to unseat hard-line Republican congressman James C. McGrew of Preston County. For his part, Dayton backed Davis in his bid for reelection to the state senate, and he won with Republican votes.[62] This accommodation between moderate Democrats and Republicans hurt Republican incumbents, who tended to be more dogmatic on Reconstruction issues, and Sen. Waitman T. Willey prophesied Republican defeat in 1870. In a September diary entry, he wrote that he had "yet seen little enthusiasm and [had] predicted to leading repubs. in confidence" that the party would be "beaten at the ensuing election."[63] Willey's prediction came true. Stevenson lost the governor's chair to Jacob, and Democrats took two of the state's three congressional seats. The Democrats gained control of both houses of the legislature through support from let-uppers among the Republicans, and through that control they handed Willey's U.S. Senate seat to Henry G. Davis.

Although Democrats won the legislature, political accommodation between moderates in both parties did not benefit them alone; let-upper Republicans earned places as power brokers in the legislature. As the most prominent of these, Spencer Dayton retained his post as chair of the influential committee on internal improvements and navigation and wielded a veto over committee appointments made by the new Democratic senate president, Lewis Baker, editor of Wheeling's Democratic newspaper. Through such power-brokering, Republicans received four of the sixteen committee chairs in the state senate. They also received Baker's support for the Flick Amendment, which went before voters in April and passed by a nearly four-to-one margin. In return for Baker's concessions to the let-upper Republicans, Dayton sponsored legislation to return the capital to Wheeling, which had lost it to Charleston the previous year in a sectional battle that had crossed party lines.[64]

A major result of the cooperation between senate Democrats and the let-uppers was a call by the legislature for a constitutional convention to revise the Republican-inspired wartime constitution. Supporters of the call claimed that the proposal fulfilled a mandate from the voters in 1870 to reform government, while the bitter-enders in the Republican Party contended that the voters had never contemplated a new constitution.[65]

The legislature set two elections on the constitutional convention, one to decide whether it would take place and one to choose delegates. Republicans split on support of the convention, Dayton's followers favoring it and others rejecting it as a sign of the erosion of their control of the state. For most Democrats, the call for a convention was a symbol of their triumph and the end of disfranchisement and proscriptions. Other Democrats who had participated in the statehood movement resisted reform of the document that they had helped create. Fewer than three thousand votes separated the supporters and opponents of the convention when voters approved it in August, and when West Virginians chose convention delegates in October, twelve of the seventy-seven winners were pledged not to change the old constitution. As a whole, the delegates formed an impressive group, with records of government service stretching back to antebellum times, including service in Virginia's constitutional convention of 1850.

As the convention prepared to assemble, David Hunter Strother, a nationally known artist-correspondent from the eastern panhandle, predicted that there would not be "much mischief from the Convention, in view of the sweeping triumph of the Republican Party in the United States." He believed that the Democrats would "be afraid to retrograde" at the convention. Strother noted that "[William H.] Travers and [Charles J.] Faulkner, members from this end, are both Democrats with Republican ideas and will favor liberal measures." He added, "If such men control the Convention its action will not impede improvement and public prosperity as it might do if its controlling influences were really Democratic."[66]

Faulkner took the temporary chair when the convention convened on January 16, 1872, and he immediately set a conservative tone in his opening remarks. He laid to rest any fears that the convention might return the state to Virginia and continued in a probusiness vein by calling for an economy "backed by a good and equitable government and suitable constitution" with "all the equal rights due to every citizen of the United States."[67] Faulkner turned the chair over to permanent convention president Samuel Price. The former lieutenant governor of Confederate Virginia observed that "parties are up today and down tomorrow" and called for a bipartisan effort in drafting the constitution.[68] But bipartisanship did not seem much in evidence, according to Barbour County delegate Samuel Woods, who wrote early in the proceedings that the "Republicans are rather quiet but are disposed to make capital out of everything" and that extremists among the ex-Confederates belabored "trivial questions of the past." A visitor alluded to troubles not just between Democrats and Republicans but within Democratic ranks when he observed that the convention was not "getting along very harmoniously" and that it was "either a very weak body" or its leaders were "acting from disguised motives."[69]

When the constitutional convention adjourned on April 9, 1872, the constitution that it presented was less remarkable for its differences with the 1863 constitution than for its similarities. It preserved many of the institutions of the Unionist government, most notably the secret ballot and free schools, but it abolished townships. Several provisions addressed states' rights and guaranteed that disfranchisement and proscriptions could not occur again. Despite expectations to the contrary, the new constitution did not allow the state government to loan money to corporations, and in one

major difference with the 1863 constitution, it did not guarantee the state's
share of the Virginia debt, apparently due to stalemated relations with Virginia. Based on the state's experience with the B&O, the constitution provided for regulation of rail rates, banned rate discrimination, and mandated
that trains stop in West Virginia towns. It discouraged railroad mergers
and pools and subjected railroad property to eminent domain. The constitution made railroad property subject to sale for delinquent taxes, and
it required railroad companies to make annual reports to the state auditor. Other changes in the constitution changed the state's land policies.
These controversial changes seemed destined to prompt much litigation
over land claims and earned the 1872 constitution the nickname "the lawyers' constitution."

The constitutional convention accentuated rifts among the wings and
factions of the Democratic Party, and just as the Unionists and Republicans
had split into factions when they dominated state politics, the Democrats
fractured when they had control of the state. Although Johnson N. Camden had expected the Democratic nomination for governor in 1872, strong
opposition arose against him and in favor of the incumbent, John J. Jacob.
After a bitter party convention, Camden managed to earn the nomination.

Partly to avoid the national rift between Republicans and Liberal
Republicans from spreading to West Virginia, the state's Republicans took
advantage of dissent among the Democrats and threw their nomination
to Jacob, who remained in the race as an independent and promised the
Republicans that he would oppose ratification of the new constitution.
In spite of this coalition, the new constitution received voter approval by
nearly five thousand votes.

With dissident Democratic and Republican support, Jacob held onto
the governorship in 1872. Following the election, the Democrats reached
a compromise that allowed Jacob's supporters, a new eastern wing of the
party, to control state affairs, while Camden's business wing controlled
national affairs for the state party. The Republicans, while in the minority,
kept the national party split from affecting them in 1872. West Virginia
Republicans also managed to take the governor's office out of Democratic
hands by throwing their weight behind the successful independent reelection bid of John J. Jacob. Although Republicans remained in the minority
until the 1890s, they continued to play power broker in coalitions with the
Democrats. Under the direction of U.S. attorney Nathan Goff Jr., they also
wielded considerable power in controlling federal patronage in the state.

The fact of the matter was that after the end of Reconstruction, the issues of statehood, disfranchisement, and African American suffrage disappeared, settled by the new constitution. Although the Republicans opposed the new constitution as a symbol of their decline, the document sustained the major institutions for which West Virginia Unionists had fought. The Democrats who had dominated the constitutional convention supported West Virginia statehood and equality in voting, and in a sense, party differences became blurred. New issues had emerged—railroad rivalries, railroad regulation, land policy, and economic development—many of which hinged upon sectional differences among the northern and southern parts of the state and the eastern panhandle. The demise of Reconstruction gave the Democrats prominence in state politics, but the coalitions that continued to exist between Democrats and Republicans in different sections of West Virginia emphasized the cooperation that existed on state and local issues. Lines often blurred between West Virginia Democrats and Republicans on national issues such as tariffs and money policy. The thin lines between groups within both parties were demonstrated when, in the 1890s, the Republicans again rose to dominance under the leadership of Stephen B. Elkins, son-in-law and political protégé of Henry G. Davis. Rather than signaling the demise of the Democrats, the change meant that the business wing of the Democratic Party had reached an accommodation with probusiness Republicans.

Notes

1. Charles H. Ambler, *Disfranchisement in West Virginia* (Morgantown, WV: privately printed, 1905).

2. Richard O. Curry, "Crisis Politics in West Virginia, 1861–1870," in *Radicalism, Racism, and Party Realignment: The Border States during Reconstruction,* ed. Richard O. Curry, 80–104 (Baltimore: Johns Hopkins Press, 1969).

3. Eric Foner, *Reconstruction: America's Unfinished Revolution, 1863–1877* (New York: Harper & Row, 1988), 417, 442.

4. *Clarksburg (WV) National Telegraph,* May 5, 1865.

5. West Virginia, Senate, *Journal of the Senate,* 1865, 54, 61–62.

6. *Charles Town (WV) Spirit of Jefferson,* November 7, 1865.

7. Ibid.

8. *Clarksburg (WV) National Telegraph,* May 5, 1865; *Morgantown (WV) Weekly Post,* June 10, 1865.

9. *Morgantown (WV) Weekly Post,* March 25, May 27, 1865.

10. *Morgantown (WV) Weekly Post,* June 10, June 24, 1865.

11. R. J. McCandlish to Jonathan M. Bennett, May 30, 1865, Jonathan M. Bennett Papers, West Virginia and Regional History Collection (WVRHC), West Virginia University, Morgantown.

12. *Parkersburg (WV) Daily Times,* August 28, August 29, 1865.

13. A. I. Boreman to Jacob Boreman, May 12, 1865, Arthur I. Boreman Papers, WVRHC.

14. *Parkersburg (WV) Daily Times,* August 19, 1865.

15. *Charles Town (WV) Virginia Free Press,* August 24, 1865; H. W. Flournoy, ed., "A. I. Boreman to Governor of Virginia," August 28, 1865, *State Papers and Other Manuscripts, January 1, 1836 to April 15, 1869* (Richmond: Commonwealth of Virginia, 1893), 2:453–55; *Charles Town (WV) Spirit of Jefferson,* November 7, 1865.

16. *Wheeling (WV) Daily Intelligencer,* January 25, 1866.

17. Thomas J. Michie to Charles J. Faulkner, September 29, 1865, Charles James Faulkner Papers, WVRHC.

18. *Parkersburg (WV) Daily Times,* September 22, 1865.

19. West Virginia, Senate, *Journal of the Senate,* 4th sess., 1866, 4, 7, 83, 155, 161.

20. Ibid., 6–9.

21. West Virginia, *Acts* (1866), 19, 74–78, 121.

22. Rufus Maxwell to Jonathan M. Bennett, February 17, 1866, Jonathan M. Bennett Papers, WVRHC.

23. *Wheeling (WV) Daily Register,* April 14, 1866.

24. Otis K. Rice, *West Virginia: A History* (Lexington: University Press of Kentucky, 1985), 157.

25. *Clarksburg (WV) Conservative,* March and April 1866, passim.

26. *Clarksburg (WV) Conservative,* May 25, June 8, June 15, 1866; *Ex Parte Hunter et al.* (1867), 2 W.Va. 122; *J. Q. A. Nadenbousch v. Sharer* (1867), 2 W.Va. 285.

27. Benjamin H. Smith to Jonathan M. Bennett, July 13, 1865, Jonathan M. Bennett Papers, WVRHC.

28. Notes of speech, 1866, Arthur I. Boreman Papers, WVRHC.

29. Gordon B. McKinney, *Southern Mountain Republicans, 1865–1900: Politics and the Appalachian Community* (Chapel Hill: University of North Carolina Press, 1978), 41–42.

30. George W. Atkinson and Alvaro F. Gibbens, *Prominent Men of West Virginia* (Wheeling, WV: W. L. Callin, 1890), 35–39, 43.

31. Hans L. Trefousse, *Andrew Johnson: A Biography* (New York: W.W. Norton, 1989), 262–67.

32. West Virginia, Senate, *Journal of the Senate,* 5th sess., 1867, n.p.

33. Felice A. Bonadio, *North of Reconstruction: Ohio Politics, 1865–1870* (New York: New York University Press, 1970), 24–25.

34. J. M. Hagans to Waitman T. Willey, January 21, 1867, Waitman T. Willey Papers, WVRHC.

35. West Virginia, *Annual Message of the Governor of the State of West Virginia* (Wheeling: John Frew, 1867), 3–4.

36. West Virginia, *Sixth Annual Message of Governor Boreman of West Virginia* (Wheeling: John Frew, 1868), 4–5.

37. J. O. Addison to Waitman T. Willey, April 10, 1868, Waitman T. Willey Papers, WVRHC.

38. *S. P. Hawver et al. v. A. Seldenridge et al.* (1867), 2 W.Va. 274; *Edwin M. Brown v. James Wylie* (1868), 2 W.Va. 502.

39. *Parkersburg (WV) Daily Times,* August 15, 1868.

40. *Parkersburg (WV) Daily Times,* August 1, September 12, 1868.

41. Atkinson and Gibbens, *Prominent Men of West Virginia,* 108–11.

42. John Alexander Williams, *West Virginia and the Captains of Industry* (Morgantown: West Virginia University Press, 1976), 5.

43. Ibid., 4.

44. *Baltimore and Ohio Railroad Company v. Supervisors and Sheriff of Marshall County* (1869), 3 W.Va. 319; *Baltimore and Ohio Railroad Company v. City of Wheeling* (1869), 3 W.Va. 372; West Virginia, *First Annual Message of Gov. Stevenson of West Virginia* (Wheeling: John Frew, 1870), 5–7.

45. West Virginia, *An Act to Incorporate the Volcanic Oil and Coal Company, Acts* (1865), 113; West Virginia, *An Act to Incorporate the Laurel Fork Oil and Coal Company, Acts* (1870), 204–5; Festus P. Summers, *Johnson Newlon Camden: A Study in Individualism* (New York: G.P. Putnam's Sons, 1937), 151, 170–71.

46. Charles A. Wingerter, ed., *History of Greater Wheeling and Vicinity: A Chronicle of Progress and a Narrative Account of the Industries, Institutions and People of the City and Tributary Territory* (New York: Lewis Publishing Co., 1912), 226–30.

47. West Virginia, *Seventh Annual Message of Gov. Boreman of West Virginia* (Wheeling: John Frew, 1869), 14.

48. West Virginia, *An Act to Amend and Re-Enact the Fifteenth Section of an Act Providing for the Completion of a Line or Lines of Railroad from the Waters of the Chesapeake to the Ohio River, Passed February Twenty-Sixth, Eighteen Hundred and Sixty-Seven, Acts* (1868), 6–8; Minutes of Stockholders Meeting of West Virginia Central Railway Co., November 3, 1869, and L. Ayer to Spencer Dayton, January 27, 1870, Spencer and Alston G. Dayton Papers, WVRHC.

49. Richard Lowe, *Republicans and Reconstruction in Virginia, 1856–1870* (Charlottesville: University of Virginia Press, 1991), 186.

50. Elizabeth Goodall, "The Virginia Debt Controversy and Settlement," *West Virginia History* 24 (October 1962): 42–74, 296–308, 332–51.

51. Michael Perman, *The Road to Redemption: Southern Politics, 1869–1879* (Chapel Hill: University of North Carolina Press, 1984), 9–16, 58–63, 67–68, 76.

52. *Wheeling (WV) Daily Intelligencer,* May 12, 1869.

53. Ross A. Webb, "Kentucky: Pariah among the Elect," in *Radicalism, Racism, and Party Realignment* (see note 2), 104–24.

54. Charles L. Wagant, "Redemption or Reaction? Maryland in the Post–Civil War Years," in *Radicalism, Racism, and Party Realignment* (see note 2), 146–87.

55. *Wheeling (WV) Daily Intelligencer,* January 11, 1870.

56. William E. Parrish, "Reconstruction Politics in Missouri," in *Radicalism, Racism, and Party Realignment* (see note 2), 25–28.

57. *Wheeling (WV) Daily Intelligencer,* March 14, 1870.

58. H. G. Davis to George Harman, September 25, 1869, Henry Gassaway Davis Papers, WVRHC.

59. West Virginia, *First Annual Message of Gov. Stevenson,* 13–16.

60. *Kanawha Republican* (Charleston, WV), June 8, June 18, 1870; *Wheeling (WV) Register,* June 10, June 20, 1870; *Clarksburg (WV) Regulator,* July 6, 1870.

61. *Parkersburg (WV) State Journal,* June 23, 1870.

62. H. G. Davis to J. S. Wheat, June 22, 1870, Henry Gassaway Davis Papers, WVRHC; H. G. Davis to Spencer Dayton, August 12, 1870, Spencer and Alston G. Dayton Papers, WVRHC.

63. Waitman T. Willey Diary, September 24, 1870, Waitman T. Willey Papers, WVRHC.

64. Lewis Baker to Spencer Dayton, November 9, 1870, Spencer and Alston G. Dayton Papers, WVRHC; West Virginia, *Manual of the Legislature and of the Executive and Judiciary Departments* (Charleston: Henry S. Walker, 1871), n.p.

65. *(Charleston) West Virginia Journal,* March 8, March 15, 1871.

66. David Hunter Strother to Emily Walker, November 8, 1871, Strother-Walker Letters, WVRHC.

67. *Kanawha Daily* (Charleston, WV), January 18, 1872.

68. *(Charleston) West Virginia Courier,* January 17, 1872.

69. C. Boggess to Gideon D. Camden, February 4, 1872, Gideon D. Camden Papers, WVRHC.

Chapter 9

A House Redivided

From Sectionalism to Political Economy in West Virginia

Ken Fones-Wolf

In 1891, nearly three decades after West Virginia achieved statehood, Gov. A. B. Fleming alerted potential investors that the "vast possibilities of the State are as yet scarcely realized." He noted that railroad companies, potential new residents, and investors had "swept heedlessly by" the state, unaware of the millions of acres of virtually "untouched" valuable original forests and "vast mineral resources." According to Fleming, no other state possessed such cheap and abundant raw materials or offered "such conspicuous opportunities for safe and profitable investment of capital."[1] Fleming spoke for a faction of the Democratic Party that sought to graft industrial capitalism onto a political organization still rooted in agrarianism and loyalty to the South. This faction feared that a growing segment of the state's voters preferred a party that would more explicitly and consistently promote industrialization.

As a border state deeply divided by Civil War–era sectionalism, West Virginia continued to straddle Southern and Northern notions of economic development at a key moment in the realignment of American politics. During the years immediately following Fleming's speech, the defection of just a few key states from the Democratic to the Republican Party broke a political deadlock that traced its origins to the Civil War. Central to this political realignment were the course of uneven economic development and the ability of the Republicans to fashion platform demands that constructed a winning electoral coalition. By including planks favoring high

237

tariffs, immigration restriction, the gold standard, and pensions for Union soldiers, the Republicans spoke for "an extremely harsh program of inter-regional [wealth] redistribution" that benefited the industrial Northeast at the expense of the agricultural export-oriented South, according to political scientist Richard Bensel. This program solidified support in that broad swath of development bordered by the Great Lakes and the Mississippi and Ohio rivers, but it also picked up key defections in the upper South, including Delaware, Maryland, and West Virginia.[2]

Fleming and his cohort of Democratic industrialists were powerless to halt the political trends that realigned both the nation and the Mountain State toward the Republicans. Abandoning the party that had controlled the state for a generation, voters in the most rapidly industrializing areas attached their future to the Republican Party's program and the country's northeastern manufacturing belt. In many ways the state remained a borderland, but one less and less captivated by its divided sectional identity and southern political and cultural institutions. Increasingly, questions about the state's economic future shaped the political divisions among West Virginians, realigning counties in conformity with the path of industrial development, not former loyalty to the Confederacy. Borderland societies, however, typically demonstrate "contrary tendencies"; they constitute "a region of intersection that is sensitive to internal and external forces that both integrate and differentiate communities and areas on both sides of the boundary line."[3] West Virginia was no less complicated. For half a century after its creation, the state's political leaders continued to be undecided about how they would identify themselves in the nation. Were they southern and agrarian, industrial and northern, or some amalgamation?

This essay will focus on the changing geography and political economy of party strength in West Virginia, from the state's founding through the first decade of the twentieth century. This political realignment within the state demonstrates both the continuing borderland nature of West Virginia and its crucial role in breaking the nation's Gilded Age political deadlock. Although the entire Appalachian South was torn over the partisan struggle for supremacy in the late nineteenth century, no other part of Appalachia had the ability to influence the outcome. West Virginia was the only state in which the mountain counties actually controlled politics, thus making it an interesting, if atypical, case study of the continuing importance of how Appalachia dealt with the aftermath of the Civil War.[4]

To the "founding fathers" of the state, Fleming's lament about economic development bypassing West Virginia would have signaled deep disappointment. Many of the leaders of the statehood movement rejected the traditionalistic political culture of the Old Dominion that created "a system of self-perpetuating county oligarchies in which membership carried life tenure and essentially passed as a family heirloom," according to historian Robin Einhorn. Cliques of local elites, lodged in county courthouses, accumulated local offices and power unthreatened by voters at least until the new state constitution of 1851.[5] New state leaders followed a different model; in the words of one historian, they "borrowed an Ohio broom to sweep away Virginian cobwebs." What this meant was that West Virginia's creators preferred a new political system that promoted education, democratic reforms (e.g., the secret ballot, annual elections, and a reorganized judiciary), and policies favoring a more modern commercial and industrial economy.[6]

This perspective reflected in part the disproportionate influence of Wheeling, which served as the host city for the founding conventions. Antebellum Wheeling was a burgeoning industrial town, more like its close neighbors in Ohio and Pennsylvania than its distant cousins in Virginia. Two out of three heads of households in Wheeling were born out of state and outside the South, either in the industrial North or Germany and Ireland. They wanted schools, railroads, tariffs, and tax policies favorable to industry, not limited government content with the traditional agricultural economy.[7] The problem for these more urban and industrial areas was Virginia's constitution. Fearing that nonslaveholding majorities might undermine slavery by imposing heavy taxes on chattel, Virginia, like most of the slave-labor states, included a uniformity clause in the state constitution that prevented any particular form of property being taxed at a higher rate than any other. In short, Virginia's legislature could not shift the burdens of taxation to encourage new commercial and industrial activity. In fact, the state taxed commerce and industry more heavily in order to protect slaveholders.[8]

The founders of the new state ultimately could not escape the Old Dominion's legacy. New statehood leaders confronted a population that did not share their outlook. Indeed, the inclusion of counties south of the Kanawha River and east of the Monongahela River within West Virginia's boundaries meant that at least one-third, if not more, of the state's voters and nearly half of its counties sympathized with the Confederacy. A much larger portion opposed the racial and the economic policies of the Republican Party once the war ended, particularly those policies that seemed to give additional powers to the federal government. Rural families in the mountain South tended to reject the nationalizing tendencies of the Republicans for an intense localism that emphasized security and household independence.[9]

Governor Arthur I. Boreman bolstered the party's short-term prospects by disfranchising ex-Confederates, but the debate over extending the suffrage to African Americans sparked by the Fifteenth Amendment split the Republicans. Liberal Republican William H. Flick sought to unify support for black suffrage by restoring the voting rights of ex-Confederates in 1870.[10] The plan backfired: Democrats regained control of the state and immediately called for a convention to rewrite the West Virginia constitution. Symbolically, the legislature now met in Charleston, a small, undeveloped town, rather than in Wheeling, signifying a shift in leadership from the North to the South. Gone from power were the founding fathers of statehood who had sought to modernize the state's economy. Gone too was the new political culture they had introduced, wiped away by Democratic redeemers.[11]

The geographic breakdown of the political shift attests to the impact of Civil War–era sectionalism. In the first presidential election following the enfranchisement of ex-Confederates, in 1872, the Republicans largely maintained their hold in those counties north of the Little Kanawha River, especially those of the upper Monongahela Valley and along the Ohio River. Four years later, amid the last gasps of Radical Reconstruction, the Democrats controlled all but thirteen of the state's fifty-four counties and all but two counties south of the Little Kanawha. Republicans still did better in the more urban and populous counties (winning thirteen of the top fifteen), in the more industrial counties (seven of the top ten), and in those with higher percentages of immigrants (nine of the top ten).[12]

For the next two decades the Democrats ruled, bolstered by a political system inherited from antebellum Virginia that restored the courthouse cliques. From 1872 to 1895, Democrats won 64 percent of the seats in the West Virginia House of Delegates and more than 70 percent of the state senate seats. Only once in those years would the Democrats fail to control both houses of the legislature.[13] During its generation of state rule, the Democrats sent mixed messages to entrepreneurs due to party factionalism. In some counties, lawyers and ex-Confederates constituted a conservative "Bourbon" faction that exploited the complex land-registry system to

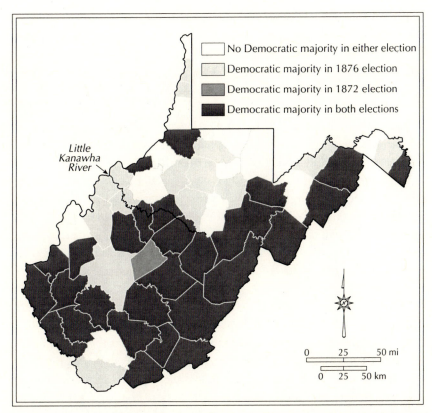

Democratic majority in the 1872 and 1876 elections. In the first presidential election following the enfranchisement of ex-Confederates in 1872, West Virginia's Republicans largely maintained their hold in those counties north of the Little Kanawha River, but by 1876, amid the last gasps of Radical Reconstruction, the Democrats controlled all but thirteen of the state's fifty-four counties and all but two counties south of the Little Kanawha.

line their pockets and facilitate the transfer of land to speculators. There was also an "Agrarian" wing that was highly critical of industrial capitalism. Finally, there was a bloc known as the "Kanawha Ring," which operated out of Charleston law firms and principally served as a conduit for patronage and party influence.[14] As a result, Democrats pursued conflicting agendas that only sporadically encouraged industrial development or manufacturing.

This is all the more ironic because the two most recognized leaders of the party, Johnson Newlon Camden and Henry Gassaway Davis, were industrialists. Camden, operating out of the Parkersburg area, had by the late 1870s obtained "complete control of West Virginia [oil] production." Davis rose to influence in the eastern portion of the state, developing a company that supplied coal and timber from the upper Potomac River region. Both men tied their fates to resource development. In Camden's case, he tired of competing against the beneficial shipping rates extracted by John D. Rockefeller's Standard Oil Company. Unable to beat the enemy, Camden merged his operations into Rockefeller's during the economic depression of the 1870s. He served West Virginia in the U.S. Senate from 1881 to 1887 and again from 1893 to 1895, often placing Rockefeller's interests above those of West Virginia. Davis had accumulated resources by supplying the Baltimore and Ohio Railroad (B&O) with coal and railroad ties, but he used his two terms in the U.S. Senate (1871–1883) to attract a powerful group of investors for a rail network connecting the vast coal and timber resources of the upper Potomac fields to the main east-west trunk line of the B&O.[15]

Throughout the Gilded Age, Camden and Davis exerted considerable influence on the state party, in large part because they had the financial resources to bankroll party campaigns and the press.[16] But they could never completely consolidate their control over a party that still relied on Civil War–era sectionalism for its political base. Indeed, many of the Democrat state leaders were ex-Confederates, and the bulk of the party's votes came from those counties that supported secession. The party divided on protective tariffs that benefited industry and shifted capital from the agrarian South to the industrializing North, and many Democrats opposed a rigid adherence to the gold standard, a currency policy that the bankers and industrialists felt was essential to securing their investments. Furthermore, there was little in state Democrat platforms that appealed to the interests of industrial workers—only meager support for restricting immigration or convict labor, and virtually nothing that strengthened the bargaining position of workers with regard to wages and working conditions.[17]

The rule of Democratic redeemers faced its first challenge from the Greenback Labor insurgency. An outgrowth of the hard times that gripped the country after the economic panic of 1873, Greenbackers proposed to cure the depression by reversing monetary policies that took silver and paper currency out of circulation. They argued that the existing tight-money policies hurt hard-pressed farmers and wage earners and discouraged investment in new enterprises. In 1876 the Greenback insurgency pulled voters away from the Democrats in the Kanawha River Valley, but in 1878 Green-backers created far more disruption, spreading through the Kanawha and Ohio River valleys. The insurgents cut into Democratic margins in each of the three congressional districts, and the Greenback candidate in the southwest carried the most industrial counties, which made the race too close for Democratic comfort. The Greenbackers also elected eighteen candidates to the state legislature, enough to push through bills that protected mechanics' liens, victims of insurance fraud, coal miners' safety, and low-cost school books.[18]

The Greenback Labor Party might have done more damage to the Democrats were it not for the lingering sectionalism of the Civil War. Wherever Greenbackers threatened to shrink Democratic pluralities, party newspapers warned "ex-Confederates of the return of the Radical Republicans to power in the state" if voters wasted their ballots on third parties.[19] Fears of "bloody shirt" politics stymied the Greenback party's fusion with the Republicans in 1880 and led to its demise. Still, as late as 1886, a Greenbacker won the state senate seat in Kanawha County and became president of the West Virginia senate. Moreover, Kanawha Valley counties with manufacturing interests joined the Republican column in the presidential election of 1880, becoming the party's entering wedge in the southern half of the state.[20]

Divisions among Democrats over politics and economics left most of West Virginia undeveloped through the Reconstruction era. In 1880 nearly half of all manufacturing jobs in the state were in the northern panhandle (Wheeling and its neighbors on the Ohio River), which had a very different political culture. These counties traced their industrial traditions back to antebellum times, and they remained committed to industry and commerce. In fact, the panhandle's control of nearly half of the state's manufacturing underestimates the lack of modern, diversified development elsewhere. Four out of every five iron and steel workers resided in just four counties, as did 85 percent of glassworkers, 65 percent of brick and tile makers, and half of foundry and machine shop employees. Outside the panhandle, only natural-resources industries like coal and salt kept the state from having virtually no industrialization at all. More than two-thirds of West Virginia's labor force toiled in agriculture.[21] Still, West Virginia's location at the southern border of the northern manufacturing belt meant that entrepreneurs in both parties wanted to challenge the direction of the state's political economy.

Cracks in the Democratic Party widened with the triumph of the agrarian wing in the 1880s. If the Greenbackers had appealed broadly to working people, the agrarians rallied discontented farmers, especially after Gov. Jacob Jackson's order for assessors to list previously exempted farm products for taxation in 1883. Howls of protest greeted the order and added to the growing anger about the state's outmoded tax system, which assessed farmers and benefited corporations that hired lobbyists to convince assessors to undervalue their property. For example, one B&O Railroad consultant accompanied assessors during their work and bragged about achieving "a reduction of six hundred dollars a mile in the valuation of both single and double track."[22] As a result of such unfair assessments, the agrarians rebelled against the regular party leadership and elected E. Willis Wilson governor in 1884. Wilson and the agrarians that entered with him introduced bills that were "inimical to trusts, combinations, and all that sort of thing," according to an agent for Standard Oil.[23] The agrarians committed the final insult to industrialists when they defeated Camden's bid to return to the U.S. Senate in 1887. Consequently, the two party leaders who cared the most about industry and national party issues—Camden and Davis—were out of the Senate and struggling to maintain influence in the state. Meanwhile, the political leaders in the ascendancy were all former Confederates, demonstrating the continuing importance of sectionalism to the party's base.[24]

Camden enjoyed some revenge in the 1888 elections, watching agrarian Democrats go down to defeat, but such personal delights cost the party. While Democrat A. B. Fleming narrowly won the governorship, voters reduced the Democratic majority in the state legislature to three and left the senate deadlocked, allowing a Greenbacker to be that body's president. Furthermore, Republicans expanded on their inroads in the southern part of the state, capturing Wyoming, McDowell, and Mercer counties, important new coal-industry sites. Clearly, the industrialist leaders of the Democrats feared for their future. Rumors circulated that Henry Gassaway Davis was consulting with leading Republicans to advance his interests and that he supported Republican Benjamin Harrison for president. Meanwhile, the Democrats struggled to maintain the support of the party's industrial wing for the pro–free trade U.S. congressman William L. Wilson.[25]

Thus, when Gov. A. B. Fleming spoke of "conspicuous opportunities" in 1891, the Democrats had proved unequal to the task of becoming the party of industrial capitalism. Although Democrats rebounded in state

elections in 1892, the partisan loyalty of several of their leading industrialists waned. In addition to concern about Davis, Camden raised eyebrows in
the party by allowing Ohio's Republican governor, William McKinley, use
of his special railroad car for campaign speeches in West Virginia.[26] Other
Democrats feared the influx of Republican votes with African American
migration into the southern coal counties. Indeed, although the Democrats
held onto the state legislature and elected William MacCorkle as governor,
the Republicans added six counties throughout the state to their side while
losing just one formerly Republican county.[27]

West Virginia's development efforts certainly had many obstacles to
overcome. Despite the state's wealth in natural resources, the increasing concentration of manufacturing in the United States made it difficult for newly

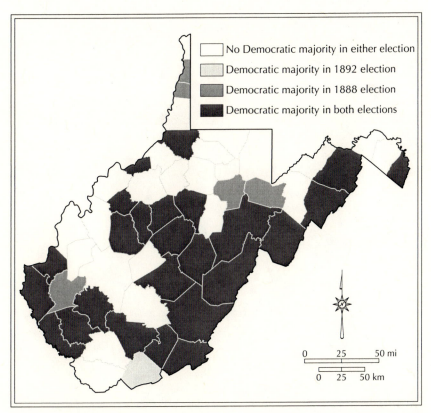

The elections of 1888 and 1892 showed the end of West Virginia's traditional Civil
War–era political divisions and foreshadowed the Republican Party's ascendancy in
the state in 1893.

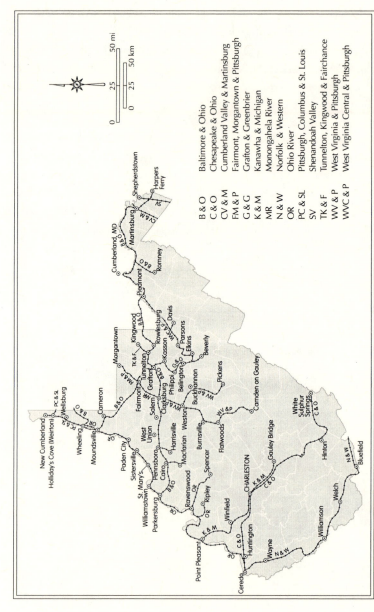

B & O	Baltimore & Ohio
C & O	Chesapeake & Ohio
CV & M	Cumberland Valley & Martinsburg
FM & P	Fairmont, Morgantown & Pittsburgh
G & G	Grafton & Greenbrier
K & M	Kanawha & Michigan
MR	Monongahela River
N & W	Norfolk & Western
OR	Ohio River
PC & SL	Pittsburgh, Columbus & St. Louis
SV	Shenandoah Valley
TK & F	Tunnelton, Kingwood & Fairchance
WV & P	West Virginia & Pittsburgh
WVC & P	West Virginia Central & Pittsburgh

West Virginia's railroads in 1893. A comparison of election results in 1888 and 1892 with an 1893 railroad map of West Virginia shows that there was a direct correlation between railroad development and increases in Republican strength. (based on a map by Frank S. Riddel, *The Historical Atlas of West Virginia* [Morgantown: West Virginia University Press, 2008], 171) developing areas to compete with established industrial regions. By 1889 nearly three-fifths of all manufacturing jobs were located in just thirty-four industrial areas, and those same areas maintained their share of manufacturing employment over the next forty years. This was the industrial core of the nation. These centers of manufacturing, according to economists and geographers, built upon their early advantages. Their population growth provided large markets, a labor pool attractive to new industries, and fertile fields for further investment in new products and advanced technologies that only enhanced their advantages. Peripheral areas like West Virginia that lagged behind in industrial development thus faced enormous obstacles in changing their relationship to the core.[28]

Even though West Virginia was a borderland for the core industrial region, mountain state capitalists faced several barriers to industrialization. The state's agricultural sector declined in the post–Civil War years, unable to compete with the fertile soils and mechanizing farms of the Midwest and the Plains. Thus, agriculture could not generate capital for investment. Moreover, West Virginia suffered the lingering effects of Virginia's antipathy to commercial and industrial development, particularly in its western counties. Many West Virginia counties had no bank at all as late as the 1890s. The state ranked near the bottom in holdings of stock in national banks, and in 1891 West Virginia had just forty-nine state banks with deposits of less than $9 million. Combined, the total investments in both state and national banks amounted to only $5 million, a paltry sum for a state with 760,000 people.[29] Consequently, such limited assets made the region dependent upon imported capital, which proved to be reluctant to finance local markets, especially those that marketed locally produced goods.[30]

Of course, there were many entrepreneurs anxious to tap the vast fuel resources essential to the second industrial revolution. Especially in the sparsely settled southern coalfields, the rush to exploit the region amounted to a virtual feeding frenzy. During the 1880s, such noteworthy national business figures as J. P. Morgan and John D. Rockefeller benefited from hastily built railroads connecting the state's coalfields to important markets. These and other entrepreneurs speculated in coal lands, purchasing deeds dating back as far as the Revolutionary War. Although the state had long ago reclaimed these lands when the original deed holders had neither registered their claims nor paid taxes, speculators convinced friendly judges to void subsequent sales and reinstate the earlier titles. By 1900 nonresident speculators owned 90 percent of Mingo, Logan, and Wayne counties and 60 percent of Boone and McDowell counties. These absentee owners included men with enormous influence in business and political circles.[31]

The role of absentee ownership is part of a long debate on the causes of the lagging economic development of West Virginia. Because outsiders owned such large portions of the resource-rich southern coal fields, the state lacked the means to develop self-sustaining economic growth. In a gloomy but insightful report in 1884, the West Virginia Tax Commission cautioned that regardless of the construction of railroads, the opening of mines, and the influx of workers, "if the entire enterprise is owned by nonresidents, if all the profits belong to persons who reside abroad, if those who are permanently identified with the locality do not participate in the harvest, the State is going backwards." The agents of powerful nonresident capital, the commission advised, were "emissaries of injurious schemes," buying up the state's resources and manipulating politics to the benefit of private interests.[32] Drawing upon such examples, some scholars blame nonresident landowners for the truncated economic growth of the state. To them, the ongoing poverty of West Virginia is the result of political, economic, and cultural domination by powerful corporations operating outside the region. Their ownership of land and mineral rights doomed the state's ability to promote a more diversified, self-sustaining growth.[33]

Other scholars warn against extrapolating the experience of the southern coalfields too broadly; they remind us that other parts of the state developed differently. The northern panhandle has already been mentioned, but it was not the sole exception. The industrialization process in the Upper Monongahela Valley also broke with the pattern of nonresident ownership that channeled investment into a single industry (coal). Instead, much of the development in this region built more gradually from a base of local (albeit small scale) commercial activity and capital accumulation begun earlier. Coal, oil, and natural gas were important, but Harrison, Marion, and other north-central counties nurtured manufacturing enterprises as well.[34] However, it is unclear whether these local entrepreneurs acted any differently from absentee capitalists when it came to pursuing a political economy that favored a balanced and self-sustaining growth over a path that emphasized exports of natural resources.[35]

In either case, even the more indigenous industrialism of north-central West Virginia never fostered a fully developed region with "the ability, the finances, and the will to generate the conditions for further development internally." Economic historians and geographers explain this situation by drawing upon a theory of world capitalist systems. According to this theory, the global spread of capitalism causes regions to develop collaterally but not equally. Regions that develop later (peripheries) become dependent upon metropolitan regions that developed earlier (cores) and are thus unable to overcome barriers to self-sustaining economic growth. Applied to West Virginia, the theory explains the state's economic backwardness as the result of its lack of capital and human resources and its inability to generate sufficient internal investment to keep profits in the state.[36]

People in the northern panhandle and the Upper Monongahela Valley were doing their best to overcome those hurdles. Upon examination of a series of factors that demonstrate levels of industrial development—manufacturing activity, accumulation of wealth, integration into capital markets, participation in technological change, and the skill level of the workforce—it becomes clear that these areas were above the national average in at least two of the categories, and several counties were above average in three categories. On a map of relative development, the northern panhandle and Upper Monongahela counties made up the southern border of the most advanced region. Not surprisingly, most of these counties, which made up the state's First Congressional District, returned majorities for Republican candidates beginning in the 1880s.[37]

They received assistance from a new generation of judges who began to interpret the law in ways that benefited railroads and industrial uses of the land over the needs of farmers. In deciding liability cases where railroads killed livestock or started fires that damaged farms, state supreme court judges like Henry Brannon routinely overturned jury awards to farmers in favor of railroad, coal, and timber corporations. Other entrepreneurs won favorable decisions on cases that involved the diversion of streams and rivers for industrial purposes, despite the harm that such changes would cause to farms. These changes, according to one historian, amounted to a virtual "legal revolution" aimed at making investment capital secure in the state.[38]

West Virginia's location—initially on the border of Civil War–era sectionalism and later on the dividing line between agrarian and industrial economies—created a hybrid Democratic Party, evident in the factions mentioned previously. Prodevelopment Democrats had injected an enthusiasm for industry into one wing of the party, but they never ruled the party unchallenged. Although Camden and Davis built a modern political organization that relied on effective communications, fundraising, patronage, and bureaucracy, they could not completely "tame" the other factions. Moreover, they appealed to a base that often still thought in terms of the Civil War party system. By 1892 Davis and Camden wondered if their party could serve as the vehicle for attracting capital investment and spurring industrialization, especially once the national party moved increasingly toward free trade and soft money in its platform.[39] In a state so unevenly reaping the fruits of economic development, the problem was how to shift the balance of power.

During the 1880s, as key individuals in the state embraced industrial development, many considered coal to be the engine of change. Whether they enticed outside speculators or generated investment from within, coal seemed like the most marketable commodity and thus the key to subsequent development. In 1893 at the Columbian Exposition in Chicago, for example, Gov. William A. MacCorkle claimed: "It is an axiom of political economy that the coal, iron and heavier products will attract the lighter products, cotton, wheat and wool and each of their products and manufactures."[40] For coal to drive West Virginia development, however, some coal operators argued that they needed tariffs to protect their markets against foreign imports.[41]

The most consistent advocates of protective tariffs were the Republicans. As interest in industrial development spread, so too did support for the party. The Republican Party provided links to the founders of West Virginia, but sectional politics limited its appeal in the state. Republicans relied mainly on those areas where railroad building, coal mining, manufacturing, and banking were already progressing. In fact, the party stronghold in the First Congressional District had more manufacturing capital and produced more manufacturing value than the other three districts combined.[42] Republicans stressed their attachments to the Union cause in the Civil War, especially through support of soldiers' pensions, but they increasingly emphasized a development-oriented economic program. In particular, the party believed that tariffs would "give employment to the labor and capital of this country" and that government surpluses could be spent on internal improvements and education, the "social capital" that would attract further investment capital.[43]

Indeed, some industrialists expected that the state's abundant fuel resources, so critical to the second industrial revolution, could enable the Mountain State to join the nation's manufacturing belt. Their philosophy migrated into West Virginia along with railroads, investment capital, and

industrial development, and it increasingly won over voters in the coal mining and industrial counties during the 1880s, particularly as party constituencies began to more closely match party economic agendas. The
Republican gubernatorial candidate in 1888, for example, received letters
of encouragement from coal miners in Fayette County as well as factory
workers in Ohio County. By 1892 the state's political map no longer resembled Civil War–era divisions.[44]

The eventual triumph of the Republicans awaited only new leaders and
a more professional party organization. Supplying the missing ingredients,
as well as some much-needed funding, was Stephen B. Elkins, son-in-law of
Henry Gassaway Davis. Davis, a Democrat, actually encouraged his Republican son-in-law to enter politics because he was so discouraged by the low-
tariff policies of his own party. Elkins, born in Missouri in 1841, had risen
to prominence in Republican circles in New Mexico in the 1870s. In 1875
he married Davis's daughter and became a partner in the family's extensive
Maryland and West Virginia enterprises. Although he wielded influence in
the Republican Party from his homes in New York and Washington, DC,
he did not enter politics in West Virginia until his father-in-law pressed
him to do so as a result of his growing frustration with the state's Democrats. Elkins's close friendship with Pres. Benjamin Harrison enabled him
to assume leadership of the party after 1890. In particular, state Republicans appreciated the money that Elkins could bring to party coffers, both
from his own substantial wealth as well as his connections. One Republican
leader rejoiced that they could now entice votes from mountaineers who
needed "encoinagement."[45]

Despite steadily growing popular support, the Republican ascendancy
did not occur until the Depression of 1893 rocked the Democrats. Because
the party trumpeted its protectionist, hard-money program, Elkins hoped
that the economic calamity would crush the free-trade, soft-money Democrat opposition in the state. Even many Democrats shared that assumption. Writing to Senator Camden in December 1893, former governor A. B.
Fleming claimed: "From day to day I am strengthened in my belief that we
can't afford free coal, either from a business or political standpoint. From
what I can learn, I have no doubt but free coal will give us three Republican congressmen and a Republican House of Delegates next fall."[46] As
the depression worsened, strikes and labor unrest swept across the state,
which Republicans blamed on Democratic policies that they claimed discouraged high wages and capital investment. Many political leaders in both

parties, particularly those who placed industrial development at the top of the state's agenda, blanched at the proposed Democratic tariff reductions in 1894. They believed that these reductions, in large part authored by West Virginia Democrat William L. Wilson, disadvantaged the state. In particular, the Wilson-Gorman tariff opened a major chasm between Wilson and Davis.[47]

This was all the help the Republicans needed. Elkins worked throughout the winter and spring to save some protections for coal, and then turned his attention to unifying the party to defeat Wilson in the November elections. His confidants predicted the impact of the Wilson-Gorman tariff: "free coal and iron meant Republicanism in West Virginia."[48] They were right. Elkins watched as the Republicans swept to a landslide victory in West Virginia, electing all four congressmen and turning a twenty-six-seat minority into a twenty-nine-seat majority in the state legislature. Davis felt vindicated by his son-in-law's triumph. More importantly, he expected some rewards: "I hope and believe that the result . . . will be to considerably increase business in the country and we should get our share," he wrote to his nephew.[49] The real payoff came in January 1895 when the state legislature elected Elkins to Camden's seat in the U.S. Senate. The party's nomination speech revealed its expectations: Elkins was the right man to develop the "unexplored wealth of coal, iron and minerals" in the state. Not only could he obtain "home capital," but he could also go into the "monied centres" and command attention.[50] The industrialists maintained an important advocate in the U.S. Senate, although the party label had changed.[51]

Elkins's first agenda item was to build a party that would guarantee unswerving support for his policies. After a generation out of power, much of the party's energy went into securing patronage positions for loyalists. To cite just a few examples, Nathan B. Scott, a Wheeling glass manufacturer and investor in coal and oil, wanted an appointment as commissioner of internal revenue; John W. Mason, a Fairmont lawyer and mine owner, sought a position in the Treasury Department; and Parkersburg newspaper editor A. B. White hoped to become a collector of internal revenue. Elkins worked hard to keep their loyalty: Scott obtained a seat in the U.S. Senate in 1899, Mason obtained a judicial appointment in 1900, and White became governor in 1901.[52] Elkins also needed to walk a tightrope among national party candidates to obtain the maximum benefits for West Virginia. In 1896, for instance, he cultivated the presidential aspirations of both Pennsylvania senator Matthew Quay and Ohio congressman William

McKinley so he could win support for a $1.13 million appropriation for dams on the Monongahela River. Elkins reminded his followers that "I do not think such success would have come to us had we been fighting the Presidential candidates that are here."[53] If the party had hoped to put a man in the Senate who could bring development dollars to West Virginia, then Elkins was the man.

The realignment of politics resulting from the critical election of 1896 solidified the Republican Party in the state for the next thirty years. When the Democratic Party hung its fate on William Jennings Bryan and his opposition to the gold standard, those areas in the state hoping to entice outside capital became firmly committed to the Republicans. Political scientist Richard Bensel asserts that "the intersection between Bryan's electoral support and congressional voting on gold may have been the closest tie between popular voting behavior and legislative policy-making in history." In West Virginia, the critical elections of 1894 and 1896 signaled a dramatic shift to popular support for the Republican economic program, and their representatives voted for sound currency and high tariffs. Between 1896 and 1908, Republicans increased their control from thirty-one to forty-two of the state's fifty-five counties. For those who saw the state's future in industrial development, the results were electric.[54]

The Republican triumph did, in fact, accelerate the economic transformation of West Virginia. Elkins threw his influence behind the resumption of high tariffs that protected coal, and the state became a prime target for investment. In the 1890s, despite four years of depression in the middle of the decade, population increased by nearly 46 percent. The patterns of that growth demonstrate even more clearly the changing nature of the state. The growth occurred in two concentrated areas: the commercial and industrial counties along the Ohio River and the leading coal counties. These concentrations accounted for only one-third of the land in the state but two-thirds of the population increase. Jobs in coal increased from 5 percent of the male labor force to 9 percent during the decade.[55] Once begun, the industrial transformation picked up pace. By 1910 the combined numbers of men in manufacturing and resource extraction topped the numbers in agriculture (see table 9.1).

West Virginia's booming development followed two paths. In the southern coal counties, investment focused on coal and coke production, the sort of development that historians have associated with the theories explaining the economic backwardness of West Virginia. These were the counties

Table 9.1. West Virginia Male Workforce Distribution by Industrial Sector

Industrial Sector	1890	1900	1910
Agriculture	57.7%	49.6%	40.2%
Trade and transportation	11.0	12.2	12.1
Services (professional and personal)	5.4	4.9	5.8
Manufacturing	18.7	20.7	25.6
Resource extraction	7.2	12.6	16.3
Total male workforce (000's)	202	295	394

Source: U.S. Census Bureau, *Thirteenth Census (1910): Population* (Washington, DC: Government Printing Office, 1914), 529–30.

where powerful nonresident investors dominated and took the state's mineral wealth to fuel the factories of the Great Lakes region. They and their agents recruited large numbers of blacks and southern or eastern European immigrants, constructed makeshift towns completely controlled by the company, and made the region as dependent as possible upon coal.[56]

The panhandle and the northern coal counties set a different pattern, one that demonstrates West Virginia's character as a borderland between the industrial political economy of the North and the agrarian South. The panhandle built upon its early industrial development and its advantages in cheaper water transportation on the Ohio River. The four panhandle counties accounted for more than one-fourth of all new manufacturing jobs between 1890 and 1930, keeping its share of manufacturing in the state above 30 percent. At the same time, the Upper Monongahela Valley of West Virginia, a ten-county coal region built around Harrison and Marion counties, experienced an economic take-off. Improvements on the Monongahela River and the opening of the Monongahela River Railroad in 1890 sparked the boom. The population more than doubled between 1890 and 1920, attracting a variety of different ethnic groups with cosmopolitan political ideas. The main county seats matured from towns with a combined population of less than nine thousand to almost fifty-eight thousand during those years. Although coal was a critical component here, the number of manufacturing establishments more than doubled, and the average manufacturing wage surpassed both the state and the national averages.[57]

It was equally important that these two regions did not follow the example of the southern coal counties in relying almost exclusively upon outside capital. The northern panhandle included a significant number of local elites who invested in the industrialization of the region's iron and steel, nail, pottery, glass, leather, and tobacco factories.[58] The Upper Mononga- hela Valley developed later, but much of the investment also came from local capital. The Watson and Fleming families in Fairmont, the Goff and the Lowndes families in Clarksburg, and Alston G. Dayton in Philippi were among the men who honeycombed the region with railroads and built fortunes and power. This group, however, split on party affiliation and economic thinking. While all could agree that railroads were essential to prosperity, their visions of economic development diverged. Democrats believed that a low-price strategy would enable coal operators to export fuel resources and accumulate investment capital. Many Republicans, in contrast, worried about exporting all of the state's energy resources. They followed the model of the northern manufacturing belt, hoping to attract more diverse investment and create a balanced and sustainable development strategy that included high wages and value-added manufacturing.[59]

Republican proponents of development emphasized protective tariffs. While Elkins preached the benefits of high tariffs to keep out coal from Nova Scotia, Democrat operators felt they could best achieve market con- trol with a low-wage, nonunion strategy. Thus, agreement on the desir- ability of development masked important policy and partisan differences. Of course, tariffs also benefited the fastest-growing manufacturing indus- tries in the state, glass and steel. Not surprisingly, then, a strong candidate to join Elkins in the U.S. Senate in 1899 was Nathan B. Scott. Born in Ohio in 1842, Scott was a Union Civil War veteran. In 1865 he located in Wheeling, where he became a glass manufacturer, banker, and coal and oil speculator. As the Republicans came to power in the 1890s, Scott's politi- cal fortunes soared. He gained favor not only among Wheeling's manufac- turers but also with its growing numbers of workers because of his support for protective tariffs and immigration restriction, issues that protected the high wages and profitability of their industries.[60] With Scott on the Senate Committee on Mines and Mining and Elkins on the Committee on Inter- state Commerce, West Virginia industrialists felt that their interests were well represented.[61]

The Republican Party's program to stimulate economic development ultimately led back to tax policy. Democrats, even proponents of indus- trialization, had argued that limited taxation was essential to attracting capital investment. The state's constitution required uniform taxation, but that placed the burden of taxes on owners of real estate at rates of 25 cents for every $100 of assessed value, plus an additional ten cents for education. One problem was that the assessment of value and the collection of taxes remained in the hands of local authorities, a problem that the Republicans did not immediately address. Another problem was the uniformity clause, which sought to shield the wealth of elites from policies that the legislature might determine to be fair and equal taxation. Uniformity clauses served the purpose of limiting the ways that legislatures could distribute the burdens of taxation. During the years of the agrarian insurgency in the Democratic Party, the state had made only modest efforts at equalizing tax burdens; an 1885 law taxed corporate charters, and in 1887 the state legislature pushed an ineffective inheritance tax. A more substantial reform effort died on the state senate floor in 1893, victim of "a powerful lobby and combinations with men and money at their command," according to the *American Agriculturalist*.[62]

Industrialization only worsened the problem. In sparsely settled counties where nonresident corporations held a commanding influence, assessments severely understated real values. Especially in counties where coal was king—McDowell, Randolph, and Marion, for example—the average value per acre of real estate declined in the 1890s, despite the presence of huge mining corporations and the growth of new towns. Similarly, the valuation of railroad property actually declined between 1894 and 1900 by half a million dollars, despite a 25 percent increase in mileage.[63]

The system generated considerable animosity. On the one hand, counties with a more diversified economy and a more politicized citizenry insisted on more accurate valuations. But this meant that property owners in these counties—primarily in the northern panhandle—paid much more in state taxes. On the other hand, many objected to the growing deficits in the state budget. Republican-dominated legislatures in the 1890s expanded the state bureaucracy as government took on the new responsibilities necessary to a more modern industrial society. Pressure from organized groups of small businessmen and industrial workers pressed government for regulatory agencies and the provision of new services. Demands ranged from pure food laws and railroad regulations to child labor and factory safety inspections, so that by 1899 the projected state budget was approximately $200,000 above expected revenues.[64]

By 1901 politicians could no longer ignore the clamor for tax reform. The legislature convened with a strong reform contingent, led by the president of the Wheeling Board of Trade. Moreover, the outgoing governor, also a Republican from Wheeling, endorsed an increase in the license tax on all corporations. Opponents of increased taxes averted political disaster by agreeing to a commission to study tax reform, one that included Democrat industrialist Henry Gassaway Davis. But the commission's report in 1902 gave an unexpected boost to progressive forces in the state, as did the new governor, A. B. White. The report recommended that property taxes go to the localities but required uniform annual assessments from the state tax commissioner. For state funds, the commission proposed a combination of license taxes that hit saloon owners more harshly than mine owners and small license and severance taxes on coal, oil, and natural gas.[65] To the proponents of reform, especially those from the increasingly Republican industrial areas of the state, the sort of economic growth that would benefit all the people of the state required a tax policy that would generate revenues from its abundant fuel resources and use them to build the social capital necessary for future development.

Initially, tax reform seemed like a winning strategy for the Republicans. William D. Hubbard, a rising star in the party from Wheeling, headed the commission and led the movement for changes that promised to make West Virginia a leader in progressive tax reform. The report won the endorsement of a wide spectrum of people in the state, ranging from many Republican businessmen to such groups as the West Virginia Grange. Indeed, Grange secretary M. V. Brown was so impressed with the efforts that Republican governor A. B. White was making on behalf of reform that he abandoned his longtime support of the Democrats. Reformers even built alliances with organized labor, which gave "substantial aid" to the cause. Moreover, the leader of the industrialists in the Democratic Party, Henry Gassaway Davis, not only served on the commission but wrote to Governor White that his recommendation for taxes on coal, oil, and gas "would have been higher; but the Commission appeared to think I was too high."[66]

However, even the modest changes proposed by the tax commission generated a storm of protest from Democrats and industrialists involved in resource extraction. Before the state legislature could meet to consider the bills drafted by the tax commission in January 1903, opponents claimed that the legislation was unconstitutional. Leading the opposition to tax reform was none other than former governor A. B. Fleming. As counsel for Standard Oil in West Virginia and as a partner of the Watson family in the Fairmont Coal Company, Fleming was an ardent foe of labor unions, tariffs, and taxes.[67] Fleming's strategy for economic development relied on exporting fuel out of the state, making cost containment the critical issue in maintaining markets. For the coal industry, the primary factor in reducing costs was labor. In the years after serving as governor, Fleming returned to Fairmont to battle the United Mine Workers, which, in his mind, received too much sympathy from state Republican leaders.[68] When glass manufacturers located their plants in Fairmont, Fleming found new reasons to despise unions and the high-tariff policies of the Republicans. The glass industry was a high-wage, unionized industry that drove up wages in the nearby coalfields. Moreover, glassworkers were reliably Republican in party affiliation, presenting a clear challenge to the local political dominance of Fleming and the Watsons. Fleming abandoned his earlier support for glass factories and helped choke off further investment in local manufacturing.[69]

Fleming also argued that new taxes on coal, oil, and gas would raise costs and make West Virginia's resources less attractive. Of course, he was not alone. He enlisted twenty-seven other prominent figures in the state to issue a manifesto opposing the commission's reforms. Signers of the document included not only key Democrats but also a number of Republican defectors. Of note were Alston G. Dayton, whom Elkins had helped win a seat in the U.S. Congress, Charles Teter, Emmet Showalter, and Romeo Freer, all men tied to the coal industry and large corporations. The opponents of reform challenged the constitutionality of the proposed legislation, the need for an expanding state budget, and the wisdom of saddling the coal, oil, and gas industries with the largest share of the burden for the state's revenues. They also launched an aggressive public relations campaign to convince legislators of the harm that reform could do.[70]

Elkins skirted an open endorsement of the reforms, hoping to hold the Republicans together. He had witnessed the factional fighting that had destroyed the Democrats' control of the state in the 1880s, and he was a master at avoiding the sort of rigid party discipline that had hampered his own party before he claimed leadership.[71] But he also worried about the possibility of more sweeping changes if the Republicans did not accept some reforms. He wrote to Governor White, "I am satisfied the gas and oil interests will submit to any reasonable taxation, and we don't want to impose any other; the coal men may stand out, if so we could compromise with them, and then we could treat the railroads fairly and I believe they would be satisfied."[72] Elkins was wrong.

Opponents successfully lined up their support to kill the bills during the legislative session of 1903. They even blocked an attempt by reformers to convene a joint session of the house and the senate aimed at preventing delaying tactics. While Republican defectors from reform cloaked their motives in statements claiming that they were protecting the party's interests and preventing legislation "inimical to the investment of capital in the state," reformers argued otherwise. The *Grant County Press* of Petersburg, among other newspapers, laid the blame on a few "money-laden capitalists" who had "scores of well-boodled lobbyists besetting the legislature at every hand in a desperate effort to thwart the will of the people."[73] Although opponents of the tax bills successfully averted reform in the 1903 legislative session, Governor White promised to call for a special session to enact the bills.[74]

Because 1904 was an election year, Elkins feared that party disunity threatened the party's hold over the state. A more likely scenario was that it might damage Elkins's hold over the party. One B&O Railroad attorney wrote to Dayton "that the business interests of the State, including the commercial, banking, mining, manufacturing, oil and gas interests, are solidly arrayed against" tax reform, and that they "hold Senator Elkins responsible for the position taken by Governor White."[75] Moreover, the front-runner for the Republicans' gubernatorial nomination was William O. Dawson, a supporter of tax reform who was certainly likely to disrupt party unity. The antireform leaders jumped at this opportunity. Believing that the Democrats had little chance of winning, A. B. Fleming decided to try to influence the Republican nomination process. He handpicked Dayton's protégé, Charles Teter, to run against Dawson and then in large part directed his campaign.[76]

Elkins acted to avert disaster, convening a meeting of key party leaders in Washington, DC, that included both reformers and opponents. Over months of negotiation, the group worked out compromise bills to unite the party and get behind Dawson, a candidate who was immensely popular with farmers and labor. Governor White would get some of his tax reform in a special session of the legislature, but the most obnoxious parts of reform to the coal, oil, and gas interests—the severance or production taxes—would not be included. Eventually, the legislature passed this compromise legislation in a special session, which represented a small shift in the tax burden toward the corporations, but omitted the proposed severance tax on coal, oil, and gas.[77] The struggle for meaningful tax reform did not end in 1904, but the forces opposing change were vigilant and determined.

Interestingly, two Democrats give perhaps the most interesting perspectives on the limited nature of West Virginia's tax reform. Henry Gas-saway Davis, the early leader of the industrialists in the party and its vice presidential candidate in 1904, lamented what he saw as a failure. Davis supported fair, "even liberal," treatment of corporations, "but they should bear their just proportion of the taxes," he wrote. "It is unnecessary for me to call your attention to the comparatively large expenditure by the State for the protection of our coal, oil and gas operations, for which the State now gets but little return," he added, "especially as a large proportion of those who reap the benefit of the mining of coal, and the production of oil and gas, live out of the State and pay practically no taxes in West Virginia."[78]

In contrast, A. B. Fleming delighted in the defeat of tax reform for par-tisan reasons but also for personal economic ones. He wrote, "Any person who will take the code of West Virginia or the statutes enacted by the leg-islatures, even during the recent period of crusade against corporations in the United States, will find that this hostility has not reached the West Vir-ginia legislatures." Instead, Fleming boasted, "We have always succeeded in defeating everything to which we objected, and that too without the use of money."[79] It was not quite as easy as Fleming had claimed; opponents of reform had spent a great deal of time and money making certain that the financial benefits of the fuel resources of the state remained in the hands of private companies. In much the same way that antebellum slaveholders had restrained majority rule to prevent voters from taxing their most valu-able asset, powerful elites in the industrial era used every means at their disposal to shield corporations from what the people deemed to be fair and equal taxation.[80]

As a result, West Virginia raised only about half of the revenues per capita through taxes that its neighbors, Pennsylvania and Maryland, raised. Although it was a borderland for the great manufacturing belt of the nation, its tax policies and resources for spurring economic development more closely matched those of its neighbors to the south, like Kentucky.[81] Indeed, the remnants of Civil War–era sectionalism resurfaced in the 1904 and 1908 elections when the Democrats chose to campaign on Jim Crow laws and black disfranchisement. Even Davis, campaigning for the posi-tion of vice president of the United States, felt that the party's best hope of regaining power in West Virginia was to appeal to its southern roots.[82]

Reformers at the turn of the century thus failed to restructure the state's finances. Some Republicans, especially a group of Progressives in the more diversified industrial areas of the northern panhandle and the northern coal counties, hoped for different results. They believed, as did Governor White, that companies engaged in resource extraction "should pay taxes for miners' hospitals, inspectors and education," among a host of other activities that a modern industrial state should provide.[83] Although White eventually capitulated on the severance tax in the interest of Republican harmony, many in the party felt that increased corporate taxes as well as a tax on the exporting of the state's energy resources might encourage more investment in manufacturing industries that would add high-paying jobs, increase the urban population, and create a growing home market for goods and services. At the same time, tax revenues would enable state government to invest in education, roads, services, and infrastructure, the social capital that could generate the conditions for further development.

Instead, a combination of low-wage resource exporters (both Democrats and Republicans) and agents of the large nonresident corporations thwarted reform. Key were men like A. B. Fleming and Alston G. Dayton, each of whom promoted a low-cost export strategy for coal. They did not worry about uneven development or policies that funneled investment into coal and other extractive industries, and for good reason. None other than the governor of the state, George Atkinson, told a group of businessmen in 1897: "West Virginia, my friends, is the *eternal center* of coal and gas and oil and timber and of stalwart Republicanism also."[84]

Eternity did not last very long. Coal absorbed the lion's share of investment capital for the ensuing generation. Manufacturing jobs began their steady decline as a percentage of the state's occupations, while coal mining kept increasing. However, when the price of coal collapsed in the 1920s, the state had little else to fall back on. Consequently, the Great Depression came early to West Virginia. Per capita incomes fell from 78.9 percent of the national average in 1920 to 65.7 percent in 1929. Even then, the Republican state government adopted the Tax Limitation Amendment just before losing power in 1932, which once again limited options for democratic reforms that might have benefited West Virginians.[85]

All this seems to conform too easily to the theories of uneven economic development that help explain West Virginia's poverty despite its abundance of valuable resources. But economic geographers remind us that "leading industrial territories do not inevitably stay in the lead, despite the many advantages leadership confers, nor are lagging territories condemned to eternal backwardness, despite their many handicaps."[86] West Virginia had its opportunities; at the start of the twentieth century it could boast of burgeoning glass, tin plate, steel, pottery, and other industries. It was a borderland for the nation's most developed region, contemplating modernizing political reforms. But Virginia's legacy remained.

Notes

1. *West Virginia State Gazetteer and Business Directory 1891–92* (Detroit: R.L. Polk & Company, 1891), 29, included in Ronald L. Lewis and John C. Hennen Jr., *West Virginia: Documents in the History of a Rural-Industrial State* (Dubuque, IA: Kendall/Hunt Publishing Co., 1991), 156–57.

2. See especially Richard Franklin Bensel, *The Political Economy of American Industrialization, 1877–1900* (New York: Cambridge University Press, 2000), chapters 2 and 3; and Robert W. Cherny, *American Politics in the Gilded Age, 1868–1900* (Wheeling, IL: Harlan Davidson, 1997), chapter 2.

3. The concept of "borderland" is becoming increasingly useful in social analysis. I have drawn from a number of studies, but the quote comes from Randy William Widdis, "Migration, Borderlands, and National Identity," in John Bukowczyk et al., eds., *Permeable Border: The Great Lakes Basin as Transnational Region, 1650–1990* (Pittsburgh: University of Pittsburgh Press, 2005), 154. See also Oscar J. Martinez, *Border People: Life and Society in the U.S.-Mexico Borderlands* (Tucson: University of Arizona Press, 1994); Jeremy Adelman and Stephen Aron, "From Borderlands to Borders: Empires, Nation-States, and the Peoples in Between in North American History," *American Historical Review* 104 (June 1999): 814–41; responses to Adelman and Aron by Evan Haefeli, John R. Wunder, Pekka Hamalainen, and Christopher Schmidt-Nowara, *American Historical Review* 104 (October 1999): 1222–39; Mabel Berezin and Martin Schain, eds., *Europe without Borders: Remapping Territory, Citizenship, and Identity in a Transnational Age* (Baltimore: Johns Hopkins University Press, 2003); and J. R. V. Prescott, *Political Frontiers and Boundaries* (London: Allen & Unwin, 1987).

4. Gordon B. McKinney, *Southern Mountain Republicans, 1865–1900: Politics and the Appalachian Community* (Chapel Hill: University of North Carolina Press, 1978).

5. Robin L. Einhorn, *American Taxation, American Slavery* (Chicago: University of Chicago Press, 2006), 34. See also John Alexander Williams, "The New Dominion and the Old: Ante-Bellum and Statehood Politics as the Background of West Virginia's 'Bourbon Democracy,'" *West Virginia History* 33 (July 1972): 329–42.

6. Williams, "New Dominion," 342. Two excellent comparisons of comparative development in Virginia and Pennsylvania are John Majewski, *A House Dividing: Economic Development in Pennsylvania and Virginia before the Civil War* (New York: Cambridge University Press, 2000); and Sean P. Adams, *Old Dominion,*

Industrial Commonwealth: Coal, Politics and Economy in Antebellum America (Baltimore: Johns Hopkins University Press, 2004).

7. Ken Fones-Wolf, "Caught between Revolutions: Wheeling Germans in the Civil War Era," in Ken Fones-Wolf and Ronald L. Lewis, eds., *Transnational West Virginia: Ethnic Communities and Economic Change, 1840–1940* (Morgantown: West Virginia University Press, 2002), 20–23.

8. Einhorn, *American Taxation,* chapter 6, brilliantly explores the emergence of sectional systems of taxation and their impact. For an excellent description of the politics of taxation in antebellum North Carolina, see John C. Inscoe, *Mountain Masters: Slavery and the Sectional Crisis in Western North Carolina* (Knoxville: University of Tennessee Press, 1989), 141–51.

9. Robert S. Weise, *Grasping at Independence: Debt, Male Authority, and Mineral Rights in Appalachian Kentucky, 1850–1915* (Knoxville: University of Tennessee Press, 2001), 9–13.

10. McKinney, *Southern Mountain Republicans,* 41–44.

11. Ronald L. Lewis, *Transforming the Appalachian Countryside: Railroads, Deforestation, and Social Change in West Virginia, 1880–1920* (Chapel Hill: University of North Carolina Press, 1998), especially chapter 8; Williams, "New Dominion," 352.

12. This characterization is compiled from the county-level voting maps created by Richard Edward Tyre for his 2007 master's thesis in the Department of Geography at West Virginia University, compared with Stanley B. Parsons, William W. Beach, and Michael J. Dubin, *United States Congressional Districts and Data, 1843–1883* (Westport, CT: Greenwood Press, 1986), 144. The political division in the state also conformed to what historian John Alexander Williams identified as its two "physiographic provinces" separated by a southwest-to-northeast axis. One of these provinces tilts toward Ohio, and the other incorporates the broad valley counties that are closer to Virginia and "connected to the Great Valley by the watersheds of the Potomac and upper New rivers." See Williams, "New Dominion," 323–24.

13. Patrick A. Carone, "The Governor as a Legislator in West Virginia" (PhD diss., Duke University, 1969), 110.

14. John Alexander Williams, *West Virginia and the Captains of Industry* (Morgantown: West Virginia University Press, 1976), 7–10.

15. Festus P. Summers, *Johnson Newlon Camden: A Study in Individualism* (New York: Putnam, 1937), chapter 7 (quote is on p. 194); Charles M. Pepper, *The Life and Times of Henry Gassaway Davis, 1823–1916* (New York: The Century Company, 1920), 27–29, 96–103.

16. Camden's and Davis's papers are filled with requests from party officials for money to run campaigns and help keep the Democratic Party solvent. See, for example, George S. Otte to H. G. Davis, November 11, 1890, box 119, Henry Gassaway Davis Papers (hereafter Davis Papers), West Virginia and Regional History Collection, West Virginia University (hereafter WVRHC); W. E. Chilton to Johnson N. Camden, October 18, 1892, box 35, Johnson Newlon Camden Papers (hereafter Camden Papers), WVRHC.

17. Bensel, *Political Economy,* chapter 3.

18. William Derrick Barns, "The Granger and Populist Movements in West Virginia, 1873–1914" (PhD diss., West Virginia University, 1946), 524–38.

19. *Weekly Register* (Point Pleasant, WV), September 11, 1878, October 2, 1878.

20. Barns, "Granger and Populist Movements," 541–50.

21. Richard Mark Simon, "The Development of Underdevelopment: The Coal Industry and Its Effect on the West Virginia Economy, 1880–1930" (PhD diss., University of Pittsburgh, 1978), 289.

22. J. A. Robinson to John T. McGraw, December 15, 1885, box 4, John T. McGraw Papers (hereafter McGraw Papers), WVRHC.

23. See, for example, W. P. Thompson to J. N. Camden, February 5, 1889, box 35, Camden Papers; J. N. Camden to John T. McGraw, March 23, 1885, and Ira Robinson to McGraw, December 15, 1885, box 4, McGraw Papers; Barns, "Granger and Populist Movements," 568–93.

24. See Charles J. Faulkner to Camden, March 2, 1887, Arthur P. Gorman to Camden, May 6, 1887, box 35, and W. E. Lively to Camden, December 8, 1888, box 6, Camden Papers; Barns, "Granger and Populist Movements," 583. The ex-Confederates included E. Willis Wilson, Roger Chew, John Sydenstricker, Charles Faulkner, and W. L. Wilson.

25. On Davis, C. B. Carney to Camden, February 1, 1887, and W. E. Lively to Camden, December 8, 1888, box 35, Camden Papers; on opposition to Wilson, C. L. Hutchins to John T. McGraw, July 28, 1888, and C. J. Faulkner to McGraw, September 30, 1888, box 5, McGraw Papers.

26. Stephen B. Elkins to Camden, October 5, 1892, box 35, Camden Papers.

27. W. E. Chilton to Camden, October 19, 1892, box 35; W. P. Thompson to Camden, November 16, 1892, box 36, Camden Papers. The voting patterns are from Richard Tyre's maps. The Republican additions included Lincoln and Fayette counties in the south, Tucker and Barbour counties in the northeast, and Ohio and Brooke counties in the northern panhandle.

28. Simon, "Development of Underdevelopment," 288–91.

29. Paul Salstrom, *Appalachia's Path to Dependency: Rethinking a Region's Economic History, 1730–1940* (Lexington: University Press of Kentucky, 1994), 28–33; *Appletons' Annual Cyclopaedia and Register of Important Events of the Year 1892* (New York: D. Appleton and Company, 1893), 794–95; Commissioner of Banking of the State of West Virginia, *Tenth Annual Report, 1910* (Charleston, WV: Tribune Publishing Co., 1911), 6; Bensel, *Political Economy,* 62.

30. Salstrom, *Appalachia's Path to Dependency,* 29.

31. David Alan Corbin, *Life, Work, and Rebellion in the Coal Fields: The Southern West Virginia Miners, 1880–1922* (Urbana: University of Illinois Press, 1981), 2–4. For more on the role of absentee ownership in Appalachia's lagging development, see Barbara Rasmussen, *Absentee Landowning and Exploitation in West Virginia, 1760–1920* (Lexington: University Press of Kentucky, 1994), and Wilma A. Dunaway, *The First American Frontier: Transition to Capitalism in*

Southern Appalachia, 1700–1860 (Chapel Hill: University of North Carolina Press, 1996).

32. West Virginia Tax Commission, *Second Report: State Development* (Wheeling, 1884), 1–3, included in Lewis and Hennen, *West Virginia,* 158–60.

33. See, for example, Williams, *Captains of Industry;* Ronald D Eller, *Miners, Millhands, and Mountaineers: Industrialization of the Appalachian South, 1880–1930* (Knoxville: University of Tennessee Press, 1982); and Helen M. Lewis and Edward E. Knipe, "The Colonialism Model: The Appalachian Case," in Helen Matthews Lewis, Linda Johnson, and Donald Askins, eds., *Colonialism in Modern America: The Appalachian Case,* 9–31 (Boone, NC: Appalachian Consortium Press, 1978).

34. Simon, "Development of Underdevelopment," 307–14; Michael E. Workman, "Political Culture and the Coal Economy in the Upper Monongahela Region, 1776–1933" (PhD diss., West Virginia University, 1995), chapter 4.

35. In *Glass Towns: Industry, Labor and Political Economy in Appalachia, 1890–1930s* (Urbana: University of Illinois Press, 2007), especially in chapter 6, I argue that it did not. Similarly, I assert in the rest of this piece that local and absentee capitalists were equally culpable in shaping the political economy that left West Virginia a poor state despite its abundant natural resources.

36. In addition to the sources above, see the rejoinder by David Walls, "Internal Colony or Internal Periphery? A Critique of Current Models and an Alternative Formulation," in Lewis et al., eds., *Colonialism,* 319–50. Also see Lewis, *Transforming the Appalachian Countryside,* 47–52.

37. Bensel, *Political Economy,* 47–54; *Official Directory, West Virginia Democratic State Committee, with the Vote of the State* (Charleston: M.W. Donnally, 1894), 6–22.

38. Lewis, *Transforming the Appalachian Countryside,* chapter 4.

39. See J. W. Goshorn to Camden, October 16, 1893; A. B. Fleming to Camden, December 17, 1893, box 36; and Stephen B. Elkins to Camden, August 25, 1894, box 37, all in Camden Papers; Williams, *Captains of Industry,* 7–16.

40. William A. MacCorkle, "Address to the Columbian Exposition," *Public Papers of Governor Wm. A. MacCorkle, of West Virginia* (Charlestown, WV: M.W. Donnally, 1894), 6–22.

41. Williams, *Captains of Industry,* 17–21. See also Jeffery B. Cook, "The Ambassador of Development: Aretas Brooks Fleming, West Virginia's Political Entrepreneur, 1839–1923" (PhD diss., West Virginia University, 1998), 161–84.

42. Stanley B. Parsons, Michael J. Dubin, and Karen Toombs Parsons, *United States Congressional Districts, 1883–1913* (New York: Greenwood Press, 1990), 159.

43. Nathan Goff Jr. to *Toledo Blade,* November 24, 1887; W. J. W. Cowden to Goff, September 12, 1888, box 9; both in Nathan Goff Jr. Papers (hereafter Goff Papers), WVRHC.

44. There are reports of mass meetings of miners and mine laborers from Coal Valley (February 6, 1888), Fayette County (January 30, 1888), the Caperton mines

(January 23, 1888), and Stone Cliff (January 25, 1888), among others, in box 9, Goff Papers. Also see Wheeling Potters Protective Tariff Club to Goff, March 6, 1888; and Nail City Lodge #3, AAISW to Goff, March 13, 1888, in box 9, Goff Papers. The confluence of party constituencies and party economic programs is discussed in Jeffrey A. Jenkins, Eric Schickler, and Jamie L. Carson, "Constituency Cleavages and Congressional Parties: Measuring Homogeneity and Polarization, 1857–1913," *Social Science History* 28 (Winter 2004): 537–73.

45. Quote from H. R. Riddle to William H. H. Flick, August 16, 1888, cited in McKinney, *Southern Mountain Republicans,* 152. There is much information on the contest between Goff and Elkins for control of the Republican Party and its patronage in 1888 in the John W. Mason Papers, box 2, WVRHC. For information on Elkins, see Williams, *Captains of Industry,* 3–7, and McKinney, *Southern Mountain Republicans,* 150–60.

46. Fleming to Camden, December 17, 1893, box 36, Camden Papers.

47. Williams, *Captains of Industry,* 57–64.

48. S. C. Neale to Elkins, July 17, 1894, in box 4, Stephen B. Elkins Papers (hereafter Elkins Papers), WVRHC. See also Elkins to H. G. Davis, December 14 and December 19, 1893, and February 10 and February 21, 1894, box 4, Elkins Papers.

49. Henry G. Davis to H. G. Buxton, November 10, 1894, cited in Williams, *Captains of Industry,* 66.

50. Nominating address of Alex R. Campbell to House of Delegates, January 22, 1895, in box 4, Elkins Papers.

51. Camden seemed almost pleased that Elkins, an industrialist like himself, was about to take his place. In fact, Elkins and Camden shared a commitment to higher tariffs that separated Camden from people like Wilson in his own party. See Elkins to Camden, March 12, 1894, August 25, 1894, and December 12, 1894, box 37, Camden Papers.

52. Nathan B. Scott to John W. Mason, January 25, 1897; A. B. White to Mason, February 25, 1897; and Elkins to Mason, March 11, April 14, 1897, all in box 3, Mason Papers; Robert E. Murphy, *Progressive West Virginians: Some of the Men Who Have Built Up and Developed the State of West Virginia* (Wheeling, WV: Wheeling News, 1905), 1, 43.

53. Elkins to Mason, April 10, April 25, 1896, in box 3, Mason Papers. Nathan Scott feared that McKinley's eventual election would hurt Elkins and his wing of the party. See Scott to Elkins, December 5, 1896, box 4, Elkins Papers.

54. Bensel, *Political Economy,* 276–77; Carone, "Governor as Legislator," 110; Tyre political maps.

55. Simon, "Development of Underdevelopment," 287, 294; Williams, *Captains of Industry,* 59.

56. Simon, "Development of Underdevelopment," 302–6; Corbin, *Life, Work, and Rebellion,* 4–9; Joe William Trotter, *Coal, Class, and Color: Blacks in Southern West Virginia, 1915–32* (Urbana: University of Illinois Press, 1990), 16–23.

57. Workman, "Political Culture," 149–53.

58. Gibson Lamb Cranmer, *History of Wheeling City and Ohio County, West Virginia and Representative Citizens* (Chicago: Biographical Publishing Co., 1902), 317–23.

59. Workman, "Political Culture," chapter 4; Charles Henry Ambler, *West Virginia: The Mountain State* (New York: Prentice-Hall, 1940), 621.

60. *Commoner and Glassworker,* December 25, 1897, 16, and December 23, 1899, 3; Williams, *Captains of Industry,* 3; Murphy, *Progressive West Virginians,* 4; Cranmer, *History of Wheeling,* 327–28.

61. See, for example, N. B. Scott to A. B. White, November 7, 1902; S. B. Elkins to White, February 9, 1903, and February 19, 1903, all in box 33, A. B. White Papers, WVRHC (hereafter White Papers). See also W. J. Showalter to Elkins, October 16, 1906, box 8, Elkins Papers.

62. Barns, "Granger and Populist Movements," 312–15.

63. Williams, *Captains of Industry,* 203–6, thoroughly explains the operation of the archaic tax system inherited from "colonial Virginia."

64. Nicholas Clare Burckel, "Progressive Governors in the Border States: Reform Governors of Missouri, Kentucky, West Virginia and Maryland, 1900–1918" (PhD diss., University of Wisconsin, 1971), 292–97; David T. Javersak, "The Ohio Valley Trades and Labor Assembly: The Formative Years, 1882–1915" (PhD diss., West Virginia University, 1977), 105–10; Williams, *Captains of Industry,* 203–4.

65. *Final Report of the West Virginia Commission on Taxation and Municipal Incorporation, 1902* (reprint, Charleston, 1925), 519–23; Williams, *Captains of Industry,* 220–21; Elmer Guy Hendershot, "Tax Reforms in West Virginia during the Administration of Governor Albert Blakeslee White" (master's thesis, West Virginia University, 1949), 29–40.

66. M. V. Brown to A. B. White, September 18, 1903, box 35, White Papers; W. W. Stathers to Alston G. Dayton, March 13, 1904, box 80, Dayton Papers; Davis to White, September 2, 1901, box 13, Davis Papers.

67. Workman, "Political Culture," chapter 4; Cook, "Aretas Brooks Fleming." Fairmont Coal Company would soon become Consolidation Coal Company.

68. See especially W. A. Ohley to Fleming, July 29, 1897, box 30, A. B. Fleming Papers, WVRHC; and Workman, "Political Culture," 218–20.

69. Owen McKinney to Fleming, January 23, 1902, box 35, Fleming Papers. For more on Fairmont, see Ken Fones-Wolf, *Glass Towns: Industry, Labor, and Political Economy in Appalachia, 1890–1930s* (Urbana: University of Illinois Press, 2007), 155–57.

70. "The New Plan of Taxation as Proposed by the Tax Commission," undated [ca. January 1903] broadside, WVRHC. On Elkins and Dayton, see McKinney, *Southern Mountain Republicans,* 155–56.

71. McKinney, *Southern Mountain Republicans,* 156–58.

72. Elkins to White, October 30, 1903, box 35, White Papers. See also Wil-

liam N. Miller to White, October 9, 1903, Elkins to White, January 19, 1904, and Scott to White, January 22, January 27, February 29, 1904, all in box 35, White Papers.

73. *Parkersburg (WV) News,* January 30, 1903; *Grant County Press* (Petersburg, WV), January 30, 1903; *Grafton (WV) Sentinel,* January 30, 1903; *Parkersburg (WV) Daily News,* January 31, 1903.

74. Arnold C. Scherr to Alston G. Dayton, March 4, 1903, box 72, Dayton Papers.

75. Hugh L. Bond to Dayton, January 15, 1903, box 69, Dayton Papers.

76. Williams, *Captains of Industry,* 224; A. B. Fleming to C. W. Watson, March 27, 1904, box 36, Fleming Papers.

77. Burckel, "Progressive Governors," 302; Williams, *Captains of Industry,* 232.

78. Davis to William D. Hubbard, January 30, 1904, box 15, Davis Papers.

79. Fleming to Chandler and Bros., May 20, 1909, as cited in Williams, *Captains of Industry,* 249–50.

80. Robin Einhorn elaborates on the importance of these points in *American Taxation,* 201–5.

81. *The Tax Problem in West Virginia* (New York: National Industrial Conference Board, 1925), 22.

82. Davis to John T. Morgan, August 12, 1904, box 15, Davis Papers; also cited in Williams, *Captains of Industry,* 227.

83. A. B. White, "First Biennial Message to the Legislature," in *Public Addresses of Albert Blakeslee White, A.M., Governor of West Virginia, during His Term of Office* (Charleston, WV, 1905), 117.

84. George W. Atkinson, "The New Old Dominion," in *Public Addresses, Etc. of Geo. W. Atkinson, LL.D., D.C.L., Governor of West Virginia, during His Term of Office* (Charleston, WV, 1901), 25. Simon, "Development of Underdevelopment," chapter 11, goes into great detail on the problems that overinvestment in coal created for the development of the state's economy.

85. Fones-Wolf, *Glass Towns,* 188–90.

86. Michael Storper and Richard Walker, *The Capitalist Imperative: Territory, Technology, and Industrial Growth* (New York: Blackwell, 1989), 123. See also Doreen Massey, *Spatial Divisions of Labor: Social Structures and the Geography of Production,* 2nd ed. (New York: Routledge, 1995).

Chapter 10

"Grudges and Loyalties Die So Slowly"

Contested Memories of the Civil War in Pennsylvania's Appalachia

Robert M. Sandow

On a late October night, as the Civil War dragged on into its third year, Deputy Marshal Cyrus Butler descended on a mountain cabin to apprehend an Appalachian farmer resisting the draft. The mountaineer, Joseph Lansberry, mortally shot the government official before escaping arrest with the help of his community. Such stories are common in the myths and history of Southern Appalachia; but this incident occurred in Northern Appalachia. While there is robust scholarship on the Southern Appalachians, a fact underscored by the essays in this collection, the Northern stretches of this mountain chain are both significant and significantly underexamined. The Northern Appalachian experience was not a mirror of wartime life in mountain communities below the Mason-Dixon line.[1] Nonetheless, like counterparts in the Confederacy, rural Northerners in the mountains of Pennsylvania experienced the war from the vantage points of their homes and communities. Traditions of localism in these "island communities," a memorable description by historian Robert Wiebe, shaped a myriad of complicated responses to the strains of fratricidal war.[2] Wartime actions led to contested memories and legacies of the conflict among the bitterly—sometimes violently—divided communities of the Pennsylvania mountains, linking attitudes and developments from the antebellum age to the fractious period of Reconstruction.

These developments occurred against a backdrop of far-reaching economic and political change that undermined the livelihoods and perceived rights of mountain communities in Pennsylvania. Republican political dominance from the late 1850s throughout Reconstruction opened the doors for expansion of industrial capitalism. Scholars continue to debate the war's impact on the larger economic structure of the nation.[3] Nevertheless, the war marked a transition toward the ascendency and government support of large-scale managerial capitalism and legal changes that favored entrepreneurial development.[4] This shift was coupled with the social impact of migrating capital and labor, particularly the influx of new immigrants in search of work. In the Pennsylvania Appalachians, these social and economic forces contributed to the rapid exploitation of the state's natural resources of timber, oil, and coal, with devastating and irreparable ecological consequences. For mountain communities, the loss of these resources signaled the erosion of economic means to maintain stability and permanence. This pattern had already begun before the Civil War, and it continued during and after the conflict, presaging the process that would affect the southern Appalachians in the postwar decades.[5]

The struggling classes of rural people did not sit idly by; they resisted these overwhelming changes controlled by outside forces. Responding from a sense of desperation, many turned to traditional communal-based grassroots resistance against outside threat.[6] Such protest had formulaic rituals reaching back to colonial antecedents. In order to legitimize resistance, communities formed collective organizations to measure broad-based democratic consensus. The prominent place of women in crowd actions attests to the informal sanction such protest carried. Public meetings helped clarify grievances, and leaders articulated principles of rights and justice in a language of republicanism stressing key themes: the rights of small farmers and producers against large-scale capitalists; the superiority of local claims to land over the speculations of outsiders; and the right to just wages for laborers.[7] Acts of resistance moved along a spectrum from economic and political protest to intimidation and bloodshed. Levels of violence can be seen as a barometer of community despair.

Ultimately, communal-based resistance failed to avert the turn toward industrial capitalism. Political and legal forces ran against mountain folk. The outbreak of civil war allowed the infant Republican Party to expand the reach of federal government in the name of national security. They were aided in the passage of developmentalist economic acts by the absence of

Southern obstructionists.[8] They were also generally successful in waging a rhetorical battle against political opponents at home, utilizing a language of wartime loyalty and patriotism that stymied any coherent challenge.[9] In the Reconstruction period, Republicans maintained their political domination through "bloody shirt" tactics nourished by wartime constructs of loyalty. This control allowed them to promote the expansion of industrial capitalism and its exploitation of mountain resources and to curb resistance as a form of disloyalty.[10] Proponents of change employed their own rhetoric to undermine the rights of land-owning small farmers. They denounced resistance to federal authority as ignorant, backward, selfish, and detrimental to the growth of the nation. In consequence, Pennsylvania Appalachians were systematically impoverished, and many inhabitants abandoned the area in search of economic opportunity.[11]

Though less majestic than the southern mountains, the substantial northern Appalachians arrested westward expansion in the colonial period. In Pennsylvania, the ancient continental collisions had thrust up a glaciated spine of ridges embracing long and fertile agricultural valleys. At the western boundary of the ridge and valley region, the Allegheny Front marked the rising mass of the fractured Appalachian Plateau forming the western and northern parts of the state.[12] Mountains and twisting, narrow river valleys characterized the plateau, as did seemingly inexhaustible stretches of old-growth white pine and hemlock forests. Clearfield County, one of the high north-central counties that contemporaries termed the lumber region, straddled the Eastern Continental Divide and was ideally located to send its timber wealth into the great watersheds of the Allegheny River and the West Branch of the Susquehanna.[13]

A challenging landscape and distance from existing settlements delayed migration into the Appalachians for decades. Opened to migrants in the 1780s, the northern lumber region gathered inhabitants slowly throughout the antebellum period. By the outbreak of the Civil War, it was the least populous portion of the state. Though representing one quarter of Pennsylvania's land area, it held a mere 6 percent of the population. Early homesteads and trade were tied to the region's networks of rivers and streams. Farms on the river flatlands were most productive. Later migrants pushed into the upland areas marked by poor, thin soils. The lumber region remained a frontier area of small farms, mixing livestock, hay, cereal crops, and varied farm products in a predominantly local economy.

Compared to farms in rich agricultural areas, those in Appalachia were smaller and less productive, and they contained a lower percentage of cleared land. The farms in Appalachian Pennsylvania fell behind statewide averages in capitalization and mechanization.[14] Climate, soils, and moisture levels contributed to this outcome, as did the relative poverty of many migrants to the region. Elevated rates of farm failure and outmigration attest to the marginal nature of many area farms. In winter, a majority of farmers and laborers supplemented their meager agricultural output by cutting timber and hauling it to the riverbanks. On spring freshets, the men piloted timber to downriver markets in the form of giant rafts. Rafting farmers looked to long-term sustainability by selectively culling forest resources.

Community ties carried great significance in the mountains and formed the basis of economic, social, and political networks. The modest agricultural settlements gave rise to few towns, none large. The whole region was only tenuously connected to the outside world before the end of the Civil War. Railroads skirted the periphery of the highlands until the final year of the Civil War brought the first trunk line.[15] Their isolation should not be overstated, however. Telegraph and newspaper communications, remarkable geographic mobility, and the economic connections to outside markets mitigated feelings of disconnectedness. Outside observers were nonetheless quick to point out the vast wild places and hardscrabble existence of most of the area's inhabitants.[16]

The war occurred in a context of industrial development and aggressive exploitation of mountain resources that stirred local resentment. Pennsylvania was the nation's leading producer of wood in the 1860s. The lumber region marked the epicenter of a shifting logging frontier that began in New England decades earlier and moved steadily westward toward the Great Lakes.[17] The rise in production marked a transition from agricultural to industrial lumbering that expanded in Pennsylvania in the 1850s. Industrial lumbering was characterized by its large scale, capital-intensive operations, technological innovation, and aggressive harvesting and processing methods.[18] Lumber companies hired armies of lumberjacks to fell trees into short sections. With spring thaws, workers unleashed log drives into the rivers that would be swept into great corrals dubbed "booms" on the river below. Boom operators sorted the timber and forwarded the logs to giant steam sawmills for processing.[19] Labor-intensive rafting could not compete with such productivity; nor could it share the rushing streams with the floating logs. Rafting declined, a victim of industrial evolution toward efficiency and nationalization.[20]

The looming threat of log drives, perpetrated by outside developers, led to an episode of resistance known locally as the Raftsmen's Rebellion of 1857. It modeled rituals of protest that would be repeated in the face of similar outside challenges during the Civil War and beyond. Rafters held public meetings in Clearfield in March 1856, printing grievances and warnings in local papers. "The floating of loose saw logs . . . and running rafts in the usual way, cannot be carried on at the same time," argued a summary of one lumbermen's meeting, and "one or the other must cease, and it becomes a question only, of whether the free and uninterrupted navigation of these valuable highways shall continue open for the enjoyment of the mass of the people, or be monopolized by a few." The lumbermen warned that "if the Legislature, to whom we have a right to appeal, turn a deaf ear to us, we must take other means to redress our wrongs."[21]

Methods of industrial logging challenged customary uses of waterways and pitted the rights of many against "monopolies" of power. These values of a "moral economy" justified localistic community resistance in defense of traditional economic and political rights.[22] Protestors understood clearly the long-term implications of the struggle. A leader of the "rebellion" described the peril thusly: "They are not woodsmen, but men backed by speculators who would sacrifice everything for the chance to make quick money. If we let them have their way they'll fill the streams with log jams, and then when there's nothing more for them to cut and float they'll go, leaving us with our business and occupation gone and our property rendered valueless."[23]

Clearfield rafters unleashed their simmering tensions against loggers in a violent but futile outburst in May 1857. Nearly fifty men took up axes and guns to confront a team of lumberjacks along Clearfield Creek. When the loggers ignored orders to clear out, the raftsmen fired warning shots and chased off the men. While the confrontation was a clear statement of local anger, state authorities continued to support the right of industrial lumbering with its log drives and booms. The act of intimidation failed to arrest the work of log-driving throughout the county. Ten of the raftsmen were convicted on charges of riot but given light fines. The court's protection of log driving signaled the shift toward industrial lumbering. By the 1870s, rafting was economically marginalized, and the effects of deforestation evident. One editor put it plainly: "That the business has seen its best days is no longer to be questioned, and this is for the best of reasons—the want of timber. The vast forests of Clearfield County are getting pretty well cleared out, not by rafting but by 'logging.' . . . Had the system of logging never been adopted, Clearfield could to-day be one of the richest counties in the state. . . . If logging had never been introduced here, Clearfield would have pine trees enough to-day to pay off the state debt and plenty of them left."[24]

Economic and political tensions remained close to the surface during the war years. Many who supported the war urged their fellows to set aside political differences and economic selfishness for the cause of the union. Despite the appeal to patriotism and loyalty, a great many Northerners came to oppose the war and the military policies of the Lincoln administration. For a variety of reasons, the Pennsylvania Appalachians proved one of the most vexatious regions of dissent for federal authorities during the war. While the two-party system fueled a generalized wartime protest, rural Pennsylvanians responded to a number of motivations. As in Southern mountain communities, this could include ambivalence about the war, disgust with national military policies such as conscription and emancipation, economic self-preservation, concerns about inflation, patterns of statewide political opposition, and persistent strains of localism in civic affairs.[25]

Republicans argued foremost that resistance was the fruit of Democratic teachings. The southern reaches of the lumber region were staunchly Democratic counties, and Clearfield routinely returned a Democratic majority. As a region of struggling farmers, many poorer folk were drawn to the party of Jefferson and Jackson, with its emphasis on limited government and states' rights. Over the course of the war, a pronounced antiwar movement expanded across the North, its adherents denounced as "Copperheads." Republicans deemed them a "fire in the rear" that materially undermined the war effort. They called war opponents Southern sympathizers and said that Democrats formed widespread secret societies that were determined to forcibly resist the federal government. Some recent scholarship continues to champion Republican mythology, largely ignoring factual reality or the social, economic, and political context of resistance.[26] In this analysis, it could be argued that these rural Pennsylvanians were part of a top-down struggle between political parties. The Democratic Party was a national institution, with national leaders and platforms, and widespread values. Its partisan newspapers conveyed party messages using common language and arguments. To focus on this structure, however, misses the grassroots origins of resistance and violence. Decisions to resist came in face-to-face meetings with neighbors in schoolhouses, homes, barns, stores, and saloons.

Outside observers also linked resistance to hypermasculine cultures of hunting, work, and leisure. Census records indicate the population imbalance of young men who labored as farmers, hunters, lumbermen, and later coal miners. Mountain men were stereotyped as rough characters with insatiable appetites for drinking and fighting. Richard I. Dodge, the provost marshal of Western Pennsylvania, revealed his preconceived notions in a report to his superior in Washington. According to Dodge, "West of the western range of mountains and extending nearly to Lake Erie is a vast wilderness (nearly one-sixth of the State), covered with virgin forests of hemlock and pine." Employing language almost identical to that used to describe Southern Appalachians, he explained that the region's "inhabitants, living almost entirely from the proceeds of their labor as lumbermen, are ignorant and easily imposed upon by designing politicians, but are hardy, vigorous, and make good soldiers."[27]

Marshal Dodge was not alone in depicting mountain folk as tough, armed, and ignorant political tools. A colleague of Republican governor Andrew G. Curtin warned the governor that "the greatest drawback to the draft to recruit the army is the lumber regions east west north and south," for "every loose fellow who is or expects to be drafted runs off to the lumber shanties into the mountains and remote districts where he finds employment and high wages. In this way the vagrants hide and lay concealed from the officers who find it impossible to catch or discover their dens."[28] Many area men who joined the army played up their "wildcat" nature. The most famous example was the Pennsylvania Bucktails, a number of whom rode rafts to the seat of war and sported bucktails on their hats as signs of their prowess as crack shots. Those who opposed the war were assumed to be hard cases who were armed and organized to resist federal authority.

While there were many acts of individual resistance, protest had widespread communal roots and sanction. The enactment of emancipation and conscription in 1863 brought issues of resistance to the fore. Attempts to enroll local men for the draft could be met with lying, threats, intimidation, and violence. Enrolling officers were attacked, shot at, and sometimes killed. One officer who was shot from his horse wrote, "Houses were shut against me and even some who gave their ages declared they would resist the draft."[29] The district provost marshal added, "other enrolling officers in that county have been driven off with stones and threats of murder and arson."[30] Women and men colluded to harass officers, conceal identities, or supply food or other necessities to men hiding in "tall timber." When drafting began, the government found few men willing to deliver draft notices, and high proportions of drafted men failed to report. Classified as deserters, these draft evaders were hunted by deputies who left pitiable accounts of their failures and mishaps. Deputies wrote of the difficulty of finding informants in tight-lipped communities. The vast, undeveloped terrain made it easy for prey to elude capture. Men accustomed to guns sometimes fought back or freed prisoners from the custody of marshals. The toughest cases lived and worked together, defying officers to challenge them.

Federal officials cited high levels of draft evasion and widespread armed resistance to justify a military expedition into Clearfield. In the draft of October 1864, 400 men refused to report out of 660 drafted. At the end of October, a deputy marshal named Cyrus Butler was mortally wounded near the town of Clearfield while arresting a draft evader named Joseph Lansberry. Authorities were unable to catch Lansberry, and he remained at large into the 1870s. To quell dissent, the Provost Marshal General's Bureau sent the undersized Sixteenth Veteran Reserve Corps regiment into Clearfield. For months, the soldiers used patrols and nighttime raids to arrest deserters and reestablish military authority.[31]

Many of the social and economic conditions animating wartime protests persisted through the Reconstruction period, giving rise to further episodes of communal-based resistance. In addition to the expansion of industrial capitalism, Appalachian folk faced the social impact of migrating capital and labor, including the influx of European immigrants, as well as the further ecological devastation and economic exploitation of natural resources that undermined their ability to maintain viable agricultural communities. These underlying conditions stemmed from continuity of Republican political power and the effectiveness of their political rhetoric beyond the war years.

Republicans maintained political dominance both nationally and within the state through a politics of loyalty.[32] Democrats fared poorly in postwar political campaigns until the 1880s in the face of Republican "bloody shirt" rhetoric. Republicans won elections by reminding voters that they were the party that had remained loyal to the government during the war. Regardless of the numbers of war Democrats, Republicans encouraged veterans to "vote as they shot." Such control gave Republicans the ability to legislatively promote the continued exploitation of resources.

During Reconstruction, aggressive logging hurried along deforestation of the state's northern mountains. Already under assault from the 1850s, rafting farmers saw extreme marginalization in the postwar period. The

1870s and 1880s were years of peak production along the West Branch.[33] As white pine became depleted, investors turned to hemlock, which fed a large tanning industry in the western part of the state. New means of extraction quickened the pace of exploitation. Earlier logging depended on use of the river to transport timber from the woods to processing centers. The late 1870s and early 1880s saw the expansion of railroad lumbering, in which a network of small-gauge rail lines stripped larger acreages of woods with ruthless efficiency. By the first decade of the twentieth century, most of the lumber railroads had been abandoned, and the large operators had relocated to other timbered areas in West Virginia and the Great Lakes region. Many of the lumber operations that moved into West Virginia in the late nineteenth century migrated out of Pennsylvania with the logging frontier.[34]

The widespread deforestation there typified the short-term profit-mindedness of outside speculators and developers. Logging caused considerable ecological damage, denuding hillsides and contributing to erosion and loss of soil nutrients. Lumbering exemplified the unrestrained exploitation of natural resources that beset the Appalachians and its early inhabitants. As timber resources gave out, area leaders ironically hoped that careful stewardship of area coal resources would maintain longer-term economic viability. On visiting a distant West Branch community, the editor of the *Clearfield Republican* remarked, "Everything looks thriving and prosperous, except the lumber business. We have often passed up the river 'after rafting,' but never saw things so ragged. . . . The depression of the lumber trade is a success. It can get no worse. . . . However, our people need not depend wholly on this trade. The prosperity in the coal business will assist a large portion of our citizens to raise enough to pay their taxes."[35]

Undergirding the vast Appalachian plateau was a tremendous reservoir of bituminous soft coal termed the Pittsburgh or Allegheny basin. During the Civil War, operators had only begun to tap the abundant seams of coal. The war marked a shift toward capital-intensive coal operations in the northern mountain counties. As much of the timber was stripped by the lumber corporations, entrepreneurs turned to the exploitation of coal. The economic significance of the mountains was extended as Pennsylvania coal fueled the industrial age.[36]

The economics of the coal business was shaped by regional market prices for coal and the competition between railroad corporations for market dominance. Most area coal was sent to eastern markets in Philadelphia and New York by the competing lines of the Pennsylvania Railroad and the Philadelphia and Erie Company. Like many industries, coal operators and their profits became shaped by the transportation rates set by railroad corporations. The Pennsylvania Railroad had been the primary force in the state since its completion in the 1850s, and it had become one of the world's largest corporations in the postwar period.[37] The company ran branch lines into the coal basins of Clearfield, particularly those lying at the southern edge of Clearfield County.[38] To put regional coal production into statistical perspective, Pennsylvania produced two-thirds of the nation's coal in the first half of the 1870s.[39]

Though their work fueled America's industrial revolution, miners struggled against extreme poverty. In the Clearfield mines, most workers lived in company houses, were indebted to company stores, and were expected to pay for their own blasting powder, lamp oil, and tools at elevated company prices. When attitudes hardened toward a strike, miners warned their employers that "they cannot live without subjecting themselves and their families to trouble and hardship."[40] Miners turned to unionism out of a sense of powerlessness and in the hope that collective action would improve their circumstances.[41] It was true that national unionizing efforts in a broad spectrum of trades were top-down attempts at education and organization. This ideal of national solidarity may have been truer of turn-of-the-century unionism in Pennsylvania, but it did not represent the reality of Reconstruction-era labor protest. Local organizations and considerations guided the goals and methods of postwar protest. Even when representatives of nascent national organizations were present, they could do little more than witness or appeal to local audiences.

Clearfield coal miners adopted grassroots union organization in the late 1860s in response to falling wages and a drop in bituminous coal prices. Unsuccessful localized strikes for higher wages occurred in 1869 and again during the winter of 1872 and 1873. Miners argued that wages were artificially depressed by the collusion of mine operators and railroad corporations that manipulated freight costs for maximum profit. Through the 1870s, both the Pennsylvania Railroad and the Philadelphia and Erie lines engaged in regional competition by rapidly extending branch lines through the coal fields. Railroad executives defined the right to set pay as a prerogative of management and attacked unionism as "criminal conspiracy."[42] Mineworkers championed their rights as producers and saw collective action as the traditional method to exert those rights and redress grievances.

Any hope for favorable adjustment of wages in Clearfield was curtailed by the onset of the Panic of 1873. Railroad executives ironically blamed unionism for the economic downturn, rather than their own disastrous speculative excess. In any regard, workers were forced to accept wage cuts in the lean years that followed. By 1875 bituminous sales had begun to revive, but area operators claimed to be unable to raise miners' wages. They positioned themselves as victims of sliding-scale charges by the Pennsylvania Railroad. Miners felt betrayed for the sacrifices they had made. One article on the "Miner's Conflict" reported, "Worse even than the loss of time and money is the bad feeling which has been engendered betwixt employer and employed. The men are irritated and sullen; they think they have been imposed upon. . . . There is in the attitude of the operators a stubbornness which does no credit to their intelligence."[43]

Angry Clearfield mineworkers advanced through stages of ritual protest toward collective action. They had met with mine operators to press their case for better wages and conditions, only to be rebuffed with refusals. They organized themselves together for solidarity, fruitlessly enlisting the aid of Miners' National Association (MNA) organizer Xingo Parks. The MNA was a recent presence in Clearfield mines, and it was unclear how the national organization could help Clearfield miners achieve local goals. Only a third of area miners were members, and while the national union called vigorously for organization, it seldom supported local strikes financially or as a matter of course. Clearfield miners thus fell back on forms of communal-based resistance.

The miners' greatest challenges in 1875 were to create both an organization and a strategy; the latter proved their undoing. Strikers achieved reasonable success in joining area miners into collective action. Initial meetings at the mines along Moshannon Creek were repeated throughout the collieries of the region in the first week of April. In a mass meeting, members of the different branch mines outlined their grievances and took responsibility for calling a general strike that began around April 12. The strike garnered national attention and lasted more than a month before collapsing in defeat. The miners' strategy failed because they could not contain violence as negotiations broke down. With standing orders for coal, mine operators naturally turned to outside laborers, among whom Italians figured prominently. Strikers actively monitored trains into the region, watching for "blackleg" strikebreakers. They threatened, intimidated, and persuaded many to go back, but always with an inherent logic to their method. Their modus operandi required that they explain their case to strikebreakers, effect a vote among them whether to continue, and force a promise not to return in exchange for paid fare home. The largest such effort involved 700 to 800 miners who confronted 190 strikebreakers, 60 of whom were Italians. They were sent back down the line at strikers' expense on a special train. Strikers also sent threatening letters to area men who continued to work in the few sites not shut down.

The strike devolved into violence on a number of occasions, especially when strikers were barred by operators from speaking with replacement workers. The turning point came at Fisher's Mine when union representatives could not communicate in Italian with the strikebreakers to negotiate their departure. An angry, impatient crowd of roughly four hundred men and women marched on the strikebreakers' boardinghouse and threw their baggage out of the window before escorting the Italians unceremoniously out of town. The Italian "blacklegs" roused their ire because they could not be reasoned with and because they so obviously represented the threat of outsiders taking their jobs.[44] With the outbreak of violence, operators pressed formal charges against strikers and called on the state to uphold their rights to free-market employment. The county sheriff reluctantly took the side of operators, arresting prominent union men, preventing strikers' access to "blacklegs," and escorting replacement workers to the mines. Without legal remedy, strikers voted to return to work, but not without two hundred being blacklisted. A month after the strike had ceased, fifty-seven men were put on trial for riot, unlawful assembly, and conspiracy; they were found guilty and punished with high fines and prison sentences. The decision against the coal miners made this a landmark case undermining the right to unionize and strike nationwide.[45] The verdict held prominent strikers liable for the violence that broke out, whether they had counseled restraint or not. The lasting effect of the trial was to discourage workers from supporting national unionism, as a minority drifted into the more secretive Knights of Labor. What unionism remained emphasized political activism as the means to achieve economic goals.

In significant ways, the 1875 strike reflected the continuation of patterns stretching into the antebellum period. Key themes included the demonization of mountain folk as violent, ignorant, and impressionable; widespread community support for protest, including the participation of women; adherence to rituals of dissent as a means of justification and legitimacy; and an emphasis on the struggle against outside forces coupled with a sobering fear of federal intervention. Predictably, mine operators, railroad executives, and unsympathetic journalists vilified rural miners as violent and ignorant.[46] The *New York Times* reported, "It is very true that miners, as a rule, are not a class of men who kindly take to argument. Their peculiar vocation is not favorable to law-abiding and law-fearing habits. Miners, the world over, are a rough set, but they are human and susceptible to generous influences."[47] Miners were also depicted as susceptible to influence, and union leaders were blamed as "turbulent spirits" goading many to strike in the first place.[48] These harsh assessments echoed those of previous outsiders. In 1864, the provost marshal of western Pennsylvania had written uncharitably of the mountain region: "Underneath almost the whole division lie immense beds of coal, the working of which gives employment to the very worst class of beings, both native and foreign, to be found in this country."[49]

As had been the case with wartime opposition to the draft, the miners' strike had widespread communal support. Though national union organizers sought to control labor negotiations, they failed to avert the strike or to contain violence. Community leaders orchestrated a collective response, including the strike, which involved hundreds of area miners who often gathered together in a massive crowd to protest. Women were prominent members of the crowd, even when events turned to violence and intimidation.[50] Community members also relied on each other for the economic support of striking families. One report describes how "thousands of men are idle; their families are in want, and are subsisting upon charitable contributions from the surrounding country."[51] Local petition drives in the aftermath of the trials helped to secure release for most of the Clearfield prisoners by December.

While the violence of the strike was unscripted, the broader outlines of the dispute adhered to civic rituals of dissent. Mine operators described crowd protest menacingly, but news reports suggest otherwise. Protest efforts were coordinated through meetings where decisions were made by voting. Miners articulated grievances in a language of republicanism, defending their economic rights as producers and residents of the mining districts. The *New York Times* explained how the geography of the Appalachians shaped the economic dynamics of the area: "The mining region is a mountainous one, where the only products are coal and lumber. Agriculture, excepting in a very limited way, is unknown, so that the strikers, unless they move away, cannot obtain employment sufficient to support them. For this reason principally it is feared they will offer a desperate resistance to the new-comers."[52] When warned of attempts to bring in strikebreakers, crowds assembled at rendezvous points and marched to meet the incoming trains. At two o'clock in the morning of May 17, two hundred miners marched from Houtzdale to the train line at Osceola "carrying flags and singing."[53] The strikers staged military pageantry as a show of solidarity. A large procession of men marched to a mass meeting on May 14 led by fifes and drums.[54] Even when confronting "blacklegs," delegations of strikers negotiated with the men, explaining their situation and asking them to vote and to pledge not to return. Only when the rituals of protest broke down did the crowds of strikers become violent.

The creation of secret organizations also paralleled wartime opposition. While the union meetings of the 1875 strike did not reflect a strong emphasis on secrecy, others both before and after did stress clandestine organization. When Clearfield coal miners first embraced unionism in the fall of 1868, they put together a group called the "Sons of Liberty." The miners created a constitution and bylaws as well as unnamed secret ceremonies.[55] They were responsible for the failed strike of 1869 that ended with the arrest of thirteen men on charges of "criminal conspiracy." After the failure of 1875, the shadowy Knights of Labor took the place of the MNA for those few miners who held faith in organized labor. The Knights had no connections to the Sons of Liberty but relied likewise on secrecy.[56] During the Civil War, men from Clearfield who opposed the draft created a mutual protection society that they named the "Democratic Castle." They also created a constitution, bylaws, and secret grips and passwords for meetings. Club members pledged to assist each other in the case of seizure by marshals. The advent of the Democratic Castle was traced to an incident in which more than a dozen men freed two prisoners from the custody of marshals in 1864.[57]

Most important of all, postwar labor protest in the region stressed the battle of local people against outside forces. Whether the threat came from distant railroad corporations or in the person of imported strikebreakers, area workers asserted their rights to their jobs and to living wages. Unfortunately, as in numerous cases before, people in mountain communities lost the fight against the power of the state and its support of industrial capitalism. In the midst of the strike, operators urged Republican governor John Hartranft to provide military or police assistance. He obliged by forwarding to the sheriff sixty stands of arms and two thousand rounds of ammunition.[58] He also commissioned police captain T. E. Clark to command a special detachment of Coal and Iron Police in the region. Captain Clark's hard stance against the miners did much to poison relations between miners and operators. The *Clearfield Republican* condemned the hastiness with which outsiders called for military enforcement: "The policy of force which has been resorted to for the last fifteen years to govern this country, seems to be taking root all over the land. It makes no difference what the crimes committed are, military and brute force seems to be uppermost in the minds of our rulers and a proportion of the people."[59] In the end, the sheriff wisely avoided confrontation, serving warrants and escorting strikebreakers alone.

For Clearfield residents, the possibility of a military presence in their communities brought back bitter memories of the war and the federal campaign to enforce the hated draft laws. Those experiences were coincidentally brought to the fore in an unrelated trial. Shortly after the 1875 strike trials, a verdict from a Pittsburgh judge brought partial vindication for a wartime act of protest. Joseph Lansberry, the Clearfield man who defied the draft laws and mortally wounded provost marshal Cyrus Butler, had been caught and brought to trial for murder. The highly publicized U.S. Circuit Court proceeding reawakened the public debate over wartime loyalty. While only a single life was in jeopardy, the outcome reflected on the mountain communities that had resisted wartime laws. An acquittal could release them from a sense of collective guilt levied on them by federal authorities during the war. The *New York Times* reporter put it plainly: "It is said that his trial will develop some important facts, and convict many persons in that section of the country with treasonable practices during the war."[60]

Lansberry's lawyers predictably argued that the conscription laws were flawed and that their client had acted in self-defense. Lansberry did not testify, but he had not denied that he shot Butler. He claimed to have not received a draft notice, and his lawyers concluded that he "was not a deserter, or non-reporting drafted man within the meaning of said act, and was not therefore liable to arrest as such."[61] Moreover, they described how Colonel Butler and his assistant came in civilian clothes and had not identified themselves clearly. The shooting occurred in a dark stairway, where only the deceased and the accused were witnesses. The attorneys lay blame on Butler for firing first, compelling Lansberry "to fire upon them to save his own life."[62]

The judge's instructions to the jury guaranteed Lansberry's acquittal.

"The jury must be convinced beyond a reasonable doubt that the defendant knew the officers, who were dressed in citizens' clothes, who visited his house in the night time, and who made every effort to surprise and capture him, were officers acting under the law."[63] He added "that an officer could not take a man unless it could be shown that the man had knowledge that he was a deserter. Without notice he was not bound to submit and surely had the right to defend his liberty."[64] After thirty minutes, the jury set Lansberry free, giving the man's friends and family cause for celebration.

The verdict in the Lansberry trial did not indicate the restoration of localism in the face of expanding federal authority. At best, it could be viewed as the lingering disdain of area juries for despised wartime draft laws. It did not vindicate the use of personal violence against federal power. In that regard, the loss of the miners' strike in 1875 was more indicative of larger patterns in which collective economic action was vilified as "conspiracy." Given no legal sanction, miners' unionism was pushed into a phase of secret local organization embodied in the Knights of Labor. This too paralleled wartime organizations that acted outside the law.

Community-based resistance may have been discredited, but the indelible traces of wartime disharmony echoed down through the generations. Those who lived through the war recalled privately how their community had been fractured by the experience. The threat of military occupation during the miners' strike of 1875 brought back visceral fears. The recollections of protest lingered on as local lore. Undistinguished novelist Herbert E. Stover used regional history as the foundation for his writings on such topics as the Bucktails and the Copperheads. His 1952 novel *Copperhead Moon* spun a fictional tale that reinforced the wildest Republican charges of conspiracy. In the brief foreword, Stover wrote: "Both grudges and loyalties die so slowly in the quiet of the wooded hill country that it is entirely possible that some of the issues touched in this book may still be controversial even to third or fourth generation people who remember old stories."[65] He knew wild places where deserters had hid from provost marshals or stood lonely sentinel for their arrival. He had been shown the locations of gunfights with federal officers and the home of a woman who baked bread for fugitives.

In recent years, the communities of Clearfield have even commemorated their wartime suffering. In December 2004 a reenactment was held on the site of "Bloody Knox," an 1864 clash between soldiers and civilians that claimed the lives of two people. When the U.S. military arrived in late 1864 to quell antidraft dissent, its first successful raid was against the "notorious" Tom Adams and his "gang." Adams represented the stereotype of the Appalachian "everyman." He was an impecunious tenant farmer who took to hard labor in the fields and woods to support his family. He had a reputation as a rough character who cavorted with like-minded men. He had joined the army only to desert the service at the first opportunity, most likely to obtain the bounty money. In the fall of 1864, he played host to a troublesome group that included fellow deserters and disaffected men. Adams and his band were having a party when the first contingents of soldiers reached the area. Angry loyalist neighbors led the soldiers to Adams's house. The army made an example of Adams by surrounding the property and breaking in upon the revelers, arresting more than a dozen men. Adams would not be taken without a fight, however, and he managed to shoot a soldier mortally before being riddled with musket balls as he fled from his house. Reenacting the event was a highlight of the county's bicentennial celebration, and the restored site today bears a roadside plaque summarizing the details. In many ways, the reenactment and the historical marker shrouded the meaning of local Civil War resistance in ambiguity. Visitors to the Clearfield County Historical Society can follow the "Civil War Shootout" brochure to "the historic site of Bloody Conflict." They read definitively that "War resistance in [the] county culminated here," but they are only told what happened, not why. What Clearfield people actually think about this curious wartime history is unknown, but it is certain that they have not forgotten.

Notes

1. Scholarship on Southern mountain communities during the war is a significant genre and reflects the diversity of experiences within the Confederacy. There are a number of works that stress this diversity and explore its connections to wartime issues on a regional or community scale. Model examples of this research include Jonathan Dean Sarris, *A Separate Civil War: Communities in Conflict in the Mountain South* (Charlottesville: University of Virginia Press, 2006); Brian D. McKnight, *Contested Borderland: The Civil War in Appalachian Kentucky and Virginia* (Lexington: University Press of Kentucky, 2006); Robert Tracy McKenzie, *Lincolnites and Rebels: A Divided Town in the American Civil War* (New York: Oxford University Press, 2006); John C. Inscoe and Gordon B. McKinney, *The Heart of Confederate Appalachia: Western North Carolina in the Civil War* (Chapel Hill: University of North Carolina Press, 2000); the essays in Kenneth W. Noe and Shannon H. Wilson, eds., *The Civil War in Appalachia: Col-*

lected Essays (Knoxville: University of Tennessee Press, 1997); and the community study by Martin Crawford, *Ashe County's Civil War: Community and Society in the Appalachian South* (Charlottesville: University Press of Virginia, 2001). This essay acknowledges and draws several themes from this fruitful scholarship, particularly ideas of localism and loyalty, the escalation of violence, the myth of Appalachian savagery, and the economic development of Appalachia.

2. Robert Wiebe, *The Search for Order, 1877–1920* (New York: Hill and Wang, 1967). Wiebe's viewpoint can be seen as a modernization thesis in which traditional personal and communal-based social values and orientations were supplanted by the values of a frequently impersonal, national, and urban-dominated society. Migration and industrialization contributed to this process.

3. A good starting point to examine this debate is Phillip Shaw Paludan, "What Did the Winners Win? The Social and Economic History of the North during the Civil War," in *Writing the Civil War: The Quest to Understand,* ed. James M. McPherson and William J. Cooper, 174–200 (Columbia: University of South Carolina Press, 1998). Paludan traces the historiography of economic analysis of the war. Charles A. Beard and Mary R. Beard fashioned a dominant interpretation stressing the ascendency of industrial capitalism in *The Rise of American Civilization* (New York: Macmillan, 1927). That view was given more weight by Louis M. Hacker's *The Triumph of American Capitalism* (New York: Simon & Schuster, 1940). Consult Paludan for ways in which the Beard-Hacker thesis has been challenged or refined over time. For an important study that traces the dominance of industrialists after the war, read Richard Franklin Bensel, *Yankee Leviathan: The Origins of Central State Authority in America, 1859–1877* (New York: Cambridge University Press, 1990). Bensel's work amplifies that of the Beard-Hacker thesis by stressing the importance of rising finance capitalists and their work as agents of economic development. The developmental role of the Republican Party receives greater treatment in Bensel's more recent *The Political Economy of American Industrialization, 1877–1900* (New York: Cambridge University Press, 2000).

4. The view that mid-nineteenth-century legal interpretations favored corporate development derives predominantly from Morton J. Horwitz, *The Transformation of American Law, 1780–1860* (Cambridge, MA: Harvard University Press, 1977).

5. Indispensible works on the economic development of the southern Appalachians include: Ronald D Eller, *Miners, Millhands, and Mountaineers: Industrialization of the Appalachian South, 1880–1930* (Knoxville: University of Tennessee Press, 1982), and Ronald L. Lewis, *Transforming the Appalachian Countryside: Railroads, Deforestation, and Social Change in West Virginia, 1880–1920* (Chapel Hill: University of North Carolina Press, 1998).

6. Altina L. Waller argued similarly that the notorious Hatfield-McCoy feud stemmed in part from conflicts between local economic autonomy and outside industrial development. Altina L. Waller, *Feud: Hatfields, McCoys, and Social Change in Appalachia, 1860–1900* (Chapel Hill: University of North Carolina Press, 1988).

7. The significance of "republicanism" as an ideology has been repeated in numerous works addressing topics from the Revolutionary War to the post–Civil War labor movement. A concise but by no means exhaustive historiographical overview can be found in Daniel T. Rodgers, "Republicanism: The Career of a Concept," *Journal of American History* 79, no. 1 (June 1992): 11–38.

8. For a comprehensive assessment of Republican wartime economic measures, consult Heather Cox Richardson, *The Greatest Nation of the Earth: Republican Economic Policies during the Civil War* (Cambridge, MA: Harvard University Press, 1997).

9. While more recent studies have built on the theme of loyalty, the classic statement is George M. Fredrickson, "The Doctrine of Loyalty," in *The Inner Civil War: Northern Intellectuals and the Crisis of the Union* (New York: Harper & Row, 1965), 130–50.

10. The exploitation of wartime loyalties was similar to that in southern Appalachia, where myths of Unionism were used to attract capital to the region in the postwar period.

11. Much of the area focused on in this essay reverted back to a state of nature, constituted anew as the Allegheny National Forest.

12. Illustration, landform regions of Pennsylvania, from David J. Cuff, William J. Young, Edward K. Muller, and Wilbur Zelinsky, *The Atlas of Pennsylvania* (Philadelphia: Temple University Press, 1989).

13. This essay draws context from the author's dissertation, titled "Deserter Country: Civil War Opposition in the Mountains of Pennsylvania" (PhD diss., Pennsylvania State University, 2003). The work is forthcoming (spring 2009) from Fordham University Press as part of the North's Civil War series. The work explores Appalachian resistance from the antebellum period through the war years, but it does not address the period of Reconstruction.

14. For a comparison of farm economics in the southern Appalachians, see Dwight B. Billings and Kathleen M. Blee, "Agriculture and Poverty in the Kentucky Mountains: Beech Creek, 1850–1910," in *Appalachia in the Making: The Mountain South in the Nineteenth Century,* ed. Mary Beth Pudup, Dwight B. Billings, and Altina L. Waller, 233–69 (Chapel Hill: University of North Carolina Press, 1995).

15. For connections between economic modernization and railroad development in the southern Appalachians, read Kenneth W. Noe, *Southwest Virginia's Railroad: Modernization and the Sectional Crisis in the Civil War Era* (Urbana: University of Illinois Press, 1994).

16. It is important to understand that myths of Appalachian uniqueness were themselves social constructions by outside observers. The seminal work on the concept of Appalachian "otherness" focusing on the southern mountains is Henry D. Shapiro, *Appalachia on Our Mind: The Southern Mountains and Mountaineers in American Consciousness, 1870–1920* (Chapel Hill: University of North Carolina Press, 1978). Shapiro's landmark study did not place the creation of this myth in a

context of lumbering and coal mining, as stressed in this essay. A compelling work from an anthropological perspective is Allen W. Batteau, *The Invention of Appalachia: The Anthropology of Form and Meaning* (Tucson: University of Arizona Press, 1990). Batteau explores the central symbolisms, including nature and poverty, that have made Appalachian myths so enduring.

17. David C. Smith, "The Logging Frontier," *Journal of Forest History* 18, no. 4 (October 1974): 96–106. To see how West Virginia lumbering illustrates the expansion of the logging frontier, consult Lewis, *Transforming the Appalachian Countryside*. A similar study that charts the shift of the Appalachian coal frontier is Raymond E. Murphy and Hugh E. Spittal, "Movements of the Center of Coal Mining in the Appalachian Plateaus," *Geographical Review* 35, no. 4 (October 1945): 624–33.

18. Thomas R. Cox, "Transition in the Woods: Log Drivers, Raftsmen, and the Emergence of Modern Lumbering in Pennsylvania," *Pennsylvania Magazine of History and Biography* 104, no. 3 (July 1980): 345–64.

19. Samuel A. King, "A Log Drive to Williamsport in 1868," *Pennsylvania History* 29, no. 2 (April 1962): 151–74.

20. Forest history has a broad literature. Two key narrative overviews are Michael Williams, *Americans and Their Forests: A Historical Geography* (New York: Oxford University Press, 1989), and David C. Smith, *This Well-Wooded Land: Americans and Their Forests from Colonial Times to the Present* (Lincoln: University of Nebraska Press, 1985). An important early reference work on American lumbering is James Elliot Defebaugh, *History of the Lumber Industry of America*, 2 vols. (Chicago: The American Lumberman, 1907). Defebaugh wrote lengthy sections on regional lumbering in Pennsylvania. Other volumes that focus specifically on the lumber region of northern Pennsylvania include R. Dudley Tonkin, *My Partner, the River: The White Pine Story on the Susquehanna* (Pittsburgh: University of Pittsburgh Press, 1958); J. Herbert Walker, ed., *Rafting Days in Pennsylvania* (Altoona, PA: The Times-Tribune Co., 1922); and James Mitchell, *Lumbering and Rafting in Clearfield County, Pennsylvania, on the West Branch of the Susquehanna River* (Clearfield, PA: n.p., 1911).

21. "Lumbermen's Meeting," *Raftsman's Journal*, July 9, 1856.

22. The classic articulation of the "moral economy" and economic resistance to outside change is James C. Scott, *Weapons of the Weak: Everyday Forms of Peasant Resistance* (New Haven, CT: Yale University Press, 1995).

23. Quote by John M. Chase in John B. Rumberger, "The 'Loggers' against 'Rafters,'" *Lock Haven (PA) Express*, June 17, 1915. Rumberger's local history is based on original documents and newspaper articles.

24. "Susquehanna Rafting," *Daily Patriot* (Harrisburg, PA), April 9, 1873.

25. The chief study of political opposition in Pennsylvania remains Arnold Shankman, *The Pennsylvania Antiwar Movement, 1861–1865* (Rutherford, NJ: Fairleigh Dickinson University Press, 1980).

26. Two important works that take decidedly different stances on the meaning

and impact of Democratic opposition are Frank L. Klement, *The Copperheads in the Middle West* (Chicago: University of Chicago Press, 1960), and Jennifer Weber, *Copperheads: The Rise and Fall of Lincoln's Opponents in the North* (New York: Oxford University Press, 2006). While Weber's work is more recent, it sheds no new light on the subject and unconvincingly maintains the Republican wartime view of "Copperheads" as traitors.

27. U.S. War Department, *The War of the Rebellion: A Compilation of the Official Records of the Union and Confederate Armies* (Washington, DC: U.S. Government Printing Office, 1880–1901) (hereafter *Official Records*), ser. 3, vol. 4: 990.

28. Joseph F. Quay to Andrew Gregg Curtin, September 2, 1864, Slifer-Dill Papers, Pennsylvania State Archives, Harrisburg.

29. David J. Cathcart to John S. McKiernan, June 19, 1863, RG-110, Records of the Provost Marshal General's Bureau, Department of Pennsylvania, Western Division, Letters Received from the Districts, Nineteenth District, entry 3140, box 36, National Archives and Records Administration (NARA), Philadelphia.

30. H. S. Campbell to James V. Bomford, June 25, 1863, RG-110, Records of the Provost Marshal General's Bureau, Department of Pennsylvania, Western Division, Nineteenth District, Letters Sent, entry 3394, vol. 6, NARA, Philadelphia.

31. There is a growing body of literature that addresses themes of Northern protest, much of it in essay form. Two excellent examples are Joan E. Cashin, "Deserters, Civilians, and Draft Resistance in the North," in *The War Was You and Me: Civilians in the American Civil War,* ed. Joan E. Cashin, 262–85 (Princeton, NJ: Princeton University Press, 2002); and Paul A. Cimbala, "Soldiering on the Home Front: The Veteran Reserve Corps and the Northern People," in *Union Soldiers and the Northern Home Front: Wartime Experiences, Postwar Adjustments,* ed. Paul A. Cimbala and Randall M. Miller, 182–218 (New York: Fordham University Press, 2002). Another fine essay that stresses the significance of localism in dissent is Kenneth H. Wheeler, "Local Autonomy and Civil War Draft Resistance: Holmes County, Ohio," *Civil War History* 45, no. 2 (June 1999): 147–59.

32. The most thorough studies of Pennsylvania politics in this period are Erwin Stanley Bradley, *The Triumph of Militant Republicanism: A Study of Pennsylvania and Presidential Politics, 1860–1872* (Philadelphia: University of Pennsylvania Press, 1964), and its follow-up: Frank B. Evans, *Pennsylvania Politics, 1872–1877: A Study in Political Leadership* (Harrisburg: Pennsylvania Historical and Museum Commission, 1966).

33. Defebaugh, *History of the Lumber Industry,* 2:602.

34. Defebaugh, *History of the Lumber Industry,* 2:614. An exceedingly relevant study of deforestation in West Virginia is Ronald L. Lewis, *Transforming the Appalachian Countryside: Railroads, Deforestation, and Social Change in West Virginia, 1880–1920* (Chapel Hill: University of North Carolina Press, 1998). Lewis's masterful work covers the broad spectrum of social and economic changes pertinent to this region, which occurred slightly later here than in the Pennsylvania lumbering counties.

35. "Good Prospects," *Clearfield (PA) Republican,* July 14, 1875.

36. The economic transformation of Southern Appalachia as exploitation shifted from timber to coal is highlighted in Ronald D Eller, *Miners, Millhands, and Mountaineers.*

37. Walter Licht, "Civil Wars: 1850–1900," in *Pennsylvania: A History of the Commonwealth,* ed. Randall M. Miller and William Pencak (University Park: Pennsylvania State University Press, 2002), 232.

38. James Macfarlane, *The Coal-regions of America: Their Topography, Geology, and Development* (New York: D. Appleton, 1873), 171–76.

39. These figures come from a contemporary source, James M. Swank, secretary of the American Iron and Steel Association. He compiled national and international coal production figures as part of an 1877 report for the Pennsylvania Board of Centennial Managers, later submitted to the Pennsylvania Legislature. Swank calculated that Pennsylvania produced 11.05 percent of the world's production of coal in 1875. James M. Swank, *Introduction to a History of Ironmaking and Coal Mining in Pennsylvania* (Philadelphia: James M. Swank, 1878), 124.

40. "The Coal-Mine Troubles," *New York Times,* May 15, 1875.

41. While postwar miners' unionism may seem unrelated to antiwar attitudes, labor historian Grace Palladino conducted research on the anthracite region of Pennsylvania that demonstrated how they were linked. She focused on regional unionism during the war among the laboring classes in anthracite coal mining. Union organization was denounced by operators as a threat to vital wartime industries. Applying a rhetoric of disloyalty to the miners' organization allowed operators to call on the authority of the federal government to quell dissent and uphold their rights to free-market hiring. Grace Palladino, *Another Civil War: Labor, Capital, and the State in the Anthracite Regions of Pennsylvania, 1840–68* (Urbana: University of Illinois Press, 1990).

42. The author is indebted to Andrew B. Arnold and his work on Pennsylvania coal mining, "Ordering Coal: Labor, Law, and Business in Central Pennsylvania, 1870–1900" (PhD diss., University of North Carolina at Chapel Hill, 2001). Arnold focuses on the same region but uses Reconstruction as a jumping-off point for the development of labor organization until the turn of the century. Arnold asserts that railroad executives "demonized" unionism and the "disruptive power of traditional, community-based activism" (5). Much of the context and significance of the 1875 strike is highlighted in Arnold's work.

43. "The Miners' Conflict," *New York Times,* May 17, 1875.

44. Arnold, "Ordering Coal," 103. Arnold argues that the crowd gave up control because the strikebreakers had "removed themselves from polite consideration" with their inability to listen to the appeal and take a vote.

45. The national impact of the Clearfield strikes is a centerpiece of Arnold's thesis. Arnold, "Ordering Coal," 111–17.

46. Ronald L. Lewis emphasized the importance of this regional stereotyping at the outset of his work on postwar logging in West Virginia. Drawing and

expanding upon Henry Shapiro's work, he summarizes how local-color writers "perpetrated, and then helped perpetuate, the myth of Appalachian otherness to facilitate absentee corporate control of the region's natural resources by marginalizing indigenous residents." Lewis, *Transforming the Appalachian Countryside*, 1. Unlike Shapiro, Lewis firmly connects the process of capitalist resource exploitation with the emphasis on the "otherness" of Appalachian residents.

47. "The Miners' Conflict," *New York Times*, May 17, 1875.

48. "The Mining Troubles," *New York Times*, May 19, 1875.

49. Richard I. Dodge to James B. Fry, December 12, 1864, *Official Records*, ser. 3, vol. 4: 990.

50. The *New York Times* reporter interviewed both strikers and mine operators to understand their opposing viewpoints. In summarizing "What the employers say," he reported: "The operators describe the men, who were accompanied by a number of women, as using violent threats and taking the miners out from their work by main force, and forcing them to march to Tyrone, a distance of twenty-five miles." "The Coal-Mine Troubles," *New York Times*, May 15, 1875.

51. "The Miners' Conflict," *New York Times*, May 17, 1875.

52. "The Coal Mines," *New York Times*, May 17, 1875.

53. "The Coal-Mine Troubles," *New York Times*, May 15, 1875.

54. "The Coal-Mine Troubles," *New York Times*, May 15, 1875.

55. It is unknown why these men chose the title "Sons of Liberty," but the name had historical significance. In a broad context, it echoed those groups of the Revolutionary era that organized political and economic protest. Curiously, during the Civil War it was alleged that there existed another group by the same name, a Democratic secret society that opposed the war and its policies. There is no evidence that the "Sons of Liberty" existed in Pennsylvania during the war. Nevertheless, as mentioned below in the text, rural Pennsylvanians did create community resistance groups stylized along similar lines as the 1868 union. For more on Pennsylvania, consult Shankman, *The Pennsylvania Antiwar Movement*. For a larger work that examines the phenomenon of secret societies, read Frank L. Klement, *Dark Lanterns: Secret Political Societies, Conspiracies, and Treason Trials in the Civil War* (Baton Rouge: Louisiana State University Press, 1984). Details about the 1868 "Sons of Liberty" union are found in Arnold, "Ordering Coal," 44. Arnold cites the *Phillipsburg Journal*, November 16, 1868.

56. The key work on labor organization in this period is David Montgomery, *Beyond Equality: Labor and the Radical Republicans, 1862–1872* (New York: Knopf, 1967), 136–42. His chapter on "Labor-Reform Organizations" highlights the origins and features of key working men's societies, including the Knights of Labor.

57. "Mutual protection society" is a term that does appear in contemporary sources, though not in materials related to the "Democratic Castle." Historians have used the term generally to characterize their intent. Klement, *The Copperheads of the Middle West*, 139, 161–63; Weber, *Copperheads*, 27, 128. For details

of the "Democratic Castle" and the military tribunals of civilians in Clearfield, consult the case against Patrick Curly, Samuel Lansberry, and Jacob Wilhelm, NARA, RG 153: Records of the Office of the Judge Advocate General, Army, Court Martial Case files, box 1968, OO 348; see also the second case against Gainer P. Bloom, George Rousher, Benjamin Boyer, Henry Yoas, and Charles Keller, NARA, RG 153: Records of the Office of the Judge Advocate General, Army, Court Martial Case files, box 1031, MM 1607.

58. "The Mining Troubles," *New York Times,* May 19, 1875.

59. "Badly Educated," *Clearfield (PA) Republican,* June 2, 1875.

60. "Arrest of a Murderer," *New York Times,* March 30, 1875, 1.

61. "Lansberry's Case," *Pittsburgh Post,* November 13, 1875, 4.

62. "Lansberry's Trial," *Pittsburgh Post,* November 13, 1875.

63. "Not Guilty," *Pittsburgh Post,* November 15, 1875, 4.

64. "Lansberry's Case," *Pittsburgh Post,* November 13, 1875, 4.

65. Herbert E. Stover, *Copperhead Moon* (New York: Dodd, Mead & Co., 1952), vii.

Chapter 11

The Lost Cause That Wasn't

East Tennessee and the Myth of Unionist Appalachia

Tom Lee

In September 2007, the History Channel premiered *Hillbilly: The Real Story.* The two-hour special included action scenes filmed at the Sycamore Shoals State Historic Area in Elizabethton, Tennessee, featuring cast members from Tennessee's official outdoor drama, *Liberty!* "You hear a lot of talk about 'branding' from high-priced consultants," said Jon Ruetz, *Liberty!* author and director, "but, as far as we're concerned, our region's brand is right here in front of us. In a real sense, we are who we were, and the stories of our heroic ancestors are the best of America." The story reenacted each summer at Sycamore Shoals—a story of pioneer settlement and heroic courage at the 1780 battle at King's Mountain—continues to resonate among East Tennesseans and tourists as a mytho-historical explanation of origins, a creation story of a distinct people and place within Tennessee, within the South, and within America. As the title of the History Channel special suggests, however, it was in the making of the image of Appalachia that the distinctive history of East Tennessee may have played the greatest role.[1]

In his 1899 *Atlantic Monthly* article, "Our Contemporary Ancestors in the Southern Mountains," William Goodell Frost describes a deep regional Unionism and rejection of slavery as characteristics that identified Appalachia as a discrete region and its people as peculiar. Moreover, he argues that the persistence of a Revolutionary heritage best explains the loyalty of the Southern mountaineers. In the last thirty years, Appalachian scholars have demonstrated that Frost's depiction of widespread Unionist sentiment in the Southern mountains belied the divisions and violence that pervaded the region during the Civil War. Yet because Frost's acceptance of a monolithic Unionism in Appalachia was central to his vision of Appalachia as a discrete region inhabited by "contemporary ancestors," the question of where and how the myth of Unionist Appalachia originated remains important. In 1965, a century after the Civil War, East Tennessee State University historian Eric Russell Lacy analyzed the prevailing theories explaining the stubborn resistance of East Tennesseans to secession. He concluded that no single theory satisfactorily explained the Unionist path chosen by East Tennesseans. Lacy did however expose a thread of continuity in the evidence. Decades before the secession struggles of 1861, political and economic disputes with the other sections of Tennessee produced among East Tennesseans a distinctive sectional identity built around a mythologized historical narrative of heroism and victimization that East Tennesseans themselves fostered and that persisted through the Civil War and into the twentieth century. In the midst of the Civil War, antebellum perceptions of East Tennessee as a distinctive section within Tennessee evolved into a perception of East Tennessee as a distinctive region within the South. By the end of the nineteenth century the mythologized narrative of East Tennessee exceptionalism had become integral to the image of Unionist Appalachia.[2]

As Northern troops moved south during the Civil War they noted the peculiarity of the land and the people, but the mountain South proved to be notable even within the South. In the 1870s and 1880s, local colorists appealed to readers both North and South with descriptions of an exotic and wanton Appalachia of lanky, shiftless mountaineers, worn-out women with cob pipes, feuds, and quaint habits and speech. Missionaries set out to educate and liberate the mountaineers from ignorance, and scholars sought to explain the apparent backwardness of white Americans who failed to fit the American pattern of progress. While William Goodell Frost accepted that mountaineers tended to be "rude and repellent," he blamed the condition on generations of isolation from the currents of the American mainstream. Predominantly of British origin and unspoiled by the heterogeneous, immigrant ethnicities pouring into Northern cities, the mountaineers represented racial purity as well as a romantic association with the British Isles. Moreover, as Frost argued, their separation from the South's aristocratic society had insulated them from the evil influences of slavery. It had preserved in them a deep commitment to liberty that their ancestors had evidenced at the defeat of the British at King's Mountain.[3]

In mountain Unionism, Frost found evidence for both mountaineer independence and his theory that the Southern mountaineers were "contemporary ancestors." "Appalachian America clave to the old flag," wrote Frost. At the outbreak of the Civil War, the "'Sons' and 'Daughters' of the Revolution" exhibited an "old-fashioned loyalty which held Kentucky in the Union, made West Virginia 'secede from secession,' and performed prodigies of valor in East Tennessee, and even in the western Carolinas." Their loyalty sprang from the wells of ethnicity and ties to a revolutionary, heroic past, but it was also a product of isolation and ignorance. Had the mountaineer not been isolated and ignorant of the economic and social ties that should have bound him to the South in 1861, he would have associated with the Confederacy. For a nation rapidly industrializing and losing touch with its rural past, however, the presence of a population that retained its "pioneer spirit" meant an opportunity for America to reconnect with vanishing virtues. It was within the South, Frost argued, that the mountain people could make their most profound contribution, for in the New South their labor and their resistance to aristocratic pretensions might well bring the whole region into accord with the nation.[4]

As president of Berea College, William Goodell Frost had a personal and professional stake in producing an image of mountaineers that would bring northern financial support. Founded by southern abolitionists in the 1850s, Berea College reopened in 1866 as a biracial school. Berea's effort to provide education to both blacks and whites proved to be problematic, however. Historian Shannon H. Wilson has argued that Berea, much like Appalachia itself, was caught in a common post–Civil War tension between "regional loyalties and national reunion." In the wake of civil war and reconstruction, northern interest in the fortunes of freedmen waned. Reunion required some avenue for understanding the war that would obscure prior differences over race and politics. By the time of Frost's article, Berea had begun shifting its outreach to mountain whites. After the passage in 1904 of a Kentucky law banning integrated education, Berea's trustees voted to continue providing education to mountain youth and to found a separate institute for African American students.[5]

Like Berea, Lincoln Memorial University in Harrogate, Tennessee, based its appeal to northern benevolence on the school's mission to the Anglo-Saxon Unionists of the mountains. For Frost and others who saw the potential for educating the mountaineers, no better exemplar existed than Abraham Lincoln—a poorly educated boy, born in a cabin and raised on the frontier, who held the Union together in the time of its greatest trial. In 1897 Union general O. O. Howard and others established Lincoln Memorial University. Howard often said that Abraham Lincoln once expressed to him a deep compassion and concern for the loyal people of East Tennessee, and the university, in addition to providing an education "of the most practical sort" to needy, white mountain children, was to be a memorial to Lincoln. More than merely a tribute to East Tennesseans' wartime loyalty, the university would be a symbol of the sectional reunion that Lincoln had sought. Lincoln's legacy as the Great Emancipator, according to Shannon H. Wilson, had become "a metaphor for freedom from ignorance, rather than a tangible witness to a 'new birth of freedom.'" The trustees chose blue and gray for the school colors and named the main building Grant-Lee Hall. The courses of Berea College and Lincoln Memorial reflected the national retreat from race that corresponded with sectional reconciliation, the powerful appeal of the mountaineer image to benevolent northerners and southerners, and the power of the Unionist myth to bind northern donors to the institutions that used it so well.[6]

Lincoln Memorial University's location in eastern Tennessee was both a practical choice and a reflection of the connection between East Tennessee's wartime loyalty and the myth of Appalachian Unionism. Indeed, during the Civil War many East Tennesseans demonstrated a devotion to the cause of the Union even when their state's secession was a foregone conclusion, but the complexities of their response to secession rose from deep in the region's history. At the approach of the Revolutionary War, settlers found themselves at odds with the British government and organized provisional governments in 1775 that led to their incorporation into the state of North Carolina. Throughout much of the war, the residents of the so-called Overmountain districts or backwoods settlements battled the Cherokees and participated fitfully in the vicious civil war between rebels and Tories raging to the east. In 1780, however, the British invasion of the South prompted the Overmountain settlers to participate in what would become an iconic episode in the mythologized history of East Tennessee. Threatened with destruction for aiding revolutionary forces in Virginia and the Carolinas, the Overmountain men trekked across the mountains to meet British loyalist forces under Patrick Ferguson. In the Battle of King's Mountain that ensued, the Overmountain men won a substantial victory.[7]

At the conclusion of the Revolution, the legislature of North Carolina first ceded the state's western lands to the new national government and then rescinded the cession. Disgruntled settlers west of the mountains held a convention and proclaimed their right to pursue statehood. The resulting State of Franklin existed from 1784 until 1788 in a dubious condition of independence. Led by John Sevier, a commander at King's Mountain and governor of Franklin, the Franklinites organized militia units, elected officials, wrote a constitution, collected taxes, negotiated treaties with Native Americans, and performed the functions of a sovereign government. Unfortunately for Sevier's followers, North Carolina continued to claim authority over the people of Franklin, and after a few years of conflict even the leaders of the Franklin experiment began to doubt the wisdom of pursuing independence. In 1789 North Carolinians ratified the U.S. Constitution and ceded their state's western lands to the new U.S. government. The rationale for Franklin ceased to exist, but the idea of Franklin continued to shape East Tennesseans' self-perception.[8]

After a period of territorial status, Tennessee became a state in 1796. Within two decades, however, burgeoning population growth in Middle Tennessee supplanted East Tennessee's dominance in state politics. By 1810 Davidson County, the location of Nashville, had a larger population than any county in East Tennessee, and in 1843 Nashville became the permanent capital of the state. While Middle Tennessee's rich soils and navigable waterways led to rapid development between 1800 and 1850, East Tennessee's fortunes stagnated. Bounded on the east and west by mountainous terrain and hampered by shallow, obstacle-filled waterways, East Tennessee developed an early antebellum agricultural economy dominated by corn and livestock that kept food on family tables but left East Tennessee's farmers starving for cash. Likewise, East Tennessee's iron and timber industries failed to develop beyond local markets. Though in 1859 iron manufacturing accounted for 26 percent of the value of commercial manufacturing in northeastern Tennessee and southwestern Virginia, only a few years earlier southern industrial advocate J. D. B. DeBow had observed that the majority of iron production in northeastern Tennessee used primitive methods little changed from the industry's frontier origins.[9]

While East Tennesseans retained the capacity to shape state politics even after 1815, they lacked the political strength to use state government to advance their own interests, especially to overcome obstacles to economic development. In 1834 East Tennesseans submitted twenty-five of thirty petitions seeking to include avenues for the gradual emancipation of slaves in a new state constitution only to have the plan blocked by Middle Tennessee delegates, who amended the new constitution to prohibit the state from emancipating slaves without the consent of the owner. In 1836 and 1838 the Tennessee General Assembly passed laws to aid internal improvements, but the primary benefit went to Middle Tennessee, and the laws were repealed in the 1840s. Finally, on February 27, 1848, the Tennessee legislature chartered and provided limited state backing for the East Tennessee and Virginia and the East Tennessee and Georgia railroads to connect Bristol, Tennessee, and Dalton, Georgia, via Knoxville, but East Tennesseans already sensed that their section was being treated inequitably within the state. In remarks favoring the railroad charters in 1848, Democratic state representative Landon Carter Haynes expressed the opinion of many East Tennesseans. "I for one," said the Washington County lawyer and future Confederate senator, "am not willing to see the noble people of that section that I have the honor to represent, left behind those of every other." East Tennesseans had begun to identify themselves as the victimized inhabitants of a specific geographic area.[10]

Recourse to a heroic past salved feelings of victimization. On December 7, 1841, Andrew Johnson, Democratic state representative for Greene and Washington counties, submitted one of three antebellum requests that East Tennessee be allowed to secede from Tennessee and form a separate state. Johnson called for the appointment of a joint committee to consider the cession of East Tennessee to the federal government and to inquire of other states if the mountain sections of those states could join a resurrected "State of Frankland." While some East Tennesseans supported Johnson's measure in hopes of achieving the manumission victory denied them in 1834, Whig newspaper editor William G. Brownlow offered another rationale for support. Improvement money, he argued, was not reaching beyond the Cumberland Plateau from Nashville, and the people of the "Little Switzerland," as East Tennessee was sometimes called, would never prosper as supplicants to the Middle Tennessee aristocracy.[11]

In 1858 Andrew Johnson, then in the U.S. Senate, turned again to the history of East Tennessee when he felt compelled to respond to aspersions cast upon the state. "I ask the Senate, I ask the people of this nation, if it is any part of Tennessee's history that her people have been ever wanting in prowess or courage?" asked Johnson. Vindication, he continued, "exists in her own history. I could recite many of her military deeds that would be ample, if her reputation was not beyond the assaults of the Senator. I could begin with the Battle of King's Mountain, which was fought before Tennessee was a State."[12]

Allusions to East Tennessee's heroic past not only provided material for defenses against forces from outside the region, but they also helped create a façade of unity in a region often torn by competing forces. From the 1830s to the early 1850s, Tennessee Whigs and Democrats fought ferociously in local, state, and national elections, and yet so powerful was the identification of East Tennessee as a distinct region with a distinct past and a distinct set of economic interests that political divisions could be set aside. In an examination of Washington County, Tennessee, historian David Hsiung found evidence of socioeconomic divisions exacerbated by the campaign for railroads. Latecomers to Washington County had little choice but to accept property in the most remote and mountainous sections of the county, argued Hsiung, and had little expectation of growing surpluses sufficient to merit interest in expanding the commercial links between Washington County and distant markets. Valley dwellers, however, stood to gain handsomely from investment in improved means of transportation such as the railroad. When Washington County's railroad boosters sought financial support for their ventures in the mountainous sections, they met disinterest and rejection. Rather than explaining the response in terms of differing economic interests, railroad boosters generalized that mountain residents were simply shiftless, lazy, ignorant, and backward. Such characterizations would be used later as explanations for the Unionism of East Tennesseans and for the backwardness of Appalachian mountaineers, but even prior to the Civil War they served the purposes of economic development proponents who would set the image of a faltering East Tennessee against images of a once-heroic past in order to make their case for state funds, not for the needy but for the region and its railroads.[13]

The completion of East Tennessee's trunk-line railroads in 1855 and 1858 linked the Deep South and Virginia and enhanced the prospects for economic development in East Tennessee, but success also directed East Tennessee commerce away from the rest of the state and linked the region with states that would later join the Confederacy. While the railroads opened the commercial connections that railroad boosters had desired, political conflict already threatened their achievements. The 1860 election of Abraham Lincoln set in motion the secession of South Carolina and the rest of the Deep South states in the ensuing months. In a February 9, 1861, referendum, Tennesseans voted overwhelmingly against holding a secession convention, and three out of every four delegates chosen for the convention that was not to be were Unionists. The results from the February referendum, however, failed to reflect the depth of commitment Unionists had to the cause of Union. Many were conditional Unionists. As early as January 1861, William G. Brownlow reflected the tensions within Unionism when he declared himself in favor of East Tennessee's separation from the state in the event that Tennessee seceded but rejected any effort by the federal government to interfere with slavery. A Bristol, Tennessee, resident wrote well-known Jonesboro Unionist Thomas Amis Rogers Nelson that Sullivan County voters were for the Union but would readily follow the South if Tennessee ever broke her ties to the federal government. The April 1861 firing on Fort Sumter and Abraham Lincoln's subsequent call for volunteers led many conditional Unionists to abandon their advocacy for loyalty. On May 6, 1861, Tennessee legislators approved a declaration of independence and scheduled a statewide referendum for June. The following day, May 7, without the approval of the people but with the consent of the legislature, Tennessee governor Isham Harris signed an alliance with the Confederate States of America.[14]

The situation in late May differed markedly from what had prevailed in February. Governor Harris had engineered the de facto secession of the state, and once-vicious political foes had joined forces. Democrat Andrew Johnson had once been castigated by Whig newspaper editor William G. Brownlow, but upon his return to East Tennessee from the Senate in the spring of 1861 Johnson received effervescent praise from the verbal pugilist for his strong stand against secession while in Washington. Moreover, Johnson and former Whig adversary T. A. R. Nelson undertook a canvass of East Tennessee together only to find that voters across East Tennessee were far less receptive to Unionist overtures. On May 30, some four hundred Unionists converged on Knoxville to attend a convention called by Brownlow and leading Unionists. While both Nelson and Johnson spoke and the delegates passed resolutions condemning secession, at least a faction of the delegates were either sympathetic to Confederate grievances or expected Tennessee's secession and were therefore loath to declare their unconditional loyalty to the Union. While middle Tennesseans had voted against a secession convention in the February referendum, on June 8 almost 90 percent of Middle Tennessee voters favored independence. Statewide, nearly 70 percent of Tennesseans voted for secession. Only in East Tennessee, where voters preferred Union by a ratio of more than two to one, did the returns show a decided preference for loyalty to the Union, but even in East Tennessee the vote was far closer than it had been in February. Sullivan County, on the Virginia border in the northeastern section of the state, and a number of counties in southeastern Tennessee voted for secession. In Washington County, Unionists won by only ninety-three votes out of more than two thousand cast.[15]

Three days after the referendum, T. A. R. Nelson called for the delegates from Knoxville to reconvene in Greeneville. With secession now confirmed, fewer than three hundred delegates attended, and divisions were even more pronounced. Once again, the idea of East Tennessee separation, based on the notion of conflicting interests with the rest of the state and with the region, emerged in the midst of conflict. Early in the convention, Nelson called for the organization of militia units for the defense of East Tennessee, called for the Tennessee legislature to permit the separation of East Tennessee and willing counties of Middle Tennessee, and promised to maintain a position of neutrality in the war unless "molested by either actual violence or insult." By mid-June the majority of Tennesseans were solidly behind the Confederacy, and Confederate troops had already begun moving into Knoxville. Well aware of the possible consequences of provoking Confederate authorities, several Knoxville Unionists led the opposition to Nelson's potentially inflammatory proposals. After much debate, convention delegates adopted a set of substitute resolutions that toned down Nelson's language, but they preserved his challenge to the legitimacy of secession, promised passivity and neutrality, and expressed a desire that East Tennessee be allowed to separate from Tennessee. "If the substitute resolutions did not accomplish all that was hoped," wrote Oliver P. Temple decades after the Greeneville convention, "they did secure the first and greatest object—the preservation of peace. They prevented the greatest of all calamities—a fraternal civil war, with all the attendant horrors." Before adjourning, convention delegates elected commissioners to carry their petition for separation to the state legislature. The legislature received the petition but took no action. In the words of Eric Lacy, "East Tennessee was left a disunited section of a factional state in a country rent asunder by civil war." Once again, East Tennesseans, although internally "disunited," attempted to project the image of a region with interests and goals distinct from those of the rest of Tennessee and the South.[16]

Cognizant of both East Tennessee's strategic importance and its loyalists, Confederate authorities hoped that time would reconcile East Tennesseans to their fate, and in the months immediately following secession adopted a policy of leniency toward East Tennessee. Unionist sentiment remained intact, however. In August elections, the voters of the First and Second Congressional Districts thwarted the hopes of Gov. Isham Harris that Confederate policies would mollify East Tennessee Union sentiment, and they elected Unionists T. A. R. Nelson and Horace Maynard to serve in the U.S. Congress, not the Confederate Congress. After a harrowing escape from East Tennessee, Andrew Johnson, the only U.S. senator from a seceding state to remain loyal to the Union, met with Abraham Lincoln and appealed for assistance for the Unionists of East Tennessee. Lincoln took particular interest in East Tennessee and the plight of East Tennesseans. The presence of Unionists in Tennessee offered an opportunity to reconstitute a state government quickly and to pave the way for the restoration of the Union. In addition, Lincoln recognized East Tennessee's strategic importance and the area's potential as a fertile ground for recruiting. While Lincoln rejected plans to liberate several centers of Unionist sentiment in the South, a plan presented by William B. Carter of Carter County drew the president's backing. On November 8, Unionists successfully burned five bridges along the East Tennessee and Virginia and East Tennessee and Georgia railroads. From Johnson County in the northeastern tip of Tennessee to Hamilton County in southeastern Tennessee, Unionists armed themselves and gathered by the tens and hundreds to await the arrival of the federal forces that William B. Carter had requested. At Elizabethton, Tennessee, a thousand Unionists collected near Sycamore Shoals, the site where the Overmountain men had gathered before departing for King's Mountain eighty years earlier. Although rumors of federal forces were rampant, the anticipated federal army failed to arrive. In the wake of the bridge burnings and the fear of an invasion of East Tennessee, a Confederate sympathizer in Jonesboro wrote Confederate president Jefferson Davis that Unionists were firmly established in East Tennessee and would never "be appeased, conciliated, or quieted." Furthermore, he argued, Unionists should be considered "alien enemies" and forced from the state. Confederate authorities reversed their policy of leniency, set about disbanding armed Unionist rebels, hanged several of the bridge burners, and began mass arrests.[17]

From the bridge burnings of 1861 until the last Confederate forces were pushed from East Tennessee in 1865, East Tennesseans endured partisan raiders, bushwhackers, armies on the march, intimidation, violence, retribution, conscription, and privation. Unionists suffered under Confederate authority and sought vengeance against their Confederate neighbors when Union forces were nearby, but all East Tennesseans felt the terror of lawlessness when neither Confederate nor federal authorities were present to preserve civil order. Threatened by violence from bushwhackers and neighbors and stripped of crops and livestock, East Tennesseans either abandoned their homes or suffered where they remained. After Confederate authorities implemented conscription in 1862, Unionist men by the thousands left their homes and families to join federal forces. In 1863 fortunes were reversed when General Burnside's federal army arrived in Knoxville and federal forces took control of Chattanooga. While Unionists continued joining federal forces and Unionist refugees swarmed to Knoxville seeking relief and protection, many Confederate sympathizers fled to areas more firmly under Confederate control. In East Tennessee they faced vengeance, the destruction or confiscation of their property, and the possibility that charges would be pressed against them for their roles in the rebellion. "We are badly broken up it is true having lost all I have made in the last 20 years," wrote N. C. Baldwin from Washington County, Virginia, to his father, who remained near Jonesboro, Tennessee. "But I have made a good crop this year, and shall have plenty to go on if the Yankees don't get in upon us again." In the same letter, Baldwin advised his father to "get your young negroes away for the Yankees will be certain to take them if they get there again." Refugees had no way to know how long their exile would last, and not all Confederates chose to leave. Historian W. Todd Groce argued that many of those who remained "simply lost the will to fight" as they recognized that secession, rather than bringing about the prosperity they had sought, was actually leading to economic ruin.[18]

In the midst of the strife, Unionists made good use of East Tennessee's distinctiveness. After being exiled from the Confederacy in March 1862, editor William G. Brownlow began a speaking tour of the Northern states, introducing a national audience to the established themes of East Tennessee distinctiveness while transposing new themes that would merge in a later mythologized East Tennessee Unionism. To establish sympathy for East Tennesseans, not least perhaps for William G. Brownlow, the "Fighting Parson" told of the depredations that East Tennessee Unionists faced under Confederate authority and told his listeners that above all East Tennesseans had wished to avoid both Northern and Southern agitators and extremists. Victims East Tennesseans were, but in an early manifestation of the bloody shirt, Brownlow proclaimed that East Tennessee Unionists were more than mere victims; they were central to the preservation of the Union. They had not only contributed soldiers to federal armies but had confounded Confederate desires to bring the war north. As for slavery, Brownlow never denied its presence in East Tennessee or that he had only a year before proclaimed his devotion to the institution in the pages of his newspaper, but before his audiences he expressed an unconditional Unionism. "We deprecate alike the fanatical agitators of one section and the Disunion demagogues of the other," wrote Brownlow in a pamphlet. "I believe I represent the views of multitudes of ever-true and now suffering patriots," he insisted, "when I declare that, Southern man and slave-holder as I am, if the South in her madness and folly will force the issue upon the country, of Slavery and no Union, or a Union and no Slavery, I am for the Union, though every other institution in the country perish."

Brownlow likewise returned to the Revolution. Both Confederates and Unionists had viewed secession through the lens of liberty and tyranny—a country-republican sensibility. Not content without a dig at his Southern opponents, Brownlow rejected Southern efforts to cast East Tennessee loyalists as the ideological descendants of Tories. Instead, Brownlow pointed to the citizens of Charleston, who in 1780 had argued for the capitulation of Charleston, as evidence of the "original Toryism of South Carolina." Here again, Brownlow indicated a potential thematic connection between contemporary events and the already mythologized Revolutionary past of East Tennessee.[19]

Two years after Brownlow's tour of the North, another East Tennessee exile began speaking to northern audiences. A witness to much of the suffering in East Tennessee, Nathaniel Green Taylor determined to escape East Tennessee and seek relief for the suffering. Born of a distinguished family and a resident of heavily Unionist Carter County, Tennessee, Taylor graduated from Princeton in 1842 and became a Methodist minister the following year. Known for his eloquence when aroused, Taylor developed an interest in Whig politics that led him to make numerous bids for state and local office between 1849 and 1857. More focused on relief for the needs of East Tennesseans than was Brownlow, Taylor spoke to large audiences in Philadelphia, Boston, and New York to plead for money and supplies to fill the want that he had personally witnessed. In Pennsylvania, Taylor spoke at the Philadelphia Academy of Music on January 29, and a relief association was immediately organized.[20]

The next month Taylor was in Boston seeking funds from the state of Massachusetts and was introduced during a public meeting at Faneuil Hall by Edward Everett, who enjoyed a tremendous reputation in the Bay State, having served as governor, U.S. senator, and U.S. secretary of state under Millard Fillmore. A well-known Whig and vice presidential candidate with John Bell of Tennessee on the Constitutional Union ticket in 1860, Everett had also held the presidency of Harvard University and spoken prior to Abraham Lincoln's delivery of the Gettysburg Address. While introducing Taylor, Everett recounted the conditions in East Tennessee and echoed William G. Brownlow's claim that Northerners directly benefited from the resistance in East Tennessee. "I will only add, fellow-citizens, that our brethren of East Tennessee are fighting our battles as well as their own, on their blood-stained soil," stated Everett. "It is our cause as much as theirs in which they have suffered the most cruel persecution; and however largely, however promptly, your relief may be extended to them, it will come too late, I fear, to rescue some of them from the horrors of starvation." In addition, Everett argued for a more geographically broad application of the Unionist image that included parts of Maryland, Virginia, North Carolina, and northern Alabama; but he reserved special honor for East Tennessee.[21]

When Everett finished his remarks, Taylor rose to great applause. Like Brownlow, Taylor presumed to speak for East Tennesseans, but while Brownlow mentioned the Revolutionary past in connection with the loyalist sentiments of the 1860s only tangentially, Taylor made the history of East Tennessee a centerpiece of his address. Taylor explained how the "pioneer heroes of East Tennessee" left their homes to battle at King's Mountain during the Revolution and in the 1830s had stood with Jackson against South Carolina when nullification threatened the Union. Another theme struck at Faneuil Hall, however, would persist for decades. In the late nineteenth and early twentieth centuries, northern industrialists, financiers, teachers, missionaries, and their agents in Appalachia would link philanthropy with investment in Appalachia. Edward Everett described East Tennessee as "a state in itself," with fertile valley soils and mountains "filled with coal and almost every variety of ore." Taylor, noting the development of Northern industry during the war and the wealth being generated from Northern mineral regions, stressed that "the desolations and ruin of this unnatural and cruel war have opened a wide field for your philanthropy and benevolence," and he asked: "Will you enter it?—will you sow it?—will you cultivate it?" As in Philadelphia a relief society quickly emerged in Boston on the heels of Taylor's address. In Knoxville, Unionist leaders like Thomas William Humes and Oliver Perry Temple organized the East Tennessee Relief Association to receive and distribute goods sent from the North and food and other necessities purchased with Northern funds.[22]

The image of East Tennessee Unionism, presented in the North by East Tennessee exiles and accepted by influential men like Everett, belied the complexities and consequences of Unionist sentiment during and after the war. Understandably, both Brownlow and Taylor glossed over the importance of Confederate sympathies within East Tennessee and the divisions that had emerged among Unionists. By presenting a monolithic image of East Tennessee Unionism and binding that image to an already mythologized heroic past, Brownlow and Taylor were both building on previous conceptions of East Tennessee distinctiveness. They were also refining the image of East Tennessee for the consumption of Northern audiences whose "philanthropy and benevolence" were much desired. In the midst of the Civil War, the antebellum image of East Tennessee as a discrete region within Tennessee came to be accepted as reality at the same time that East Tennessee's exceptionalism was applied to a broader swath of the mountain South.

Even as the myth of a monolithic Unionism grew, however, divisions continued to plague East Tennessee. Many former Confederates faced charges of treason, had civil cases and indictments pressed against them, and had their lands confiscated. Some, such as Confederate senator Landon Carter Haynes, spent the rest of their lives in exile. Other major supporters of the Confederacy in eastern Tennessee, such as John C. Vaughn and David McKendree Key, left the state in the immediate aftermath of the war but returned to East Tennessee when conditions improved. Unionists, meanwhile, struggled with their own issues. Once again there was talk of separation from Tennessee. "The people of this section, long before the war, had just cause of complaint against the people of Middle and West Tennessee in the aggregate," said the *Chattanooga Gazette.* Many conservative Unionists objected to Andrew Johnson's iron fist, to the recruitment and use of black soldiers, and to the Emancipation Proclamation.

In 1864 T. A. R. Nelson called for the delegates of the Knoxville and Greeneville conventions to reassemble in Knoxville. Johnson rushed to Knoxville, where conservative delegates led by Rev. W. B. Carter of Carter County, originator of the 1861 bridge-burning scheme, argued against abolition or any hint of black equality and in favor of gradual emancipation that included payment to Unionists and paroled former Confederates. By April 15 convention delegates had reached an impasse. After four days of debate and internecine strife between Johnson supporters and those who opposed the direction of his policies, delegates agreed to adjourn. Subsequently, Johnson and his supporters organized a "grand mass meeting" in Knoxville to rally support for amending the state constitution to abolish slavery and endorse the policies of both Johnson and Abraham Lincoln. According to Noel Fisher, "The tragedy of East Tennessee Unionists was that they fit comfortably into no region and no party. Conservative Unionists could not follow the South in 1861, but they also could not accept many Northern policies during the war and Reconstruction." The strife in Knoxville in 1864 foreshadowed the rift between conservative Unionists and Radicals that deepened when William G. Brownlow became governor and that led eventually to the emergence of the Republican Party in East Tennessee, but it also reflected the fact that no monolithic Unionism had ever existed in East Tennessee. The issue of race was itself a divisive factor that undermined the myth—a myth that excluded African Americans from participation in the heroic past.[23]

As in antebellum East Tennessee, however, the promise of regional economic development overwhelmed political and ideological divisions within the region. Under Governor Brownlow, East Tennessee received state funds for internal improvements that stopped rapidly when conservatives and Redeemers captured control of the state government. Nonetheless, by the late nineteenth century, the economic development dreamed about by antebellum East Tennesseans seemed at hand. Across the South boosters like Henry Grady proclaimed the emergence of a progressive New South that was built on industrial growth and was rapidly challenging the North for economic supremacy. Across Appalachia plans burgeoned for new railroad ventures, iron furnaces, and mines. East Tennessee was among the first areas to see the consequences of Northern investment. The war hindered development but failed to derail it completely.[24]

Some of the new investment resulted from the activities of former Union soldiers who had seen the mineral wealth of the mountains during the war and returned to see that it was exploited. In 1867 Gen. John Wilder founded the Roane Iron Company with a capitalization of a million dollars, mostly northern capital. The Roane Iron Company was but one of Wilder's investments in East Tennessee and one of several iron manufacturing establishments in Chattanooga. Indeed, Chattanooga became the first city in the South that could claim to have a permanent steel mill. Not all the ventures were entirely new and not all were tied to former Union soldiers. As early as the 1830s, iron manufacturers recognized the quality of the iron ore at Cranberry in Mitchell County, North Carolina, and East Tennessee railroad promoters used the presence of the ore and the promise of a railroad connection to the ore in the promotion of their own railway projects. On May 24, 1866, the Tennessee General Assembly chartered the East Tennessee and Western North Carolina Railroad (ETWNC) to run from a point on the East Tennessee and Virginia Railroad to the Cranberry ores in North Carolina. Among those listed on the charter were Unionists Henry Johnson, generally considered the founder of Johnson City, and Rev. William B. Carter, the man responsible for the 1861 bridge burnings. Five years later, and after redeemers gained control of the state government, Tennessee's commissioner of delinquent railroads sold the ETWNC to recoup state funds invested in the railroad during Reconstruction. The buyers included a number of prominent Unionists from Carter County, many of them investors listed in the original charter, and former Confederate brigadier general Alfred Eugene Jackson, who had been instrumental in the construction of the East Tennessee and Virginia Railroad.

By 1874 the president of the ETWNC was seeking buyers, and in 1875 a new set of investors purchased the railroad. Among the investors were Confederate general and North Carolinian Robert F. Hoke, and Pennsylvania iron, timber, and rail baron Ario Pardee. Two years before the purchase, a corporation that included Hoke and Pardee purchased the Cranberry mines. Aware that rail access to the Cranberry ores would improve the value and productivity of their mines, Hoke, Pardee, and their partners set about constructing a narrow-gauge rail line from Johnson's Depot on the then-consolidated East Tennessee Virginia and Georgia Railroad.[25]

In the decades following the Civil War, the economic development that had for so long besotted East Tennesseans trumped the potential for conflict over the meaning of the past. The inflow of northern capital made possible East Tennessee's economic resuscitation, but the need for capital provided an impetus to reconciliation. Again, the notion of a distinct East Tennessee history both softened reunion and appealed to northern audiences. For former Confederates in East Tennessee, the utility and predominance of the Unionist myth meant that their own past was often obscured. By the end of the nineteenth century, for instance, East Tennessee had only fifteen United Confederate Veterans camps, most between Knoxville and Chattanooga. Only a single organization covered the entire area from Knoxville to Bristol. Likewise, even in southeastern Tennessee, few towns saw fit to raise statues and civic memorials to the Confederate dead. If openly recognized, the Lost Cause had to be harmonized with the history of Unionist victory, and the memorialization of a shared history of East Tennessee provided an avenue to cooperation. In 1876 Unionist O. P. Temple and former Confederate General Alfred E. Jackson served together on a committee celebrating East Tennessee's role in the first hundred years of the United States' existence. In Nashville the centennial jubilee included the reading of a speech by East Tennessee Confederate J. G. M. Ramsey entitled "The Iliad of Patriotism" in which Ramsey, by then president of the Tennessee Historical Society, told again of the heroes of King's Mountain. No less an engineer of the Lost Cause mythology than novelist Thomas Nelson Page claimed that the era of Thomas Jefferson had been the most authentic exhibition of southern heritage, for it was in the years of the Early Republic that the South joined all other sections in an optimistic nationalism. Thus, memorials to a common past and Revolutionary-era history allowed both Confederate and Union supporters to claim a common heritage of nationalism and patriotism. In East Tennessee, the mythologized past worked to maintain internal unity in much the same way that the myth of the Lost Cause worked in the rest of the South.[26]

The dual role of East Tennessee's past as internal mediator and external promotional tool became apparent in the memorials to East Tennessee's past that followed the Civil War. Even among Unionists who memorialized the war, time softened the harsh realities of the conflict, and allusion to a shared prewar history made reconciliation possible. In 1887 Union veteran, politician, and Knoxville newspaper editor William Rule addressed the Ohio Commandery of the Military Order of the Loyal Legion. Rule began his address, entitled "The Loyalists of Tennessee in the Late War," with an imagined narrative of James Robertson and Daniel Boone leaving the Yadkin River valley for a hunt into the Watauga country, where they would found a "colony" that was "composed of men and women of a heroic mold, filled with inspirations of patriotism." Rule then explained to his audience that the descendents of these earliest settlers formed the basis of his remarks. The settlement had become the "Switzerland of America," and he reminded his listeners of the manumission heritage of the area and of the first abolitionist paper in Jonesboro. The majority of East Tennesseans, he said, had been opposed to slavery. Over time, the descendants of the pioneers had "made honorable records on the battle-fields of every war ... from King's Mountain to Appomattox." To reinforce the Revolutionary connection, Rule added that the leaders of East Tennessee Unionists had been denounced as Tories and traitors.[27]

Rather than merely promote the Unionist story, however, Rule tailored his remarks to appeal to his audience of Union veterans and Republicans. While Rule praised the bravery and patriotism of East Tennesseans, he allowed that he would not "forget the thousands of colored men who enlisted from the rebellious states ... and who demonstrated that black skin is no barrier to manly courage." Nor, he argued had Knoxvillians forgotten the Union dead buried in Knoxville who were "buried among friends." As for East Tennessee, Rule even admitted that East Tennessee had been divided and that the bitter strife and fatal feuds of the war years might have been predicted, but the excesses were "committed on both sides." The passions of the war had subsided, and things had changed:

> Now all want the "Yankee" to come, whether from the land of "baked beans" or from the great pushing, driving, restless Northwest; and the more of him the better. Now instead of the flashing flames from burning cottages, log cabins, and more pretentious homes, which lit up the hills and valleys of this "Switzerland of America," we can show a far more pleasing picture. We can show dense clouds of black smoke curling aloft from hundreds of smoke-stacks, that mark the location of busy manufacturing establishments, the products of which are the contributions of the New South to the Nation's wealth.

The war had passed, but while the people of East Tennessee were "losing something of their individuality, and becoming more cosmopolitan in character," the patriotism displayed by East Tennesseans remained and only awaited the nation's call to be reanimated. Infused with the activity of the New South, the people were once again chasing the prize of economic development.[28]

In 1888 Thomas Humes, a minister and president of East Tennessee University and of the East Tennessee Relief Association, authored *The Loyal Mountaineers of Tennessee*. He echoed the central themes of the East Tennessee Unionist history, but with an almost religious fervor. That East Tennessee Unionists had acted in a "scene in a momentous tragedy, thus presented in a region of country so isolated from the great world that its actors could have no stimulus to their constancy in the heard applause of admiring spectators, was phenomenal, even in that time of heroic deeds." Again, Humes told of the Wataugans and King's Mountain, but unlike Rule he included reference to the State of Franklin. Clearly, the point of Franklin had been independence, but masterfully Humes chose to empha- size the reconciliation of the Franklinites to the government of North Caro- lina. Their "broad patriotism" had "triumphed over a spirit of revolutionary separation, in retaining the allegiance of the people of Frankland to the mother State of North Carolina." Also like Rule, Humes recited the history of the manumission movement in East Tennessee and tied East Tennes- see's history to industrial development. Humes quoted from the Pennsylva- nia Relief Association's 1864 report on conditions in East Tennessee: "East Tennessee, with its fertile lands, its rich mines and valuable water-power, presents a fine field for the application of Northern labor and capital; and when this calamity is overpast, and a direct railroad communication with the North is secured, it will prosper as never before." The words resem- bled those of Nathaniel Taylor, whose religious faith during his exile in the North during the war Humes lauded. The cause of relief, it seemed, had divine sanction.[29]

Other than wartime victimization, Humes failed to deal with the messy realities of Unionism in East Tennessee under Confederate rule, and neither would Oliver Perry Temple in his 1899 book *East Tennessee and the Civil War*. As he explains in the preface to his book, Temple sought to "rescue from oblivion" the "historical facts" of the struggle in East Tennessee dur- ing the Civil War and to "vindicate the course of the Union people of East Tennessee in separating from their friends and kindred in the South." Yet Temple also expressed a desire to present the facts "without offensiveness." Although a slaveholder and "bound to the South by ties of interest, associa- tion, and many long friendships," Temple was nonetheless "drawn toward the North by a strong love of the Union." Besides, time had "softened his feelings, and to a certain extent modified his views regarding some of the questions formerly dividing the two sections." For Temple, then, reconcilia- tion was an integral part of the story of East Tennessee's Civil War.[30]

So, too, was the mythologizing and memorializing of the past. Of twenty-six chapters, Temple dedicated the first three to the early settlers of Tennessee, particularly emphasizing the Watauga Association and King's Mountain. "For one," wrote Temple, "I would uncover my head, at the name and in the presence of the majestic men of the Revolution." While Thomas Humes made John Tipton rather than John Sevier the hero of the State of Franklin story, Temple praised John Tipton for his Revolutionary record and then chose to avoid the dilemmas inherent in the Franklinites' bid for independence from North Carolina by excluding the episode from his book. Like memorialists before him, he sought to unite the events of the Civil War with the Revolutionary generation, but Temple included both Confederates and Unionists in his collection of heroes. "These old soldiers of East Tennessee, on both sides, are what their hero fathers were," wrote Temple. Probably for the same reason that he opposed T. A. R. Nelson's resolutions at the Greeneville convention, and perhaps to rationalize his own actions, Temple condemned Unionist rebellion in 1861 as an affront to law and order. For Temple, civil strife and lawlessness, not Unionists or Confederates, bore the burden of the evils that haunted East Tennessee during the Civil War.

There was yet another division in East Tennessee to be healed, however. Temple, accepting the prevailing ethnic explanations for mountaineer distinctiveness, actually attributed the heroic history of East Tennessee to the Scots-Irish heritage of East Tennesseans. Reminiscent of antebellum distinctions, the aging author also differentiated between the inhabitants of the valley and of the mountains, declaring that "the people dwelling in this territory above the valley are a genuine mountain race." He explained that someone meeting the mountain people would find a lack of education, few material comforts, low intelligence, and "in some localities, a deplorable state of morals," but, he continued, "this is not the general and certainly not the universal, condition. On the contrary, a majority of the people have due respect for the Sabbath, love of the Bible, regularly attend church and Sunday school, and outwardly observe in their humble walks the common decencies and proprieties of civilized life." Anyone expecting to see "wild, uncivilized savages, would surely be disappointed." Indeed, Temple decried writers North and South who "represent the people of this region as being ignorant, immoral, intemperate, and lawless" and "find in this region a people scarcely known to those of us familiar with it from our infancy."

His third chapter presented material on education, religion, and life on the frontier in an effort to challenge prominent theories relating contemporary mountain whites to uncultured forbearers and to demonstrate that "the first settlers of East Tennessee were an educated people and the friends of education." William Goodell Frost and O. O. Howard argued that mountaineers merited education and the benevolence of northern donors, who by the late nineteenth century had grown weary of the repercussions of war; Temple asserted that East Tennesseans, even mountaineers, were worthy of similar benevolence: "A new race of men is in the lead. These are the men who, with the aid of Confederate soldiers, are helping to push the state forward, and saving it from retrogression. Contrary to all expectations, the war made the soldiers of both armies better citizens." Reconciliation required that the divisions rent by the Civil War be obscured, but even as he reinterpreted the meaning of the war, Temple clung to the idea that East Tennessee's Unionism defined the region and made it worthy of recognition.[31]

As in antebellum decades, it was perhaps in the realm of politics that the role of East Tennessee's peculiar history gained its fullest expression. Few East Tennessee politicians used East Tennessee's past to greater advantage than did Walter P. Brownlow. Born in 1851 in Abingdon, Virginia, Brownlow had only three years of formal education before running away at thirteen to try joining a federal cavalry unit. After failing to be enlisted, he trekked to Nashville to seek aid from his uncle, Gov. William G. Brownlow, who refused to help his nephew. After a varied series of jobs, Brownlow purchased the *Jonesboro Herald and Tribune* and soon after began his political ascent. In a series of positions that included doorkeeper of the House and superintendent of the Senate Folding Room, Brownlow used every opportunity to secure loyalty in the First Congressional District and among southern Republicans. After being elected to Congress from the First Congressional District of Tennessee in 1896, Brownlow secured large quantities of federal favors for his constituents, especially Union veterans.[32]

In 1900 Brownlow put forward legislation to create a branch of the National Home for Volunteer Soldiers at Johnson City, Tennessee. When news reached Johnson City, the Democratic editor of *The Comet*, Cy Lyle, lauded the Brownlow measure, claiming that its strength was "the poetic justice in the proposition that it should be located in East Tennessee, the great mountain union stronghold of the south." Initially, the managing board of the soldiers' home rejected Brownlow's plan, but Brownlow arranged a five-minute meeting with the board, and once before them repeated the oft-told story of East Tennessee's loyalty during the Civil War. After only three minutes, according to the editor of *The Comet*, the board adopted Brownlow's proposal unanimously and increased the funding requested from a quarter million to a million dollars. At Brownlow's suggestion, Lyle quickly collected funds from "cheerful citizens" so that the Johnson City Board of Trade could print and mail 10,000 copies of the board's report to every Grand Army of the Republic post in the country. When Brownlow's bill came before the House of Representatives in January 1901, only one representative spoke against the bill, and the House passed it unanimously. Government expenditures on the Mountain Branch of the National Home for Volunteer Soldiers amounted to $1.8 million. Visitors to the home brought $30,000 annually to Johnson City, and inmates, as residents were called, brought more than $40,000 in pensions.[33]

Still, Brownlow wanted more. In 1906 Brownlow persuaded Congress to accept from the descendants of Andrew Johnson ten acres in Greeneville that contained the grave of the former president and to establish Johnson's grave and the adjoining land as a fourth-class national cemetery. The following year he attached a request for funds for the improvement of the cemetery to a civil appropriations bill. When a northern representative moved that Brownlow's request be removed from the bill because only four Union soldiers were buried there, Brownlow responded with what the *New York Times* called a "ringing oration of five minutes on the patriotism of Andrew Johnson." "The First Congressional District of Tennessee," thundered Brownlow, who seldom spoke on the floor of the House, "furnished more soldiers to the Union service during the dark days of the rebellion than any Congressional district in the United States; and yet we were 100 miles inside the Confederate lines." Continued Brownlow, "Oh, Mr. Chairman, when these soldiers left Eastern Tennessee they were followed by bloodhounds; they bid their wives, their daughters, and their sweethearts good-bye by moonlight at the old home spring and went across the mountains into Kentucky and joined the Union Army." Then Brownlow expressed indignation that "here from this Northern section of the country comes the opposition to doing honor to these people of the mountains who were loyal to the cause of the Union." Finally, calling Johnson the "only Senator of his party, North or South, that stood by Abraham Lincoln" and "taking his surroundings and his acts and comparing them," Brownlow asserted his belief that Johnson was "the greatest patriot of the civil war." Brownlow's speech saved the $32,000 appropriation.[34]

At each step in the mythologizing process, the image of Unionist East Tennessee served the purposes of myth by constructing a history that reinforced a sense of unity with northern audiences and northern capital while obfuscating the complexities and divisions within East Tennessee. Walter

Brownlow's defense of Johnson, like the mythologized history of East Tennessee that he utilized, was more than a bid for funds and northern benevolence; it was a rallying point for East Tennesseans jealous of their pride and sensitive to slights made against them, and thus a means of maintaining unity. In September 1908 Congressman Brownlow published "Defense and Vindication of Andrew Johnson" in the *Taylor-Trotwood Magazine,* in which he disputed assertions made about Johnson's character and personal habits, and he challenged critics who spoke "sneeringly of Mr. Johnson as having sprung from the 'poor whites' of the South." At the time of his death in 1875, national opinion of Andrew Johnson remained overwhelmingly negative, but by the 1908 centennial of Johnson's birth an effort was underway to rehabilitate the image of the East Tennessean. According to the *New York Times,* Johnson "was a type of the true American of his hour, of lowly birth, of great courage and tenacity of purpose, of high ideals. He served his State and country well in many offices, local and National." On May 31, 1909, thousands of East Tennesseans attended the first memorial celebration held in the National Cemetery. Martin Littleton, a member of the House of Representatives from New York and a native of East Tennessee, addressed the crowd and predicted that "the day would come when the entire country would do homage to his [Johnson's] memory."[35]

In 1959 and again in 1961, the future Republican congressman from the First Congressional District, Jimmy Quillen, proposed to the Tennessee legislature the resurrection of the State of Franklin. In his 1961 bill he spoke of East Tennessee as being "composed of the descendants of those great men who originally carved out of a wilderness the State of Franklin, which said section of the State is indigenous to the stalwart characteristics and qualities of leadership which contributed so greatly to the establishment and preservation of our nation." Like so many East Tennesseans, Quillen utilized the history of East Tennessee in a struggle against perceived inequity. Mythically, the State of Franklin was a symbol of resistance to faraway state governments on behalf of liberty, but as the memorialists of Unionist East Tennessee recognized, history often proved to be more complicated than myth. It was ironic, perhaps—and telling—that it was Andrew Johnson, the great commoner and a First Congressional District congressman, who in 1841 proposed the revival of the State of Franklin and who fit neatly into neither the Republican nor the Democratic Party. He died in Carter County, Tennessee, near the town of Elizabethton, where two hundred years after Johnson's birth producers of *Hillbilly: The Real Story* filmed the cast of *Liberty!* at Sycamore Shoals, where the Wataugans mustered for King's Mountain and where in 1861 East Tennessee Unionists awaited the arrival of a federal army that never came.[36]

Notes

1. "Making History Channel," *Johnson City (TN) Press,* September 18, 2007, 1A, 8A.

2. William Goodell Frost, "Our Contemporary Ancestors in the Southern Mountains," *Atlantic Monthly* 83 (March 1899), 313–14; Eric Russell Lacy, *Vanquished Volunteers: East Tennessee Sectionalism from Statehood to Secession* (Johnson City: East Tennessee State University Press, 1965), 189; W. Todd Groce, *Mountain Rebels: East Tennessee Confederates and the Civil War, 1860–1870* (Knoxville: University of Tennessee Press, 1999), 156; Kenneth W. Noe, "'Deadened Color and Colder Horror': Rebecca Harding Davis and the Myth of Unionist Appalachia," in *Back Talk from Appalachia: Confronting Stereotypes,* ed. Dwight Billlings, Gurney Norman, and Katherine Ledford (Lexington: University Press of Kentucky, 1999), 68; Henry D. Shapiro, *Appalachia On Our Mind: The Southern Mountains and Mountaineers in the American Consciousness, 1870–1920* (Chapel Hill: University of North Carolina Press, 1978), 86. For analysis of Appalachian Unionism, see: Martin Crawford, *Ashe County's Civil War: Community and Society in the Appalachian South,* A Nation Divided: New Studies in Civil War History (Charlottesville: University of Virginia Press, 2001), 142; Kenneth W. Noe, *Southwest Virginia's Railroad: Modernization and the Sectional Crisis* (Urbana: University of Illinois Press, 1994), 20–30; Jonathan Dean Sarris, *A Separate Civil War: Communities in Conflict in the Mountain South* (Charlottesville: University of Virginia Press, 2006), 9, 79; and Brian D. McKnight, *Contested Borderland: The Civil War in Appalachian Kentucky and Virginia* (Lexington: University Press of Kentucky, 2006), 225–35.

3. Theodore Roosevelt, *The Winning of the West,* vol. 2, *From the Alleghanies to the Mississippi, 1777–1783* (New York and London: G.P. Putnam's Sons, 1889; New York: Knickerbocker Press, 1912), 214, 221, 294; Nina Silber, "'What Does America Need So Much as Americans?': Race and Northern Reconciliation with Southern Appalachia, 1870–1900," in John C. Inscoe, ed., *Appalachians and Race: The Mountain South from Slavery to Segregation* (Lexington: University Press of Kentucky, 2001), 245–258, 246; Shannon H. Wilson, "Lincoln's Sons and Daughters: Berea College, Lincoln Memorial University, and the Myth of Unionist Appalachia, 1866–1910," in Kenneth W. Noe and Shannon H. Wilson, eds., *The Civil War in Appalachia: Collected Essays* (Knoxville: University of Tennessee Press, 1997), 243; Shapiro, *Appalachia,* 91–92; Frost, "Our Contemporary Ancestors," 313.

4. Frost, "Our Contemporary Ancestors," 319.

5. David Blight, *Race and Reunion: The Civil War in American Memory* (Cam-

bridge, MA: Belknap Press of Harvard University Press, 2001), 1–5; Wilson, "Lincoln's Sons and Daughters," 242–44, 248.

6. "A College for Mountaineers," *New York Times,* May 23, 1899; "Topics of the Times," *New York Times,* October 26, 1902; Wilson, "Lincoln's Sons and Daughters," 245, 259.

7. Max Dixon, *The Wataugans* (Nashville: Tennessee American Revolution Bicentennial Commission, 1976), 4–11, 55–61; Brenda C. Calloway, *America's First Western Frontier: East Tennessee* (Johnson City, TN: Overmountain Press, 1989), 27–28, 40; Robert E. Corlew, *Tennessee: A Short History,* 2nd ed. (Knoxville: University of Tennessee Press, 1990), 41, 62–69.

8. Noel B. Gerson, *Franklin: America's "Lost State"* (New York: Crowell-Collier Press, 1968), 18–26.

9. William and Nancy Thomason to William and James Moore and Families, November 23, 1842, Moore Family Papers, Moore-Ward Correspondence, McClung Collection, Knox County Public Library, Knoxville, Tennessee; "Mines, Minerals, and Manufacturing in East Tennessee," *DeBow's Commercial Review,* 17 (1854): 303; J. G. M Ramsey, *The Annals of Tennessee to the End of the Eighteenth Century* (Knoxville: East Tennessee Historical Society, 1967), 298; Samuel Cole Williams, "The Journal of Events of David A. Deaderick, 1825–1873, I," *East Tennessee Historical Society's Publications* 8 (1936): 132–33; Charles Faulkner Bryan, "The Civil War in East Tennessee" (PhD diss., University of Tennessee, 1978), 12; *Goodspeed's General History of Tennessee* (Nashville: Goodspeed Publishing Company, 1887; Nashville: Charles and Randy Elder Booksellers, 1973), 361; David C. Hsiung, *Two Worlds in the Tennessee Mountains: Exploring the Origins of Appalachian Stereotypes* (Lexington: University Press of Kentucky, 1997), 97, 98; Tom D. Lee, "Continuity and Change in Washington County, Tennessee, 1835–1885" (master's thesis, Wake Forest University, 1993), 20; Susanna Delfino, "Antebellum East Tennessee Elites and Industrialization: The Examples of the Iron Industry and Internal Improvements," *East Tennessee Historical Society's Publications* 56–57 (1984–1985): 102–19; David Hsiung, "How Isolated Was Appalachia? Upper East Tennessee, 1780–1835," *Appalachian Journal* 16, no. 4 (Summer 1989), 346; V. N. (Bud) Phillips, *Bristol, Tennessee/Virginia: A History—1852–1900* (Johnson City, TN: Overmountain Press, 1992), 3, 4, 25–36; William H. Nicholls, "Some Foundations of Economic Development in the Upper East Tennessee Valley, 1850–1900," *Journal of Political Economy* 64, no. 4 (August 1956): 287; Paul Fink, "The Bumpass Cove Mines and Embreeville," *East Tennessee Historical Society's Publications* 16 (1944): 54–55; Corlew, *Tennessee,* 149–83; Gerson, *Franklin,* 18–20; Calloway, *America's First Western Frontier,* 120–22; Lacy, *Vanquished Volunteers,* 183; Groce, *Mountain Rebels,* 4–5.

10. *Knoxville (TN) Register,* February 23, 1848; Durwood Dunn, *An Abolitionist in the Appalachian South: Ezekiel Birdseye on Slavery, Capitalism, and Separate Statehood in East Tennessee, 1841–1846* (Knoxville: University of Tennessee Press, 1997), 3–25; Gavin Wright, *Old South, New South: Revolutions in the Southern*

Economy since the Civil War (New York: Basic Books, 1986), 19–21; J. W. Holland, "The Building of the East Tennessee and Virginia Railroad," *East Tennessee Historical Society's Publications* 4 (1932): 83–101; Stanley J. Folmsbee, *Sectionalism and Internal Improvements in Tennessee, 1796–1845* (Knoxville: East Tennessee Historical Society, 1939), 116–18, 131; Constantine Bellissary, "Industry and Industrial Philosophy in Tennessee, 1850–1860," *East Tennessee Historical Society's Publications* 28 (1956): 46–57; James W. Bellamy, "The Political Career of Landon Carter Haynes," *East Tennessee Historical Society's Publications* 28 (1956): 102–26; Lee, "Continuity and Change in Washington County," 38; Bryan, "Civil War," 19; Groce, *Mountain Rebels,* 6–7; Lacy, *Vanquished Volunteers,* 54, 100–101.

   11. Andrew Johnson, "Resolutions for the Establishment of the State of Frankland," in Leroy P. Grad and Ralph W. Hoskins, eds., *The Papers of Andrew Johnson* (Knoxville: University of Tennessee Press, 1972), 1:61; Stanley J. Folmsbee, "The Beginnings of the Railroad Movement in Tennessee," *East Tennessee Historical Society's Publications* 5 (1933): 87; Dunn, *Ezekiel Birdseye,* 3–25; Lacy, *Vanquished Volunteers,* 114, 115, 122.

   12. James W. McKee, "Alfred E. Jackson: A Profile of an East Tennessee Entrepreneur, Railway Promoter, and Soldier," *East Tennessee Historical Society's Publications* 49 (January 1977): 34–35; Constantine Belissary, "Industry and Industrial Philosophy in Tennessee, 1850–1860," *East Tennessee Historical Society's Publications* 23 (1951): 46–57; Lacy, *Vanquished Volunteers,* 54, 100–101; Folmsbee, *Sectionalism,* 9, 116–18, 131; Hsiung, *Two Worlds,* 186–87; Bryan, "Civil War," 12–13, 19; Wright, *Old South, New South,* 19–21; Groce, *Mountain Rebels,* 6–7; Delfino, "Antebellum East Tennessee Elites," 110–12; Williams, "Deaderick," 133.

   13. *Knoxville (TN) Register,* February 23, 1848; Lee, "Continuity and Change in Washington County," 38; Hsiung, *Two Worlds,* 124, 186–87.

   14. William Cullom, Esq., Monroe, TN, to Dear Son, November 18, 1860, Acc. 180, 5:3, Correspondence 1845–65, Murray Family Papers, Archives of Appalachia, East Tennessee State University, Johnson City, Tennessee (hereafter Murray Family Papers); Paul H. Bergeron, Stephen V. Ash, and Jeanette Keith, *Tennesseans and Their History* (Knoxville: University of Tennessee Press, 1999), 36, 37, 133, 134; Kyle Osborn, "'Bondage or Barbarism,' Parson Brownlow and the Rhetoric of Racism in East Tennessee, 1845–1867" (master's thesis, East Tennessee State University, 2007), 38–61; Robert Tracy McKenzie, *Lincolnites and Rebels: A Divided Town in the American Civil War* (New York: Oxford University Press, 2006), 63; Thomas B. Alexander, *Thomas A. R. Nelson of Tennessee* (Nashville: Tennessee Historical Commission, 1956), 74; John Savage, *The Life and Public Services of Andrew Johnson, Seventeenth President of the United States* (New York: Derby, Miller, Publishers, 1866), 111; Lacy, *Vanquished Volunteers,* 128, 165, 166, 168–69, 175, 181.

   15. J. Milton Henry, "The Revolution in Tennessee, February, 1861, to June, 1861," *Tennessee Historical Quarterly* 18 (June 1959), 104–19; Charles F. Bryan, "A Gathering of Tories: The East Tennessee Convention of 1861," *Tennessee Historical*

Quarterly 39, no. 1 (Spring 1980): 39, 46; Daniel W. Crofts, *Reluctant Confeder-ates: Upper South Unionists in the Secession Crisis* (Chapel Hill: University of North Carolina Press, 1989), 21–25, 341–52; Bergeron, Ash, and Keith, *Tennesseans,* 136; McKenzie, *Lincolnites and Rebels,* 82, 131; Alexander, *Thomas A. R. Nelson,* 75–78; Lacy, *Vanquished Volunteers,* 177, 180, 217.

16. Oliver Perry Temple, *East Tennessee and the Civil War* (Nashville, TN: Fisk University Black Heritage Library Collection, 1899; Freeport, NY: Books for Libraries Press, 1971), 347, 359, 361; Bergeron, Ash, and Keith, *Tennesseans,* 139; Lacy, *Vanquished Volunteers,* 181, 182. See also John C. Inscoe, "Mountain Unionism, Secession, and Regional Self-Image: The Contrasting Cases of West-ern North Carolina and East Tennessee," in *Looking South: Chapters in the Story of an American Region,* ed. Winfred B. Moore Jr. and Joseph Tripp (Westport, CT: Greenwood, 1989), 115–29.

17. Albert G. Graham to Jefferson Davis, November 12, 1861, in Lynda Lass-well Crist and Mary Seaton Dix, eds., *The Papers of Jefferson Davis* (Baton Rouge: Louisiana State University Press, 1992), 7:411; William Rule, *The Loyalists of Ten-nessee in the Late War* (Cincinnati: H. C. Sherick & Co., 1887), 9–10; Noel Fisher, *War at Every Door: Partisan Politics and Guerrilla Violence in East Tennessee, 1860–1869* (Chapel Hill: University of North Carolina Press, 1997), 4, 44, 52–61, 123; Hans L. Trefousse, *Andrew Johnson: A Biography* (New York: W.W. Norton, 1997), 142–43, 146; Richard Nelson Current, *Lincoln's Loyalists: Union Soldiers from the Confederacy* (Boston: Northeastern University Press, 1992), 29; William W. Freeh-ling, *The South vs. The South: How Anti-Confederate Southerners Shaped the Course of the Civil War* (New York: Oxford University Press, 2001), 201; William Charles Harris, *With Charity for All: Lincoln and the Restoration of the Union* (Lexing-ton: University Press of Kentucky, 1997), 33; Lacy, *Vanquished Volunteers,* 181; Bergeron, Ash, and Keith, *Tennesseans,* 142.

18. N. C. Baldwin, Washington Co., VA, to Dear Father, September 30, 1864, Acc. 180, 5:3, Correspondence 1845–65, Murray Family Papers; Landon C. Haynes, Knoxville, TN, to Jefferson Davis, January 27, 1862, in Crist and Dix, eds., *The Papers of Jefferson Davis,* 8:29; M. S. Temple, Greeneville, to O. P. Temple, October 4, 1864, MS-21, 2:6, O. P. Temple Papers, Special Collections, Hoskins Library, University of Tennessee, Knoxville (hereafter O. P. Temple Papers); "Ref-ugees from East Tennessee," *New York Times,* August 9, 1863; Thomas William Humes, *The Loyal Mountaineers of Tennessee* (Knoxville, TN: Ogden Brothers & Co., 1888; Spartanburg, SC: The Reprint Company, 1974), 139, 299, 301; Groce, *Mountain Rebels,* xv; McKenzie, *Lincolnites and Rebels,* 220–21.

19. W. G. Brownlow, *Sketches of the Rise, Progress, and Decline of Secession* (Philadelphia: George Childs, 1862), 6–8; James Welch Patton, *Unionism and Reconstruction in Tennessee, 1860–1869* (Chapel Hill: University of North Caro-lina Press, 1934), 68–69; Robert Tracy McKenzie, "Contesting Secession: Parson Brownlow and the Rhetoric of Proslavery Unionism, 1860–1861," *Civil War His-tory* 48, no. 4 (December 2002): 294; Lacy K. Ford Jr., *Origins of Southern Radi-*

calism: The South Carolina Upcountry, 1800–1860 (New York: Oxford University Press, 1988), 372.

20. Edward Everett, *Account of the Fund for the Relief of East Tennessee* (Boston: Little, Brown, and Company, 1864), 7; *Report to the Contributors to the Pennsylvania Relief Association for East Tennessee* (Philadelphia: Printed for the Association, 1864), 6; Oliver P. Temple, *Notable Men of Tennessee from 1833 to 1875: Their Times and Their Contemporaries,* comp. Mary B. Temple (New York: Cosmopolitan Press, 1912), 198–99, 202; Humes, *Loyal Mountaineers,* 309, 311.

21. Everett, *Account,* 12–13, 15; Temple, *Notable Men,* 200.

22. "Refugees from East Tennessee," *New York Times,* August 9, 1863; Everett, *Account,* 10, 11, 16, 20, 31, 32; *Pennsylvania Relief Association,* 7, 8; Humes, *Loyal Mountaineers,* 317, 318, 322, 323; Martha L. Turner, "The Cause of the Union in East Tennessee," *Tennessee Historical Quarterly* 40, no. 4 (Winter 1981): 366–80.

23. Henry Hoss, Jonesboro, to O. P. Temple, December 14, December 20, 1866, 2:22; George Grisham, Jonesboro, to O. P. Temple, April 21, 1868, 2:30; A. E. Jackson, Abingdon, VA, to O. P. Temple, June 16, 1866, 2:20; A. E. Jackson, Jonesboro, TN, to O. P. Temple, November 20, 1871, 2:45; and O. P. Temple, Knoxville, to General A. E. Jackson, Jonesboro, December 14, 1871, all in O. P. Temple Papers. I. Harris, Pulaski, VA, to Dr. Murray, September 2, 1866, Acc. 180, 5:4; N. C. B., near Marion, VA, to Dear Father, October 1, 1866, Acc. 180, 5:4; N. C. Baldwin, Friendship, Virginia, to Dear Father, September 21, 1865, Acc. 180, 5:3; G. L. Burson, Washington City, to Dear Bro. and Sister, September 22, 1865, Acc. 180, 5:3; Receipt from Marshall's Sale, October 5, 1867, Acc. 180, 4:6; and Ephriam Murray to E. F. French, serving Auditor of the Treasury, Washington, DC, February 8, 1869, all in Murray Family Papers. "Dividing the State of Tennessee," *New York Times,* March 21, 1864; *Acts of the State of Tennessee Passed by the General Assembly Passed at the First Session for the Years 1851–2* (Nashville: Bang and McKennie, Printers to the State, 1852), 439; "Legal 'Chancery Sale of Land,'" *Jonesboro (TN) Herald and Tribune,* February 29, 1872; David Abshire, *The South Rejects a Prophet: The Life of Senator D. M. Key, 1824–1900* (New York: Frederick A. Praeger, 1967), 175–76; John Cimprich, "Slavery's End in East Tennessee," in John C. Inscoe, ed. *Appalachians and Race: The Mountain South from Slavery to Segregation,* 189–98 (Lexington: University Press of Kentucky, 2001); Ray Stahl, *Greater Johnson City: A Pictoral History* (Norfolk, VA: Doning, 1983), 43; Williams, "Journal of Events," 108; Harris, *With Charity for All,* 215, 216; Groce, *Mountain Rebels,* 119, 147; Fisher, *War at Every Door,* 160–65.

24. "Captain Chamberlain Dead," *New York Times,* March 16, 1916; Ronald D Eller, *Miners, Millhands, and Mountaineers: Industrialization of the Appalachian South, 1880–1930* (Knoxville: University of Tennessee Press, 1982), 48–52; Constantine Belissary, "The Rise of Industry and the Industrial Spirit in Tennessee, 1865–1885," *Journal of Southern History* 19 (May 1953): 198, 202, 204; Michael J. McDonald and William Bruce Wheeler, "The Communities of East Tennessee," *East Tennessee Historical Society's Publications* 58–59 (1986–1987): 12; Nicholls,

"Some Foundations," 288; Bergeron, Ash, and Keith, *Tennesseans,* 189; Belissary, "Rise of Industry," 207. In the 1870s, capital invested in industry increased by some 400 percent.

25. "North Carolina Western Railroads," *Rail Road Journal and Family Visitor,* February 11, 1854; Thirty-fourth General Assembly, *Acts of the State of Tennessee, 1865–66* (Nashville: S.C. Mercer, 1866), 260; North Carolina General Assembly, *Public Laws and Resolutions Together with the Private Laws of the State of North Carolina, 1872–1873* (Raleigh: Stone and Uzzell, 1873), 454; *Records of the Proceedings of the Chancery Court, Elizabethton, Tennessee, in Regards to the Sale of the East Tennessee and Western North Carolina Railroad,* 1–2, East Tennessee and Western North Carolina Railroad Collection, Miscellaneous File, Archives of Appalachia; "Good for Johnson City E.T. & W.N.C.R.R.," *Jonesboro (TN) Herald and Tribune,* August 12, 1875; "Bristol Enterprise," *Bristol (TN) News,* January 13, 1874; Daniel W. Barefoot, *General Robert F. Hoke: Lee's Modest Warrior* (Winston-Salem, NC: John F. Blair, 1996), 335; Mallory H. Ferrell, *Tweetsie Country: The East Tennessee and Western North Carolina Railroad* (Boulder, CO: Pruett Publishing Co., 1976), 1–5; Nancy Susan Reynolds, *Reynolds Homestead, 1814–1970,* ed. Nannie M. Tilley (Richmond, VA: Robert Kline and Company, 1970), 48–49; Barbara Babcock Millhouse, ed., *Recollections of Major A. D. Reynolds, 1847–1925* (Winston-Salem, NC: Reynolds House, 1978), 28; Robert S. Loving, *Double Destiny: The Story of Bristol, Tennessee-Virginia* (Bristol, TN: King Printing Co., 1955), 158, 160, 206; C. J. Harkrader, *Witness to an Epoch* (Kingsport, TN: Kingsport Press, Inc., 1965), 201, 206–7; Patrick Reynolds, *The Gilded Leaf: Triumph, Tragedy, and Tobacco: Three Generations of the R. J. Reynolds Family and Fortune* (Boston: Little, Brown, 1989), 51; Phillips, *Bristol, Tennessee/Virginia,* 88–90, 92, 243.

26. "Two Hundred Civil War Veterans Attend Annual Reunion," *Bristol (TN) Herald Courier,* September 16, 1915; "Bristol Will Pay Tribute to Major Reynolds Today," *Bristol (TN) Herald Courier,* Friday Morning, September 25, 1925, p. 1; J. G. M. Ramsey, *The Iliad of Patriotism,* reprinted in Frederick Saunders, ed., *Our National Centennial Jubilee: Orations, Addresses, and Poems Delivered on the Fourth of July in the Several States of the Union* (New York: E.B. Treat, 1877), 543; "Address of the Centennial Executive Committee of East Tennessee," *Jonesboro (TN) Herald and Tribune,* June 10, 1875; Lyman C. Draper, *King's Mountain and Its Heroes* (Cincinnati: Peter G. Thomson, Publisher, 1881), iv; Paul M. Gaston, *The New South Creed: A Study in Southern Mythmaking* (Baton Rouge: Louisiana State University Press, 1970), 52, 67, 168–69, 173; Charles Reagan Wilson, *Baptized in Blood: The Religion of the Lost Cause, 1865–1920* (Athens: University of Georgia Press, 1980), 1, 145–46, 151, 164–66; Roosevelt, *Winning of the West,* 221; Groce, *Mountain Rebels,* 156.

27. Rule, *Loyalists of Tennessee,* 3, 4, 6–7; Current, *Lincoln's Loyalists,* 211.

28. Rule, *Loyalists of Tennessee,* 17, 19, 21–23.

29. Humes, *Loyal Mountaineers,* 8–9, 35, 37, 64, 304–5. East Tennessee University is now the University of Tennessee, Knoxville.

30. Temple, *East Tennessee*, vii, 530–31; McKenzie, *Lincolnites and Rebels*, 130.

31. Temple, *East Tennessee*, 63, 71, 80, 527.

32. Helen Still Beeson, "Walter P. Brownlow, Republican" (master's thesis, East Tennessee State University, 1967), 75.

33. "Rural Free Delivery," *Journal and Tribune* (Knoxville, TN), November 24, 1900; "Thanks to Brownlow," *The Comet* (Johnson City, TN), January 24, 1901; "East Tennessee Claim for a Home Strong Points for the Brownlow Bill," *The Comet* (Johnson City, TN), February 22, 1900; "Johnson City Will Get Branch Soldiers' Home," *The Comet* (Johnson City, TN), January 24, 1901; "Are Feeling Very Good," *Knoxville (TN) Journal*, January 22, 1901; John Lewis Gillin, *Poverty and Dependency: Their Relief and Prevention*, The Century Social Science Series (New York: The Century Company, 1921), 443; Beeson, "Brownlow," 3, 4, 6–9, 11, 14, 20, 23, 25, 34, 88–89, 90–93, 96–98, 103, 107, 109–11. It is worth noting that the land for the Mountain Branch of the Home for Disabled Volunteer Soldiers was purchased from J. P. Lyle, a Confederate veteran from Washington County. See Linda Vance Gordon, "Johnson City," in *History of Washington County, Tennessee,* ed. Joyce and W. Eugene Cox (Jonesborough, TN: Washington County Historical Association, 2001), 664–68.

34. "Andrew Johnson Eulogized," *New York Times*, February 24, 1907; Beeson, "Brownlow," 99–101.

35. "Honor Andrew Johnson," *New York Times*, June 1, 1909; "The Family of Andrew Johnson," *New York Times*, March 15, 1884; Walter P. Brownlow, "Defense and Vindication of Andrew Johnson," *The Taylor-Trotwood Magazine* (September 1908): 493, 501–2.

36. "Truck Measure in House for Consideration," *Kingsport (TN) Times,* March 10, 1959; "State of Franklin May Rise Again," *Kingsport (TN) Times-News,* March 5, 1961; S. D. Gilbreath, Homestead Hotel, Kingsport, TN, to Dear Jimmie, March 10, 1959, Acc. 498, 492:3, James H. Quillen Collection, Archives of Appalachia; James H. Quillen to Honorable H. Nick Johnson, Senator, Twenty-first District, Harlan, Kentucky, Acc. 498, 492:3, James H. Quillen Collection, Archives of Appalachia; "An Act entitled an Act to establish and create the territory of Franklin, and to authorize said territory to petition for admittance as the 51st sovereign State of the United States of America," typed manuscript, Acc. 498, 492:3, James H. Quillen Collection, Archives of Appalachia.

Chapter 12

"A Northern Wedge Thrust into the Heart of the Confederacy"

Explaining Civil War Loyalties in the Age of Appalachian Discovery, 1900–1921

John C. Inscoe

The first comprehensive codification of southern Appalachian life and culture came in the early twentieth century. Regional commentaries through much of the nineteenth century had been primarily travel narratives, first-hand descriptions of scenic vistas and flora and fauna along with observations of the often quaint customs and folk life of southern highlanders, or local-color writing, which conveyed much of the same in fictional form.[1] But by the turn of the century, these impressionistic, localized, and often anecdotal accounts began to give way to more serious and systematic ethnographic assessments of mountain people by missionaries, social workers, and academics. The work of Horace Kephart, William G. Frost, John C. Campbell, Emma Bell Miles, and others quickly became the foundational base for much of the way in which twentieth-century America came to know and understand the highland South.[2] Because of these writers' scholarly credentials and commitment to the region and its residents, their characterizations of its populace—even while perpetuating already established generalizations, distortions, and stereotypes—gave their work a credibility and endurance that came to be scrutinized and challenged only toward the end of the twentieth century.

Curiously, the Civil War played a relatively small role in this particular body of work on southern Appalachia. Only four or five decades removed

from the conflict, and at a time when an obsession with "the late unpleas-
antness" manifested itself in the ideological and ceremonial trappings of
the Lost Cause throughout much of the rest of the former Confederacy,
the war's legacy became increasingly simplistic, vague, and detached from
historical context in the masterworks of this age of Appalachian discovery. And yet, even given the minimalist treatment accorded the war by so
many of these writers, almost all of them drew upon the issue of Southern
highlanders' wartime loyalties as one means of gauging or explaining the
character and ways of life of their subjects—sometimes in positive ways,
sometimes negative.

Henry Shapiro was the first modern scholar to seriously consider how
the war's legacy was carefully shaped by Appalachians seeking to portray
themselves and their region in a beneficial light. In his seminal *Appalachia on Our Mind* (1978), Shapiro suggests that there had been a concerted
effort in the immediate postwar years to downplay or avoid any reference
to the war in the outpouring of writings on the Southern highlands that
appeared in the popular press. Only from about the mid-1880s did region-
alists come to acknowledge highlanders' role in the war, and then only as
Unionists, whose loyalty became a valuable means of winning favor for
southern mountaineers as integral parts of the nation at large.[3]

More recent scholars have offered other perspectives on treatments
of wartime Appalachia during the 1870s and 1880s. In perhaps the most
pointed treatment of the "myth" of Unionist Appalachia, Kenneth Noe
has examined how and why "the southern mountains' slaves and Johnny
Rebs [were] swept under the nation's intellectual rug." Looking at popular
fiction produced in the first two postwar decades, Noe demonstrates that
the war was not as ignored as Shapiro and others had claimed and that the
assumption of a solidly Unionist Appalachia was not yet firmly in place, as
indicated by portrayals of loyalist individuals and families as beleaguered
minorities in Confederate-dominated parts of the region.[4] Shannon Wilson
has explored more self-conscious efforts by educators within Appalachia to
cast the region as a bulwark of patriotism and loyalty to the Union cause,
and even to embrace Abraham Lincoln himself as a product and reflection of highland character and virtues.[5] James Klotter and Nina Silber have
explored the perceived "whiteness" of southern Appalachians after the war
as explanations for its attraction to northern social workers and philanthropists, but only Silber made wartime loyalties a significant part of her
analysis.[6]

Yet none of these scholars pushed their examination of these issues past the turn of the century to examine how the far more influential writings of that era incorporated the Civil War into their portraits of the region and its people.[7] While the trends detected in late-nineteenth-century accounts of the war are very much in evidence in the outpouring of writing in the early twentieth century, significant variables emerge in that work as well that reflect newly evolved agendas and perspectives by this next generation of Appalachian chroniclers.

Several traits distinguish this new era of scholarship from the travel writing and local-color fiction of previous decades. By the end of the nineteenth century, Henry Shapiro has noted, "the 'old-fashioned' quality of mountain life seemed to demand explanation, both as an abstract problem and as an aspect of the American dialogue on the nature of American civilization." This in turn led to a redefinition of Appalachia as a discrete region of the nation and its residents as a distinct population, and with it an assumption of a social and cultural coherence and homogeneity throughout this vast geographical entity that embraced parts of at least seven different states. From these new perceptions emerged a different stage of Appalachian portraiture that was far more systematic in its attempts to embrace the region as a whole.[8]

Just as they claimed to portray the region as a whole, these writers were also far more inclusive of the regional experience they chose to document. Adopting an ethnographic approach taking shape among academics at the turn of the century, they devoted chapters or sections of their books to a vast range of topics such as religion, language, folkways, kinship, community, and work, as well as moonshine, humor, and other "quaint" attributes of southern Appalachian life. Several worked from the assumption that southern highlanders had little sense of their own history, and they themselves vary in terms of their own use of the historical past as explanatory forces in assessing mountain life and culture.

Most of these new chroniclers were sympathetic toward their subjects; some displayed outright affection for mountaineers and admiration for their stalwart traditions, love of land, and the simplicity of their lifestyles. While they often portrayed mountain life and attitudes in bemused or condescending tones, they saw themselves as advocates for and often defenders of this perceived constituency. Closely related to this attitude is the other biggest distinction in their writing over that of previous decades: all of these writers had specific agendas that drove their writings and shaped their characterizations for particular readerships. As ministers, educators, social workers, or merely as scholars, they sought to portray mountain people as worthy of attention and of help, whether philanthropic, educational, or mission-driven. Some saw themselves as culture brokers who sought to preserve and promote the distinctive music, folklore, and handicrafts of which they themselves had become so enamored. In whatever form of "uplift" their agendas took, these writers looked to northern readers, benefactors, and organizations as the primary targets of the books and articles they produced. Although their characterization of highland life was basically presentist in outlook and emphasis, they also had to acknowledge the Civil War and to explain the role of Southern highlander participants in ways conducive to what were, in effect, elaborate sales pitches on their behalf.

The most seminal of these works was not a book, but a mere eight-page article. Published in 1899 in the *Atlantic Monthly*, William Goodell Frost's "Our Contemporary Ancestors in the Southern Mountains" embodies almost all of these traits and served as an influential model for much of the subsequent scholarship on the region.[9] The grandson of an abolitionist and the son of a Congregational minister in upstate New York, Frost was educated and then taught at Oberlin College before moving to Berea College in Kentucky, which he served as president from 1892 to 1920. His leadership had much to do with reviving the college, which had faced serious setbacks in the postwar decades in terms of finances and enrollment. By shifting its mission and identity from a biracial student body to one that served the sons and daughters of Appalachia to its east, Frost made himself one of the era's most influential spokesmen for educating and uplifting the mountain people.[10]

In "Our Contemporary Ancestors," Frost articulated for a national readership a portrait of southern highland society that resonated for many years afterward. Folklorist W. K. McNeil has called it "perhaps the most famous essay ever written about Appalachia," while Allen Batteau has credited Frost, in perhaps a bit of an exaggeration, with having "invented Appalachia as a social entity."[11] As the title of his essay suggests, Frost casts the region as a remnant of America's pioneer past, with highlanders living in log cabins and living off the land with none of the trappings of modern technology or ideas. While at first glance an outsider might have found such backwardness "rude and repellent," Frost stresses the virtues they retained—among them, the purity of their Anglo-Saxon heritage, unpenetrated by foreign contamination, an abiding patriotism that emerged during the American Revolution, and an abhorrence of slavery. As a result of these traits, Frost maintains, "when civil war came, there was a great surprise for both the North and the South. Appalachian America clave to the old flag. It was this old-fashioned loyalty that held Kentucky in the Union, made West Virginia 'secede from secession,' and performed prodigies of valor in East Tennessee and even in the western Carolinas."[12] Somewhat more vaguely, he celebrates the "independent spirit" that inspired this loyalty and its rejection of slavery, though he did no better than any other writer of the era in clarifying the linkage between Unionism and this rugged individualism.

None of these ideas originated with Frost (the notion of the region's predominant Unionism, as we have seen, was well established by then). But by making them so integral a part of his sweeping characterization of mountain society and culture, Frost paved the way for much of what followed, and the traces of his claims, his assumptions, and even his phrases continued to appear in the work of his successors. It is clear that he was seeking substantial aid for the region; he even called his essay a "call for the intervention of intelligent, patriotic assistance." "Appalachian America is a ward of the nation," he claimed, and the means by which its residents "are to be put in step with the world is an educational one."[13] Essential to that effort was to create both sympathy and admiration for its people, and as with an earlier generation making a similar plea, one means of doing so was to stress their devotion to the Union at a time when other Southerners rebelled against it. Frost very consciously linked the word "Appalachian" with "America" (repeating the term at least seven times in his essay), thus reminding readers of the most basic commonality they shared with readers, even while delineating their "otherness."

Equally important to Frost, and to those who followed in his wake, was his emphasis on the Revolutionary War. That conflict proved a much safer historical context in which to place these highlanders, given that it evoked far more consensual sentiments among Americans, North and South. That most of Southern Appalachia was only sparsely settled in the 1770s, and that its few frontier inhabitants were likely as divided or detached as their descendants were during the Civil War, were facts even easier to ignore than the messier realities of 1861–1865.[14] As evidence of that "Revolutionary patriotism," Frost posited a single event to stake his claim: the battle of King's Mountain, where, he claimed all too simply, "backwoodsmen of Appalachian America annihilated a British army." To further accentuate how closely tied later generations of Appalachians were to that era, he stated: "Cedar kegs used as canteens, and other accoutrements which saw service in that enterprise, may still be found in mountain cabins."[15]

Another, far more obscure essay produced at about the same time echoes Frost's themes. In an essay on "The Mountaineers of Madison County, N.C.," Mrs. D. L. Pierson, a Presbyterian mission worker based at Hot Springs, just north of Asheville, dismisses the Civil War as irrelevant to their present backwardness. "We can not charge his poverty to the war," she wrote of the typical mountaineer she observed there. "He never was a slaveowner and his uninviting little home was unmolested by the invading armies."[16] Such a claim took on particular irony, even absurdity, given that Madison County was notorious for the guerrilla warfare waged in its more remote sections and was the site of one of the war's most notorious atrocities, the infamous Shelton Laurel massacre, in which a Confederate regiment, the Sixty-fourth North Carolina—mostly home-grown and based in the county seat of Marshall—invaded the Shelton Laurel community, where it captured and then executed thirteen suspected Unionists.[17] To make no reference to that internecine violence a mere thirty-five years later seems to be a blatant oversight, intentional either on the part of the writer or on that of the local populace who may have shielded her from that bitter but unspoken past.

Yet Pierson did not neglect the more common theme in such pleas for sympathy and support. "The mountain people have a peculiar claim upon us, because they are purely American born," she stated. "Probably ninety per cent of them would be eligible 'Sons and Daughters of the Revolution.'" In an even greater stretch than Frost's evoking of King's Mountain, she harkened back to pre-Revolutionary incidents, from the Battle of Alamance in 1771 and the Mecklenburg Declaration of Independence of 1775, which she claimed were somehow the "work of their ancestors" and thus made them worthy of assistance now, though neither locale was even remotely Appalachian.[18]

Another Kentuckian, John Fox, was even more influential than William Frost in conveying southern highland life to a national readership in the early twentieth century. A native of the Bluegrass region, Fox spent most of his adult life in Big Stone Gap, in the heart of Virginia's Blue Ridge Mountains, though most of his writing focuses on Kentucky.[19] Best known for his fiction (his novels *The Little Shepherd of Kingdom Come* [1903] and *The Trail of the Lonesome Pine* [1908] were major best-sellers), Fox wrote of encounters between uncouth and primitive mountaineers and urbane, sophisticated lowlanders, which play out through cross-regional romances, politics, and even the Civil War, which forms the setting for *The Little Shepherd*. Fox characterized mountain life in nonfictional form as well. In 1901 he published a collection of twelve essays contrasting the two sections of the state, entitled *Bluegrass and Rhododendron: Outdoors in Old Kentucky*. In the first of that volume's essays, a broad overview of "The Southern Mountaineer," Fox makes a forceful case not only for Appalachia as a solid Unionist bastion but also for its military significance in preventing the Confederacy from winning its independence, a claim made by few others referenced here.

Obviously influenced by Frost's 1899 essay, Fox took his argument to a new level, claiming that it was Confederate military leaders who first discovered the American mountaineer when they learned, through sad experience, that the Mason-Dixon line was not necessarily a firm demarcation between Northern and Southern loyalties. He cites the plan of a Captain Garnett who was charged with moving Confederate troops through the Virginia mountains and into Ohio in an effort to sever the Midwest from the Northeast but who got no farther than Harper's Ferry. "When he struck the mountains," Fox writes, "he struck enemies who shot at his men from ambush, cut down bridges before him, carried the news of his march to the Federals, and Garnett himself was felled with a bullet from a mountaineer's squirrel rifle at Harper's Ferry."[20]

Only then, Fox states, "did the South begin to realize what a long, lean powerful arm of the Union it was that the southern mountaineer stretched through its very vitals." In a passage obviously derived from Frost's essay, he builds his case state by state:

> For that arm helped hold Kentucky in the Union by giving preponderance to the Union sympathizers in the Blue-grass; it kept the East Tennesseans loyal to a man; it made West Virginia, as the phrase goes, "secede from secession"; it drew out a horde of one hundred thousand volunteers, when Lincoln called for troops, deleting Jackson County, Kentucky, for instance, of every male under sixty years of age and over fifteen; and it raised a hostile barrier between the armies of the coast and the armies of Mississippi. The North has never realized, perhaps, what it owes for its victory to this non-slaveholding southern mountaineer.[21]

Fox was highly selective in making his case for highlanders' attachment to the Union, having made no mention of those areas of Appalachia—in Virginia, the Carolinas, or Georgia—where Confederate sentiment was much more in evidence; nor did he acknowledge the guerrilla warfare waged not only in those areas, but in the very areas he suggests were solidly in support of the Union. Nevertheless, the very specificity with which he defined Unionist Appalachia lent credibility to that assumption and would be reinforced in his novels still to come.

In 1906 another Presbyterian and another college president sought to explain the southern mountaineers to the rest of America. Samuel Tyndale Wilson, the president of Maryville College on the western edge of the Great Smokies in Tennessee and just east of Knoxville, published his small book of that title *(The Southern Mountaineers)* through the Presbyterian Home Missions Board in New York City. Born to missionary parents in Syria and educated at Maryville, Wilson himself served a brief stint as a missionary in Mexico. He returned to teach at his alma mater in 1884 and spent the rest of his career there, assuming the presidency in 1901.[22] Wilson was forthright in stating of his title characters that his was a "story told by one who has been all of his lifetime identified with them, and loves them, and has been their ready champion whenever occasion offered." Wilson echoed the themes of both Frost and Fox. As a Presbyterian, he stressed the Scots-Irish roots of most highlanders; in an early section entitled "Service to the Nation," he declares them "possessed by a fierce love of freedom," and proceeds through the usual litany of the Mecklenburg Declaration of Independence and the Battle of King's Mountain, in which "mountaineers had, without order, without pay, without commission, without equipment, and without hope of monetary reward, struck a decisive blow for the entire country."[23]

For all of his rhapsodizing about highlanders' valor, patriotism, and sacrifice in America's wars—he gives nearly equal attention to their roles in the War of 1812, the Mexican War, and the Spanish American War—Wilson was more willing to acknowledge the very real divisions within the region during the Civil War, stating up front that "many on the Virginian side of the mountains and among the North Carolina, Georgia, and Alabama mountains espoused the cause of the Confederacy, and made as good soldiers as the valorous hosts of the South could boast." He also notes that Stonewall Jackson was a "mountaineer indubitably of the first class" and that his famous brigade was made up "largely of the men of the hills."[24]

Yet once he has given due lip service to the pro-Confederate Appalachians (in a mere two sentences), Wilson moves on to his real focus—nearly two pages extolling the Union loyalists of West Virginia, Kentucky, and East Tennessee. He makes his case in quantitative terms: "The Federal forces actually recruited from the southern Appalachians were as considerable in number as were the armies of the American Revolution gathered from all the thirteen colonies," he asserts, "and considerably exceeded the total of both mighty armies that fought at Gettysburg." He boasts that his own congressional district "claims the distinction of having sent a larger percentage of its population into the Union army than did any other congressional district in the entire country." He notes that these Appalachian loyalists "cleft the Confederacy with a mighty hostile element that not merely subtracted great armies from the enrollment of the Confederacy, but even necessitated the presence of other armies for the control of so large a disaffected territory."[25]

Wilson stresses as well the risks taken by mountain Unionists and suggests that their contribution to federal forces may have tipped the conflict's ultimate resolution. "Their soldiers," he maintains, "were not conscripted or attracted by bounty, but rather in most cases ran the gauntlet through hostile forces for one, two, or three hundred miles to reach a place where they could enlist under the flag of their country" (a half-truth at best, because it hardly applied to those very areas of Union strength that he had just documented so forcefully). Like both his predecessors and those who followed, he suggests that while it might have been an exaggeration to say that "the loyalty of the Appalachians decided the great contest, that loyalty certainly contributed substantially to the decision."[26]

The two most notable female chroniclers of the highland South during this era made little reference to the war and were less explicit or categorical in their characterizations of Appalachia's wartime loyalties. Both Emma Bell Miles in *The Spirit of the Mountains* (1905) and Margaret W. Morley in *The Carolina Mountains* (1913) wrote only fleetingly about the war, yet they made very different suggestions as to what it meant to their highland subjects.

Born in Indiana and raised, until the age of ten, in north-central Kentucky, Miles spent her adolescence and most of her adult life in and around Chattanooga. Her parents taught school on Walden's Ridge (now known as Signal Mountain), which overlooked the city yet seemed quite remote from its influences, both economically and culturally. It was the residents

Emma Bell Miles became one of the most notable female chroniclers of the highland South during this era, with her publication of *The Spirit of the Mountains* in 1905. (frontispiece, original edition of *The Spirit of the Mountains*)

of Walden's Ridge whom Miles took as her archetype Appalachians, drawing on their customs, beliefs, and simple lifestyle to generalize about the southern highlanders as a whole. The result is a study that is as much that of a folklorist as an ethnographer. While she exhibits a genuine affection for her subjects and frequently identifies herself with them, Miles is often patronizing in extolling the virtues of their isolation, their harmony with the natural world, and their long-held traditions. She downplays the more degenerate attributes of feuding and moonshine so prevalent at the time, dismissing them with only the slightest of rationales. "Feuds are part of the price we pay for the simplicity and beauty of mountain life—for its hospitality, for its true and far-reaching family ties," she wrote. She even suggests that they were a mere phase to be withstood: "I do not say the inevitable price, for the lawless fighter, along with illicit whiskey, is bound to disappear; but these ugly features are, under present conditions, the price of the tribal bond."[27]

Miles displays remarkably little sense of history in her descriptions of southern mountain life. It seems especially odd that someone who spent so much of her life in and around Chattanooga would have no more sense of the Civil War's impact than Miles demonstrates in her book, given the tangible trappings so evident there—battlefields, monuments, and Confederate veterans' reunions, all of which made the most of the crucial engagements that played out in and around the city in 1863. And yet, Miles devotes a mere two sentences to her highland subjects' role in the war.

She opens a chapter on "Neighbors" with the statement that there is no such thing as a community of mountaineers, one of the common misconceptions long perpetuated by outside observers of the region. "They are knit together, man to man, as friends," she suggests, "but not as a body of men." There was no core or axis between the family and the state in this remote rural setting that would fit the definition of a community. As a result, she concludes that "our men are almost incapable of concerted action unless they are needed by the Government." It was, of course, war and war alone that defined that need in the nineteenth century, and Miles suggests that it was an innate impulse that drew Southern highlanders into military service. "It was the living spirit of '76 that sent the mountaineer into the Civil War—they understood very little of what it was all about." But unlike most other regional chroniclers, she did not assume that they remained loyal to the Union. "I even venture to say that had the Southerners fought under the Stars and Stripes," she wrote, "most of our people would have been found on that side, following the flag they knew."[28] In short, she seemed to think that, like Southern sheep, they blindly joined the Confederate cause, simply because their fellow Southerners or the state of Tennessee did as much.

The fact that Miles assumed that her subjects were pro-Southern in their sympathies and service—even if rather indiscriminately so—was most likely a function of her Chattanooga base. Compared with other parts of heavily Unionist East Tennessee, there was certainly more Confederate support in this crucial railroad center on the state's southeastern border,[29] but to assume that those in its highland outskirts were equally of one mind is, of course, a gross oversimplification that is indicative of Miles's generalizations throughout her book.

Although hers was the first book-length treatment of Appalachia in this era of discovery, *The Spirit of the Mountains* seems to have enjoyed only

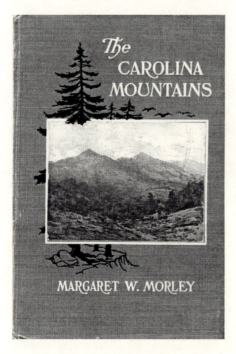

The original cover of Margaret W. Morley's *The Carolina Mountains,* a popular travel narrative and analysis of mountain life published in 1913 for the many tourists who were finding their way to western North Carolina at the turn of the century.

limited sales and had relatively little influence compared to the later successes of Kephart and Campbell; it was only with a 1975 reprint edition that scholars have embraced both Miles and her work.[30] Similar in tone and sympathies, Margaret Morley's *The Carolina Mountains* proved much more popular than *The Spirit of the Mountains* when it appeared eight years later. As much a travel narrative as an analysis of mountain life, it was aimed more specifically at the many tourists who were finding their way to western North Carolina at the turn of the century, which also contributed to its wide circulation.[31] Perhaps for the same reasons, her book is much less valued now and receives far less attention from current scholars.

Morley was far more of an outsider to the region than was Miles, having discovered the area only in middle age after a teaching and writing career based in the Midwest and New England. In the early 1890s she and a companion visited the summer home of prominent actor William Gillette in Tryon, North Carolina. She became a regular visitor to this thriving artists' and writers' colony at the base of the Blue Ridge Mountains, and eventually she moved there to practice both pursuits. It proved to be a convenient base from which she explored both the Smokies and the Blue Ridge, the result of which was *The Carolina Mountains*, one of her last and most successful publications. (Most of her earlier output had been children's books on botany, natural history, and even sex education.)[32]

Far more than Miles or any other regional chronicler of the era, Morley was as fully attuned to the cities and the resorts of the highlands as she was to the primitive and picturesque "backcountry" on which most others limited their attention. She seemed enamored of the wealth in the region—perhaps because of her own social standing among New England intelligentsia—and devoted whole chapters to Asheville, Flat Rock, Highlands, and other tourist destinations, including the Biltmore House, with which she was particularly enthralled. Nevertheless, her primary focus remained on the same backward inhabitants, and she describes their customs, beliefs, and way of life with the same fascination and interest as do her contemporaries, though occasionally she seems more bemused than anything else. "We're powerful poor around here, but we don't mean no harm by it," she quoted one "ancient native of the forest who does not think himself poor at all."[33]

Morley demonstrated a far greater sense of the region's history than did Miles, and yet, for her too, the Civil War was never more than of marginal interest. Her several references to it throughout the book are brief and serve only to illustrate other points about her subjects. Like Miles, she grants the mountaineers very little agency or sense of purpose in terms of their military service in the war. She quotes another elderly highlander, who in reminiscing about the war said that he was drafted into Confederate service against his will but claimed no understanding of the circumstances or the issues behind the war or his role in it. "When you asked him about it he knit his brows, 'studied' a minute, and then slowly said, 'Law, which side was I on?'" Although he may have been puzzled by "the meaning and the advantages [an odd term] of the War of the Rebellion," which he characterized simply as "a rich man's war and a poor man's fight," one should not mistake his disdain for participating as cowardice, Morley insists. She is quick to remind her readers that when he did understand what the fight was about, as at King's Mountain, he was more than willing to join the Union cause.[34] Once again, the Revolution served as a far safer and less ambiguous touchstone than any reference to the Civil War.

Miles and Morley both seemed to use the ignorance of the mountaineer as a reflection of his innocence. He may have fought in the war—as either Confederate or Unionist—but he did so with either little sense of purpose or against his will, and thus could be absolved of any allegiance that might offend current readers from either section of the country. Both were quick to extrapolate from an individual to the populace as a whole, and in so doing not only embraced the values of the current generation but, following Frost's lead, evoked the patriotic virtues of earlier generations as well.

Both women seemed to view their subjects as an endangered species in the wake of what Miles calls "the oncoming tide of civilization, that drowns as many as it uplifts." For her, that meant an influx of summer people and the trappings of wealth that could prove so corruptible to the character and the simple lifestyle of the backwoodsmen she championed.[35] Morley, first and foremost a tourist at heart, acknowledges that the idea of progress may have scared the Carolina highlanders in its path, but she was optimistic as to its likely effects. "Let the new order be better than the old," she proclaims, and she prophesies, rather naively, that "the mountains [will] continue to develop in the direction of sanitation, safety, and ever-increasing beauty."[36] Yet neither scenario for the region's future relied much on its past, particularly that of the Civil War, which seemed to have been ultimately irrelevant to the circumstances in which the mountain people now found themselves.

Later in the same year in which Morley's book was first published, another far more influential and lasting work made its first appearance: Horace Kephart's *Our Southern Highlanders* (1913). Generally acknowledged as one of the two "classics" of its time and genre (John C. Campbell's *The Southern Highlander and His Homeland* being the other), Kephart undertook his masterwork with a less definite agenda than did most of his contemporaries. Also an outsider, with roots in the Northeast and much of his career spent in the Midwest, he was, in Allen Batteau's description, "an alcoholic-librarian-turned-journalist." His retreat to the Great Smokies in North Carolina in 1904 represented a retreat from academia and from his drinking problem into a natural world that satisfied what he called his "inborn taste for the wild and romantic" and his yearning "for a strange land and people that had the charm of originality."[37] At forty-two years of age and nearing a nervous breakdown, Kephart left family and career behind him and moved to North Carolina for therapeutic purposes, ultimately settling in a remote settlement on Hazel's Creek in the heart of the Smokies. He later moved to nearby Bryson City, where he lived until his death in an automobile accident in 1931.[38]

Kephart's first books reflect his recreational interests in the area—*Camping and Woodcraft* (1906), *Camp Cookery* (1907), and *Sporting Fire-*

arms (1907)—but gradually he became more enamored of the people and culture in whose midst he found himself. Once an impassioned student of the American frontier, he discovered in the Smokies survivals of that early American history. "In Far Appalachia," he wrote, "it seemed that I might realize the past in the present, seeing with my own eyes what life must have been to my pioneer ancestors of a century or two ago."[39] Despite constant observation and notes made at Hazel Creek and Bryson City, Kephart was hesitant to draw broad conclusions on the region based on those areas alone, but after travel throughout the highlands of Tennessee, Georgia, and Kentucky, he concluded that "southern mountaineers everywhere [were] one people." And while he fully acknowledged the socioeconomic variables within the towns, valleys, and highlands throughout the region, he devoted the vast majority of his attention to the same traditional "mountaineers" as did other authors, maintaining that the segment of the populace that most typified those traditions were "the great multitude of little farmers living up the branches and on the steep hillsides, back from the main highways, and generally far from the railroads. These, the real mountaineers, were what interested me; and so I wrote them up."[40]

Some critics have found Kephart's book a significant step forward in terms of its approach to mountain life—one recent scholar called it "probably the most vigorous and honest book written on the Appalachian South"[41]— and yet his interest in his subjects lay largely in the more primal aspects of their existence. He devotes multiple chapters to moonshining, bear hunts, and other activities, along with the obligatory chapters on religion, dialect, and living off the land that differ from others of the genre only in the lively, engaging—sometimes sensationalistic—style and the wide array of literary and historical allusions sprinkled throughout the narrative.

Yet Kephart's historical perspective is among the book's weakest and most pejorative components, and one built upon the worst of the stereotypes so rampant at the time. Despite an abiding interest in Daniel Boone and early settlement patterns, he was quick to portray Appalachia as a quagmire for the thousands of poor whites whose migration forced them into a land of no return. Their deterioration began as soon as "the best lands, the river valleys, were claimed by a class of citizens superior to the average mountaineers." Once pushed back along the creek branches and up along the steep, they quickly became the isolated and ignorant mountaineers with "nothing in [their] environment to arouse ambition. The hard, hopeless life of the mountain farm, sustained only by a meager and ill-cooked diet, begat laziness and shiftless unconcern." As for why they didn't follow so many other Americans who sought new opportunities farther west, Kephart's explanation adds insult to injury: "They were so immured in the mountains, so utterly cut off from communication with the outer world, that they did not know anything about the opportunities offered new settlers in far-away lands."[42]

And so they remained until the Civil War, which to Kephart served only as a "thunder-crash" that aroused those highlanders languishing in a "Rip Van Winkle sleep" (an image borrowed from Frost). Not that that was a good thing, given that "throughout that struggle, the mountain region was a nest of bushwhackers and bandits that preyed upon the aged and defenseless who were left at home," a situation for which it paid a heavy price after the war: "an evil legacy of neighborhood wrongs and private grudges." And because most mountaineers incurred strong resentment from the rest of their states by remaining loyal to the Union, "after Appomattox, they were cast back into a worse isolation than they had ever known." That alienation from their states was compounded by new federal tyranny in the form of "a prohibitive excise tax imposed upon their chief merchantable commodity." So, he concludes, now that the highlanders were "inflamed by a multitude of personal wrongs [and] habituated to the shedding of human blood . . . it was inevitable that this fiery and vindictive race should speedily fall into warring among themselves. Old scores were not to be wiped out in a reign of terror. The open combat of bannered war was turned into the secret ferocity of family feuds."[43]

Kephart was thus the first twentieth-century writer to see the war as a significant turning point in the course of Appalachian development and to acknowledge the internal warfare Southern highlanders endured, even if, ironically, it returned them to the same primitive and unchecked impulses that had characterized them before the war. Given the degenerate state to which the war had reduced (or merely returned?) these backwoodsmen, any progress—or civilization—imposed on the region, whether it be timber or mineral enterprises, would be a welcome impetus for change. Kephart insisted that "this economic revolution," bringing with it "good schools, newspapers, a finer and more liberal social life," should be celebrated as a vast improvement in Appalachians' lives, whether or not they wanted it or recognized it as something better than their current way of life.[44]

Far different in both tone and purpose was John C. Campbell's posthumous treatise on the region that appeared in 1921, two years after

Horace Kephart's *Our Southern Highlanders* is generally acknowledged as one of the two classics of its time and genre. Kephart was the first twentieth-century writer to see the Civil War as a significant turning point in the course of Appalachian development and to acknowledge the internal warfare southern highlanders endured. (frontispiece of *Our Southern Highlanders*, 1922)

Campbell's death and, perhaps not coincidentally, a year before a new and expanded edition of Kephart's *Our Southern Highlanders*. Campbell was another Midwesterner, Indiana born, who spent most of his early career as a teacher in the southernmost Appalachians, most notably at Piedmont College in the north Georgia mountains. A research grant from the newly established Russell Sage Foundation in New York led Campbell to mount an extensive and systematic study of southern Appalachia's social and economic conditions. Based in Asheville from 1909 on, he served as secretary of the Foundation's Southern Highland Division. His book was the culmination of his research and increasing activism. He organized the Conference of Southern Mountain Workers and worked closely with his wife, Olive Dame Campbell, who was a major force in her own right as both scholar and activist in pursuing and promoting the music, crafts, and folk life of the region for more than thirty years after Campbell's death in 1919. The first major task she undertook as a widow, however, was the completion of his book, which was published by Russell Sage.[45]

Campbell's characterization of the region was both more sophisticated and more balanced than most of those that preceded it. An odd but often effective mix of social science data and literary descriptions (perhaps a function of Olive's input), the book recognizes and readily acknowledges both the region's geographical variables and how they shaped a far more diverse socioeconomic structure among southern Appalachians. Historian John Alexander Williams has even suggested that had Campbell lived longer and been able to expand upon these ideas—indeed, these realities—the scholarly stranglehold on the stereotypes and misconceptions of the region might have been broken a full half century sooner than they were.[46]

Nevertheless, Campbell was not immune to many of the same generalizations and clichés already in circulation. He took on the war in a chapter of his book dealing with individualism. He opens the chapter by challenging both the notion that Appalachia "was thrust like a Northern wedge into the heart of the Confederacy" and the rationale behind that claim. He notes up front that "speakers who have sought to raise money in the North for mountain work have been wont to dwell upon the part played by the Highlander in the Civil War." The impression left by these claims is that "the Highlander is in reality a Northerner in a Southern environment. The impression is far from the real truth."[47] Yet Campbell was not willing to cast his stock highlander as fully Southern either; hence his emphasis on his independence. "Heredity and environment have conspired to make him an extreme individualist," Campbell claims. "His dominant trait is independence raised to the fourth power."[48]

In explaining the wartime loyalties and the reasons behind them, however, Campbell falls back on the same tenuous connections that his predecessors had propounded, which have little to do with any independence of thought or spirit. "They held, withal, a deep though distant attachment to the Federal Government, for which they had fought in the Revolution, the War of 1812, and that of Mexico." He does acknowledge the same general division as that laid out by Samuel Wilson: that West Virginia, eastern Kentucky and East Tennessee "stood firm for the Union," while western North Carolina and Virginia "showed a larger Confederate element."[49]

Campbell admits that the war provoked "the bitterest of feeling" among mountaineers, especially those from Tennessee and Kentucky, where "the roughness of the country led to a sort of border guerrilla warfare," and even provides anecdotal evidence of the harassment suffered by mountain women and children at the hands of bushwhackers and "rebel raiders." And yet he assures his readers that there were no lingering after effects from such atrocities, which he based on firsthand yet fairly impressionistic evidence.

He notes that in the "little community at the southern end of the mountains" where he first taught, a town named Joppa, Alabama, many veterans had settled, some Union and more Confederate. "At his hearth sat often a man who had stood with the 'Rock of Chickamauga,' and another who had starved with Pemberton at Vicksburg or taken his tender farewell of Lee at Appomattox"; and yet, Campbell claims, "there was no bitterness or rancor between them." He told of another highland community where a Blue and Gray Camp was organized, due to the number of sympathizers from both sides. On Southern Memorial Day, veterans of both sides gathered at the school hall "to listen to declamations on patriotism by the school boys . . . while above them on one side hung the picture of Lee between the Stars and Stripes, and on the other, framed in Southern garlands, the picture of Grant."[50]

So what are we to make of these various treatments of the war's impact on Southern Appalachia, or Southern Appalachians' impact on the war, given the agendas of their authors and the audiences they hoped to reach? Shannon Wilson made this observation of certain college administrators in the region in the 1870s and 1880s raising funds for their schools: "The memory of the war experience was manipulated artfully to project a way of seeing and perhaps a means of thinking about Appalachia in a defined and particular manner."[51] Much the same could be said about those chronicling the region in the early twentieth century, although both how and why they "artfully manipulated" the war's legacy differed in several telling respects.

At one level, it is obvious that these authors still sought to woo northern philanthropists and organizations by depicting Appalachians as deserving and worthy recipients of their largesse. Certainly an easy means of winning that sympathy and support was to stress their wartime loyalty to the Union; thus it is no surprise that every writer but one made that loyalty integral to their coverage of the war. (Only Emma Bell Miles assumed a Confederate majority among her mountaineers, but even she held them blameless in that decision, asserting that they had little understanding of what they were doing or why.)

Of the rest, there is considerable variation in terms of the extent, the significance, and the rationale behind the Unionism they claimed was so predominant among Southern highlanders. Only Wilson and Campbell took seriously the fact that some areas of Appalachia were more supportive of the Confederacy, but both minimized that reality, offering no explanation as to why some mountaineers would cast their lots with the South.

Most others followed the lead of Frost and Fox by linking Unionism to a deep-seated patriotism that mountain people had demonstrated from the American Revolution through even the Spanish American War, and falling back on the same few examples to demonstrate that point. On the other hand, some attributed that loyalty to less worthy factors, either to mountaineers' ignorance or apathy of the world beyond their own, and hence to a lack of ability to make a reasoned commitment to either cause. Even Frost quoted a "fine old Southern lady . . . in a border city" who explained mountain Unionism to him: "If those mountain folks had been educated they would have gone with their states!" Frost's response: "Probably she was right."[52] Curiously, the presence of slavery or the lack thereof played little part in the explanations offered. John Campbell was among the few who even raised the issue directly, and said only: "The doctrine of States' Rights, separated from its slavery bias, was but an abstraction to them." In effect, he suggested, as others had, that the issues that drove the sectional crisis—whether slavery or something else—were irrelevant to mountain people.[53]

Others focused more on the effects than on the causes of Appalachian loyalties. Several suggested that the manpower the region provided to the federal war effort and denied to the Confederacy was significant; indeed, it may even have tipped the scales in favor of the North and its ultimate victory. Both John Fox and Samuel Wilson pushed that claim and insisted that such a commitment by highlanders entailed far more risk and sacrifice than joining Confederate forces would have. Campbell's description of the region's role as "a Northern wedge thrust into the heart of the Confederacy" vividly makes the same point.

On the other hand, it is equally striking that the coverage of the Civil War in all in these works was only fleeting. One could hardly have written comprehensively about any other part of the South at the turn of the century and not made the war's impact a central part of a characterization of the region. And yet, most of the book-length works examined here devote no more than a page or two to the war, while the essays or journals include a paragraph or two at best. Such minimal attention reflects in part an ahistorical approach to their subjects. In seeking to explain the origins of mountain people and what made them what they became, most of these writers fell back on the platitudes and misconceptions about patriotism, individualism, sacrifice, and other unspecific but value-laden terminology. Yet these writers may also have felt that only by downplaying Appalachia's role in or impact on this most central event of the nation's history could they make a convincing case for the isolation or insulation of its inhabitants. If they were to remain the simple, backward "contemporary ancestors" that would make them so palatable to potential benefactors, the less said the better about the complexities of guerrilla warfare, divided loyalties, and homefront atrocities—not to mention the political wranglings of influential leaders such as Andrew Johnson, Zebulon Vance, and Joseph E. Brown, which would paint a much messier portrait of Southern highland agendas and agency.

Also curious is how little firsthand information about the war these chroniclers derived from the many local residents that they came to know and certainly relied on for much material on so many other topics. The fact that the only direct quote from Carolina highlanders that Morley could muster was the question "Law, which side was I on?" says a great deal about what she chose to overlook or not pursue in terms of local memories or sentiments. The same can be said of most of her fellow authors as well. John C. Campbell drew on firsthand observation only to stress the reconciliatory spirit of highlanders after the war's end, though one is sure that he must have heard just as many or more reminiscences about the waging of the war itself, none of which he acknowledges in his book.

By the same token, the fact that Campbell was based in Asheville, a center of Confederate enlistment, mobilization, and even manufacturing; that Emma Bell Miles was in Chattanooga, another center of Confederate activity and military action; and that Mrs. D. L. Pierson seemed so oblivious to the Shelton Laurel massacre in her portrait of Madison County, North Carolina, all suggest intentional silences used to obscure a very different reality that would not have jived with the sympathetic and simplistic portraits each sought to present.

In short, by the turn of the century, the particulars of how the war was actually fought in the mountain South, and why, entailed far more inconvenient truths that did not always lend themselves to the image of mountain people these writers worked so hard to create and convey. To sell the remoteness and "otherness" of highland life required that the Civil War—so central a trauma and turning point to the rest of the South—be granted only a marginal place in explaining southern Appalachia, where people were so set in their ways that even an upheaval of that nature had little lasting effect on their lives. If their loyalties could not be linked to an innate—or even blind—patriotism or long-standing sense of duty to the federal government, then it could be explained as something far less flattering but even more useful: the assumption that they simply did not understand what the war was about and were therefore innocent pawns drawn into the conflict—on whichever side—without even the option of making that decision themselves.

The easiest way to make that case was to minimize the war, its impact, and its relevancy to Appalachia. Despite ample private and communal memories of the region's residents that were still very much alive during the early twentieth century, these writers created a version of their war experiences all their own—one that became firmly embedded in popular perceptions for far too much of the century to follow.

Notes

1. W. K. McNeil, ed., *Appalachian Images in Folk and Popular Culture,* 2nd ed. (Knoxville: University of Tennessee Press, 1995); Kevin E. O'Donnell and Helen Hollingsworth, eds., *Seekers of Scenery: Travel Writing from Southern Appalachia, 1840–1900* (Knoxville: University of Tennessee Press, 2004); and Katherine E. Ledford, "A Landscape and a People Set Apart: Narratives of Exploration and Travel in Early Appalachia," in Dwight B. Billings, Gurney Norman, and Katherine E. Ledford, eds., *Confronting Appalachian Stereotypes: Back Talk from an American Region,* 47–66 (Lexington: University Press of Kentucky, 1999).

2. Henry Shapiro, *Appalachia on Our Mind: The Southern Mountains and Mountaineers in the American Consciousness, 1870–1920* (Chapel Hill: University of North Carolina Press, 1978); Cratis Williams, "The Southern Mountaineer in Fact and Fiction" (PhD diss., New York University, 1961); and Allen W. Batteau, *The Invention of Appalachia* (Tucson: University of Arizona Press, 1990), chapters 4 and 5.

3. Shapiro, *Appalachia on Our Mind,* 87–90. Most of his discussion of this issue is limited to East Tennesseans. Kenneth Noe has noted that of thirty-nine works considered by Shapiro that were published between 1865 and 1883, only nine made any reference to the Civil War.

4. Kenneth W. Noe, "Toward the Myth of Unionist Appalachia, 1865–1883," *Journal of the Appalachian Studies Association* 6 (1994): 67–74, which appeared in an expanded version as "Deadened Color and Colder Horror: Rebecca Harding Davis and the Myth of Unionist Appalachia," in Billings, Norman, and Ledford, eds., *Confronting Appalachian Stereotypes,* 67–84.

5. Shannon H. Wilson, "Lincoln's Sons and Daughters: Berea College, Lincoln Memorial University, and the Myth of Unionist Appalachia, 1866–1910," in Kenneth W. Noe and Shannon H. Wilson, eds., *The Civil War in Appalachia: Collected Essays,* 242–64 (Knoxville: University of Tennessee Press, 1997).

6. James C. Klotter, "The Black South and White Appalachia," *Journal of*

American History 66 (March 1987): 42–62; Nina Silber, "What Does America Need So Much as Americans? Race and Northern Reconciliation with Southern Appalachia, 1870–1900," in John C. Inscoe, ed., *Appalachians and Race: The Mountain South from Slavery to Segregation,* 244–58 (Lexington: University Press of Kentucky, 2001).

7. Shapiro extends his treatment of Appalachia and its chroniclers to 1920, but he has nothing to say about the Civil War in his coverage of 1900 through 1920.

8. Shapiro, *Appalachia on Our Mind,* 116–17, 132–33. With the exceptions of John Fox and Margaret Morley, all of the writers discussed in this essay at least claimed that their observations and conclusions applied to all parts of southern Appalachia.

9. William G. Frost, "Our Contemporary Ancestors in the Southern Mountains," *Atlantic Monthly,* March 1899, reprinted in McNeil, ed., *Appalachian Images,* 91–106. (Subsequent references to the essay are to the version appearing in the McNeil volume.)

10. The best biographical information on Frost is found in his memoir, *For the Mountains: An Autobiography* (New York: Fleming H. Revell Co., 1937), and in two histories of Berea College: Elisabeth S. Peck, *Berea's First 125 Years, 1855–1980* (Lexington: University Press of Kentucky, 1982), 68–74; and Shannon H. Wilson, *Berea College: An Illustrated History* (Lexington: University Press of Kentucky, 2006), 78–81, 90–111.

11. McNeil, ed., *Appalachian Imagery,* 91; Batteau, *The Invention of Appalachia,* 74. Both Shapiro and Batteau offer insightful analyses of Frost's essay: Shapiro, *Appalachia on Our Mind,* chapter 8, and Batteau, *The Invention of Appalachia,* 74–80.

12. Frost, "Our Contemporary Ancestors," 99.

13. Ibid., 105–6.

14. On the strength of British loyalists of the southern backcountry, see Robert S. Lambert, *South Carolina Loyalists in the American Revolution* (Columbia: University of South Carolina Press, 1987); Carole W. Troxler, *The Loyalist Experience in North Carolina* (Raleigh: North Carolina Division of Archives and History, 1976); and Robert M. Calhoon, *The Loyalists in Revolutionary America, 1760–1781* (New York: Harcourt Brace Jovanovich, 1973).

15. Frost, "Our Contemporary Ancestors," 99. John C. Campbell wryly noted that "few discourses on mountain questions are complete without this reference [to King's Mountain]. The audiences for whom such addresses are given . . . would feel cheated without it. They look for it as expectantly as the Bostonian does for the closing phrase in the Governor's Thanksgiving Proclamation, 'God Save the Commonwealth of Massachusetts.'" John C. Campbell, *The Southern Highlander and His Homeland* (New York: Russell Sage Foundation, 1921), 8.

16. Mrs. D. L. Pierson, "The Mountaineers of Madison County, N.C.," *Missionary Review of the World,* November 1897, 823.

17. For a more detailed account of the Shelton Laurel massacre and how it was

remembered locally, see John C. Inscoe, "Unionists in the Attic: The Shelton Laurel Massacre Dramatized," *North and South* 10 (October 2007): 56–65.

18. Pierson, "Mountaineers of Madison County," 828. The Battle of Alamance was the final showdown between the Regulators and North Carolina's royal governor, William Tryon. Neither it nor the Mecklenburg Declaration of Independence took place in North Carolina's backcountry; instead, they occurred in the state's piedmont, much farther east.

19. On Fox's life and Appalachian writing, see Darlene Wilson, "The Felicitous Convergence of Mythmaking and Capital Accumulation: John Fox Jr. and the Formation of An (other) Almost-White American Underclass," *Journal of Appalachian Studies* 1 (Fall 1995): 17–29; Wilson, "A Judicious Combination of Incident and Psychology: John Fox Jr. and the Southern Mountaineer Motif," in Billings et al., ed., *Confronting Appalachian Stereotypes,* 98–118; and Batteau, *The Invention of Appalachia,* 64–74. On the significance of *The Little Shepherd of Kingdom Come* in particular, see Silber, "What Does America Need So Much as Americans?" 254–56.

20. John Fox Jr., *Bluegrass and Rhododendron: Outdoors in Old Kentucky* (New York: Charles Scribner and Sons, 1901), 6. Brig. Gen. Robert S. Garnett took Confederate command of northwestern Virginia in June 1861, having been informed beforehand that "there is great disaffection in this and adjoining counties and opposition to the lawful action of the State authorities is certainly contemplated." *Official Records of the War of the Rebellion* (Washington, DC: U.S. Government Printing Office, 1880), ser. 1, vol. 2, 843. He was killed in a battle against Gen. George McClellan's forces at Laurel Hill, in what would be West Virginia, on July 11, 1861.

21. Fox, *Bluegrass and Rhododendron,* 6–7.

22. Biographical information on Wilson is lacking; this information comes from his own description of his early life in Samuel Tyndale Wilson, *A Century of Maryville College, 1819–1919: A Story of Altruism* (Maryville, TN: Directors of Maryville College, 1919), 159.

23. Samuel Tyndale Wilson, *The Southern Mountaineers* (New York: Presbyterian Home Missions, 1906), preface, 27–31.

24. Ibid., 33.

25. Ibid., 34.

26. Ibid.

27. Emma Bell Miles, *The Spirit of the Mountains* (1905; reprint, Knoxville: University of Tennessee Press, 1972), 82.

28. Ibid., 71–72.

29. On the stronger Confederate sentiment in the Chattanooga area than elsewhere in East Tennessee, see W. Todd Groce, *Mountain Rebels: East Tennessee Confederates and the Civil War, 1860–1870* (Knoxville: University of Tennessee Press, 1999), 39. Groce reports that 89 percent of the city's voters supported secession in the referendum of June 8, 1861, the highest concentration in the region. On Con-

federate enlistment in Chattanooga and elsewhere in East Tennessee, see John D. Fowler, *Mountaineers in Gray: The Nineteenth Tennessee Volunteer Infantry Regiment, C.S.A.* (Knoxville: University of Tennessee Press, 2004), 18–22.

30. David Whisnant, "Introduction" to the University of Tennessee Press's reprint edition, xv. Other scholarly work on Miles includes Grace Toney Edwards, "Emma Bell Miles: Feminist Crusader in Appalachia," in Robert J. Higgs, Ambrose N. Manning, and Jim Wayne Miller, eds., *Appalachia Inside Out,* 2:709–12 (Knoxville: University of Tennessee Press, 1995); and Kay Baker Gaston, *Emma Bell Miles* (Signal Mountain, TN: Walden Ridge Historical Society, 1985). For a particularly favorable assessment of *The Spirit of the Mountains* and of Miles's treatment of her subjects, see McNeil, "Introduction," *Appalachian Images,* 3–4.

31. Foreword to Margaret W. Morley, *The Carolina Mountains* (1913; reprint, Fairview, NC: Historical Images, 2006), xix. In 1926 the Grove Park Inn in Asheville commissioned a special deluxe edition of *The Carolina Mountains* and placed it in each guest room.

32. Ibid., "About Margaret W. Morley," xi–xiv.

33. Ibid., 12–13.

34. Ibid., 13. Morley's other significant reference to the war is a chapter on the history of Asheville, in which she states that "deserters from both sides took refuge in the mountains. Desperadoes of the worst sort lived in caves and raided the country" (102). While this is one of very few acknowledgments of guerrilla warfare in any of the works under discussion, Morley fails to mention Asheville as a center of Confederate recruitment and armament production, as a target of Stoneman's Raid at war's end, or as the home base of Zebulon B. Vance, North Carolina's Civil War governor.

35. Miles, *The Spirit of the Mountains*, chapter 10, quote, 190.

36. Morley, *The Carolina Mountains,* 123; see also 292–95.

37. Batteau, *The Invention of Appalachia,* 89; Horace Kephart, *Our Southern Highlanders: A Narrative of Adventure in the Southern Appalachians and a Study of Life among the Mountaineers* (New York: Macmillan Co., 1913, 1922), 29. The book was much expanded in 1922, when the subtitle was added. That edition is the one cited here.

38. The fullest biographical treatment of Kephart is George Ellison's "Introduction" to a 1972 reprint of *Our Southern Highlanders,* ix–xlvi.

39. Kephart, *Our Southern Highlanders,* 29–30.

40. "Horace Kephart by Himself," *North Carolina Library Bulletin* 5 (June 1922), 52, quoted in Ellison, "Introduction," xxxvii.

41. Batteau, *The Invention of Appalachia,* 90.

42. Kephart, *Our Southern Highlanders,* 429, 443–45. Nearly half of Kephart's coverage of the war consists of lengthy block quotes from John Fox and William Frost, discussed earlier in this essay.

43. Ibid., 447, 449–50.

44. Ibid., 40–51.

45. Biographical information on Campbell remains surprisingly thin. Among the most thorough accounts of his life are those found in the inventory of the John C. Campbell and Olive Dame Campbell Papers, Southern Historical Collection, University of North Carolina at Chapel Hill Library, and in David Whisnant, *All That Is Native and Fine: The Politics of Culture in an American Region* (Chapel Hill: University of North Carolina Press, 1983), 106–7, although Whisnant focuses more fully on Mrs. Campbell's work after her husband's death.

46. John Alexander Williams, *Appalachia: A History* (Chapel Hill: University of North Carolina Press, 2001), 207–8.

47. Campbell, *The Southern Highlander,* 90.

48. Ibid., 90–91.

49. Ibid.

50. Ibid., 96–97.

51. Wilson, "Lincoln's Sons and Daughters," 244.

52. Frost, "Our Contemporary Ancestors," 99.

53. Campbell, *The Southern Highlander,* 91. For more on how several of these authors dealt with race in their work, see John C. Inscoe, "Race and Racism in Nineteenth Century Appalachia: Myths, Realities, and Ambiguities," in Dwight B. Billings, Mary Beth Pudup, and Altina Waller, eds., *Appalachia in the Making: The Mountain South in the Nineteenth Century* (Chapel Hill: University of North Carolina Press, 1995), 103–31.

Chapter 13

Civil War Memory in Eastern Kentucky Is "Predominately White"

The Confederate Flag in Unionist Appalachia

Anne E. Marshall

On a cold December day in 2004, Jacqueline Duty, a defiant-looking teenager from Greenup County, Kentucky, stood outside the federal courthouse in Lexington. In her hands she was holding a strapless dress emblazoned from bust to toe with red, blue, and silver sequins in the shape of a Confederate battle flag. Duty had worn the dress seven months earlier on the night of her senior prom in May 2004. According to court documents Duty and her lawyers filed that December day, Duty had long dreamed of wearing such a dress, and she had spent several years designing it. She never got to attend the dance, though. Instead, as she and her boyfriend tried to disembark from his car in the Russell High School parking lot on prom night, they were stopped by her principal and two police officers, who turned Duty away. As her lawyer later explained in pathetic tones, "Her only dance for her senior prom was on the sidewalk to a song playing on the radio."[1]

In the days before the prom, however, Russell High principal Sean Howard heard about the dress and, fearing that it would spark controversy, entreated her to find alternate attire. Duty, who did not have another dress to wear, decided to wear the dress and go anyway, and in doing so launched a chain of events that resulted in her filing suit against the Russell independent school district for violating her First Amendment rights to free speech and her right to "celebrate her heritage." Claiming that she had lost numerous college scholarships because the incident had painted her as racist, she asked for $50,000 in punitive damages.[2]

In front of the court building, Duty stood flanked by her lawyers, Kirk Lyons from the South Carolina–based Southern Legal Resource Center, an organization dedicated to defending symbols of southern heritage, and local attorney Earl Ray Neal. She defiantly answered the questions of journalists, explaining that she had been motivated to wear the dress because she wanted to "show part of [her] Southern heritage." When asked about the politics of the flag, she admitted that it was an offensive symbol to some. "Everyone has their own opinion," she remarked, "but that's not mine. I'm proud of where I came from and my background." Referring to her fellow students, she added, "We've all worn Confederate flags to school before."[3]

In fact, Duty and her lawyers contended that neither her dress nor the Confederate symbols worn by other students at Russell High were disruptive because there were few African American students who attended the school. This idea was also echoed in media coverage of her suit. The *New York Times* referred to both Russell High's geography and its racial makeup, noting that it was "in eastern Kentucky" and "predominately white." Within a few days, Jacqueline Duty's story had become national news and she appeared on Fox News's *Hannity and Colmes* show, as well as the radio talk show hosted by Los Angeles–based black libertarian Larry Elder. Her case became a cause célèbre among Confederate heritage groups, and the Sons of Confederate Veterans began soliciting donations to help fund her lawsuit.[4]

Duty's prom dress drama is but one of several high-profile incidents involving Confederate symbolism to come out of eastern Kentucky in recent years. In 2004 two rival motorcycle clubs from Bath and Bell counties took a fight over the right to be called "The Southern Brothers," and to wear a signature patch depicting a Confederate soldier superimposed atop a Confederate flag, to U.S. District Court. From a legal standpoint, however, the most consequential decision regarding Confederate symbolism in eastern Kentucky came in 2002, when the Sixth District U.S. Court of Appeals ruled in favor of a high school student in Madison County who had been suspended from school for wearing a Hank Williams Jr. T-shirt bearing the stars and bars. This case set an important legal precedent as First Amendment rights in public schools have emerged as the most significant front line in the fight over Confederate symbolism. More recently, in

2006, controversy erupted over the Confederate mascot at a Floyd County high school.[5]

In one sense, these recent disputes are simply part and parcel of the ongoing national dialogue about the meaning and political correctness of Confederate symbols. The outline of the debate is familiar. Opponents of the Confederate flag cite its connection to the defense of slavery during the Civil War, its later incarnation as a symbol of white resistance to black civil rights, and its adoption by hate groups like the Ku Klux Klan and the American Nazis. Those who support displaying the flag everywhere from car bumpers to the grounds of southern state capitols claim that it represents "Heritage not Hate" and that prohibiting such displays is in violation of First Amendment rights.

In historical context, however, the critical mass of controversy that has emerged over this Confederate symbolism in eastern Kentucky stands at odds with the Unionist Civil War narrative that Americans assigned to the region in the late nineteenth century. From the 1880s through the early twentieth century, eastern Kentucky developed an identity as a region that had resisted the tide of secession to remain loyal to the Union during the Civil War. According to this theory, highlanders were integral to keeping Kentucky in the Union, and along with the rest of the mountain South formed a bulwark against complete Confederate domination of the South. By contrast, the latter-day embrace of Confederate symbolism in a region that was celebrated for its unwavering loyalty to the Union during the Civil War seems improbable.

Upon closer examination, however, the references to a latent Confederate past are not a simple yet ironic turn in historical memory. Recently, historians of Appalachia have examined the complexity of Civil War loyalties in the region, revealing that many mountain Southerners had a vested interest in the politics of slavery and states' rights. Residents of the Southern mountains were just as divided in their sectional sentiments as lowlanders. What does make this turn of Civil War memory in Appalachia noteworthy, however, is that both the foundations of the late-nineteenth-century Unionist identity and the modern-day discourse surrounding neo-Confederate expressions center around the supposed whiteness of the region. They are predicated on the idea that Appalachia was and is overwhelmingly Anglo-Saxon, with African Americans virtually nonexistent in the region. In yet another incarnation of Appalachian exceptionalism, the idea of a racially homogenous Appalachia has shaped the discussion of Civil War memory in the region, with the tacit implication that whether Unionist or Confederate, the memory of the Civil War should be understood differently in the region. Furthermore, the latest variations on historical memory perpetuate the myth of an all-white Appalachia.[6]

The suggestion that eastern Kentucky had a distinctive Civil War heritage first came at the hands of late-nineteenth-century journalists, local-color writers, and social scientists. During the postwar period, white Kentuckians in other parts of the Bluegrass State famously experienced a bout of historical amnesia, seemingly forgetting that the Commonwealth had remained in the Union throughout the conflict. Along with former Rebels, many Unionists began casting a Confederate Civil War history for themselves. They erected scores of Confederate monuments, published Southern sectional periodicals, and generally embraced the Lost Cause as their own. It was in opposition to this latter-day rebellion that writers like James Lane Allen began to assert that there existed "Two Kentuckys," each with its own divergent Civil War experiences. One featured the landed, slave-owning Bluegrass aristocrats who sided with the South out of custom, kinship, and a proslavery position. In the other was the Kentucky mountaineer who, according to contemporary literature, had little or no contact with the peculiar institution but had by virtue of his century-long isolation and undiluted devotion to democratic institutions and nationalism, sided with the Union. These ideas emerged within the context of the American reading public's "discovery" of and fascination with Appalachia as a distinctive region. From the 1880s through the 1910s, millions of middle-class readers, ambivalent about the increasingly homogenized national culture, enjoyed reading about what Henry Shapiro calls "the peculiarity of life in the 'little corners' of America" in magazines such as *The Century, Scribners, Cosmopolitan,* and *Harpers New Monthly Magazine.*[7]

Furthermore, at a time when white Americans were concerned about the effects of foreign immigration and took extreme measures to segregate whites and African Americans, eastern Kentucky and the rest of southern Appalachia appeared to the nation as the last untouched bastion of Anglo-Saxon heritage. Perhaps the scholar who best defined this idea was Louisville, Kentucky, native and geographer Ellen Churchill Semple. Semple utilized a new theoretical method known as anthropogeography, which posits that environmental factors directly determine human characteristics. In an 1899 article entitled "The Anglo-Saxons of the Kentucky Mountains:

A Study in Anthropogeography," Semple argues that the isolated mountain communities of her home state were the site of "the purest Anglo-Saxon stock in all the United States." As descendents of the English and Scots-Irish settlers of Virginia and North Carolina, "with scarcely a trace of admixture," they "[bore] about them in their speech and ideas the marks of their ancestry as plainly as if they had disembarked from their eighteenth-century vessel yesterday," she claims.[8] As a people, "kept free from the tide of foreign immigrants," argues Semple, "the Kentucky mountaineers were sturdy threads in the national fabric."[9]

Along with this bifurcated geography and demography, Kentucky gained another distinctive Civil War narrative. Despite the fact that the Bluegrass State had not seceded from the Union during the Civil War, from the 1860s on politicians, writers, and journalists emphasized Kentucky's postwar Confederate proclivities. Turn-of-the-century chroniclers of Appalachia, however, regularly emphasized the region's supposedly steadfast Unionism during the war. As Ellen Semple claimed, "Such was their zeal for the Union, that some of the mountain counties of Kentucky contributed a larger quota of troops, in proportion to their population, for the Federal army than any other counties in the Union."[10]

Nationally best-selling author James Lane Allen suggested that these internal geographical and sectional divisions within the state determined nothing less than the ultimate outcome of the war. Without the mountain "wall," he wrote, "the history of the state—indeed the history of these United States—would have been profoundly different. Long ago, in virtue of its position, Kentucky would have knit together, instead of holding apart, the North and the South. The campaigns and the result of the Civil War would have been changed; the Civil War might never have taken place." But for the existence of Appalachia, and therefore, "two Kentuckys," the state would have been free of division, Allen asserted.[11]

The idea of a Unionist Appalachia became a common theme not only in local-color sketches but in historical fiction as well. William E. Barton's *A Hero in Homespun: A Tale of the Loyal South,* which focuses on the forgotten loyalties of the mountain South, typifies this movement. During the Civil War, Barton argues, the Southern mountaineer "emerged from his obscurity and turned the tide of battle" only to later return to "his mountain fastness" and to be subsequently forgotten. Though the book was based mainly on the fictional experiences of loyal Unionist soldiers from East Tennessee, Barton took care to map out Kentucky's allegiances. In his story, two men from East Tennessee must travel through the Kentucky mountains to enroll in the Union Army in the central part of the state. One character explains the geography of sectional loyalty in the state: "Wall, the Bluegrass thar is secesh, same as West Tennessy is. But the mountings is fur the Union, same's here. An' they'r goin' to raise troops, an'let the Gov'nor go to grass."[12]

This Unionism, asserted many scholars and chroniclers of the region, was rooted in the supposed absence of slavery in Appalachia. While Kentucky's status as a slave state figured prominently in the Confederate memory, the postwar narrative of Appalachian Kentucky was notable for the absence of slavery. As Ellen Semple declared, the mountains had "kept out foreign elements" but "still more effectually . . . excluded the negroes." "There is no place for the negro in the mountain economy," she wrote in 1901, "and never has been." The impracticality of large-scale agriculture in the mountains, Semple argued, "made the whole Appalachian region a non-slave-holding section." When the Civil War began, "this mountain region declared for the Union, and thus raised a barrier for disaffection through the center of the Southern States." By the early twentieth century, this history supposedly manifested itself in relative racial egalitarianism and loyalty to the Republican Party.[13]

Like Kentucky's Confederate past, the notion of Unionist mountain Kentucky was grounded in both truth and exaggeration. In actuality, residents of Kentucky's eastern, mountainous counties distinguished themselves from their lowland counterparts during the Civil War and Reconstruction era in several ways. While slave ownership was not uncommon in the Kentucky mountains, it was certainly less widespread than in the rest of the state. Landholdings were often much smaller and staple crop farming even less tenable in the mountainous terrain. Though its prevalence varied widely from county to county, slavery certainly existed in eastern Kentucky. In Jackson County in 1860 African Americans made up less than 1 percent of the population, while in Clay County, enslaved and free blacks composed just over 5 percent and 4 percent of the population respectively, for a total of nearly 10 percent. Mountain residents were well aware of the buying and selling of slaves, as the mountain passes and rivers provided the southward and westward routes of the interstate slave trade. Mountain towns like London, Pikeville, and Manchester also held regular slave auctions.[14]

Nevertheless, prior to the war, much of the state's antislavery activity took place in eastern Kentucky, with the foothills of Madison County pro-

viding the base of operation for both John Fee and Cassius Clay. Some historians maintain that many residents of eastern counties were more likely
to hold antislavery sentiments. This, however, did not translate into a lack
of racism or concern for the well-being of African Americans. By the time
fighting broke out in 1860, John Alexander Williams has pointed out,
"the mountaineers' resentment of slaveowners and their war was coupled
with an even stronger dislike of the slaves themselves and of black people
generally."[15]

With the failure of Kentucky's neutrality policy, most mountain residents, like their lowland counterparts, remained loyal to the Union. They
enlisted in the Union army over the Confederate by a ratio of about four
to one. In the Big Sandy Valley counties of Floyd, Johnson, Lawrence, and
Pike, which bordered what would become West Virginia, three times as
many men enlisted in the Union Army as in the Confederate. Suggesting that slave ownership was not a significant determinant of loyalty, both
Union and Confederate enlistments in these counties owned slaves in similar numbers.[16]

After the war, however, many Kentucky mountain whites marked
themselves distinct from their lowland counterparts when their loyalty to
the government during the war translated into voting Republican. During
the fifteen years that followed the war, the state's mountain counties proved
the state's only major white base of Republican strength. In some places, the
contrast in political geography was striking. In 1865, when Lincoln garnered only 30 percent of Kentucky's vote, more than 90 percent of Whitley
and Johnson County voters cast their ballots for him. Overall, however,
political sentiment was uneven and varied from county to county. In the
Big Sandy region, for instance, between 1865 and 1872 Johnson County,
which prior to the war had been the most Democratic county, became solidly Republican by a two-to-one margin, Floyd and Pike counties remained
marginally Democratic, and Lawrence County residents cast ballots in proportions similar to those before the war.[17]

Eastern Kentuckians' propensity to vote Republican, however, by no
means translated into racial egalitarianism. Despite their purported ignorance of African Americans, they were just as attuned to racial issues as
other white Kentuckians, and their loyalty to the Republicans was contingent upon the party's moderate conservatism. In 1869, when the Republican state convention endorsed the Fifteenth Amendment, many mountain
counties "revolted" from the "radical program," and some previously

staunchly Republican counties supported Democratic candidates. Furthermore, Republican voting in the mountains showed its most marked increase when the state party toned down its antagonistic anti-Confederate rhetoric in 1870 and 1871, choosing instead to campaign on such issues as internal improvements and education.[18]

In spite of a variegated pattern of Civil War participation and postwar political alignments, and racial attitudes that, on the whole, diverged little from their lowland counterparts, by the 1880s eastern Kentucky had developed wartime and postwar narratives distinct from those of the rest of the state. These narratives, moreover, were based on the notion that, like African Americans, slavery and racism had been all but absent from the region. Thereafter, many Americans began to view "Holy Appalachia" as both pure of blood and heart.[19]

Perhaps the earliest and most influential source of Union identity for Appalachian Kentucky was Berea College. Located in the foothills of the Cumberland Mountains, the small college was founded in 1855 by Kentucky's two most famous abolitionists, John Fee and Cassius Clay, with a mission to educate free African Americans and southern mountain whites. The school shut its doors during the upheaval of the Civil War, and when it reopened them, school officials began to emphasize the educational needs of the "hardy and loyal men" it served.[20]

In promotional pamphlets aimed at northern philanthropists, the school strategically sets its constituency apart from the rest of Kentucky's population, implicitly setting the mountain yeomanry against the advantaged heirs of slavery. One brochure argues that in the South, education was a privilege that had always been "monopolized by the wealthy class of planters." Underscoring the mountaineers' service to the nation, the tract notes that several counties proximate to the school had surpassed the draft quota, and inquires: "Can any part of the North show so good a record?" "Now that these men, their ideas enlarged and energies developed by the War, are asking for the key to knowledge, their wants must be met." College promoters reasoned, "having periled their lives for the Union, the least their grateful countrymen can do, is give them those Christian Seminaries necessary to the full development of their manhood." In another pamphlet, college boosters describe Berea's educational mission in terms of the "three distinct classes in Kentucky, namely: the inhabitants of the Blue Grass (ex-slaveholders), the colored people (confined almost entirely to the same region), and the mountain people."[21]

The idea of an Appalachia unbesmirched by slavery was a common theme in Berea's promotional efforts. In 1870 Berea president Charles Fairchild gave a speech to the American Missionary Association in which he emphasized that it was mountain whites who "made an antislavery church and school in a slavery state," implying that the rest of the state was proslavery. He admonished his listeners to "remember that this whole section was loyal in the battle for a united country unstained by slavery." An 1888 pamphlet remarks that "the mountain people have been almost entirely separate from slavery and slaveholders, and have had little interest in them, and have been, in the main independent of them."[22]

William Frost, who served as Berea's president between 1893 and 1920, employed the notion of highland faithfulness and racial naiveté in his efforts to solicit donations to the college from northerners. In the widely read and influential tract "Our Contemporary Ancestors in the Southern Mountains," which appeared in the *Atlantic Monthly* in 1899, Frost claims that the "old-fashioned loyalty" of mountaineers had "held Kentucky in the Union." "The feeling of toleration and justification of slavery, with all the subtleties of states' rights and 'South against North,' which grew up after the Revolution did not penetrate the mountains. The result was that when the Civil War came there was a great surprise for both the North and the South. Appalachian America clave to the old flag."[23]

No one, however, more effectively established the notion of mountain Kentucky Unionism than Bluegrass-born, Harvard-educated John Fox Jr. Fox wrote a number of books and essays that touted eastern Kentucky's Civil War Unionism, but it was his best-selling 1903 novel, *The Little Shepherd of Kingdom Come,* that indelibly etched the image of the loyal Kentucky mountaineer on the minds of the American reading public. *Little Shepherd* tells the story of Chad Buford, an orphan who descends from his home in the heart of the Cumberland Mountains to the valley of Kingdom Come. In the valley, Chad encounters African American slaves for the first time in his life. "Dazed" by their appearance, Chad asks his new acquaintance, Tom, "Whut've them fellers got on their faces?" Laughing, Tom replies, "Lots o' folks from your side o' the mountains nuver have seed a nigger. . . . Sometimes hit skeers 'em." Unruffled, Chad replies, "Hit don't skeer me."[24]

Chad eventually settles in Lexington and begins to conform to the refined behavior of lowland Kentuckians. He transforms from a mountain waif into a "highbred, clean, frank, nobly handsome" man, embodying "the long way from log-cabin to Greek portico"—the progress of man from semibarbarity to civilization. His new life is interrupted, however, by sectional tensions. When the Civil War breaks out, Chad must decide whether to cast his lot with the Confederacy or the Union. Though most of his patrician Bluegrass acquaintances in Lexington side with the South, Chad follows his primordial highland sensibilities and rides off to join the Union Army.[25]

In Fox's telling, the Kentucky mountains, marked by near "uniformity" of Union sentiment, offer a sharp contrast to the divided Bluegrass. The basis of this Unionism is an innate patriotism that had never been corrupted by slavery, an institution, according to Fox, unknown to mountaineers. Having little knowledge of and even less vested interest in the institution frees them from the politics surrounding it. To these mountaineers, Fox explains, slaves are seen only in their biblical context as "hewers of wood and drawers of water." Before coming to the Bluegrass, Chad had read *Uncle Tom's Cabin* and smiled incredulously at the tale, for "the tragedies of it he had never known and he did not believe." While some valley folk, like Chad's first adoptive family, the Turners, own slaves and decide to fight for their human property, "as they would have fought for their horses, their cattle, or their sheep," most "Southern Yankees," state Fox, "knew nothing about the valley aristocrat, nothing about his slaves, and cared as little for one as for the other."[26]

Fox's mountaineer, incarnate in Chad Buford, presents an alternative Kentucky Civil War character. Unsullied by connections to slavery and unencumbered by radical abolitionism, he is a white Southerner with no sectional and racial baggage, a holdover from a time when Americanism was purer and simpler. "Unconsciously," Chad "was the embodiment of pure Americanism," who, "like all mountaineers . . . had little love of State and only love of country—was first, last and all the time, simply American." This identification, furthermore, is not based upon reason but is instinctual. Just as Appalachians are arrested in their development in other ways because of their isolation, so are they in politics. They had crossed over the mountains after the Revolution, taking their Revolution-era politics with them, and there in this isolated land they had incubated without change for almost a century. Mountaineers have, since 1776, known only one flag and had "never dreamed there could be another." Chad "was an unconscious reincarnation of that spirit, uninfluenced by temporary apostasies of the outside world, untouched by sectional prejudice of the appeal of the slave."

Therefore Chad, the pure American, ultimately sacrifices his relationship with nearly everyone he loves for his primordial loyalty to the Union, and rides off to join the Union army, albeit astride a horse named "Dixie."[27]

More than 100 years passed between the time the American reading public was introduced to the simple, ennobled Chad Buford and the time they saw the AP photos of the indignant Jacquelyn Duty holding up her dazzling prom dress for reporters outside the Fayette County Courthouse. Most modern-day Americans have never heard of John Fox Jr. or Chad Buford. The idea that eastern Kentucky had been overwhelmingly Unionist is not as prevalent as it once was, thanks in no small part to the recent high-profile controversies over Confederate symbolism. Significantly, however, the dialogue surrounding these modern-day debates hinges on a reading of Appalachian racial demography that varies little from late-nineteenth-century assumptions. Both then and now, the idea of a racially homogenous Appalachia has shaped the perception of Confederate symbolism as much as it did eastern Kentucky's historic Unionist identity.

The notion of African American absence in eastern Kentucky has been especially prominent in the controversy surrounding Confederate symbolism at Allen Central High School. Located in mountainous Floyd County, Allen Central was founded in 1972, when four county schools consolidated. When school officials settled on a mascot, they chose a gray-clad Confederate soldier, who often appears against the backdrop of the St. Andrew's cross on the school's athletic banner. There is nothing sparing about the presence of Confederate symbols at Allen Central. The word "Rebels" is emblazoned across the school's cheerleading uniforms and on the basketball goal post covers. A large mural featuring the excitable soldier waving the stars and bars dominates the school's lobby, while a Confederate flag hangs over tables on the wall of the lunch room, and another is inset with blue bricks in the school's courtyard.

In 2006 Prestonsburg lawyer and Floyd County school board member Mickey McGuire expressed concern that the school's use of the Confederate flag and rebel mascot might be less than politically correct. Little did he know that his concerns would ignite a heated debate between defenders and detractors of the school's mascot and would garner national attention for the small school. Predictably, discussion soon turned to the racial meaning of the flag. Allen Central students and other flag proponents were quick to deny racial connotations of the flag. One school cheerleader explained to a newspaper reporter, "To us, it's not about the hatred. I have colored friends around here and they never say anything." This remark later earned her an on-air drubbing by MSNBC's Keith Olbermann, who named her to his nightly list of "worst people." Another student avowed that the flag was simply Allen Central's "tradition." "If I was black," he conceded, "it probably would bother me. But if they could understand it wasn't put toward them in hatred, it wouldn't be an issue." While some students clearly understood that the flag bore a racist connotation, they still insisted that *their* use of the symbol transcended such associations.[28]

The comments of students are consistent with recent findings regarding racial and regional views of mountain southerners. A survey conducted during the 1990s by the University of North Carolina's Southern Focus Polls found that more Appalachian whites view the Confederate battle flag "as an expression of southern pride" than as "a symbol of racial division." The same study also revealed that mountain whites are highly conscious of their racial identity and, according to sociologists Larry Griffin and Ashley Thompson, have a strong regional identification with the South. Furthermore, they were more likely to answer "yes" than were lowland southerners when asked whether they thought the South would be better off now if it had won the war and were a separate country. The 2008 Democratic presidential race seemed to underscore these findings when the national press attributed Hillary Clinton's overwhelming victories over Barack Obama in the West Virginia and Kentucky primaries to both the region's whiteness and its perceived racism.[29]

Unlike Jacqueline Duty, most defenders of Allen Central's mascot did not try to make a direct connection to a Confederate heritage. Rather, they cited more intangible qualities that it represented. Allen Central principal Lorena Hall recalled that at the time of the school's creation, those who selected the symbol "took the rebel soldier as being independent, ready to stand up for ourselves. The flag just came along with it. . . . It has nothing to do with racism. It's a part of us." Hall's assertions echoed the common refrain of the flag apologists who have tried to divorce the symbol from overt racism by concentrating on its association with secession and the South's struggle for state sovereignty, and by relation the abstract ideals of individualism and strength of character. Significantly, these were also traits ascribed to mountaineers by late-nineteenth-century authors, who considered them the very qualities that led Appalachian Southerners to stand strong for the Union.[30]

Such efforts to divorce the rebel flag from Confederate experience underscore the malleability of the flag's modern-day meaning. While the emblem is proudly defended by the Lost Causers, southern nationalists, and white supremacists, it also has garnered a much broader constituency. People around the world have adopted the flag as a symbol of national self-determination and anti-authoritarianism. The stars and bars have come to communicate class as well as racial distinctions. As historian James C. Cobb has written: "In a real sense, the Rebel flag had become a signifier not just of racial but of class differences as well, and not simply the economic distance between white and blue collar but the emotional distance between believing the system is there for you and believing that it is there for every-one but you." It is not hard to see how this connotation of Confederate symbolism might resonate with residents in one of the most economically depressed areas of the United States.[31]

The media coverage surrounding the Allen Central controversy, how-ever, focused solely on the racial implications of Confederate symbolism. Particular attention was paid to the small African American population, noting the overwhelming whiteness of many eastern Kentucky school dis-tricts and citing the fact that in Floyd County, in which Allen Central is located, the thirty-three black students in the county made up less than 1 percent of the student population, while in neighboring Pike County, black students constitute only half of 1 percent of the total. The small black school population reflects the overall demographics of the county. Accord-ing to the 2000 census, 97.6 percent of Floyd County residents were white, and 1.4 percent were African American. The rhetoric of flag defenders com-bined with the emphasis on the small African American population seemed to present a twist on the tree-in-the-forest riddle: "If a Confederate flag flies in Appalachian Kentucky, and there are no African Americans there to offend, is it still offensive?"[32]

The African American students from neighboring school districts cer-tainly thought so. A black basketball player from Pikeville High School expressed his dismay not only at the Confederate flags he was forced to see when his team played Allen Central but also at the perception that black students were not bothered by them. Before the 2006 controversy, how-ever, African American students had not spoken out against Confederate symbolism, because, according to newspaper accounts, they felt "outnum-bered" by whites in eastern Kentucky.[33]

Like Jacqueline Duty's trial, the Allen Central commotion drew in both supporters and detractors from around the region. The regional commander of the Sons of Confederate Veterans commended the school for retaining the symbol, declaring, "It has nothing to do with race except in the minds of those who think it does." The leaders of the Justice Resource Center, a Louisville-based civil rights group, disagreed, however, and traveled to Floyd County to express their concerns to school officials. Rev. Louis Coleman, who headed the organization, explained: "The rebel flag to African Americans represents something very bad—it represents slavery. . . . This community is still in the past." Coleman's choice of words was unwittingly ironic given the historic denial of the presence of the peculiar institution in the region. In January 2007 the Center filed a complaint with the Kentucky High School Athletic Association.[34]

The controversy over Allen Central's mascot widened when another Floyd County basketball team decided to boycott its game against the Rebels. According to the team's coach, Ned Pillersdorf, the eight-member team from the David School, which included one black player, voted unanimously to cancel their scheduled match against Allen Central. Pillersdorf claimed that the Confederate flag was a "form of taunting," a practice prohibited by the Kentucky High School Athletic Association. The basketball boycott turned what had been a local altercation into a national one. Wire stories ran in newspapers across the country, hundreds of people weighed in with their thoughts on Weblogs, and members of the Allen Central faculty began to receive hate mail. The situation became further muddled when the David School's board of directors issued a statement claiming that Pillersdorf, and not the team, had made the decision to boycott and had done so without proper consent of school administrators. Overriding the coach's wishes, they kept the game with Allen Central on the basketball schedule.[35]

Meanwhile, at a public meeting that was heavily attended by flag supporters, the Floyd County school board decided to further defuse the situation by removing Confederate symbols from the gymnasium. They noted, however, that they could not prevent fans from bringing in their own flags. In the face of escalating tensions, the principals of both schools decided to postpone the game because of "safety concerns." When the game was finally played more than two weeks later, the Allen Central gymnasium was closed to the public and to the press.[36]

Throughout the tumult, flag proponents continued to shrug off any claim to racist associations of the Allen Central mascot. Even Mickey McGuire, the Floyd County school board official whose concerns initiated the controversy, claimed that the students were ignorant of the historical and racial implications of Confederate symbolism. "I feel really sorry for the children," he declared, "because they sincerely have no racial motives and see no racial connotations to that flag whatsoever." Underscoring the notion that Appalachia had a different racial history, he added that "our children don't know that, because the Floyd County school system never taught them the strong racial connotations that flag has almost anyplace else." In the eyes of people like McGuire, then, the students of Allen Central share the same racial innocence as their nineteenth-century Unionist counterpart, Chad Buford. The trouble with embracing this notion is that it not only erases the presence of African Americans but also the presence of racism, both in the past and in the present. As a result, sociologist Barbara Ellen Smith has adroitly observed, "the contemporary predominance of whites in Appalachia becomes a benign demographic fact rather than a product of active practices characterized in part by persistent white supremacy. Racial innocence is preserved."[37]

In the past twenty years, scholars of Appalachia have begun to focus on the history of African Americans in southern Appalachia, and to address the concept of "black invisibility" in the region, revealing that Appalachia shares a heritage of slavery, racial violence, and oppression with the rest of the South. Their work illustrates that the limited African American presence in the Appalachian South is not simply happenstance, but is a result of deliberate human decisions and actions throughout the past several centuries. As the contemporary dialogue surrounding Confederate symbolism in eastern Kentucky reveals, though, these findings have yet to alter the denial, historical or contemporary, of black presence in the region. This latest variation of Civil War historical memory in eastern Kentucky underscores the continuity of the notion of an all-white Appalachia. The new focus it brings to prejudice in the region, however, seems to mark the end of the region's myth of "racial innocence."[38]

Notes

1. *Lexington (KY) Herald-Leader,* December 21, 2004.

2. Ibid.

3. Ibid.

4. Ibid.; *New York Times,* December 22, 2004; *Lexington (KY) Herald-Leader,* December 30, 2004.

5. *Lexington (KY) Herald-Leader,* October 12, 2004.

6. On conflicting Civil War loyalties in Appalachia, see John C. Inscoe, "Race and Racism in Nineteenth-Century Appalachia: Myths, Realities, and Ambiguities," in *Appalachia in the Making: The Mountain South in the Nineteenth Century,* ed. Dwight B. Billings, Mary Beth Pudup, and Altina Waller, 103–31 (Chapel Hill: University of North Carolina Press, 1995); John Inscoe and Robert Kenzer, eds., *"Enemies of the Country": New Perspectives on Unionists in the Civil War South* (Athens: University of Georgia Press, 2001), 158–86; Kenneth W. Noe, "Deadened Color and Colder Horror: Rebecca Harding Davis and the Myth of Unionist Appalachia," in *Backtalk from Appalachia: Confronting Stereotypes,* ed. Dwight B. Billings, Gurney Norman, and Katherine Ledford, 67–84 (Lexington: University Press of Kentucky, 1999); Jonathan Sarris, *A Separate Civil War: Communities in Conflict in the Appalachian South* (Charlottesville: University of Virginia Press, 2006); Brian D. McKnight, *Contested Borderland: The Civil War in Appalachian Kentucky and Virginia* (Lexington: University Press of Kentucky, 2006). On the "whiteness" and homogeneity of southern Appalachia, see: Nina Silber, *The Romance of Reunion: Northerners and the South, 1865–1900* (Chapel Hill: University of North Carolina Press, 1996), and "What Does America Need So Much as Americans? Race and Northern Reconciliation with Southern Appalachia, 1870–1900," in John Inscoe, ed., *Appalachians and Race: The Mountain South from Slavery to Segregation,* 245–58 (Lexington: University Press of Kentucky, 2001); David E. Whisnant *All that Is Native and Fine: The Politics of Culture in an American Region* (Chapel Hill: University of North Carolina Press, 1983).

7. For more on the creation of Kentucky's postwar Confederate identity, see Anne Marshall, "A Strange Conclusion to a Triumphant War: Memory, Identity, and the Creation of a Confederate Kentucky" (PhD diss., University of Georgia, 2004).

8. Ellen Churchill Semple, "The Anglo-Saxons of the Kentucky Mountains: A Study in Anthropogeography," *Geographic Journal* 17 (June 1901): 592.

9. Ibid., 592–93.

10. Ibid., 611.

11. James Lane Allen, "Mountain Passes of the Cumberland," *Harper's New Monthly Magazine,* September 1890, 562–63.

12. William E. Barton, *A Hero in Homespun: A Tale of the Loyal South* (Boston: Lamson, Wolfe, and Company, 1897), viii–xi, 24.

13. Semple, "The Anglo-Saxons of the Kentucky Mountains," 594, 612.

14. Richard B. Drake, "Slavery and Anti-Slavery in Appalachia," 17–18, and Wilma Dunaway, "Put in Master's Pocket: Cotton Expansion and Interstate Slave Trading in the Mountain South," 118–30, both in Inscoe, ed., *Appalachians and Race.*

15. Richard B. Drake, *A History of Appalachia* (Lexington: University Press of Kentucky, 2001); John Alexander Williams, *Appalachia: A History* (Chapel Hill: University of North Carolina Press, 2002), 154.

16. John David Preston, *The Civil War in the Big Sandy Valley of Kentucky* (Baltimore: Gateway Press, 1984), 81–82; Williams, *Appalachia: A History,* 163;

Gordon McKinney, *Southern Mountain Republicans, 1865–1900: Politics and the Appalachian Community* (Chapel Hill: University of North Carolina Press, 1978), 20. For a county-by-county percentage of Union enlistments, see James E. Copeland, "Where Were the Kentucky Unionists and Secessionists?" *Register of the Kentucky Historical Society* 71 (October 1973): 344–63.

17. McKinney, *Southern Mountain Republicans,* 50, 27; Preston, *The Civil War in the Big Sandy Valley of Kentucky,* 86–89.

18. McKinney, *Southern Mountain Republicans,* 58; Gordon McKinney, "Southern Mountain Republicans and the Negro, 1865–1900," in Inscoe, ed., *Appalachians and Race,* 202.

19. Allen Batteau, *The Invention of Appalachia* (Tucson: University of Arizona Press, 1990), 78.

20. My ideas about the importance of Berea College in the formation of a Unionist Appalachian war narrative are greatly informed by Shannon Wilson's article, "Lincoln's Sons and Daughters: Berea College, Lincoln Memorial University, and the Myth of Unionist Appalachia, 1866–1910," in *The Civil War in Appalachia: Collected Essays,* ed. Kenneth Noe and Shannon Wilson (Knoxville: University of Tennessee Press, 1997), 246.

21. Ibid.; pamphlet, ca. 1888, Record Group 5.23 7–1, Office of Information, Berea College Archives.

22. Pamphlet, ca. 1888, Record Group 5.23 7–1, Office of Information, Berea College Archives; Shannon H. Wilson, "Lincoln's Sons and Daughters," 246.

23. William Goodell Frost, "Our Contemporary Ancestors in the Southern Mountains," *Atlantic Monthly,* March 1899, 313–14; *Berea Quarterly* 2 (February 1897): 13–14. Works that discuss Frost's role in defining Appalachia include: Batteau, *The Invention of Appalachia,* 74–85; James Klotter, "The Black South in White Appalachia," *Journal of American History* 66 (March 1980): 843–48; Henry D. Shapiro, *Appalachia On Our Mind: The Southern Mountains and Mountaineers in the American Consciousness, 1870–1920* (Chapel Hill: University of North Carolina Press, 1978), 113–32; and Shannon H. Wilson, "Lincoln's Sons and Daughters." Berea's efforts to educate African Americans faltered in 1904 when, in a direct effort to undermine Berea's original mission, the Kentucky legislature passed the Day Law, which barred interracial education.

24. John Fox Jr., *The Little Shepherd of Kingdom Come* (Lexington: University Press of Kentucky, 1987), 42, 24.

25. Ibid., 149, 87, 309, 104.

26. Ibid., 192, 188–89.

27. Ibid., 188–91.

28. *Lexington (KY) Herald-Leader,* December 10, 2006.

29. *Journal of Appalachian Studies* 10 (Spring/Fall 2004): 8, 21–30. For examples of the focus on Appalachian whiteness and racism in 2008 Democratic primary press coverage, see "Skirting Appalachia," *New York Times,* May 17, 2008, and "The Race in Eastern Kentucky," *New Yorker,* April 25, 2008.

30. *Lexington (KY) Herald-Leader,* December 10, 2006, December 22, 2006.

31. James C. Cobb, *Away Down South: A History of Southern Identity* (New York: Oxford University Press, 2005), 292. For a thorough treatment of the uses of and controversies surrounding the Confederate flag, see John M. Coski, *The Confederate Battle Flag: America's Most Embattled Emblem* (Cambridge, MA: Belknap, 2005).

32. *Lexington (KY) Herald-Leader,* December 10, December 19, 2006, January 19, 2007; U.S. Census Bureau, State and County QuickFacts, Floyd County, Kentucky, http://quickfacts.census.gov/qfd/states/21/21071.html (accessed March 22, 2008).

33. *Lexington (KY) Herald-Leader,* December 10, 2006, December 19, 2006.

34. *Lexington (KY) Herald-Leader,* December 10, 2006, December 19, 2006, January 19, 2007.

35. *Lexington (KY) Herald-Leader,* December 22, 2006, January 19, 2007; *New York Times,* December 22, 2006.

36. *Lexington (KY) Herald-Leader,* January 19, February 9, 2007.

37. *Lexington (KY) Herald-Leader,* January 19, 2007; Barbara Ellen Smith, "De-gradations of Whiteness: Appalachia and the Complexities of Race," *Journal of Appalachian Studies* 10 (Spring/Fall 2004): 4.

38. The following are valuable studies on African Americans in the Appalachian South: Joe William Trotter Jr., *Coal, Class, and Color: Blacks in Southern West Virginia, 1915–1932* (Urbana: University of Illinois Press, 1990); William H. Turner and Edward J. Cabbel, eds., *Blacks in Appalachia* (Lexington: University Press of Kentucky, 1985); Ronald L. Lewis, *Black Coal Miners in America: Coal, Class, and Community Conflict, 1780–1980* (Lexington: University Press of Kentucky, 1987); Inscoe, "Race and Racism," in Billings, Pudup, and Waller, eds., *Appalachia in the Making;* and Inscoe, ed., *Appalachians and Race.*

Contributors

Mary Ella Engel is an assistant professor of history at Western Carolina University, where she teaches courses in nineteenth-century American history, religious history, and Appalachian history. She received her PhD from the University of Georgia in 2009. Her dissertation, which deals with the intersection of religion, family, and violence in nineteenth-century Appalachian Georgia, is currently under revision for publication.

Ken Fones-Wolf is the Stuart and Joyce Robbins Distinguished Chair in History at West Virginia University, where he teaches American working-class and social history. He is the author of numerous articles and two books, *Trade Union Gospel: Christianity and Labor in Industrial Philadelphia* and *Glass Towns: Industry, Labor, and Political Economy in West Virginia, 1890–1930s*. He is also coeditor of three books, most recently *Transnational West Virginia: Ethnic Groups and Economic Change, 1840–1940*.

Randall S. Gooden is an assistant professor of history at Clayton State University in Morrow, Georgia, where he teaches public history and archival studies and fills an assignment with the Georgia Archives as its circuit rider archivist. Gooden completed his PhD in history in 1995 at West Virginia University and wrote about the post–Civil War era in his dissertation, "The Completion of a Revolution: West Virginia from Statehood through Reconstruction." He has worked as executive director of the Geauga County (Ohio) Historical Society, head of the archives library at Ohio Historical Society's Youngstown Historical Center of Industry and Labor, and assistant curator of the West Virginia and Regional History Collection at West Virginia University. He also has taught history at Ursuline College, Youngstown State University, and West Virginia University.

Keith S. Hébert is an assistant professor of history at the University of West Georgia. He received his PhD from Auburn University under the direction of Kenneth W. Noe. He is currently writing a history of the Fifty-first Alabama Partisan Rangers under a research grant supplied by the Friends of the Alabama Archives and the Bradley Hale Foundation.

T. R. C. Hutton is a lecturer at the University of Tennessee in Knoxville. He received his PhD in history from Vanderbilt University in 2009. He has written articles and reviews for the *International Social Science Review, The Journal of Material Culture,* and the forthcoming *Encyclopedia of the Culture Wars*. With the support of the Social Science Historical Association–Rockefeller Graduate Student Award and the Gordon Family Research Fellowship, he finished his dissertation, "'Bloody Breathitt': Power and Violence in the Mountain South," and is now working on turning it into a book.

John C. Inscoe is University Professor at the University of Georgia. He is the author of *Mountain Masters: Slavery and the Sectional Crisis in Western North Carolina* and *Race, War, and Remembrance in the Appalachian South,* and he is coauthor, with Gordon B. McKinney, of *The Heart of Confederate Appalachia.* He has edited several essay collections on Appalachia or the Civil War. He also is the editor of the *New Georgia Encyclopedia* (online) and is secretary-treasurer of the Southern Historical Association.

Tom Lee is an assistant professor of history at East Tennessee State University. He received his MA from Wake Forest University and his PhD from the University of Tennessee. He has taught at the University of Tennessee–Knoxville, Roane State Community College, and Hiwassee College. He is the author of *The Tennessee-Virginia Tri-Cities: Urbanization in Appalachia, 1900–1950,* and is currently working on a history of burley tobacco in southern Appalachia.

Anne E. Marshall is an assistant professor of history at Mississippi State University. She received her PhD from the University of Georgia in 2004. Her publications include an article in the *Register of the Kentucky Historical Society* and an essay in the forthcoming *The Great Task Remaining before Us: Reconstruction as America's Continuing Civil War.* Her book, *Lost Cause, Gained Identity: History, Memory, and the Creation of a Confederate Kentucky, 1865–1930,* is forthcoming from the University of North Carolina Press.

Gordon B. McKinney is professor of history and department chair at Berea College. He earned his BA from Bates College and his MA and PhD from Northwestern University. He has taught at Valdosta State University, Western Carolina University, and Berea College. In addition, he was an administrator at the National Endowment for the Humanities and Executive Director of National History Day at the University of Maryland. He is the author of three books, including *The Heart of Confederate Appalachia,* coauthored with John C. Inscoe.

Steven E. Nash is a postdoctoral fellow at East Tennessee State University. He received his BA from Pennsylvania State University in 1998, his MA from Western Carolina University in 2001, and his PhD from the University of Georgia in 2009. His dissertation is titled "The Extremest Conditions of Humanity: Emancipation, Conflict, and Progress in Western North Carolina, 1865–1880."

Kyle Osborn is a doctoral candidate at the University of Georgia. He received master's degrees in history and education from East Tennessee State University in

2007. He is currently studying the ways Georgia residents imagined northern society and its people in the generation prior to the Civil War.

Robert M. Sandow is an associate professor in the Department of History, Political Science, and Economics at Lock Haven, University of Pennsylvania, where he teaches courses on the Civil War era, military history, and early America. He received his PhD from Pennsylvania State University in 2003. He is the author of *Deserter Country: Civil War Opposition in the Pennsylvania Appalachians* and has presented numerous articles and conference papers.

Andrew L. Slap is an associate professor of history at East Tennessee State University. He is the author of *The Doom of Reconstruction: The Liberal Republicans in the Civil War Era* and articles in *Civil War History* and *The Historian*.

Paul Yandle is a visiting assistant professor at Middle Tennessee State University. He received his MA from Wake Forest University and his PhD from West Virginia University, where he won the history department's William D. Barns Award for outstanding graduate student in West Virginia or regional history. His two-part article, "Joseph Charles Price and His 'Peculiar Work'" appeared in *North Carolina Historical Review* in 1993, and his essay "'Different Colored Currents of the Sea': Reconstruction North Carolina, 'Mutuality' and the Political Roots of Jim Crow, 1872–1875" appears in Paul D. Escott, ed., *North Carolinians in the Era of the Civil War and Reconstruction*.

Index